TEMPLARS OF THE PROLETARIAT

TEMPLARS OF THE PROLETARIAT

ALEXANDER DUGIN

ARKTOS
LONDON 2023

ARKTOS

Arktos.com fb.com/Arktos @arktosmedia arktosmedia

ISBN

978-1-915755-24-7 (Paperback)
978-1-915755-25-4 (Hardback)
978-1-915755-26-1 (Ebook)

Translation

Charles Ybdis

Editing

Constantin von Hoffmeister

Layout & Cover

Tor Westman

CONTENTS

I. An Unexpected Synthesis 1

The Metaphysics of National Bolshevism 1

II. Revolutionary Rus' 29

"Until the Number of the Beast Has Been Fulfilled..." 29

Katekhon and Revolution 58

"There's a Spirit of Autocracy in the Commisars". 67

L'age d'argent ou l'age mordoré?. 87

III. A General Theory of Rebellion 105

The Subject without Limits 105

Der Arbeiter (On Ernst Jünger) .114

Guy Debord Is Dead: The Spectacle Continues 117

The Threshold of Freedom 122

IV. Mustard Seed 129

Templars of the Proletariat 129

The Royal Labor of the Peasant .133

Our Motherland Is Death 138

The Reign of the Crowned and Conquering Infants 143

Under the Banner of the Goddess. 149

I Swear by the Declining Day 153

The Gnostic 158

V. Guardians of the Threshold 165

The Solar Dogs of Russia 165
Pentagram 174

VI. Chaos Magic 185

The Man with a Falcon's Beak 185
Absolute Beginners 194
Liapunov Time 201
De Sitter's Universe 206
The Fascists Arrive at Midnight 211
The Aquatic Regime 219

VII. The Kingdom of Saturn 229

The Star of the Invisible Empire 229
Orion, or the Conspiracy of Heroes 240
Venus Victrix 245
Lunar Gold 255
Hounds 262

VIII. The Guest From Within 275

Russian Вещь 275
Dark Is the Water 279
A Parallel Motherland 292
The Two-Headed Seagull 307
The 418 Masks of the Subject 317
My Name Is Axe 326
Mother Blood 344
"It Seems to Me That the Governor Yet Lives..." 364

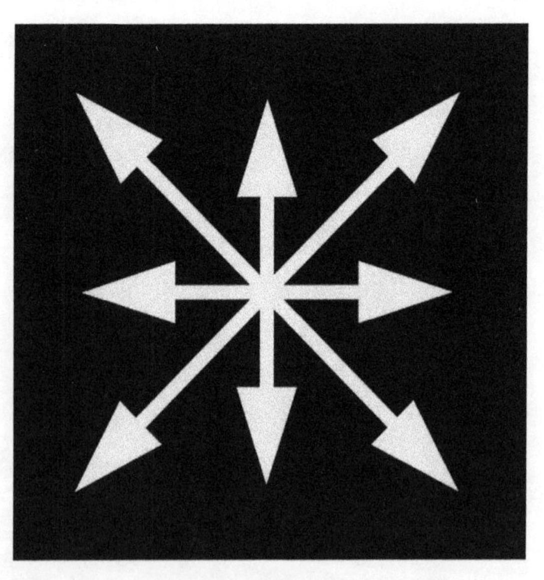

PART I

AN UNEXPECTED SYNTHESIS

The Metaphysics of National Bolshevism

A Deferred Definition

The term 'National Bolshevism' can refer to quite a few different things. It experienced a practically parallel emergence in Russia and Germany as a means, adapted by some political thinkers, of solving the riddle of the national character of the Bolshevik revolution of 1917, hidden behind the internationalist phraseology of orthodox Marxism. In the Russian context, the term was adopted to describe those communists who oriented themselves toward the preservation of State and (consciously or otherwise) continued in the geopolitical lineage of the historical Great Russian mission. These Russian National Bolsheviks were found both among the 'Whites' (Ustrialov, the *smenovekhovtsy*, and left Eurasianists) and the 'Reds' (Lenin, Stalin, Radek, Lezhnev, etc.).[1]

1 In the final years of the Soviet regime, the term 'National Bolshevik' characterized certain conservative circles within the Communist Party of the Soviet

An analogous phenomenon was associated with extreme-left forms of nationalism in 1920s and 1930s Germany, where ideas of unorthodox socialism were combined with a national line and a positive attitude toward Soviet Russia. Among German National Bolsheviks, the most radical and consequential figure was undoubtedly Ernst Niekisch, though we may also place other conservative revolutionaries within this movement — Ernst Jünger, Ernst von Salomon, August Winnig, Karl Paetel, Harro Schulze-Boysen, Hans Zehrer, the communists Laufenberg and Wolffheim, and even certain far-left National Socialists such as Otto Strasser and, for a given period, Joseph Goebbels.

In actuality, the concept of 'National Bolshevism' is much broader and all-encompassing than the political trends listed above. But to adequately understand it, we must turn our sights onto the more global theoretical and philosophical problems bearing upon the distinction between 'right' and 'left,' the 'national' and the 'social.'

The word 'National Bolshevism' contains within itself a deliberate paradox. How can two mutually exclusive concepts combine in one and the same name?

Despite the distance which the reflections of historical National Bolsheviks have gone, necessarily limited by the specifics of their milieu and temporal context, the very idea of approaching nationalism 'from the left' and approaching Bolshevism 'from the right' presents a surprisingly fertile and unexpected logic that opens up entirely new horizons of interpretation — this is a new logic of history, of social development, of political thought. We ought not to take concrete political

---

Union (the so-called 'statists'), and in this sense the word acquired a kind of derogatory meaning. But firstly, these late-Soviet 'National Bolsheviks' never agreed to such a name; and secondly, they never made any coherent attempt to formulate their views in a way that could even remotely be conceived of as a worldview. Of course, 'National Bolsheviks' such as these can be traced back in a definite manner to those of the 1920s and 1930s, but this connection is more likely predicated on inertia and has often lacked a rational conception.

factography as our starting point — 'Niekisch wrote this, Ustrialov understood some phenomenon in such and such way, Savitsky raised that argument,' etc. — but we ought rather to pursue an attempted glimpse of the phenomenon from the unexpected position which made the configuration of 'National Bolshevism' possible in the first place. Then, not only will we be able to describe this phenomenon, but we will also be able to understand it and, through it, many other strange aspects of our paradoxical times.

Karl Popper — Our Invaluable Helper

When it comes to the complex matter of determining the essence of 'National Bolshevism,' it is hard to imagine a better aid than the sociological research of Karl Popper — more particularly, his fundamental work *The Open Society and Its Enemies*. In this exhaustive work, Popper proposes a rather convincing model, according to which all kinds of society can be crudely divided into two basic categories — the 'open society' and the 'unopen society' (or 'the society of enemies of the open society').

As Popper would have it, the 'open society' is based on the centrality of the individual and his fundamental characteristics — rationality, discreetness, activities unmotivated by a global teleology, etc. One derives the sense of the 'open society' from its rejection of all forms of the Absolute incompatible with individuality and its nature. A society such as this is 'open' in as much as the various combinations of individual atoms know no bounds (just as they lack both a goal and a meaning); and, theoretically, this society must strive to achieve an ideal dynamic balance. Popper considers himself a convinced partisan of the 'open society.'

Popper defines the second type of society as 'inimical to the open society.' He does not refer to it as a 'closed society,' anticipating possible rebuttals, but frequently employs the term 'totalitarian.' In any case, starting from either the acceptance or the rejection of the 'open society,' Popper delineates political, social, and philosophical doctrines belonging to one or the other camp.

The enemies of the 'open society' are those who would rail against the individual and his central position, promoting various alternative models founded on the Absolute. The Absolute, even when it is affirmed voluntarily and spontaneously, makes a rapid incursion into the sphere of the individual, abruptly changes its evolutionary process, and does violence to the integrity of the atomized personality, subjecting it to a supra-individual impulse. The individual is swiftly limited by the Absolute, as a result of which the society of persons loses its quality of 'openness' along with its prospect of developing in any and all directions. The Absolute dictates goals and tasks; it sets dogmas and norms, violates the individual as a sculptor does with his clay.

Popper begins his genealogy of enemies of the 'open society' with Plato, in whom he sees the father of totalitarian philosophy and 'obscurantism [мракобесия].' Further on, he transitions to Schlegel, Schelling, Hegel, Marx, Spengler, and other modern thinkers. They are all united in his classification by one criterion — their affirmation of metaphysics, ethics, sociology, and economics that are founded on principles which negate the 'open society' together with the centrality of the individual. In this respect, Popper is entirely correct.

The most important aspect of Popper's analysis consists in how his category of 'enemies of the open society' includes thinkers and political figures regardless of their orientation toward 'right' or 'left,' 'reaction' or 'progress.' He selects an alternative, more meaningful and fundamental criterion which, at first glance, unites the most wildly different and opposing ideas and philosophies along both poles. Among the 'enemies of the open society' are Marxists, conservatives, fascists, and even some social democrats. In addition, among the 'friends of the open society' are to be found liberals such as Voltaire and reactionary pessimists such as Schopenhauer.

And so Popper's formula can be read as follows: "either the 'open society' or 'its enemies.'"

The Sacred Union of Objectivity

National Bolshevism can be most successfully and completely defined as follows: "National Bolshevism is a super-ideology shared by all enemies of the open society." That is to say, it is not simply one of the ideologies inimical to such a society, but rather it is that society's total, deliberate, and essential antithesis. National Bolshevism is a worldview constructed upon a total and radical negation of the individual and his centrality, while the Absolute, in whose name the individual is rejected, possesses the broadest, most general meaning. One could go out on a limb and say that National Bolshevism stands for *any* version of the Absolute, for *any* motivation leading to a negation of the 'open society.' One clearly perceives in National Bolshevism a will to universalize the Absolute at any cost, to promote the ideology and philosophical program which will best embody within itself all intellectual forms that are inimical to the 'open society,' reduced to a common denominator and integrated into a unified conceptual-political bloc.

Of course, in the history of the various political directions that have been inimical to the open society, the factions have often also fought among themselves. The communists indignantly denounced any likeness they might have borne to fascists, while conservatives disowned both the former and the latter. Practically no group falling into the category of 'enemies of the open society' has recognized its kinship with other analogous ideologies, considering such a comparison to be nothing more than derogatory criticism. By the same token, however, all the different versions of the 'open society' itself have developed in solidarity with one another; they have done this in full awareness of the shared philosophical bonds of their worldview. The principle of individualism was able to unite England's Protestant monarchy with the democratic parliamentarianism of North America (and in the latter case, liberalism initially had no problem finding a conjunction with slavery).

It was precisely the National Bolsheviks who launched the first attempt at creating a coalition of differing ideologies against the 'open society.' The National Bolsheviks, just like their ideological opponents, perceived a certain general axis which united all possible alternatives to individualism and the society that had been built upon it.

The first historical National Bolsheviks, applying the strategy of 'double criticism,' based their theories on this deep impulse, which has rarely been acknowledged. Both for the 'right wing' and the 'left wing,' the target of this National Bolshevik criticism was individualism (for the right, an economic individualism — the 'theory of the market'; for the left, political liberalism — the 'legal society,' 'human rights,' etc.). In other words, the National Bolsheviks, reaching into the beyond of ideologies, grasped the essence both of the enemy camp and of their own metaphysical position.

In philosophical language, 'individualism' is practically identical to the concept of 'subjectivity.' If we transpose the National Bolshevik strategy onto this level of discourse, it is possible to suggest that National Bolshevism categorically opposes the 'subjective' and categorically represents the 'objective.' This is not a question of whether materialism or idealism takes primacy. It is rather a question situated between two different poles: one must choose either objective idealism and objective materialism (on one side of the barricades!), or subjective idealism and subjective materialism[2] (on the other!).

---

2 If the first three concepts ('objective materialism' or just 'materialism,' 'objective idealism,' and 'subjective idealism') are quite broadly employed, the term 'subjective materialism' calls for further explanation. 'Subjective materialism'

And so, the philosophical lineage of National Bolshevism affirms an essential unity of worldviews predicated on a recognition of the centrality of the objective, equated with the Absolute and independent of how that objectivity is understood. One could say that the highest metaphysical maxim of National Bolshevism is the Hindu formula 'Atman is Brahman.' In Hinduism, 'Atman' is a person's highest transcendental 'I,' which stands on the other side of the individual's 'I,' but within this second 'I' as its most intimate and enigmatic part, constantly shrinking away from the capture of immanence. 'Atman' is the internal Spirit, but it is an objective and super-individual Spirit. 'Brahman' is absolute reality, enveloping the individual from the outside; it is external objectivity raised to its supreme origin. The identification of 'Atman' with 'Brahman' in a transcendental unity is the crowning achievement of Hindu metaphysics and, most importantly, the foundational path toward spiritual realization. This point is shared among all sacred doctrines without exception. In each case, what is at stake is the main purpose of human being—self-determination, an escape beyond the boundaries of the minor, individual 'I,' in which the path beyond this 'I' (either inward or outward) leads to one and the same triumphant result. Here we encounter the initiatic paradox of Traditionalism, embodied in the well-known evangelical phrase: '[W]

is a worldview, typical of consumer society, in which the basic motivation of human acts is the satisfaction of individual desires—primarily those of a material, physical character. In this instance, the whole of reality is situated not within the structures of individual consciousness (like in subjective idealism), but in a complex of individual sensations, base emotions, fears and enjoyments, the lowest layers of the human psyche connected with its vegetative, corporeal levels. In the field of philosophy, this state corresponds to sensualism and pragmatism, in addition to certain schools of psychology such as Freudianism. Furthermore, every attempt at political revisionism regarding the communist movement, beginning with 'empiriocriticism' and Bernsteinism and ending with Eurocommunism, has been accompanied on the philosophical level with an appeal to the subjectivist line and to different versions of 'subjective materialism,' one of the most recent manifestations of which has been 'Freudo-Marxism.'

hosoever will lose his life for my sake shall find it.'[3] The same understanding is to be found in Nietzsche's ingenious assertion: 'Man is that which must be surpassed.'

The philosophical dualism between the 'subjective' and the 'objective' has been historically reflected in a more concrete field — ideology; more specifically, in politics and the particularities of social order. Various versions of 'individualistic' philosophy were gradually concentrated within the ideological camp of the liberals and in liberal-democratic politics. And this is the macro-model of the 'open society' about which Karl Popper writes. The 'open society' is the terminal result of individualism, transformed into an ideology and manifested in concrete politics. But then we must pose a question to ourselves regarding the ideological model most common among partisans of the 'objective' approach, the universal politico-social program of the 'enemies of the open society.'

As a result, we will discover nothing else than the *ideology of National Bolshevism.*

In parallel with the radical novelty of this philosophical division, realized vertically in this case with respect to traditional schemas (idealism — materialism), National Bolsheviks affirm a new watershed in politics. Leftists and rightists are respectively separated into two sectors. Far-leftists, communists, Bolsheviks, and all heirs to Hegel from 'the left' merge into a National Bolshevist synthesis with radical nationalists, statists, proponents of the 'New Middle Ages' — in brief, all of Hegel's heirs from 'the right.'[4]

3 [Translator's note]: Matthew 16:25.

4 The opposite process occurs on the opposing side: Kantian revisionists of social democracy, left liberals, and progressives acknowledge their similarities with right-wing conservatives who recognize the values of the market, free exchange, and human rights.

The enemies of the 'open society' are returning to the metaphysical womb which they all share.

The Metaphysics of Bolshevism (Marx Viewed from the Right)

We now turn to an elucidation of that which is to be understood, in a strictly metaphysical sense, by the two constituent terms of 'National Bolshevism.'

The term 'Bolshevism' originally emerged, as is well-known, during discussions held by the Russian Social-Democratic Workers' Party [RSDWP] aimed at proscribing that faction which stood in support of Lenin. We remind the reader that the Leninist line in Russian social-democracy consisted in an orientation toward extreme radicalism, refusal to compromise, accentuation of the party's elite character, and 'blankism' (the theory of 'revolutionary conspiracy'). Later, 'Bolshevik' became a synonym for the communists who had brought about the October Revolution and had seized power in Russia. Almost immediately after the revolution, the term 'Bolshevik' lost its limited meaning and came to be seen as coterminous with ideas of 'the majority,' 'universal representatives of the people [всенародности],' 'national integration.' At a particular stage, 'Bolshevism' was eventually perceived as a strictly Russian, national version of communism and socialism, standing in opposition to the abstract dogma of classical Marxists, as well as to the conformist tactics of other social-democratic movements. A concept such as 'Bolshevism' was in large part characteristic of Russia and almost unilaterally dominated in the West. However, no evocation of 'Bolshevism' in conjunction with 'National Bolshevism' should be limited only to this historical understanding. Under discussion here is a certain lineage common to all radically leftist tendencies — both of a socialist and communist bent. One could call this the 'radical,' 'revolutionary,' 'anti-liberal' lineage. By this we mean that aspect of leftist doctrines which Popper situates among 'totalitarian ideologies,' or among the doctrines of the 'enemies of the open society.' In this respect, 'Bolshevism' is not only a legacy of the Russian element's influence on social-democratic doctrine. This is a sort of constantly present component in all leftist philosophy which could only have developed so fully and openly in Russian conditions.

Recently, the most objective historians are constantly asking themselves the following question: "Is fascist ideology really 'right-wing?'" Naturally, the presence of such doubt suggests the possibility of formulating 'fascism' as a much more complex phenomenon, possessing a plethora of typically 'leftist' traits. As far as we are aware, a symmetrical question — "Is communist ideology really 'left-wing?'" — has yet to be raised. But this question is even more crucial and relevant. It must be asked.

It is difficult to deny the presence of authentically 'leftist' traits in communism — an appeal to rationality, progress, humanism, egalitarianism, etc. But, together with these, one detects aspects which fall unequivocally into the framework of 'the Right' relating to the sphere of the irrational, the mythological, the archaic, the antihumanistic, and the totalitarian. *This complex of 'rightist' components in communist ideology should also bear the name of 'Bolshevism' in its widest understanding.*

One already finds within Marxism itself two fundamental components which appear quite doubtful from the perspective of authentically 'leftist,' progressive thought. These are the legacies of the socialist-utopians and Hegelianism. Only Feuerbach's ethics, which lend a terminological patina of humanism and progressivism to the whole discourse, are excluded from the essentially 'Bolshevist' ideological construction of Marxism.

The socialist-utopians, whom Marx includes wholesale in the ranks of his predecessors and teachers, are the representatives of a particular mystical messianism — heralds of the return of the 'golden age.' Practically all of them were members of an esoteric milieu, in the midst of which a spirit of radical mysticism, eschatology, and apocalyptic portents reigned supreme. This was a world which combined the motifs of sectarianism, the occult, and religion, whose essence could be distilled into the following scheme: "The modern world is hopelessly rotten. It has lost its sacred dimension. Religious institutions have become abominations and have been stripped of God's grace (a general theme for radical Protestant sects, 'Anabaptists,' and Russian schismatics). The world is governed by evil, materialism, deceit, lies, and egoism. But holy men know that the approach of the golden age is near at hand and, by way of their mysterious rituals and occult acts, collaborate with its coming."

The socialist-utopians projected this motif, common for Western messianic esotericism, onto social reality and imbued the coming golden age with sociopolitical features. Of course, this idea bore a suggestion of rationalizing the eschatological myth, but along with this, the supernatural character of the coming Kingdom, the Regnum, can clearly be perceived in their social programs and manifestoes, in which one catches a hint of the coming miracles of communist society (riding on dolphins, controlling the weather, sharing women, human flight in the air, etc.). It is entirely obvious that this lineage takes on an explicitly traditional character, and it is completely logical to classify such a radical eschatological mysticism not only as a 'right-wing' component, but even a 'far-right' one.

Now on to Hegel and his dialectics. It is broadly known that the political convictions of the philosopher himself were extremely reactionary. But this point doesn't get to the heart of the matter. If one carefully analyzes Hegel's dialectic, the method which underpins his philosophy (and it is precisely the dialectical method which Marx adopts on a broad scale), one will notice a strictly traditionalist and even eschatological doctrine swathed in idiosyncratic terminology. Moreover, this methodology represents none other than an initiatic, esoteric structural approach to the problems of knowledge, as distinct from the profane, everyday logic of Descartes and Kant; these latter rely on 'common sense' and gnoseological norms of 'everyday consciousness,' whose fervent apologists, we shall note a propos, are all liberals — chief among them being Karl Popper.

Hegel's philosophy of history is a version of the traditional myth adjoined with a strictly Christian teleology. The Absolute Idea is alienated from itself and becomes the world (we shall recall the formulation found in the Qur'an: "Allah was the secret treasure that wished to be known"[5]). Finding an objectivity within history, the Absolute Idea acts upon people from outside as the 'cunning of cosmic Reason,' determining in advance the providential fabric of events. But ultimately, as a result of the Son of God's Second Coming, the apocalyptic perspective of a totally comprehended Absolute Idea opens up on the subjective level, which then ceases to be 'subjective' and becomes 'objective.' "Being and thought become one." Atman coincides with Brahman. And this all takes place in a certain chosen kingdom — the Final Empire — which the German nationalist Hegel identified as Prussia.

The Absolute Idea is the thesis, its alienation within history is the antithesis, and its comprehension within the eschatological kingdom is the synthesis.

It is upon this vision of ontology that Hegel bases his gnoseology. Unlike the usual rationality founded on laws of formal logic, operating only within positivist parameters, and linked by actual, causal relations, Hegel's 'new logic' appraises a particular ontological dimension in tandem with the potential aspect of things, inaccessible to 'everyday consciousness,' but actively employed by the mystical school of Paracelsus, Boehme, the Hermeticists, and the Rosicrucians. For

5 [Translator's note]: Found in the Hadith Qudsi.

Hegel, the fact of an object or affirmation (by which Kant's 'everyday' gnoseology is exhausted) is merely one of three hypostases. The second hypostasis is the negation of that fact, which is not then understood as pure nothingness (as formal logic sees it), but as a certain super-rational mode of being for the thing or affirmation. The first hypostasis is the *Ding für uns* (the 'Thing for Us'), while the second is the *Ding an sich* (the 'Thing in Itself'). But unlike with Kant, this 'Thing in Itself' is not to be understood as something unknowable and purely apophatic, as gnoseological non-being, but should be understood as a gnoseological other-being. Both of these relative hypostases are then resolved in a third, which emerges as a synthesis, encompassing both affirmation and negation, thesis and antithesis. If one scrutinizes this thought process with care, one finds that the synthesis follows upon the moment of 'negation' as a second negation — i.e., the 'Negation of the Negation.' The synthesis embodies both affirmation and negation simultaneously; here, the thing coexists with its own death, weighed upon a particular ontological and gnoseological scale not as a void, but as the other-being of life, the soul. Kant's gnoseological pessimism, the root of liberal meta-ideology, is turned on its head, revealed to be an 'insufficiently developed thought [недомышление],' while the *Ding an sich* ('Thing in Itself') becomes a *Ding für sich* (a 'Thing for Itself'). The cause of the world and the world itself are amalgamated in an eschatological synthesis, in which existence and non-existence are mutually present without excluding one another. The Final Earthly Kingdom, governed by a caste of holy men (the ideal Prussia), is conjoined with the New Jerusalem, descending from on high. This marks the beginning of the End of History and the era of the Holy Spirit.

Marx alludes to this eschatological, messianic scenario, applying it in a somewhat different sphere — the field of industrial relations. One is curious to know why he chose such a route. Garden-variety 'rightists' will explain this as a 'deficit of idealism' or will write it up to Marx's 'crude nature' (if not to his subversive intentions). This is an astonishingly stupid explanation which, nonetheless, enjoys a wide popularity among certain generations of reactionaries. It is more likely, however, that Marx, in the course of his careful studies of English political economics, was shocked by the correspondences between the liberal theories of Adam Smith, who saw history as a progressive movement toward an open free-market society and a universalization of the material/monetary common denominator, with Hegel's conceptions related to the historical antithesis, i.e., the alienation of the Absolute Idea within history. Marx ingeniously identified the limits of this alienation of the Absolute from itself with *Capital* — that societal formation which actively crushed Marx's contemporary Europe beneath itself. Through his analysis of the structure of capitalism and the history of its emergence, Marx gained a knowledge of alienation — a knowledge of the alchemical formula which governs it. His comprehension of this mechanism, the 'antithetical formula,' was the first and most indispensable condition of the Great Restoration or the Final Revolution. For Marx, the coming kingdom of communism was not only the inevitable result of 'progress,' but that of an *overturning*, a 'revolution' in the etymological sense of the word. It is by no accident that he refers to the primordial stage of human development as 'cave communism [пещерным коммунизмом].' The thesis is 'cave communism,' the antithesis is Capital, and the synthesis is world communism. Communism is synonymous with the End of History, the era of the Holy Spirit. Marx's materialism and his accentuation of economics and labor relations are evidence not of the worldliness of his interests, but of his magical attempt to transform reality — to issue a radical refusal against the compensatory fantasies of irresponsible dreamers, whose inactivity only aggravate the forces of alienation. It is just as easy to accuse the medieval alchemists of 'materialism' and a thirst for riches, provided one turns a blind eye to the deeply spiritual and initiatic symbolism hidden behind their discourses on the distillation of urine, the production of gold, the transmutation of minerals into metals, etc.

It was precisely this gnostic line, shared by Marx and his forebears, which was taken up by the Russian Bolsheviks; these latter had been reared in an environment where the hidden forces of Russian sectarianism, mysticism, folk messianism, secret societies, and the passionate, romantic natures of Russian rebels amassed themselves against the alienated, secular, and deformed monarchist regime. "Moscow is the Third Rome. The Russian people are the god-carriers [богоносец]. The nation is the Pan-Human [Всечеловек]. Russia is called upon to save the world." These ideas saturated Russian life, resonating with esoteric narratives latent within Marxism. But unlike any purely spiritual formulations, Marxism proposed an economic, social, and political strategy—something clear and concrete that even a simple person could comprehend, and which provided a basis for further socio-political moves.

In Russia, it was precisely 'right-wing Marxism' which reigned supreme, having been given the name 'Bolshevism.' But that is not to say that these conditions were found only in Russia. One can find a similar lineage in communist parties and movements the world over, provided of course they don't degenerate into a social-democracy that conforms to the liberal spirit. In this respect, it is no surprise that, other than Russia's October 1917, the socialist revolutions have only managed to occur in the East—China, Korea, Vietnam, etc. Once more, this serves to underline the fact that the most traditional, least progressive, and least modern peoples and nations ('alienated from spirit'), which are, by implication, the most 'conservative' and 'right-wing' peoples and nations, were able to recognize in communism a mystical, spiritual, 'Bolshevist' essence.

National Bolshevism belongs precisely to this lineage of 'right-wing communism,' which recedes into the depths of ages, harkening back to ancient initiatic societies and spiritual doctrines. Here, the economic aspects of communism are not reduced or negated, but rather viewed as a theurgical mechanism, a magical praxis, a concrete instrument with which to transform reality. The only thing which should be discarded is the inadequate, historically exhausted discourse found in Marxism, which is informed by accidental themes of a bygone humanist, progressivist epoch. The Marxism of the National Bolsheviks is Marx minus Feuerbach — i.e., minus evolutionism and a less frequently encountered inert humanism.[6]

The Metaphysics of the Nation

The other half of the term 'National Bolshevism' — 'national' — also requires some elucidation. The very concept of the 'nation' is far from unequivocal. One finds at different turns its biological, political, cultural, and economic interpretations. One can understand nationalism with an emphasis both on 'racial purity' or 'ethnic homogeneity,' as well as on the unification of atomized individuals for the sake of attaining optimal economic conditions within a limited socio-geographical space. The national component of National Bolshevism (to include both its historical and metahistorical, absolutist variants) is completely unique.

Historically, National Bolshevist circles distinguished themselves through a staunch orientation toward imperial, geopolitical understandings of the nation. Ustrialov's adherents and sympathizers, the Left Eurasianists, to say nothing of the Soviet National Bolsheviks, understood 'nationalism' as a super-ethnic phenomenon connected with geopolitical messianism, with 'local development [месторазвитием],' with culture, with the state on a continental scale. Likewise, with

6 [Translator's note]: In a later version of this passage, found in the 1997 publication of *Templars of the Proletariat*, Dugin has simplified this thought to: "The Marxism of the National Bolsheviks is Marx minus the Enlightenment."

Niekisch and his German comrades, we encounter the idea of a continental empire 'from Vladivostok to Flessingue,' as well as the idea of the 'Third Imperial Figure' ('*Die dritte imperiale Figur*'). In both cases, we are dealing with a geopolitical and cultural understanding of the nation, devoid of even the slightest hint of racism, chauvinism, or 'ethnic purity.'

This geopolitical and cultural understanding of 'nation' was based on a fundamental geopolitical dualism, which received its first lucid description in the work of Mackinder, after which it was taken up by the school of Haushofer in Germany and the Eurasianists in Russia. The imperial conglomerate of Eastern peoples, coalescing around the Russian 'heartland,' formed the skeleton of a potential continental state, united in their choice of 'ideocracy' and in their rejection of 'plutocracy,' their orientation toward socialism, and revolution against capitalism and 'progress.' It is telling that Niekisch insisted on the foundational potential of a socialist and Protestant Prussia, genetically and culturally bound with Russia and the Slavic world, all the while dismissing the centrality of Catholic Bavaria with its gravitational pull toward the Roman, capitalist model.[7]

But parallel to this 'pan-continental' version of nationalism, which, by the way, corresponds exactly to the universalist messianic pretenses of a strictly eschatological and 'pan-human' Russian nationalism, there existed in National Bolshevism a subtler understanding of the nation that did not contradict the scale of empire, but refined it on a more down-to-earth level. In this sense, the idea of 'nation' was analogous to the populist understanding of 'the people [народ]'—i.e., as a certain

7 Niekisch had already prophetically recognized the catastrophe constituted by the victory of Hitler's Austro-Bavarian, Slavophobic path in 1932, which he went on to express in his book *Hitler—Germany's Evil Fate.* It is striking that Niekisch had already managed to foresee the tragic consequences of Hitler's victory for Russia, Germany, and the idea of the Third Path as a whole.

organic, integral being, irreducible to anatomical parts, which possessed its own specific fate and unique constitution.

According to Tradition, each people is assigned a designated angel, a heavenly being. This angel is the historical meaning of a given people which stands without time and space, while maintaining a constant presence in every historical peripeteia of that people. This is the foundation of a nation's mysticism.

The national angel is neither obscure nor sentimental. It is a luminous, intellectual essence — a 'thought of God,' according to Herder's phrasing. One may analyze the angel's structure within a people's historical accomplishments, in the social and religious institutions which define it, in its culture. The entire fabric of national history is a narrative text describing the qualities and form of this luminous national angel.

In traditional society, the national angel carried a personified expression — in the form of 'divine' tsars, great heroes, shepherds, and saints. But in its capacity as a superhuman reality, this angel is completely independent of any human carrier. As a result, after the monarchist dynasties have been crushed, the angel can incarnate in collective form, such as in an order, a class, or even a party.

The 'people,' taken as a metaphysical category, is identified not with a concrete mass of individuals sharing the same blood, culture, and language, but with a mysterious angelic being, emerging throughout history. This is analogous to Hegel's Absolute Idea, but in a minor form. It is a national reason, alienating itself in a multitude of individuals before once more reintegrating (in a self-conscious, 'recorded [отснятом]' manner) into the nation's elite during particularly eschatological periods of history.

Here we approach a very important moment: these two concepts of the 'nation,' equally acceptable for the National Bolshevik worldview, share a point of communication — a magical point at which they converge into one. This comes down to Russia and her historical mission. It is telling that German National Bolshevism, in the capacity of a cornerstone, was precisely Russophilic. It was from this affective position that all of their geopolitical, social, and economic views flowed. The Russian (and to an even greater degree, the Soviet) understanding of the 'Russian people' as an open mystical society, called upon to provide the world with the light of salvation and truth [истины] during the end of times, lends itself favorably to both the 'pan-continental' and 'historico-cultural' aspects of the nation. And in this way, Russo-Soviet nationalism becomes the focus of National Bolshevik ideology, not only with regard to Russia or Eastern Europe, but on a planetary scale. The Angel of Russia is discovered to be the angel of integration—a certain luminous being who teleologically strives to unite within itself other angelic entities without defacing their individuality, but rather elevating their individuality to a universal, imperial breadth. It is no accident that Erich Müller, a student and close associate of Ernst Niekisch, wrote the following in his book *National Bolshevism*: "If the First Reich was Catholic, and the Second Reich was Protestant, then the Third Reich must be Orthodox." It must be Orthodox and Soviet simultaneously.

In this situation, we are met with quite the curious query. Because the national angels are quintessentially different individuals, the fates of peoples in history and, consequently, their sociopolitical and religious institutions reflect a picture of the disposition of power in the angelic world itself. One is stricken by the degree to which this purely theological idea can be so brilliantly affirmed through a study of geopolitics; one quickly perceives the mutual link between the geographical and topographical conditions in which a people, together with its culture, psychology, and even its sociopolitical preferences, exists. Gradually, one discovers an explanation for the dualism between East and West, doubled by an ethnic dualism: the land-faring [сухопутная], 'ideocratic' Russia (the Slavic world plus other Eurasian ethnicities) against the island-borne, 'plutocratic' Anglo-Saxon West. The angelic Eurasian horde against the Atlanticist hosts of capitalism. In this scheme, it is easy to guess at the true nature of Capital's 'angel' (as per Tradition, his name is 'Mammon')...

Traditionalism (Evola Viewed from 'The Left')

Whenever Karl Popper 'unmasks' the enemies of the 'open society,' he makes constant use of the term 'irrationalism.' This is the logical route, since the 'open society' itself is based exclusively on norms of rationality and postulates of 'everyday consciousness.' As a rule, even the most explicitly anti-liberal authors seek to justify themselves by this yardstick and to dispel any accusations of 'irrationality' leveled against them. The National Bolsheviks, following Popper's schema in its negative sign, embrace this rebuke. Indeed, the fundamental motivation of the 'enemies of the open society' and its most fervent, fastidious foes — the National Bolsheviks — is entirely alien to the edifice of rationalism. We shall find particular support in this question with reference to the works of the Traditionalists and, first among them, René Guénon and Julius Evola.

Both Guénon and Evola expound a meticulous mechanics of the cyclic process, in which a degradation of the earthly sphere (as well as human consciousness, by extension) and a desacralization of civilization take place. They analyze modern 'rationalism' (with all of its logical implications) as one of the final stages of this degradation. The 'irrational' is understood by Traditionalists not as a purely negative and deprecative category, but as a gigantic field of reality, inaccessible to inquiries posed through purely analytical, rational methods. Consequently, the Traditionalist doctrine does not dispute the witty conclusions drawn by the liberal Popper, but rather agrees with them, reorienting his signs into the diametrically opposite position.

Tradition is founded on superrational knowledge, on initiatic rituals which provoke a rupture in consciousness, and on doctrines that find their expression through symbols. Discursive rationality bears only a supplementary character and, as a result, holds no definitive sway over meaning. Tradition's center of gravity lies in a sphere not only of the irrational, but also of the Inhuman, in which credibility is assigned not to intuitive hunches, anticipations, or assumptions, but to authentic experiences of a particularly initiatic sort. The irrational, which Popper defines as a central feature of his doctrine of enemies of the open society, is in fact nothing other than the axis of the sacred, the foundation of Tradition.

If we take this as a given, then all the various anti-liberal ideologies, to include 'leftist' revolutionary ones, must align in some relation to Tradition. If in the case of the 'far-right' and the hyper-conservatives this seems obvious, then it is rather problematic in the case of 'the left.' We have already broached this question in relation to the concept of 'Bolshevism.' But we must consider yet another moment: the revolutionary anti-liberal ideologies, particularly communism, anarchism, and revolutionary socialism, call for the radical annihilation not only of capitalist relations, but also such traditional institutions as the monarchy, the church, and all cult religious organizations. How does one reconcile this aspect of anti-liberalism with Traditionalism?

It is instructive to consider how Evola himself denied the Traditional character of revolutionary doctrines and considered them to be the maximal expression of the spirit of modernity, degradation, and fallenness (To a certain degree, Guénon also leaned in this direction. But it is difficult to ascribe such a firm position to him, since he never formulated as unequivocal a relation to 'the left' as did Evola, who openly aligned himself with radical conservatives and the far-right). However, in the personal fate of Evola, there were periods—his earliest and latest—during which he took up almost nihilistic, 'anarchistic' positions in relation to the surrounding reality, proposing that his followers should do no more and no less than 'ride the tiger' (i.e., make a compact with the forces of decay and chaos in order to overcome the critical point known generally as the 'decline of the West'). But we do not only concern ourselves here with Evola's historical experience as a political figure. We assign immensely greater importance to the fact that, even in his works of the middle, 'high-conservative' period, one notes his constant accent on the necessity of adopting a particular esoteric tradition; to put it lightly, such an esoteric tradition is far from inscribed in the monarcho-clerical models so characteristic of the politically European conservatives, whom he held in such high regard. In this respect, we should consider not only his anti-Christian sentiments, but also his consuming interest in tantric traditions and Buddhism, which, in the context of traditional Hindu conservatism, are considered quite heretical and subversive. Moreover, Evola's sympathy for figures such as Giuliano Kremmerz, Maria de Naglowska, and Aleister Crowley, whom Guénon numbered unequivocally among the 'counter-initiators' (the negative, destructive tendency in esotericism), was an utter scandal. In the work of Evola, who constantly spoke of 'Traditionalist orthodoxy' and chastised the subversive tactics of 'the left,' one frequently encounters direct appeals to open heterodoxy. It is still more telling that he considered himself to be among the esoterics walking the 'left-hand path.'

It is at this point that we approach the metaphysics of National Bolshevism. In this esoteric current, it is not simply the political antipodes (the 'right' and the 'left'), not the apparently mutually exclusive philosophical systems (idealism and materialism) that are paradoxically fused together; rather, it is the two threads found in Traditionalism itself—the affirmative (the orthodox) and the negational (the subversive)—which are combined. And in this sense Evola is an exemplary author of the highest order, although between his metaphysical doctrines and his political views one detects a definite dissonance, predicated in our view on certain inertial prejudices proper to the 'far-right' circles in the Central Europe of his day.

In his magnificent book on the tantric 'Yoga of Power,' Evola describes the initiatic structure of tantric organizations (*kaula*) and their attendant hierarchy.[8] This is a hierarchy which rises vertically in relation to the equally sacred hierarchy of Hindu society. It is as though the Tantra (like Buddhist doctrine) and one's participation in its traumatic initiatic experiences alters the entire system of everyday life, affirming the maxim that "those who walk the short path require no external support." In the tantric chain, one's status as either a *brahmin* (the highest class) or a *chandala* (the bottom class of untouchables) is absolutely irrelevant. All that matters is the success one finds in carrying out a set of complex initiatic operations and the reality of that transcendent experience. This is a kind of 'left sacrality,' based on a convicted belief in the inadequacy, degeneration, and alienation of the usual sacred institutions. In other words, 'left esotericism' sets itself in opposition to 'right esotericism,' not through pure negation, but rather as a result of a certain paradoxical belief in the authenticity of experience and the concrete nature of transformation. Both in the case of Evola and in that of mystics grouped near the sources of socialist and communist ideologies, we undoubtedly find ourselves regarding the reality of 'left esotericism.' The destruction of the churches is not simply a negation of religion — it is a specific ecstatic form of the religious spirit that insists upon absoluteness, concreteness of transformation 'here and now.' The phenomenon of self-immolation with the Old Believers or the ecstatic rites of the *Khlysty* belong to the same category.

8 This work's descriptions of tantric sects are surprisingly reminiscent of trends in European eschatology, Russian schismatic thought, the doctrines of the *Khlysty* and… ideas held by revolutionary organizations!

Guénon himself, in his article entitled "The Fifth Veda" dedicated to tantra, writes that during those certain cyclical periods immediately preceding the end of the 'iron age' (the Kali-Yuga), many ancient traditional institutions lose their vital force and, in order to reach metaphysical realization, one must adopt unorthodox paths and methods. Therefore, he declares the study of the Tantras a "Fifth" Veda, despite the fact that there are only four of them, canonically speaking. In other words, commensurate with the degree to which degeneration has wracked traditional conservative institutions (such as the monarchy, the church, the social hierarchy, the caste system, etc.), the more relevant and necessary these specialized, dangerous initiatic practices — associated with the 'left-hand path' — become.

Traditionalism, which is integral to National Bolshevism in the most general sense, is without a doubt a form of 'left esotericism,' reproducing through its fundamental features the principles of the tantric *kaula* and the doctrine of 'destructive transcendence.' The individualist variants of rationalism and humanism, operating from the inside, have defeated even those organizations of the modern world which bear a nominally sacral character. It is impossible to affirm Tradition to its true extent by gradually improving the state of society. This 'right-hand path of esotericism' is doomed in advance by its eschatological surroundings. Furthermore, any appeal to evolution and gradualism can only ever play into the hands of liberal expansion. Therefore, the National Bolshevist reading of Evola places an accent on the moments directly related to 'left-hand' doctrines — a traumatic spiritual realization sustained through concrete revolutionary and transformative experience, beyond the pale of convention and habit which has lost its sacred justification.

National Bolsheviks understand the 'irrational' not as 'un-rational,' but as an "aggressive and active destruction of the rational," as a struggle with 'everyday consciousness' (and 'everyday behavior'), as an immersion into the raw elements of the 'new life' — of the magical existence of a 'differentiated man' who has cast off all externally imposed norms and prohibitions.

Third Rome — Third Reich — Third International

Among the innumerable doctrines of the 'enemies of the open society,' only two were capable of securing a temporary victory over liberalism: these are Soviet (and Chinese) communism and central-European fascism. Nestled between them as a unique and unrealized historical possibility, as a subtle stratum of political seers, we can observe the National Bolsheviks, who were forced out of necessity to act on the fringes of fascism and communism and whose integrative ideology and political activity was condemned to obscurity. In German National Socialism, the abortive Catholic-Bavarian strain was fatefully dominant, while the Soviets stubbornly refused any open admission of their ideology's latent mysticism, thereby spiritually exsanguinating and intellectually castrating the Bolshevik movement. The first to fall was fascism, and then it fell to the last anti-liberal citadel — the USSR — to do the same. At first glance, it would appear that 1991 marked the final page of an epic in which a geopolitical entity had stood up against Mammon, the demon of the Atlanticist West and the perverted 'angel of cosmopolitan Capital.'

But by the same turn, it is growing crystal-clear that National Bolshevism is not only a metaphysical verity, but has also been vindicated by its founders' absolute historical prescience. The only political discourse of the 1920s and 30s that has maintained relevance to this day is to be found in the texts of the Russian Eurasianists and the German 'Left' Revolutionary Conservatives. National Bolshevism is the last refuge of the 'enemies of the open society' if these latter wish not to insist upon their obsolete, historically inadequate, and utterly ineffective doctrines. If 'far-leftists' refuse to be mere appendages of an opportunistic and prostitute social-democracy, if 'far-rightists' want to avoid serving as a breeding ground for the extremist wing of the liberal repression apparatus, and if those people who are possessed by a religious feeling find no satisfaction in the squalid moralist surrogates with which the priests of insipid cults and primitive neo-spiritualists regale them — they are left with only one way out: National Bolshevism.

Beyond 'right' and 'left' is a unified and indivisible Revolution: it lies in the dialectical triad, "Third Rome — Third Reich — Third International."

The rule of National Bolshevism, its Regnum and Final Empire, is a complete realization of the greatest Revolution in history, continental and universal. It is the return of angels, the resurrection of heroes, the revolt of the heart against the dictatorship of reason.

It is the Final Revolution — the mission of the Acéphale, who is the headless carrier of cross, hammer, and sickle, crowned by the eternal swastika of the sun.[9]

9 Article first written in 1994 (originally in French), first published in 1997 (in Russian) in the journal *Elements* [*Элементы*] (No. 8; "Dossier: 'National Bolshevism'").

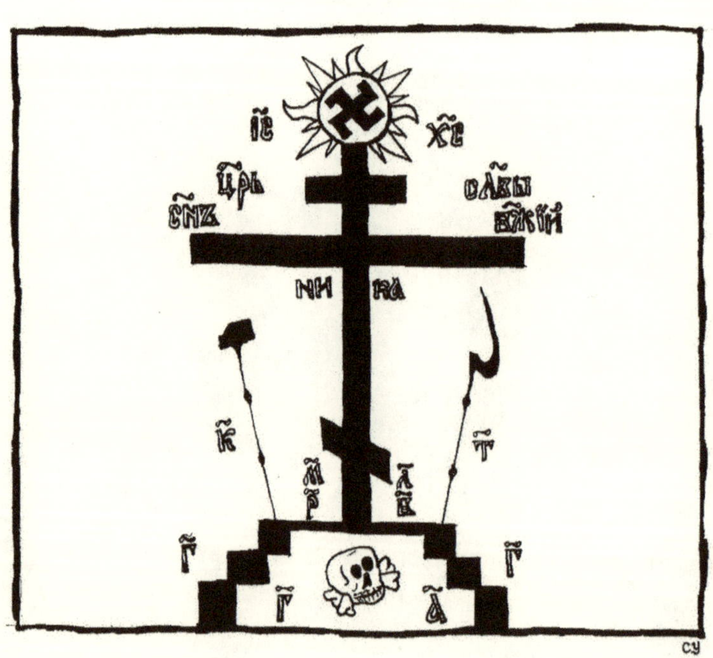

ІС
ХС
ЦРЬ
СЛАВЫ
СНЪ
БЖІЙ
НИ
КА
К
Т
М
Р
Л
Б
Г
Г
Г
А
СУ

PART II

REVOLUTIONARY RUS'

"Until the Number of the Beast Has Been Fulfilled..."

(On the Eschatological Essence of the Russian Schism)

Sergei Zenkovskii's Book

In 1995, a book entitled *The Rites of the Russian Old Believers: Spiritual Movements of the Seventeenth Century* was reissued; the author of this book is Sergei Zenkovskii, a famous slavist and historian of religion. Within its pages, he gives a detailed description of the spiritual history of the Russian schism — the most important, cataclysmic moment in the sacred history of Rus'. Here, Zenkovskii touches upon the most essential aspects of the schism related to Traditionalism's central concepts: the relationship between spiritual dominion and temporary power, the idea of eschatology, geopolitical spheres of influence, the role of rites and doctrines, etc.

Rus', Chosen by God

In his book, Zenkovsky aptly notes that "in Russia — in ancient Rus' — the idea that the Russian people, gifted with the Orthodox faith, occupy a special position in the world was already developing in their first century as Christians." In the *Sermon on Law and Grace*, Metropolitan Hilarion, the first ethnically Russian head of the Russian Orthodox Church, wrote on the Russian nation's special status as elected by God: "The old saying *about us* [our italics — A.D.] will come to pass: the Lord hath made bare his holy arm in the eyes of all nations; and all the ends of the earth shall see the salvation of our God."[1]

After the fall of Byzantium, intuitions about the chosen status of the Russian people effectively became religious doctrine. And so, in the *Sermon on the Eighth Council* of 1461, one already finds the following edict: "The greatest Orthodoxy and the highest Christianity[2] in the eastern lands is White Rus'." In 1492, Metropolitan Zosima developed this idea and spoke of Ivan III as of a direct descendant of the Byzantine emperors, a carrier of their mystical and eschatological mission; Zosima goes on to name him "the new Tsar' Constantine of the new Constantinople — Moscow and all the Russias."

We encounter a similar idea in the words of Zosima's contemporary, the renowned Russian saint Iosif Volotskii, who says in his *Enlightener* [Просветитель], "[…] Just as the Russian land overcame ancient impieties, so now will it master all with its piety."[3]

The messianic status of Rus' assumed an especially cultivated form in the *Chronicle of the White Hood*, in which it is historically situated for the first time. It is possible that this text was written in the circle of

---

1 "Открыет Господь мышцу свою святую пред всеми языки и узрят все концы земли спасение, еже от Бога нашего."

2 One should read this superlative in a literal sense.

3 «[…] Яко древние нечестие м превзыде русская земля, так ныне благочестием всех одоле.»

the Novgorod Archbishop Genadii — Iosif Volotskii's ally in routing the heresy of the "Judaizers [жидовствующих]."

Zenkovskii writes that the 'White Hood' is a symbol of the purity of Orthodoxy and of the 'luminous third-day Resurrection of Christ.' According to legend, it was gifted by Emperor Constantine to Pope Sylvester. From Rome, the White Hood found its way to Constantinople — the Second Rome, which for many long centuries[4] was the center of Orthodoxy. From there, the Hood (once more, according to legend) was 'sent to Novgorod,' to Rus', since it was 'there, indeed, that one [found] the glorious faith of Christ.' The White Hood's presence in Rus' is quite significant (according to the legend), since this presence indicates not only that "the Orthodox faith is now respected there and is glorified more than anywhere else on earth," but that it has also ensured the spiritual glory of Russia. In the opinion of the legend's authors, "[...] In the Third Rome, which exists on Russian land, the blessings of the Holy Spirit shine forth."

Another argument which lends itself to the chosen status of Rus' is the apocryphal story of the prophetic apostle Andrei, who sermonized the Gospels in northern Greece and Scythia. According to his chronicler, the apostle, having halted on the shores of the Dniepr, foretold

4 For some reason, religious historians rarely mention the fact that the New Rome, Constantinople and the Orthodox Byzantine Empire itself, did not merely exist for "many long centuries," but for approximately 1,000 years, which demonstrates its eschatological, sacred meaning, its identity with the 'Millennial Kingdom' written of in the Holy Scripture. This was the fundamental argument of those promoting 'eschatological pessimism,' who opposed the 'eschatological optimists'; these latter believed that the 'Millennial Kingdom' was a matter of the future. Such argumentation is easily penetrated by the Orthodox consciousness (despite its ultimate choice of eschatological perspective, either acknowledging this identity or rejecting it), while for Catholics (to say nothing of Protestants) the ecclesiastical cyclology was far more entangled. It is precisely thanks to the influence of Catholicism in Russia that a confusion arose with regard to this question, making it all but unsolvable already toward the beginning of the eighteenth century.

the following: "God's grace shines forth from these hills, where He will raise many churches together with a great city."[5]

In the very beginning of the sixteenth century, the elder monk Filofei provided Rus' with a conclusive formulation of its divine chosenness. Filofei specified the sacred mission of Moscow and that of the Muscovite tsar', developing the ideas of Metropolitan Zosima. In an address to the great prince of Moscow, Filofei wrote:

> For the churches of the Old Rome have fallen in their unfaithfulness and Apollinarian heresy; the churches of the Second Rome, that of Constantinople, have had their doors hacked down by the axe-wielding Hagarites. Now rises this new Third Rome—the holy Catholic Apostolic Church of your mighty domain—which, to all the ends of the celestial empire and the universe shines brighter in its Orthodox Christian faith than the sun… Two Romes have fallen, the Third now stands, and there will not be a Fourth: after your Christian tsardom, no other shall remain.[6]

Moscow (the Third Rome) and the Orthodox tsar' are endowed with an eschatological function: to gather under their saving shadow all the peoples of the world before the end of days. As the same Filofei writes, "As the end neared, all of Christendom assembled and came together into the unified tsardom of our sovereign which, according to the prophetic books, is the Russian tsardom. Two Romes have fallen, the Third now stands, and there will not be a Fourth."[7]

---

5 "На сих горах воссияет благодать Божия, имать град великий и церкви многи Бог воздвигнути имать."

6 "Старого убо Рима церкви падося неверием аполинариевы ереси; второго же Рима, Константинова града церкви, агаряне-внуци секарами и оскордми рассекоша двери. Сия же ныне третьего нового Рима державного твоего царствия святая соборная апостольская церковь, иже в концах вселенныя в православной христианской вере во всей поднебесной паче солнца светится… два Рима падоша, а третий стоит, а четвертому не быти: уже твое христианское царство инем не останется."

7 "Все христианские царства снидоша, придоша в конец и снидошася во единое царство нашего государя, по пророческим книгам, то есть

These eschatological doctrines relating to the chosenness of Rus' have found their reflection in the idea that the rites of the Russian church, having preserved (in the eyes of sixteenth-century Russians) their ancient structure, which has been lost or perverted in all other Orthodox churches, are particularly pure. Both the doctrine of Rus' as God's chosen nation and of the perfection of the Russian rites were reinforced during the convening of the "Stoglav Synod [Стоглавый собор]" in 1551. Zenkovskii rightfully points to the importance of cyclicity in the Russians' understanding of their sacred history.

Constantinople, the citadel of Orthodoxy, fell in 1453 — i.e., shortly before the end of the seventh century of the Orthodox calendar, as per biblical chronology. This end was supposed to have come in 1492. Consequently, Holy Rus' more or less concluded the sacred history of the world through Her faithfulness to Orthodoxy and Her political independence. She became the recipient of a mission, passed on from fallen Byzantium, to be the 'chosen land,' the eschatological space of New Israel, prepared to serve as the usher of the Second Coming, the appearance of the New Jerusalem. But because Byzantium itself, in accordance with Orthodox doctrine, was the universal kingdom in which all salvation was held and preserved and which determined the conclusion of world history, Moscow (Byzantium's heir) had also acquired this function as world-historical arbiter. The White Russian tsar' was identified with the Tsar' of the World, while the Russian people became the chosen vessel of grace — the saviors, the God-carriers, the nation of the Holy Spirit.

In certain versions of eschatological prophecy — particularly in the so-called *Book of Kirill* [Кириллова книга] — a different date of apocalypse was indicated: 1666. Thusly did several theologians interpret the secret number 666 as it was mentioned in the Apocalypse.

Российское царство. Два Рима падоша, а третий стоит, а четвертому не быти."

Eschatological expectations required a slight adjustment to the date of the End of the World in this case, but theologians' attitudes remained generally the same. It should be added in light of these points that the problem of the eschatological Kingdom was originally of central importance in the Christian worldview. The unified Orthodox Church, distinguished by its symphony of powers (i.e., the harmony shared between the church hierarchy and imperial power) was construed by Christians as the most important theological element — as the '*katekhon* [ὁ κατέχων],' the 'one who withholds,' about whom the apostle Paul speaks.[8] The Catholic West's falling away from Byzantium was interpreted as a consequence of the symphony's disruption, as an unsanctioned usurpation of secular functions carried out by Rome. In other words, Catholicism was seen as a 'heresy' which distorted the soteriological proportions found in the structure of the Final Kingdom, inflicted upon the '*katekhon*.'

---

8 [Translator's Note]: The *katekhon* is perhaps one of the single most important ideological nodes in Alexander Dugin's political and philosophical system. The concept is derived from a passage in 2 Thessalonians in the New Testament, in which Paul says the following: "Let no man deceive you by any means: for that day shall not come, except there come a falling away first, and that man of sin be revealed, the son of perdition [i.e. the Antichrist]; who opposeth and exalteth himself above all that is called God, or that is worshipped; so that he as God sitteth in the temple of God, shewing himself that he is God. Remember ye not, that, when I was yet with you, I told you these things? And now ye know *what witholdeth* that he might be revealed in his time. For the mystery of iniquity doth already work: only *he who now letteth* will let, until he be taken out of the way" (2 Thessalonians 2:3–7). In his book *Nomos of the Earth*, Carl Schmitt interprets the *katekhon* as the "historical power to restrain the appearance of the Antichrist and the end of the present eon" [Schmitt, Carl. *The Nomos of the Earth in the International Law of the Jus Publicum Europaeum* (Telos Press; 2003), pp. 59–60]. For Schmitt, the representative of this withholding force has historically been an orthodox (in the generic sense) regulatory state such as the Roman Empire. Undoubtedly, Dugin derives at least some of his understanding of this concept from Schmitt's thought.

Byzantium Herself (the indissoluble unity of the Eastern Church and the Eastern Kingdom) remained the *katekhon* even after the West's withdrawal. However, political motivations (were they not a reflection of providential, cyclical principles?) forced Constantinople to sign the Florentine Union in the presence of the Turkic conquerors, which amounted to no less than a disavowal of the unambiguous legitimacy of their eschatological doctrine. On the heels of this despairing concession, which symbolically stripped Byzantium of Her messianic function, She then went on to lose Her political independence as a result of the Turkic invasion. Because, in the Orthodox consciousness, secular power was irreducibly connected with the religious sphere of the Church, and because these two societal pillars were immediately combined with an exegesis of the cyclical moment of sacred history, these events (the Florentine Union and the fall of Constantinople) were seen as the beginning of a single apocalyptic process: a removal from the sphere of the 'withholder' and the total triumph of the Son of Perdition. Without the holy Christian kingdom and the symphony of powers, the usual paths to salvation were even less acceptable... Christian consciousness butted up against a most difficult problem — the earthly existence of the victorious Antichrist.

The only exception to be found during the post-Byzantine period was Orthodox Rus', a unique kingdom in which both aspects of the *katekhon* had been preserved — political might, an immense tsarist power which paid heed to no outside authority, and the Orthodox faith, which was the sole dominating canonizer of the symphony of power and the firm preserver of the ancient rites and dogmas.

Profane historians might write these coincidences and attendant shifts in worldview down to 'accident' or explain them as a 'distorted reflection of social transformations'... The consciousness of Tradition understands them as a deep ontological and cyclical fact.

Rus' *truly* became the chosen kingdom; Russians *truly* shouldered the eschatological mission.

Church and Tsardom before the End of the World

Already before the first predicted end of the world in 1492, alarming signs were emerging in the Russian church: on one hand, there was the emergence of the Judaizers' heresy, while on the other the followers of Iosif Volotsky fell into conflict with the Zavolzhe monks over monastic estate holdings. The proximity of the end times activated in religious consciousness the idea of Christianity's corruption, which must logically occur in the final, 'Laodicean' church according to the Apocalypse. Real inadequacies of hierarchy, frequent miscalculations, and the like were perceived in a hypertrophied manner. The angel of the Laodicean church, which was "neither cold nor hot, but lukewarm," had cast its shadow over all Russian Orthodoxy.

In one respect, the need for reform—for a purification of the faith—caused many to opt for the 'Old-Testament path.' The heresy of the 'Judaizers' called for a return to Judaic sources as a means of returning also to the sources of Christianity. It is possible that the Judaizers were influenced by a certain esoteric trend which had come from the West rather than from any true Judaic influence. References to the 'laws of the stars [звездозаконии]'—to astrology, which was much more proper to European Hermetic organizations than to orthodox Judaism—are characteristic in this regard. It is undoubtedly the case that, for the Judaizers, criticism coming from the church hierarchy was closely associated with aspects of eschatology. The Judaizers offered their path as a way to amend the situation. At the same time, one can clearly sense Latin influences in this conflict, and it is quite likely that agents sent by the Vatican did all they could to make use of the eschatological moods prevalent in Rus'; they sought to embed their (extremely politicized and opportunistic) version of the end of history—the union of all Christians under the Papal tiara. The second eschatological trend was the hesychastic movement of Nil Sorsky [Nilus of Sora], who demanded that the church renounce all secular power, that monks return to absolute poverty, and that the church be desocialized. It could be that Nil Sorsky and the Zavolzhe monks were influenced by the situation in Greek Athos, where Orthodox hesychasts (belonging geopolitically to a now unorthodox power) developed preferential practices of personal spiritual realization and individual salvation while utterly rejecting social problems. After all, they had found themselves in a desacralized kingdom—a world of apostasy over which the Antichrist ruled... Russians could soon expect the same. Eschatological optimists, such as Iosif Volotsky or the Novgorod Metropolitan Gennadii, were generally inclined to deny the impending fall of Rus', which in their opinion may miraculously avoid apostasy and bind itself to the New Jerusalem in the last moment of sacred history.

But the end of the world did not come in 1492.

Rus' remained an Orthodox power, and a new date up ahead could be seen by its malevolent glimmer—1666. In the lead-up to this year, eschatological problematics were inflamed with a new strength. Suspicions surrounding the 'corruption' of the church hierarchy grew as the middle of the seventeenth century neared. This idea was prevalent in the movement of the 'forest elders,' students of a certain Kapiton. The movement was particularly active in the 1630s and 40s. It was precisely in the Zavolzhe area that the 'forest elders' propagated themselves. This was the favored place for those monks and hermits who sought salvation from the world. It cannot be ruled out that followers of Nil Sorsky infused threads of their doctrine into Kapiton's. The 'forest elders' were known for their extreme asceticism, strict fasting, total focus on spiritual practice, and abandonment of all worldly responsibilities. Kapiton was at one time close to Tsar'

Mikhail Fyodorovich, who treasured the elder as a boon of prophecy and vision. There was even a certain period during which the church authorities approved of him, but his disdain for the church hierarchy and his extreme ascesis eventually provoked their ire. Both Kapiton and his followers were denounced as heretics and driven out of the church. Hiding out in the woods, the elders saw their excommunication at the hands of the hierarchy as nothing less than a confirmation of their spiritual truth and a pretense for further suffering. And so the eschatological fervor grew.

At that time, the 'forest elders' and their followers already observed the strictest of fasts (among other forms of extreme ascesis), which often resulted in death.

Another more optimistic trend of that period was the movement of the *Bogoliubtsy*, led by Ivan Neronov. These were representatives of the secular clergy [белого духовенства] — priests and archpriests — who, unlike the 'forest elders,' belonged to the lineage of Iosif Volotsky; that is to say, they were oriented toward the grace of the Orthodox tsardom, peacebuilding in accord with the eschatological role of Holy Rus'. But they, too, harshly criticized the church authorities, maintaining the idea of corruption in the hierarchy and even in certain elements of the church rites.

The *Bogoliubtsy* insisted on 'monophonic chanting [единогласии]' (i.e., the sequential pronunciation of the liturgy in its entirety, as opposed to the simultaneous chanting of various fragments of the service in order to shorten its length [polyphonic chanting — многогласие], broadly practiced by the church of their time). Besides this, the *Bogoliubtsy* were extreme moralists and taught literal observance of Christian ethics.[9] Despite their earnest commitment to the Orthodox rite, they were notable for many 'Protestant' traits.

9 René Guénon once pointed out that the first legal processes in the 'hunt for witches' in Europe coincided with the formal prohibition of carnivals (i.e., folk

Tsar' Alexei Mikhailovich himself held the *Bogoliubtsy* in great favor. Besides Neronov, other members of this circle include the tsar's confessor Vonifatiev, the future Patriarch Nikon, the archpriest Avvakum, and other brilliant religious figures. Despite the resistance of several bishops, the *Bogoliubtsy* managed to realize their reforms. But along with this, they raised quite a violent stir in the spiritual life of Rus', placing certain aspects under question which had previously seemed unshakeable and sanctified by the authority of antiquity. The *Bogoliubtsy* set the precedent of appealing to the past, to tradition, to antiquity, all for the sake of manifesting changes, 'novelties [нововедений],' in the present. In the later history of Russian Orthodoxy, this approach is taken more than once.

The question of how the Church was related to tsarist Power emerged in Russian society with renewed strength. The 'forest elders' de facto rejected the sacred character of the tsar's authority along with that of the external church, recognizing extreme asceticism as the only spiritual path. But they had already moved beyond the confines of Orthodoxy. The *Bogoliubtsy* desired an increased gravity of religion in society and insisted on a literal observation of Christian laws on

---

processions in which the church service was profaned, the anti-Pope was coronated, and other strange rituals reminiscent of the Saturnalia were performed). From Guénon's point of view, up to a certain moment, the medieval Church was an integral institution, encompassing the fulness of human existence — exalting the spiritual, but also neutralizing the indispensable dark aspects of man and society with its attentions and control. As soon as these moralistic tendencies came to dominate in the Church itself and the Saturnalia were formally banned, dark cults began to stand apart from it and posed an external threat, giving way to Satanic sects, sorcery, etc. It is typical that we encounter analogical features in the *Bogoliubtsy*: a campaign against alcoholism in the clergy, the imposition of liturgical practices and prayer on newcomers which were more befitting of church fathers and monks, and especially persecution of the *Skomorokhi*, who in Rus' fulfilled the function of sacralizing those phenomena of life not related to the Church, preserving and continuing the most ancient national traditions which tied several generations of Russians together.

the part of the laity and the clergy. Sometimes, they even promoted the "superiority of church over tsardom," which says much about the degree to which Catholicism had a hand in their thinking… But their fidelity to the Orthodox symphony of powers was nonetheless maintained.

The first serious departure from this symphonic model was instantiated by the activities of Patriarch Nikon. In his thought, notes of total and unambiguous superiority of the church over the state are clearly to be perceived. During the tsar's absence, he conducted himself as the Russian autocrat. In Nikon's character, the theocratic features inherent in the *Bogoliubtsy* reveal themselves at full strength.

Toward the middle of the seventeenth century, not long before the fatal year of 1666, Patriarch Nikon harshly disrupted the harmony of powers. The 'Textual Revision [Книжная справа],' which he initiated, took as its goal the same theocratic dream — to transform the throne of the Moscow patriarch into the prime instance of the Orthodox world, to become the Orthodox 'pope.' As a means toward this end, Nikon chose to regulate the Orthodox rite, which was expressed in the adjustment of the Russian rite in favor of the contemporary new-Greek one (the latter having been disseminated also among the Orthodox populations of Poland, Little Russia, White Russia, and the southern Slavic regions).

Dogmatic Grounds for the Schism

Nikon was not merely a facilitator for the radical tendencies of the *Bogoliubtsy*. He ultimately brought about the most important reform of the rite (and did so, as Zenkovsky convincingly shows, in a rash and glancing manner). Regarding the arguments over these rites, which served as the main pretense for the Russian schism, there was a plethora of varying opinions which depended on the position (that of

Nikon or that of the Old Believers) assumed by the author. In analyzing this question, Zenkovsky is careful to dot his i's and cross his t's.

Toward the beginning of the twentieth century, efforts of Russian historians such as Kapterev, Borozdin, and Golubinsky did much to elucidate the meaning of the rite debates of the seventeenth century. Zenkovsky writes the following: "During the years when Rus' was converting to Christianity, there were two statutes (similar but nonetheless differing) which dominated in Byzantium: in the east, the most commonly encountered was the so-called statute of Jerusalem, established by Sabas the Sanctified, while the so-called Studite or Constantinople statute prevailed in the west. When Rus' had adopted Christianity, the Greeks imported the Studite or Constantinople statute, which went on to become the fundamental Russian statute just as the Jerusalem statute (of St. Sabas) was taking over in Byzantium (during the twelfth and thirteenth centuries). Around the end of the fourteenth and beginning of the fifteenth centuries, Moscow Metropolitans Photius and Kiprian (the former a Greek; the latter a Bulgarian of the Greek school) began to introduce the Jerusalem statute in Russia in place of the Studite statute. But they were unable to take their reforms to their conclusion. And so, there were many ancient, archaic early Byzantine traits from the Studite statute latent in the Russian one — more so than were to be found in the Greek statutes of the fourteenth and fifteenth centuries. Because there had been no further Greek metropolitans after 1439,[10] the Russian church was able to preserve this transitory statute, whose archaic Studite elements distinguished it from everything to be found in the new-Greek Jerusalem statute, until the middle of the seventeenth century. But, unfortunately, this history of changing statutes was lost

10 This was the year in which the Florentine Union was adopted; for the Russian Orthodox consciousness, this was a year of spiritual apostasy in Byzantium. It follows quite naturally that Russian relations to the Greek Church were at this stage radically changed. From this point on, Byzantium had lost its eschatological position as the *katekhon*.

to both the Greeks and the Russians, and the former, having forgotten the Studite statute, considered the old ways of the Russian rite to be nothing more than Russian inventions." The Russian statute, then, was both archaic and the more authentically Byzantine Orthodox statute, and was in no sense a provincial church's divergence from the universal lineage of the Eastern Church as a whole.

Consequently, the idea of rejecting the Russian regulation and the two-finger method of crossing [перстосложение] (which was the original Christian, early Byzantine way) lacked any justification from the perspective of historical theology. Moreover, the idea of unifying the Orthodox rite under the new-Greek model flew radically in the face of the church's fundamental worldview at that time, which saw Rus' as the only power left that had preserved Orthodoxy in its pure state. As Zenkovsky rightly observes, Nikon revised Russian theological texts in accordance with new-Greek publications printed in Italy.

It goes without saying that Nikon was influenced precisely by Russian messianism. He hoped that the throne of the Russian patriarch would become the highest in the Orthodox world, and that the Russian empire would liberate the Orthodox nations, unifying them under a Russian dominion. Nikon himself saw this unified rite as a pragmatic means of expanding the particular influence of the Russian church. But an approach such as this constituted a deviation from Russian eschatological tradition that was far too grave. It would have been one thing if the fallen peoples and churches had approached Holy Rus' and the Russian tsar' on their own as to a bastion of salvation and purity—as to a chosen people and a promised land; but it was quite another thing to sacrifice the most important foundations of Russian Orthodoxy in the interest of geopolitically expanding the tsardom. Indeed, one cannot but notice in Nikon that obvious deviation from the Orthodox symphony and the Russian eschatology of Moscow-the-Third-Rome which the 'eschatological pessimists' so dreaded.

But Nikon was not the final precipitant of the schism, even though his struggle with partisans of the old rite bore a repulsively cruel, unmitigated, and crudely violent character (not unlike that of Neronov, one of the most respected spiritual authorities of Rus' in that day). Russian traditionalists were especially outraged at how the Textual Revision was overseen by absolute newcomers, such as the Greek opportunist Paisios Ligarides, who more than once changed his confession according to what was most materially advantageous. Nikon's reforms were a prelude to a truly horrific event — the church council of 1666–67. Around this time, Nikon had already been deposed. During the first portion of the council, only Russian bishops were in attendance, even though, immediately before the council began, the tsar' had especially insisted on the authority of foreign Orthodox patriarchs (in Constantinople, Antioch, and Jerusalem) to determine Russian loyalty to church reforms. In other words, Tsar' Alexei Mikhailovich himself now spoke at the council on behalf of Rus', while acknowledging as the highest spiritual authority Orthodox patriarchs who hailed from countries (and this is of utmost importance) where the Orthodox symphony of powers had long since vanished and where relations between spiritual Orthodox authorities and secular power had nothing in common with the Orthodox doctrine which saw the *katekhon* as the eschatological function of the Christian kingdom.

The council of 1666 served as the first radical step toward the secularization of tsarist power and the transition of Rus' from the Orthodox model of the eschatological kingdom to the European model of secular empire (in which Orthodoxy was only a nominal feature). The 1666 council signaled a decisive step away from Nikon's not-quite-Orthodox theocracy toward an utterly non-Orthodox secular empire in a semi-Protestant vein. The second half of the council (lasting from the end of 1666 to the beginning of 1667) was completely horrific. The Greek Orthodox patriarchs anathemized practically the entire period of Holy Rus', condemning the 'Stoglav Council,' rejecting the eschatological function of Moscow as the Third Rome, submitting the Russian rite, as a 'heretical innovation,' to ruthless criticism (never mind that they were condemning the early-Byzantine Studite regulation!). They also exiled all who supported the 'ancient faith [древней веры]' and affirmed a totally non-Orthodox adherence to the will of the tsar' above (or almost above) the spiritual dominion of religion. Though the Greeks' argumentation was formally Orthodox (struggle against Nikon's papist, theocratic proclivities), instead of returning to an authentic symphony of powers, they canonized a quasi-English surrogate which aggressively denounced all that had established the singularity and superior purity of the religious experience in Holy Rus'. Peter and the other Romanovs arrived to a desert. They were all the descendants of 1666 and its metaphysical Russophobia, to which foreign newcomers, serial turncoats, and agents of states and churches inimical to Russia devoted their every effort.

If we add to all that we have noted the undoubted fact that the defenders of the Old Believers have been totally vindicated in their position with regard to the antiquity of the Russian rite, then this entire council, which occurred exactly during that fateful year of 1666, appears indeed to have been a diabolical delusion, a national apostasy, a strange dulling of eschatological consciousness which, up to that moment, had been so painfully obvious to Russian bishops and tsars. It is as if a fascination—whether theocratic, absolutist, or individualist—took hold of Rus' in 1666... And all the terrible, mighty, beatific, and heroic proclamations of the Old Believers, their desperate resistance to apostasy, their absolute devotion to the idea of Holy Rus' could not quell the tenacious incursion of the Antichrist, who operated so cunningly with his 'good intentions,' speculating on the national feelings of the great god-bearing people... From the dogmatic point of view of Orthodoxy, the Old Believers—especially during the first moments of their resistance—were absolutely correct when they saw their opponents affirming and carrying out actions under the naked banner of apostasy. The tsars and bishops of Moscow, with their own bare hands and in collaboration with international opportunists, annihilated the last eschatological citadel of the White Tsardom... After 1666, Holy Rus' disappeared. She escaped to the woods, to the pyres, and to the far provinces of Russia.

The eschatological prophecy came to pass, even if the period spanning the initial deviation and the Second Coming turned out to be unexpectedly long. The first Christians, awaiting the End of the World as an imminent event, had experienced something similar in their own time. No one knows the true scale of the end times. Nonetheless, there are certain eschatological signs that have increasingly and compellingly demonstrated their accuracy.

Holy Rus' on the Run and Set Ablaze

From the moment that the Old Believers found themselves outside the confines of the law (both religious and social), they were obliged somehow to define their relationship to the surrounding reality. It was clear that their internal spiritual world was incompatible with the contemporary Russia; they lived in an alternative world, just as Holy Rus' is the alternative to the fallen Rus'. As a result, one frequently finds the Old Believers among politically radical circles—in company with rebellious Cossacks, in the ranks of Stepan Razin, etc. But no matter the path they might choose from that point on, the essence of their position came down to an absolute rejection of their country, her church, her everyday life, her political establishment, her authorities...

The ideas of the Old Believers were soon divided into a plethora of interpretive frames or accords. Their doctrines differed in their minor details, but their essential tenet—the rejection of the existing social order—was shared universally among them. In general, one can divide their interpretations into two fundamental trends: priestly and non-priestly. The priestly Old Believers recognized the priesthood, but believed that it was necessary to subject any priest entering their order to a purifying ritual. But for those who supported priesthood, the question of where they would find a foundation for their hierarchy soon became extremely important; this was because there was not a single figure belonging to the Old Believers who had attained the rank of bishop. As a result, it became impossible for them to induct new priests or create a religious hierarchy, and the alternative — counting solely on refugees from the official church — was difficult to countenance.

The priestly Old Believers were the least radical in their theological principles and, while recognizing the apostasy of the external church, refrained from any rejection of marriage or the sacrament. They considered self-immolation to be a form of fanaticism and avoided direct social resistance to authority. One can perceive in their ideas a particular adherence to the motifs of the *Bogoliubtsy* — extreme moralism, a love for ritual, and a meticulous observance of all aspects of their rites. In their eyes, Holy Rus' had retreated into her cell, into the villages of the Old Believers. But she nonetheless lived, even if only in an underground state. All she must do was patiently await the Second Coming while doing everything in her power to preserve her faithfulness to tradition, ritual, rites, etc.

The non-priestly Old Believers, who, in their own right, were divided into several sects, were more radical. They believed that the apostasy of Rus', as the last retreat, signified a complete victory of the Antichrist over the world. Salvation became problematic not only in the official church (of which nothing more need be said), but was generally put into question. The apostolic transmission of grace had been exhausted. The sacrament had lost its mystical strength. And so, from that point forward, the situation of man — Russian man — had become utterly tragic. All that remained was a total negation of the external world and a hope in the inexpressible and super-rational grace of Christ himself.

The most extreme of the non-priestly types, whose lineage emerges from the followers of Kapiton and the 'forest elders' (and it is not out of the question that they also descended from the Zavolzhe monks of Nil Sorsky), stood for the cruelest possible ascesis, refused to marry, and encouraged voluntary suicide—either through starvation[11] or

11 Fasting until starvation and death is clearly reminiscent of the ascetic practices of the European Cathars, who also committed suicide through starvation, *endurra*. The forerunners of the Cathars—the Bogomils—were an Orthodox sect which emerged in the northern territory of Byzantium and, from there, spread through the Balkans and the Alps into the Pyrenees and the lands of Provence. The priests of the Cathars, the 'perfected,' wore tall headpieces similar to the mitres of Orthodox hierarchs and, after reading "Our Father," included a glorification from the Orthodox service, pronounced by the priest as follows: "Such is Your kingdom and power and glory of the Father and the Son and the Holy Spirit, now and forever and for all time, amen [яко Твое есть царство и сила и слава Отца и Сына и Святаго Духа, и ныне и присно и вовеки веков, аминь]" (nothing of the sort is found in the Catholic mass). Of course, we have yet to reach a discussion of the historical links between the European Cathars and the Russian Old Believers, even though many features of the two movements are strikingly similar. The Cathars believed that the kingdom of the Light of Jesus Christ and the Holy Trinity is separated from modern humanity by a barrier and that the Catholic Church is not a road to salvation, but an obstacle in the way, a usurpation, a vessel of the Devil and the anti-Christ. The Russian Old Believers held almost the exact same views of the external Church after Nikons reforms and the council of 1666. The accusations meted against the Cathars of dualism and dual deism are doubtful, and much less so in the case of the Old Believers: rather, they merely affirmed the catastrophic distance between the human world and the world of the divine or, more precisely, that of the Church, of a light infused by rays of exaltation. And this distance was the result of certain extreme eschatological conditions. Considering the role of the Bogomils in the emergence of the Cathars, we can assume that they had obliquely drawn their idea of the heresy of Catholicism and the apocalyptic function of the Roman Pope from Orthodox sources. And if this is the case, we are dealing with very similar eschatological movements in Christianity which perceive the negative moments of the end of the cycle with an identical clarity and strength.

We observe equally obvious parallels between the doctrine of Joachimus Florensis, who announced the arrival of the 'Kingdom of the Holy Spirit,' and

self-immolation. Salvation before the end of the world could only be gained by extreme means. Love for the departed Holy Rus' that had become inaccessible was so great that only the expurgating pyre could lead the way toward saving light. Avvakum himself said: "Those who set themselves alight will find favor; just as those who die of fasting are doers of good."[12] He also wrote the following about preachers who had self-immolated: "Those dear Russian sons, it isn't so! — they crawl into the flames, but do not abandon the good faith…"[13] Comparing the self-immolators to mosquitoes, Avvakum is quoted to have said: "Similarly, the poor Russian sons[14], even if stupid, are glad: they awaited their

---

the idea of Holy Rus' in the *Chronicle of the White Hood*. Many authors among the Old Believers used the expression 'The Eternal Gospels,' which was a characteristic phrase of Joachimus Florensis. One of the tracts of Father Avvakum himself is titled *The Book of Denunciations or The Eternal Gospel*. Generally speaking, these details all point us toward the necessity of tracing the presence of Orthodox elements in all European anti-Catholic tendencies after the schism and the fall of the Latinizing West. As an example, the Ghibelline emperors of the Staufen dynasty (and, later, the Ghibelline Dante) stood precisely for the symphonic Orthodox arrangement of the state in opposition to the papistry of the Guelphs. Many Greek-Orthodox features are found as well in European secret societies, Christian and anti-Catholic simultaneously. It is not impossible that one might find something similar in the origins of Luther's reforms. But such speculation calls for further research.

12 «Иже сами себя сжигают, тому же прилично; яко и с поста умирают, добре творят».

13 «Русачьки же, миленькия, не так! — во огнь лезет, а благоверия не предает…»

14 One must pay attention to the way in which Avvakum uses the word 'Russian sons [русачки/русаки].' It is as though he speaks not of the nationality of the self-immolators, but of a mysterious spiritual brotherhood, united by a supreme unity. The officials of the state — the followers of Nikon and the fallen tsar' — had not only lost their status as Christians and become heretics for Avvakum, but had also become non-Russians! These expressions contain the totality of the natural and intuitive idea that Holy Rus' is identical with the land of the final salvation, and that the Russian people are identified as the final fulfiller of the universal world mission. It is precisely such an intensive eschatological, universal concept of the Russian nation that lay the foundation for such radical forms of religiosity,

tormentor; they braved the fires in their leagues for Christ the Son of God — of light."[15]

They entered the physical fire for the sake of metaphysical light. This victory of fire and light, in the eschatological situation, somewhat prefigures the very moment of the Second Coming. The return to Holy Rus' — the path to the New Jerusalem through the flames.

Descriptions of these pyres are astonishing: mothers threw themselves into the blaze with newborns in their arms; sisters leapt in together while holding hands; men cried tears of ecstasy and serene joy... So tangible, concrete, fleshly, and true was the Holy Orthodox Motherland, the Rus' of the Holy Spirit, the final tsardom for Avvakum's 'Russian sons.' In comparison with this reality, average earthly life became a hell; to lose such a reality was more horrific than tortures and death. It is no surprise that the Old Believers met their executioners with joy. In doing so, they avoided the sin of suicide.

But this applied to only the most radical non-priestly types, who were galvanized by their assurance of the coming end of the world and the closeness of the Second Coming. They were only slightly responsible for its hastening...

Other groups of a non-priestly persuasion were considerably less radical. Some of them recognized the institution of marriage, condemned suicide, etc. However, they all shared in their complete refusal of the clergy and their sacraments, which were considered to have lost their potency.

In latter days, the non-priestly Old Believers generated a number of Russian sects ranging from the *Skoptsy* [eunuchs] and the *Beguny*

---

leading all the way up to self-immolation. It was neither fanatics nor heretics who went into the pyres, but a 'nation,' an 'ethnos' which understood itself to be the society of New Israel, guided not through the sea like Moses's Jews, but through an eschatological fire, through the apocalyptic 'lake of fire.'

15 "Так же и русаки бедные, пускай глупы, рады: мучителя дождались; полками во огнь дерзают за Христа Сына Божия — света."

[fleers] to the *Khlysty* [self-flagellators]. Some of these sects evinced profound influences from even non-Orthodox—predominantly Protestant—heresies.

In any case, at a certain point, the paradigm of the Old Believers became the foundational formula for spiritual opposition—spiritual revolution—in Russia. And this was a deeply conservative revolution, upholding the super-conservative ideal of Holy Rus' in opposition to apostasy and the contemporary world of the Antichrist.

Beginning in 1666, the schism became the spiritual basis for all radical social and religious movements in Russia, even in those cases when they appeared externally to evoke western doctrines and were animated by a wailing appeal to social justice. Pugachev was an Old Believer; both the revolutionary democrats (Herzen) and, later, the populists [народники] made appeals to the credo of the Old Believers; many Old Believers themselves supported the Bolsheviks during the early stages of the revolution. Generally speaking, Russian 'nihilism,' in distinction from its western counterpart, was deeply compatible with national religious instincts and was structurally similar to the radical non-priestly currents. One of the non-priestly currents (the Spasovo accord) was known as 'Naysaying [нетовщина],' since its proponents broadly denied any possibility of salvation except that which came by means of the direct and unmotivated will of the Lord.

Schism through the Lens of Integral Traditionalism

If we adopt the language of Traditionalism (in a Guénonian key) for our expression of the phenomenon, then the history of the Russian schism presents itself as a rupture between the epoch of tradition and the beginning of the modern world in the Russian context. If we bracket for a moment the particularities of Christianity as a unique religious and metaphysical doctrine and examine Russia as merely one of many European (or Eurasian) countries, then when it comes to the schism, we can reframe this rupture as having occurred between social being and governmental structure on one hand, and an authentic spiritual tradition on the other. Guénon himself believed that all true bearers of the esoteric tradition had finally disappeared from Europe around that very time — 1648, near the end of the Thirty Years' War. Immediately afterward, the West began an active movement down the path of the profane, rationalism, individualism; this marked the dawn of the 'modern world' as Traditionalists understand it — i.e., the total and all-encompassing negation of Tradition and its eternal superhuman truth.

In this light, it is impossible to view the Old Believers as the legitimate carriers of tradition during the centuries following the schism, as they were forced to live out an underground existence, to hide themselves from the investigations of the authorities. Their doctrine(s) gradually and inevitably took on the character of a sect, which was in many respects heretical. Their fracturing into schools and accords only exacerbated matters. Like Protestantism, this sincere and metaphysically grounded spiritual revolt slowly changed into what was almost its antithesis. But this is in no way to suggest that the Old Believers did not preserve many esoteric aspects that had been lost to official Orthodoxy in the ensuing eras. One must grant the same credit to the various sects (especially those stemming from Orthodoxy) which occasionally managed to preserve certain esoteric doctrines and cults in a stunningly pure state. This especially applies to hesychastic practices, which enjoyed massive dissemination among radical Old Believers. Many authorities of the Old Believers, beginning with the archpriest Avvakum[16] himself, persistently repeated themselves regarding their observance of the 'Jesus Prayer [молитвы Иисусовой].'

---

16 In this regard, the beginning of the Pustozerskii Compendium [Пустозерский сборник] in which Avvakum describes his life is quite telling. In this text, Avvakum includes a fragment by the Venerable Abba Dorofei in which the

fundamental model of correspondence between the esoteric and the exoteric is described in Christian language. This is a model (revered by Guénon, who derives it from Islamic esotericism) made up of three parts — the center of the circle, its perimeter, and a line adjoining the periphery to the center. In esoteric Islam, these elements all correspond: the perimeter to *Shariat* (the external law), the center of the circle to *Haqiqat* (divine truth/reality), and the radius to *Tariqat* (the esoteric path from the external to the internal). Guénon himself interprets Tradition primarily on the basis of this symbol which, for him, was a formula of the utmost importance that allowed one to structure and order the immense field of traditional data. We include this excerpt from the life of Avvakum which provides a framework for the terminology of an original Russian Orthodox esotericism: "Seek to join yourselves one to another: for inasmuch as one joins himself to the truth, he joins himself to the divine. And the river from the Father will be set before you, and you will know the power of the word. Let us imagine a circle on the earth, like the outline of a kind of sphere made with a pointed stick; and let us take this pointed stick and place it in the center of the circle, just at the point. Now place your mind within this model: we will take this circle to be the world, and the center to be God; this is the path leading from the outer circle to the center, or a human life. In the degree to which the initiated approach the center, wishing to draw near to God, they are as near to God as they are to each other; and in the degree to which they draw near to each other, they draw near also to God. The same is true for distance: for when one leaves God and returns to the outer circle, it is just as when one departs from God and, in so doing, departs one from another disciple; and when one distances oneself from other disciples, to the same degree does he distance himself from God. Thus is the nature of love: when we are outside and do not love God, we are each removed from the divine truth, just as when we love God, we draw near to God in our love; and when we draw near to Him, we join ourselves through love to those close to us; and as we join ourselves to divine truth, we join ourselves to God. May God grant that we hear what is good for us and do as he commands, that we not be angry with one another and abstain from wrath. See the circle of the outline, about which the holy Abba speaks." In Old Russian, the fundamental esoteric terms are voiced as follows: the center is the 'point [остенъ]' (a 'barb' or 'sharp extrusion'); the perimeter is the 'sphere [облое]' (the 'surroundings'); the radius is the 'path [стезя],' like the '*Tariqa*' in Islam. And of extreme importance here is the explanation of the esoteric meaning of Christian love for those nearby (for 'the divine truth') — the closer one draws to the center of the circle, to the 'axis of the world,' and God, the closer all who walk the path draw one to another, constantly coming together as the individual paths come deeper inward; consequently, they almost melt into each other. In other words, love of God (the first commandment of Christ) and love of one's neighbor (the second commandment of Christ) are practically identical in the course of initiatic realization (i.e., as one follows the spiritual path).

We learn much from the fact that, further on, Avvakum transitions from his life to citations of Pseudo-Dionysius the Areopagite, who is one of the most esoteric authors of the Christian tradition. One should also take note of the symbolic image which Avvakum includes after this passage. This is the circularity (the 'sphere'), in the center (the 'point') of which the word 'God' is written. There are five (!) rays (five 'paths') that converge on this point, describing an upright five-pointed star. Inside of the circle, there are also five human heads with five Orthodox eight-pointed crosses and five labels of 'saint [святый].' Outside of the circle, on what would appear to be an opposing set of points on an inverted (!) five-pointed star, there are another five heads with the names of the chief hierarchs who persecuted the Old Believers. Below, in the place corresponding to the downward orientation of the outer pentagram (!), Patriarch Nikon himself is depicted.

If the moral and metaphorical dimensions of this symbol are apparent (departure from the truth on the part of the reformers and their separation from divine and human love, their transition over to the side of the anti-Christ), then the depiction of the five rays is shocking, as in all the most varied esoteric traditions, the interval between the exterior and the center always corresponds to the symbolism of the number 5 or the five-pointed star! In esoteric Islam, this is referred to as the 'five under the mantle' (Muhammed, Fatima, Ali, Hasan, and Hussein); in Freemasonry, it is the number of the Fellowcraft degree (intermediate between the Entered Apprentice and the Master Mason). The opposed 'Satanic' meaning of the inverted star is also obvious. Moreover, this image can be interpreted as a direct reference to the idea that only the tenets of the Old Believers have preserved a knowledge of true Orthodox esotericism, lost in Avvakum's opinion and that of his followers to Nikon's church.

Still further, Avvakum gives his initiatic interpretation of the concept of 'divine truth [истина],' discussing the refusal to use the symbol of faith in relation to the Holy Spirit in the expression "The Holy Spirit, the true and life-Giving Lord [Дух Святой, Господь истинный и животворящий]." For Avvakum, who here follows Dionysius the Areopagite, 'truth' coincides with being, knowledge with the object of knowledge; by this logic, the refusal to refer to God as the 'True Spirit [Дух истинный]' implies a blasphemous attempt to strip Him of his ontology, to turn him into an abstraction or a concept, as did the 'Roman heretics,' i.e. the 'Catholics.' Avvakum sees the 'reforms' not as a convention, not through a scientific critical lens, and not from a purely linguistic position. He sees this all as a profoundly *ontological* problem. And it is precisely though such a living, spiritual, initiatic, sacred connection of words and reality, preserved in Russian tradition and the Russian people, that one can explain the strife and

And so, through the optics of strict Traditionalism, the Old Believers come to be seen as the fragmentary legacy of a proper tradition, while official Russian Orthodoxy, from the middle of the seventeenth century, is identified with the purely exoteric and Russian society itself becomes progressively more profane. To put it differently, the Russian schism is nothing more or less than a moment in the general cycle of degradation in the Christian world and one of the many signs of that cycle's approaching end.

But if we observe our object from a rigidly Orthodox point of view, things take on an even more tragic and dramatic sense.[17] From this perspective, the Catholic West, even during its best period (the middle-ages) was practically a heresy and a delusion, a world of apostasy whose faith was decayed both in the letter and in the spirit. To translate this into the language of the Traditionalists, one could say that Catholicism (here, we refer only to Catholicism after its departure from Orthodoxy) was initially a mere form of the exoteric which negated the esoteric, distinguishing itself in doing so from the authentic Orthodox Christian tradition of the East (which had always preserved both dimensions — the internal/esoteric and the external/exoteric — in their sanctity). Even in its final centuries as Byzantium, the Orthodox world saw an ascendancy of hesychasm together with St. Gregory Palamas; and hesychasm constitutes not only an initiatic Christian practice, but also an authentic Orthodox metaphysics. It was precisely the inadequate presence of initiation in the western church that led to

---

the spiritual drama of the schism. For the Old Believers, the 'word' was not an abstract concept, the result of a conventional correspondence of one term to another; rather, it was something concrete, a theological quality, a contemplation of living spiritual reality, experienced in an immediate manner.

17 The interrelation between Orthodox metaphysics and Guénonian Traditionalism is elaborated in A. Dugin's *Metaphysics of the Good News (Orthodox Esotericism)* [Метафизика Благой Вести (православный эзотеризм)]. There, he develops certain cyclical and eschatological themes in greater detail.

the emergence of extra-clerical initiatic organizations—orders, secret societies, Hermetic brotherhoods, guilds, ateliers, and fellowships.

If Byzantium was the 'thousand-year kingdom,' in which the ancient serpent was for a time shackled and tamed (on the esoteric level, this is deciphered as the achievement of symphonic relations between spiritual dominion and secular power), then the fate of the eastern Church and the Orthodox doctrine (including its rite) is truly the résumé of world history, the chief and central event of the sacred cosmos, the cornerstone of ecclesiastical reality. In this case, the cycles of Byzantine history become far more important and are filled with more eschatological meaning than all other events to have ever occurred in the Christian and non-Christian world. Constantinople's theological apostasy (the council of Florence) and military defeat at the hands of the Turks which soon followed allude objectively to the end of the 'Chiliastic regime,' the conclusion of the triumphal period of ecclesiological ascension. The apostasy historically dates from the middle of the fifteenth century. It is precisely from this moment that authentic Orthodox tradition should begin counting the epoch of the Antichrist's reign, the arrival of the Son of Perdition. If the fall of Byzantium had been accompanied by a loss of political independence for all other remaining Orthodox states, or if these governments had switched their confessions and rejected the fundamental dogmas of the Orthodox church, then today all Orthodox Christians would find themselves in the same position; nothing would remain for them but to separate the spiritual from the secular and either revolt against the non-Orthodox world or make their peace with it and adapt themselves to existence on a planet ruled by the Son of Perdition. But the Russian tsardom existed—an exception to the apocalyptic situation in the Orthodox East. And so it was logical to defer the arrival of the Son of Perdition for yet another stretch of time. Holy Rus', Moscow-the-Third-Rome, having assumed the eschatological function, was to continue for a 'short time' the complete ecclesiastical eon: the period of the 'thousand-year kingdom.' For a time, the Russian tsar' became the sole personified carrier of the *katekhon* mission, the 'withholder,' while the fate of the Russian people and the Russian church became the expression of all creation. This marks the appearance of universalist motifs in the Russian national idea.

Despite the tumult, the time of troubles [смутное время], dismay, and catastrophe — this arrangement continued right up to the middle of the seventeenth century, when the history of Holy Rus' ended amid Nikon's reforms. In fact, this was the true end of the world, since, for the Orthodox consciousness, the last centuries of Russian history were the last centuries of history in general, having unfolded in the dramatic events of the last legitimate Christian kingdom. That which occurred in Russia after 1666 lacked that meaning with which the previous events had been saturated. The world was indeed ending, and its final flashes of brilliance were the glowing auras of immolation devouring the Old Believers…

"They braved the fires in their leagues for Christ the Son of God — of light."

The meaning of the Russian schism is most terrible, even if we understand it through the terminology of Traditionalism. Its horror is far more singular than that of the Bolshevik Revolution, which had merely formally altered the last external attributes of traditional society. But if we regard within Christianity and Orthodoxy the final truth, the sole and highest metaphysical testament that concludes world history, then the essence of the Russian schism reveals itself in an utterly frightening light. All of the Old Believers' apocalyptic allegories and affirmations take on an objective meaning. The visions of archpriest Avvakum cease to be metaphors and stylistic figures and become horrific, exultant revelations, descriptions of the Antichrist are to be taken literally.

Deacon Feodor, the highest authority of the Old Believers and the author of *The Answer of the Orthodox* [Ответа Православных], once wrote: "And until now, the all-cunning enemy has laid his eyes several times upon our Russian Orthodox tsardom, thinking of how he might turn us away from the righteous faith. But God would not allow it until the scriptures were fulfilled along with the number of the beast, 666 and a thousand (i.e. 1666)."[18]

The sufferings sustained by the jealous guardians of the ancient faith were cyclically justified; their understanding of eschatological symbolism was entirely correct; and events that followed — the tsardom of Peter the Great, who removed the patriarchy and transferred the capital from holy Moscow-the-Third-Rome to a deserted swamp in the north, the profanity of European culture instituted by tsars and tsarinas in his wake and, finally, the fall of the throne and the church's persecution at the hands of the Bolsheviks — these are all no more than aftershocks of that one fatal and apocalyptic event: 1666. From then on, neither in Russia, nor in the world at large, were there *any substantial occurrences*.

It was not fanaticism or religious hysterics that motivated the Old Believers to carry out their desperate spiritual feats: they were penetrated, body and soul, by the meaning of sacred Russian history. They were truly Russian people, of the holy nation chosen by God, the life of which was inseparable from the being of the Holy Spirit and the drama of its house-building [домостроительной] fate.[19]

18 "И в наше православное русское царство, до сих времен многажды вселукавый враг заглядывал, мысля от веры правыя отступити нас, но непопустившу Бога тогда, яко не у исполнися писание и число звериное, по тысяче лет 666 (т. е. 1666)."

19 Article first written in 1995, first published in 1996 in the journal *Tender Angel* [Милый ангел] (No. 3 — "The End of the World").

Katekhon and Revolution

The Third Rome

The history of Russian National Bolshevism stems back to the depths of Russian history as a whole. Irrespective of the apparently modern appearance of National Bolshevism, which appropriates 'progressive' Western terminology, its content and spirit are as ancient as the Russian people.

Russian National Bolshevism is a modernist expression of those messianic aspirations that were fundamental to the Russian people from the moment of Constantinople's fall; but these aspirations then came to be expressed alongside socio-economic notions about the creation of Russia as an eschatological society, based on the principles of justice, truth, equality, and other attributes of the 'thousand-year kingdom,' recontextualized into novel socio-political doctrines.

Russian messianism goes back to the fifteenth century, i.e. to the moment when Holy Rus' became the last powerful Orthodox state, and when, in accordance with the Orthodox doctrine of symphonic power, the Russian people and the Russian tsar' took on the previously Byzantine mantle of 'serving as a bulwark against the coming of the Son of Perdition."[20] Rus' had become 'Holy,' and the Russian people where transformed into the sole God-bearers [богоносца] in the fifteenth century. This was neither an emotional conviction, nor some official doctrine for bolstering national independence — it was an utterly obvious and theological fact of the Orthodox creed. Elder Filofei's formula of 'Moscow-the-Third-Rome' laid the ground for the self-awareness of the Russian church, which in turn defined the very identity of the Russian national soul. To 'be Russian' after the fall of the

20 "служить преградой приходу сына погибели."

Byzantine Empire was to 'be chosen for apocalyptic resistance against the liberated Satan immediately before the End of the World.'

This leads to the Russian accentuation of a legitimate Orthodox state, complete with an Orthodox patriarch and an Orthodox tsar' at its head — a state that is absolutely independent from any conceivable external factor: geopolitically, spiritually, and culturally. This is what it means to be chosen for eschatological messianism.

It follows, then, that we distinguish the eschatological function of the final Orthodox empire, the *katekhon* or 'withholder,' from 'Paul's second epistle to the Thessalonians' (chiliasm, or the idea of a 'thousand-year kingdom' which, in accordance with Judaic doctrine, would come in the future). In fact, the Orthodox Church teaches that the 'thousand-year kingdom' was already here in the Byzantine Empire from the moment of Christ's arrival. And this 'New Empire' — with its capital in Constantinople, the 'New Rome' — was of a miraculous era, during which the dragon (the ancient serpent) was bound. The fall of Byzantium was the end of the 'thousand-year kingdom,' and only Orthodox Russia, having adopted this mission from the New Rome, was able to stand for a time as the bastion of Orthodoxy in a world of universal apostasy. Holy Rus' (the Third Rome) was a sort of miraculous continuation of the 'thousand-year kingdom,' but was a far cry from its initial period or its moment of blossoming. Rather, in a certain sense, Holy Rus' took on this mission after it had ended, paradoxically preserving it in a special, providential territory chosen by God: a geopolitical ark.

Every Russian bears the stamp of the Third Rome upon his soul. This is the central paradigm of our historical consciousness. And here it is important to emphasize the intimate connection between the national, governmental component and the eschatological, metaphysical truth of the Orthodox faith. Already in its earliest forms, the Russian national consciousness was directly linked with a mystical, esoteric understanding of the social and the political. Holy Rus' was not simply one among many governments; Russians are not simply one among the multitude of Orthodox peoples, with their heroes, convictions, institutes, and customs. This is the sole New Israel on earth, having become such precisely during the fifteenth century and having been chosen to fulfill its mission from that point forward. By extension, Russian social life must base itself on a certain 'fantastic,' unique idea — on the Truth of Christ [Христовой Правде] and the Taboric Light [Фаворском Свете].

Schism as a National Paradigm

But there is no vanity in the 'elect' status of the Third Rome. Rather, it is a troubled 'chosenness,' fully of catastrophic premonitions. After all, Rus' is not the beginning of the 'thousand-year kingdom,' but its end which immediately precedes the arrival of the anti-Christ. The schism is this very catastrophe. It is of no importance whether the followers of Nikon or the 'jealous defenders of ancient piety' were historically correct. What matters is that, just on the heels of the schism, there followed a real desacralization of Rus', an unambiguous departure from its messianic role. The Russian patriarchy is dissolved; the capital is transferred from the Third Rome to the graceless swamps of the western borderlands. Russia is fissured. And for all time to come, Her national-political messianic spirit is cleaved in two.

Henceforth, the New Israel exists simultaneously in two hypostases — conservative and revolutionary. On one hand is the tsar', the state, and the official church hierarchy, inertially reproducing the external aspects of Holy Rus', but violating both the *spirit* and the *letter* of the messianic testament (even the nation itself takes on a new name — a Latinized 'Russia,' instead of the Slavic 'Rus''). On the other hand, there are the marginals, the schismatics, the sects, the conspirators, the rebels, the revolutionaries. But the deep justice of their pretensions and doctrines are cast in extreme, distorted, sometimes sacrilegious forms. At this pole, the *spirit* and the *letter* are also distorted. The messianic 'wholeness [цельность]' is destroyed, hacked in twain. Instead of a unified sociopolitical truth, reflecting a single metaphysical doctrine, two semi-truths emerge into which that doctrine is divided.

Russian Order [Русский Порядок] and Russian Revolt [Русский Бунт] are the two essential aspects of our national messianism. After Peter the Great, they became an inseparable pair. Conservatism and Revolution — mutually opposing and locked in mortal battle — flow out from a shared root, from the idea of the Third Rome which has been so foundational for Russian history.

The conservatives adhere to the affirmative, monarchic-inertial aspect of this ideology. They fear even the suggestion of dangerous questions regarding Peter and the post-Petrine legitimacy of power from the point of view of authentic Orthodox doctrine. And this is completely understandable, since such formulations are always immediately followed by 'sedition' and 'revolution,' a justification of the metaphysics of 'Russian Revolt.' Alternatively, the revolutionaries (who in fact base themselves on a feeling even more conservative than that of the most radical conservatives) are either debased by their catacomb existence, heretical excesses, and folk obscurantism [мракобесием], or are seduced by Western theories formulating the Russian revolutionary idea in terms alien to the national essence. Russian Revolution, from the times of the schism, Pugachev, and, later, the Decembrists and populists — right up until the Bolsheviks — expresses its true intuition in a chaotic manner, in a mixed-up and discordant manner, but always with a spirit of the eschatological, the fanatic, the national, the religious. Against the alien tsar', they hold up the 'rightful tsar" (whether that be Pugachev, Konstantin of the Decembrists, Lenin and Stalin of the Bolsheviks, etc.); against corrupted faith, they defend the true faith (be it the ancient piety [древлее благочестие], eunuch-hood [скопчество], or self-flagellation [хлыстовство]—'Russian Truth [Русская Правда]' or the dictatorship of the proletariat).

Ultimately, we perceive a collision between two distorted pictures of the same national, sociopolitical ideal—the Third Tsardom, the society of justice and righteousness, the ark of salvation in a world that has perished in the flood of the anti-Christ. Dmitrii Merezhkovsky felt this particularity with striking depth. His plays and novels on Russian history meticulously show the secret connection between the Russian monarchs and the Russian rebels, which reached its culmination with Alexander I, the founder and godfather of the Secret Society, the chief goals of which were the murder of the tsar' and the establishment of a 'government of the people [народовластие]'! It is most striking that we can trace the same paradigm, specifically relating authority and revolt in the Russian context, not only in the epochs described by Merezhkovsky (Peter, Pavel, Alexander I, the first years of Nikolai I), but in all periods of the Romanov dynasty, and even during the Soviet history of Russia. Merezhkovsky does not describe historical characters, but sacred paradigms; as a result, their truth is not merely a function of historical concreteness. Stalin is just as much a hero of the 'Kingdom of the Beast [Царства Зверя]' as the Romanovs, even if he emerged from the very depths of Revolution.

The Bolsheviks and Their Forebears

Now let us return to National Bolshevism. Historically, 'National Bolshevik' was a name applied to certain thinkers of the Russian émigré community who had discerned the 'conservative,' deeply nationalist character of the 1917 Bolshevik Revolution and had evaluated it as an extreme outburst of the Russian Messianic Idea. The dialectical approach to Russian history had definitively manifested a schism in the messianic complex of the Third Rome. There was the external conservatism of the Romanovs' Petersburg tsarism without the internal life of a truly Orthodox 'eschatological' *katekhon* on one hand, and the externally lawless, atheistic anti-nationalism, nourished by a most ancient and fundamental messianism — the 'society of Truth,' the 'ark of salvation,' the 'land where the laws of apostasy and the anti-Christ do not hold sway' — on the other. Both segments are insufficient on their own, doomed to the perpetual shame of dualism. A synthesis was indispensable: a saving unification of authority and revolt, conservatism (national, religious, governmental) and revolution (eschatologically honed, sacrificial, actively renewing life). But this synthesis was not to occur in the airless space of abstract, rational sociopolitical doctrines; rather, this great merger was destined to take place under the sign of Russian truth and in the spirit of the Russian mission.

National Bolshevism, in the eyes of its theorizers, was just such a synthesis. Its signs could be seen in the transferal of the capital from St. Petersburg to Moscow, the uprising of the church patriarchy in Rus', the national-governmental 'rebirth' in the form of Bolshevik power, the bolstering of geopolitical strength, etc. The National Bolsheviks did much to continue the legacy of Konstantin Leontiev with his famous maxim: 'socialism + monarchy.'

The genealogy of Russian Bolshevism, taking its roots in the schism (it is no coincidence that Old Believer merchants and sectarian capital in general took such vigorous part in the financing of the Russian Social-Democratic Workers' Party; we shall point also to the heightened attention afforded to Russian sectarianism by the Bolshevik God-seekers [большевиков-богоискателей] and God-builders [богостроителей] to Russian sectarianism, particularly in the case of Bonch-Bruyevich), draws its line through the Masons and Rosicrucians at the end of the eighteenth century, the Decembrists, the populists, etc. We should note also that, among all of these trends (so seemingly disparate), one can clearly trace a consistent messianic component — a 'national-utopianism,' a passionate, lively desperation and longing for the 'kingdom of salvation,' the 'sacred kingdom,' the 'kingdom of God,' which, in its capacity as an absolute reality of life, cannot be a mere object of rational, transcendental affirmations or a sphere of apophatic faith; but, in its culminating moment, it must be (or become) an absolute and immediate fact of sacred history, the flesh of a renewed and flaming being. And this 'Kingdom,' along with all its universality and pan-humanity [всечеловечностью] had an intimately national Russian character, which presented itself not as a result of ethnic pride, but as the direct result of its loyalty to the authentic Orthodox doctrine—especially to those elements relating to the eschatological meaning of the 'Orthodox symphony' of powers and the general apocalyptic function of the *katekhon* as Empire, State, and, more broadly, the people (society).

The eschatological character of Bolshevism was correctly perceived by authors such as Norman Cohn, Henri Besançon and, in their wake, Igor Shafarevich among others. But it was Mikhail Agurskii who provided the fullest picture of this fact. Unlike other studies into the matter, Agurskii's text clearly evinces a sympathy with National Bolshevism, as well as a deep understanding of its meaning, all while other authors satisfied themselves with what they considered to be disparaging and revelatory allusions to the irrational nature of eschatology and messianism in general. To some degree, this can explain the politically liberal, anti-socialist inclinations of Cohn and Besançon, who distinguished themselves from Shafarevich with their unambiguous Russophobia. Agurskii, utilizing the method of Cohn and other Western authors who, starting from Augustus Wyatt, began a careful study of the influence of eschatological ideas (particularly, the theories of Joachim de Fiore [Joachimus Florensis] regarding the 'kingdom of the Holy Spirit,' etc.) on the contemporary, externally atheistic culture and ideology, traced the national-messianic components of the Russian revolutionary movement up to several centuries before Marxism and outlined a brief history of the 'right-wing' sources of Russian communism. We refer the reader to the broad factology constituted by his work 'The Third Rome,' a part of which was published in Russian in a separate publication (*The Ideology of National Bolshevism* [Идеология национал-большевизма]). If, after Agurskii, one revisits the works of Merezhkovsky, his deliberate and providential freight of Russian National Bolshevism becomes an obvious and irrefutable truth.

The Heritage of Truth

If it had been a relatively simple task to determine the correct side to take in recent times, if there had existed some kind of dependable doctrinal method of doing so, then the very dramatism of eschatology in its Christian understanding would have been pale and lifeless; there would have been far more of the righteous and saved, and a witheringly small number of the tempted. If the choice were static — a decision between one thing or another, between order and revolt, affirmation and negation, then the structure of the world itself would seem nothing more than a banal mechanism, whose birth could only come by means of a depraved demiurge, deprived of fantasies. Therefore, the moralistic rhetoric of all ideological camps — both those of the revolutionaries and those of the conservatives — leaves a painfully pathetic impression. Unreflective monarchism is just as absurd as orthodox communism. The orthodoxy of the church is no more convincing than the ideas of the sectarians. This is not the fault of individual persons, but rather the essence of that most complex period of humanity in which Russia lives, thinks, and settles on Her decision.

One arrives at adequacy only through an incredible strain of spirit, when the intellect, intuition, the voice of the blood, the church doctrine, the subtlest elements of inherited culture, a fervent interpretation of that which is occurring together with a passionate desire to decipher that meaning — when all of this, taken together, becomes inflamed by awakening, reinforced by a desperate longing for national truth. No doubt, the Russian national idea is dialectical, paradoxical. A colossal labor of the soul is required in order to make sense of it. When one starts along this path, one must not reject any conclusions, even those which appear the strangest and wildest at first glance. But, in this matter, banality, complacency, and lukewarmness are murderous. It is better to err than to mark anything with a stamp of refusal, an irresponsible appeal to some conception derived from 'cultural' or even clerical authority, never having thought it through on its own terms (and, perhaps, having ignored its general fallacy). The meaning and content of Russian history is a question addressed these days to everyone.

National Bolshevism as a spiritual method, a national dialectics; an analysis of the Russian people's fate and that of the Russian state as a messianic path taken by an Orthodox order, chosen to achieve an eschatological feat, with every extremity, excess, and paradox that comes with translating this unique ideal into a sociopolitical substantiality — this all comes closer than anything else to deciphering the mystery of Rus'. And since today's time is indeed that of the *end*, he who correctly understands will act correctly. And depending on this act of sons and grandsons is the final lot of those generations who suffered and burned with a great will — the Russian will to Truth, passed down in the blood, the language, the state, and culture — passed down by the grace of the Orthodox baptism to *us*.[21]

21 Article first written in 1996, first published in 1997 in the journal *Elements* (No. 8 — Dossier 'National Bolshevism').

"There's a Spirit of Autocracy in the Commisars"

(a genealogy of Russian National Bolshevism)

What has changed? The signs and flagheads?
The same hurricane sweeps every path:
There's a spirit of autocracy in the commisars,
There are bursts of revolution in the tsars.[22]

— Maximilian Voloshin

The red murderer is holier than the chalice![23]

— Nikolai Kliuev

To date, the most complete and interesting study of Russian National Bolshevism is Mikhail Agurskii's book. Agurskii was a dissident and emigrated from the USSR to Israel in the 1970s. But despite that, his relationship to Soviet National Bolshevism remains objective in the highest degree. In some cases, his evaluations belie a deep sympathy, even. In our view, Agurskii's work is the most serious piece of writing dedicated to the Soviet period of Russian history and helps us to understand its deep spiritual significance.

Bolshevism's Recognition of the Nation

Agurskii defines the essence of Russian National Bolshevism as follows:

---

22 "Что менялось? Знаки и возглавья? Тот же ураган на всех путях: В комиссарах — дух самодержавья, взрывы революции в царях." From Maximilian Voloshin's 1920 poem "Northeast [Северовосток]."

23 "Убийца красный святей потира!" From Nikolai Kliuev's 1918 poem "We shall exalt the Revolution and the Mother of Light [Революцию и Матерь света в песнях возвеличим]..."

"From the very beginning of the Bolshevik Revolution, Bolshevism and the newly minted Soviet state were recognized both by various émigré groups and by groups within Russia as a proper response to real Russian interests regarding the nation and even religion. The number of these groups was relatively underwhelming, and they were not always influential, but their voice was audible and, from their point of view, was known to broad circles both within and without the Party. Bolshevism's recognition of the nation was considerably diverse.

"Bolshevism was considered a national phenomenon by both the left and the right, humanitarians and engineers, civilians and soldiers, the clergy and sectarians, poets, writers, and artists. The so-called movement of '*Smenovekhovtsy* [changers of signposts],' having emerged relatively late in right-wing circles of the Russian emigration, was crowned with the greatest success. It was precisely within the framework of this movement that National Bolshevism received its first formulation; though, to be fair, almost any early form of nationally oriented Bolshevism could be credited in this regard, to include Scythianism [скифство]. Outside of Russia at the outset of the 1920s, Ustrialov turned out to be the central figure of émigré National Bolshevism, while Lezhnev assumed that role in Russia.

"If this had all stayed within the boundaries of non-Bolshevik circles, it would hold a far more limited interest. But this is not what happened..."

"A Change of the Signposts"

Theses of Russian National Bolshevism first appeared among the radical Cadets, associated to one degree or another with Nikolai Ustrialov. However, another Cadet by the name of Yuri Kliuchnikov was the one who alerted Ustrialov to the possibility of moving from 'white' to 'red' nationalism. At some point, having understood the inevitability of the Whites' defeat and taking their (in many ways populist) theory of history as a point of departure — a theory affirming that it is precisely the spirit of a people, expressed in a sometimes paradoxical manner and utilizing the most unexpected ideologies and sociopolitical instruments, which creates history — these nationalist Cadets arrived at a radical reevaluation of their anti-Bolshevik positions and promoted the idea that the most consequential nationalist-statists at the moment in Russia were the Bolsheviks.

Of course, this idea was not immediately cast in such radical terms, but its fundamental traits had already revealed themselves in the first National Bolshevist texts, collected in *A Change of Signposts* [Смена вех], published in Prague in early 1921. The authors were Yu. Kliuchnikov, Yu. Potekhin, S. Chakhotin, A. Bobrishchev-Pushkin, the former procurator of the Holy Synod S. Lukyanov, and others. But it was Ustrialov himself who took on the leading intellectual role in this movement, which received the tenacious title of 'Signpost-Changing [сменовеховство].'

The *Smenovekhovtsy* were ecstatically received by the Bolsheviks themselves — especially by Lenin, Trotsky, and Stalin, who could sense the potential for a certain *intermediary* ideology, capable of attracting 'specialists' and significant strata of civil society, who were still unprepared to accept unadulterated communism. It was through the medium of the *Smenovekhovtsy* and their ideology that the Bolshevik authorities achieved what amounted to a unification with broad swaths of society. But the strength of ideas is such that they are practically never adapted to purely pragmatic ends; ideas always include their opposite tendency. As the Bolsheviks took advantage of the *Smenovekhovtsy* to achieve their goals, the *Smenovekhovtsy* themselves yielded an active influence on Bolshevik ideology. Agurskii shows how the most orthodox Marxists, particularly Zinoviev, took perfect stock of this situation and struggled from the very beginning against National Bolshevism, despite the practical benefits it offered to the Bolsheviks in their most critical period.

In parallel with the *Smenovekhovtsy*, another tendency, quite close in essence to it, was developing—Eurasianism (or at least its left wing). Both the Smenovekhovtsy and the 'Left Eurasianists' ended up in full support of the Bolshevik regime, and most of them returned to the Soviet Union, integrating with socialist society. Agurskii numbers the authors having undergone this evolution (Kliuchnikov, Bobrishchev-Pushkin, Kirdetsov, Lukyanov, Lvov, etc.) among the 'Left National Bolsheviks,' whom he distinguishes from the 'Right National Bolsheviks' on account of the latter group's leader and highest spiritual authority Ustrialov. Ustrialov remained outside of Russia in Harbin until the mid-1930s and observed a definite distance from the Soviet system in spite of his sympathies toward it.

In Agurskii's book, the idea that National Bolshevism was not simply a complex and internally heterogeneous movement, but a principally double phenomenon, clearly comes to the fore. However, there is no passage to be found in which Agurskii speaks plainly to this effect. The National Bolshevism of his treatise is divided into two constituent parts, corresponding to its two ideological aspects.

Essentially, he discusses the doubled nature of Conservative Revolution as such, and specifically how its historical expression was Russian National Bolshevism. It is telling that, as Agurskii notes, in the context of National Bolshevism, the term 'revolutionary conservatism' (first employed by the Slavophile Samarin and then appropriated by German nationalist ideologues) was used by none other than Isaiah Lezhnev, the pillar of Soviet 'Left National Bolshevism.'

Left National Bolshevism

Every revolution has 'conservative' underpinnings. These are expressions of an archaic paradigm, long forgotten and lost to an everyday conservatism which lacks any hint of radicality or revolution, which are set in opposition to the actual order of things—to the System. Externally, this tendency is often so 'nihilistic' and 'destructive' that it becomes extremely difficult to discern its 'conservative,' 'archaic' origins. It is precisely this aspect which we should think of as a 'Left National Bolshevism.'

Agurskii shows Left National Bolshevism to have originated with Russian eschatological sectarianism, the Old Believers, and populist apocalypticism. Later, certain 'Slavophiles' became its promoters—the most extreme representatives of which (as distinguished from moderate conservatives) viewed the entire 'Petersburg period' of the Romanov dynasty with the wildest unmitigated hatred; they considered this period a perversion of the true national Orthodox order. Then there were the 'populists [народники]'—from Herzen and Ogarev all the way up to Bakunin, Tkachev, and Nechaev, as well as the left Social-Revolutionaries. This trend is dominated by 'mystical nihilism': the idea that 'salvation' (i.e., the social good, the building of a just society, etc.), given the current social conditions, cannot be attained through any traditional, conventional, established path, as these routes had forever lost their legitimacy and effectiveness. Only the paradoxical path of 'holiness through sin' or 'creation through annihilation and downfall' remained.

Left National Bolshevism began with the self-immolations of the Old Believers, the radical tendencies of the non-priestly types such as the 'naysayers [нетовцы]' (or the 'Spasovo accord'), as well as the association arising from the 'spiritual Christians' known as the *Khlysty* [self-flagellators]. In this environment, assumptions that the 'anti-Christ' had already come to the world and that the Russian government, along with the official church, had fully fallen under his influence were widespread. Against such a desacralized state and a graceless church, the sectarians promoted the idea of an 'invisible city [невидимого града]' and a 'society of the chosen [общины избранных],' who, pursuing most terrible paths, hastened toward a redemption through protest, destruction, and a special path of 'sacrilegious sanctity' (at least from the usual point of view).

One must understand the terroristic populists and, in part, Nechaev, precisely through this lens of 'religious nihilism,' so characteristic of the Russian national essence. This attitude should be regarded as an informal, parallel ideology which rarely enjoyed a rigorous formulation, but which was nonetheless always potentially present in the broad masses of the people.

As Agurskii further suggests, one of the echoes of this idea, now issuing from a strictly intellectual milieu, was the Russian mystical renaissance — the so-called 'new religious consciousness' connected with Vladimir Soloviev and the entire movement of Russian symbolism, upon which he wielded such a consummate influence. Soloviev approached the same mystical, nihilistic reality from a different angle: Western mysticism, Hegelianism, an interest in gnostic and kabbalistic doctrines. We can clearly detect in Soloviev's thought the mechanism, thanks to which the gnostic idea (fundamental to the Anabaptists, the Cathars, the Albigenses, etc.) is incarnated in the modernist idea of 'progress.' Agurskii refers to Soloviev's conception as an 'optimistic eschatology,' according to which the social and technological development of society is flowing back toward a 'golden age.' Agurskii writes: "In order to reconcile the fact of the undeniable progress at the end of the nineteenth century with the no less undeniable fact of Christianity's fall, both in the people at large and in the intelligentsia (the carrier of this progress), Soloviev arrives at a paradoxical conclusion: that the Spirit of God [Дух Божий] rests not within the believers, but within the non-believers." In principle, the most radical 'nay-sayers' of the Old Believers affirmed the same concept, generally dismissing the very possibility of salvation by means of external rituals and holding that the sole path to salvation was to be gained only through the super-rational and inscrutable will of Christ. They held no regard for the merits of the faithful — some of the most extreme among them refused even to view faith as superior to a lack of faith.

Of course, the 'new religious consciousness' is in no way comparable to 'Left National Bolshevism,' but it served as an important theoretical premise, developed by only the most radical thinkers, either in joining the Bolsheviks or departing from their ranks.

Left National Bolshevism relates to the most extremist variant of the ideology, associated with a theoretical justification for the bloodiest and most horrific aspects of revolution. It is most characteristic of the left Social-Revolutionaries — particularly for that portion of their membership which entered history under the name of 'Scythianism.' In some sense, the very term 'Scythianism' can be interpreted as a synonym of Left National Bolshevism.

Scythianism

Between the end of 1917 and the beginning of 1918, two collections appeared under the name of *The Scythians*, in which the ideology of Left National Bolshevism found its first reflection. This ideology derived its meaning from an analysis of the October Revolution as a mystic, messianic, eschatological, and deeply nationalist phenomenon. The main ideologists of 'Scythianism' were the left Social-Revolutionary Ivanov-Razumnik, a member of the presidium of the All-Russian Central Executive Committee (VTsIK) S. Mstislavskii, and the poet-author Andrei Bely (Bugaev). Around this core, a group of equally famous poets and authors formed, having become classics of Soviet literature: Aleksandr Blok, Sergei Esenin, Nikolai Kliuev, Alexei Remizov, Evgenii Zamyatin, Olga Forsh, Alexei Chapygin, Konstantin Ehrberg, Evgenii Lundberg, etc.

Characteristic of the Scythians was their 'barbarian apologetics' (against Western Civilization), their appeal to the archaic elements of the nation, their praise of destructive spontaneity, leading to the creation of a 'new world.' Some authors espoused the Christian idea (in its Old-Believer—for Kliuev—or simply its non-Orthodox, nonconformist mode—as with Blok and Esenin).

The following pronouncement of Blok, directly anticipating the theses of Spengler, is typical of the era: "[...Civilized] people have grown exhausted and lost their cultural values. In times such as these, it is the freshest barbarian masses who turn out as the unconscious preservers of culture." We may consider Blok's great poem *The Twelve*, in which Bolshevism and revolution are explicitly bound with Christ, as a programmatic expression of Scythianism.

We may also associate certain purely religious phenomena with Left National Bolshevism—including the movement known as 'Renovationism [обновленчество]' and the project of the 'Living Church [Живой Церкви],' which were both actively promoted by partisans of 'Christian Socialism,' and which saw the manifestation of true Christian ideals in the form of revolution.

Valerii Briusov, having connected the Revolution not with Christian, but with magical, pantheistic renovationism and with a return to the theurgy of ancient pre-Christian cults, developed the pagan version of the very same eschatological complex.

Among figures of the young Soviet regime, Isaiah Lezhnev particularly distinguished himself as the founding ideologist of National Bolshevism in Russia and as the main promoter of the 'signpost-changing' tendencies of the émigré National Bolsheviks. Lezhnev took as his point of departure principles of an absolute 'people's spirit [народного духа],' which, for him, was the apotheosis and main axis of history. If the people resort to revolution, they do so in correspondence with their internal necessity; although, in the fulfillment of their will, they can employ any ideological, conceptual, or sociopolitical instrument. For Lezhnev, revolutionary destruction and tumult was justified precisely by national necessity and, as a result, these conditions carried within themselves the loftiest providential meaning, obscured behind a façade of barbarism. The same idea was capaciously expressed by another National Bolshevik: professor N. Gredeskul, one of the founders of the Cadets, who arrived at the idea of 'signpost-changing' independently of Ustrialov. He wrote: "Either Soviet Russia is some kind of monstrous bastard, in which case the fault for its advent falls upon the shoulders of the Russian people and it possesses no justification, for the whole people must voluntarily submit to a cabal of thieves, or Soviet Russia is an embryo — the embryo of a new humanity, an attempt by the toiling masses to materialize their eternal aspirations." Lezhnev harbored no doubt that 'Soviet Russia' was the 'embryo of a new humanity.'

We might look at the 'fellow travellers [попутчиков]' as yet another manifestation of Left National Bolshevism — B. Pilnyak, K. Fedin, A. Tolstoy, L. Leonov, Vs. Ivanov, V. Lidin, etc. One easily finds in their art all the characteristic motifs of the phenomenon.

Take, for example, this excerpt from a novel by Boris Pilnyak: "Now, in the wake of revolution, Russia has arrived at the seventeenth century in its everyday life [бытом], its mores [нравом], its cities. There has never been joy in Russia, but now there is… The Revolution, the people's revolt, had no need of the foreign [чужое]. It's the people's revolt — they have come to power and are creating their truth — authentic Russians creating an authentic Russian truth." The fellow travellers glorified the national elementality of revolt, perceiving in Bolshevism the 'new uprising of Pugachev [новую пугачёвщину],' a primordially Russian, broadly archaic phenomenon.

In some sense, one may also relate Left National Bolshevism to Maxim Gorky, who attempted to create a dedicated people's religion, the definite aspects of which were almost identical to the ideas of the radical German nationalists.

Gorky wrote: "The immortal folk [народушко бессмертный], I believe in its spirit, I profess its strength; it is the sole and unmistakable beginning of life — the father of all gods past and future." We encounter something similar with the theorists of the German Conservative Revolution, and even with the Nazis. Gorky also shares with them a fascination with Nietzsche…

Right National Bolshevism

The second principal side of National Bolshevism can be called 'Right' — 'conservative.'

'Right National Bolshevism' results from the following logic: the life of the nation, the state, and the people constitute a certain organic process which always preserves its core in an unadulterated state. In the course of all dynamic transformations — including crises, revolutions, and uprisings — the dialectic of the 'people's spirit' shows forth, leading toward providential goals, independent of the desires and will of the most immediate participants of the events. The nation remains identical with itself — like a living organism — at various stages of its existence even its infirmity is, at times, a syndrome of renewal, a means of fortification. The people's being is deeper and more absolute than their sociopolitical history.

Consequently, any change that occurs within the framework of the nation is a *conservative* phenomenon, regardless of the external forms by which it incarnates. This conception of Right National Bolshevism was incrementally and fully formulated by Nikolai Ustrialov. For Ustrialov, Bolshevism and revolution were merely stages of the history of the Russian nation, aimed at a dialectical surmounting of a state of crisis, which alone had made the revolution possible. In other words, Ustrialov and other Right National Bolsheviks saw the 'conservative' element neither in the theory of revolution itself, nor in the very essence of 'nihilistic gnosticism' (as did the Left National Bolsheviks), but solely in the constancy of the national context, which subordinated to itself every available sociopolitical instrument — including revolution.

Ustrialov's National Bolshevism was assonant with the ideas of certain 'White' ideologues, the left wing of the Cadets, a certain faction of the monarchists (Shul'gin being the most brilliant representative of this trend), and especially the Eurasianists, who arrived through their analysis of the revolution to practically the same conclusions as those of the Right National Bolsheviks.

Right National Bolshevism distinguishes itself from the 'Left' variant (with which it nonetheless shares a great deal of features) in that it does not take 'revolution,' 'barbarism,' or 'destruction' as a self-sufficient value. The elementality of religious negation — so essential for Left National Bolshevism and the gnostic impulse at its roots — is alien to the 'Right National Bolsheviks,' who saw in the revolution nothing more than a temporary, transitory evil which was immediately overcome by the positive principle of a new national affirmation. It is telling that the 'Right National Bolsheviks,' more often than not, took up the cause of the 'Whites' during the Revolution and the Civil War, having abandoned the 'old order' while they still could; but, as soon as the 'task of the Whites' had fully played itself out, they began to greet and support everything in the new authority that was also assonant with *order*, even if a 'new' one. On their part, the Left National Bolsheviks did not greet that in the new Bolshevik regime which manifested as 'order,' but that which was proper to a '*new* order.' They were concerned not with the continuity and constancy of some imperishable reality, always identical with itself, but with 'fracture [рывок],' the 'mystery of renewal,' the radical transformation of the world, 'transcendence,' going beyond boundaries. It was for this reason that the 'Left National

Bolshevik' Esenin wrote: "I never joined the Russian Communist Party (RCP) because I feel myself to be much farther left than them."

Ustrialov himself never hid the fact that he saw "National Bolshevism as a means of surpassing Bolshevism." To put it differently, he regarded the revolution and the Bolsheviks from a purely pragmatic perspective — as a force which, alone at that given moment, could provide Russia with the most effective nationally centralized power. Ustrialov believed that 'Bolshevism,' under the influence of Russian national elements and the pressure of the geopolitical and historical scale of the state, would become a 'fascist caesarism' — i.e., a totalitarian regime, oriented toward the defense of Russian national interests, both in the political and economic spheres.

Those in favor of Right National Bolshevism despised the most radical aspects of communist ideology and felt that the optimal thing for Russia would be a return to the market and to a peasant order. But, generally speaking, their relationship to economics was a purely pragmatic one (as with the Nazis): whatever economic mode was most beneficial to the nation was the one to adopt. Ustrialov found the petit-bourgeois regime to be the most effective, which was why he so rapturously greeted the New Economic Policy (NEP), which, in ideological terms, he had both formulated and potentially hastened, since many party leaders paid heed to Ustrialov's opinions, to include Lenin himself.

Many communist critics of this development — Zinoviev, Kamenev, and later Bukharin — took pains to emphasize the particular 'NEP' orientation of Ustrialov's ideology; and it was precisely on this basis that they attacked National Bolshevism, silently skirting the more delicate and subtle moment of pure nationalism.

If the most non-conformist elements of the milieu falling outside of the Bolsheviks (terrorists, neo-populists, left Social-Revolutionaries, radical sectarians, etc.) had been attracted to Left National Bolshevism, then, on the contrary, it was the hyper-conformist types who were attracted to Right National Bolshevism — the specialists, military cadres (Brusilov, Altfater, Polivanov, etc.), and, though strange it may seem, reactionary circles within the clergy and even the Black Hundreds. They were all united in their sympathy for the 'iron fist,' 'centralism,' the authoritarian regime which had clearly been installed while the Bolsheviks had been bolstering their power. According to Agurskii, the simple folk even made use of the following formula: "Whom do you support: the Bolsheviks or the Communists?" The 'Bolsheviks' were associated with representatives of the radical Great Russian state, with its attendant expressions of the people's essence, while the 'Communists,' to the contrary, were seen as the dogmatic defenders of internationalism and the 'Westernizers.'

Appended to the far-right flank of National Bolshevism were many Eurasianists, who had generally kept themselves at arm's length from any total and uncompromising acceptance of Bolshevism for religious and ethical reasons.

Resonance in the Party

National Bolshevist tendencies (both right and left) were the product of intellectual activity on the part of non-communist theorists. But they enjoyed massive resonance with the All-Russian Communist Party (VKP). Moreover, as Agurskii handily demonstrates, it is precisely the latter's relationship to National Bolshevism that provides a key to understanding the 'Aesopian' language of the inner-party polemics prevalent during the early Soviet period; it was this language which prefigured the final consolidation of unilateral power in the party of Stalin. If we rely on the formal aspects of party discussions during those years, then we shall collapse into an unintelligible chaos of paradoxes and obvious contradictions. Only by taking National Bolshevism as our fundamental interpretive criterion will we manage to construct the whole picture of the ideological struggle which occurred during this period.

Left National Bolshevism impressed Lev Trotsky beyond all others, and Agurskii fairly notes that it is high time we asked the following question: "Was Trotsky indeed of the left?"[24] It was none other than Trotsky, in his book *Literature and Revolution*, who voiced a positive reaction to the 'fellow-travellers' and the representatives of 'Scythianism,' whose pathos resonated completely with Trotsky's revolutionary spirit. In some regard, even the theory of 'permanent revolution' and the idea of its 'export to the West' fail to contradict the messianic tendencies of those who promoted 'national barbarism.' In a purely pragmatic way, National Bolshevism allowed Trotsky to strengthen his own power within the party and the army, relying on the national spirit and making direct appeals to the patriotic feelings of the Great Russians. At this stage, Zinoviev emerged as his most consequential adversary, who, however he may have disdained Great Russian National Bolshevism as the head of the Communist International (Comintern), evinced a pragmatic sympathy for German National Bolshevism and even leftist strains of Nazism. Lenin himself held extremely positive opinions regarding the *Smenovekhovtsy*, though it is difficult to say with any certainty which aspect of these opinions dominated — pragmatic Machiavellianism or a sincere identification with 'mystical nihilism.'

For its own part, Right National Bolshevism is bound with the figure of Joseph Stalin, who, as Agurskii again justly notes, was always much closer in spirit to the pragmatic conservative Ustrialov than to the Scythians and other revolutionary radicals. And even though Stalin, in his inner-party struggle with Trotsky, had initially formed a bloc with Zinoviev and Bukharin, he would gradually defeat the

---

24 [Translator's note]: "А так ли Троцкий лев?" This is a play on Trotsky's first name, 'Lev' (sometimes rendered in English as 'Leo'), which can also serve as a short-form adjective in Russian denoting someone of a left-wing persuasion.

two of them precisely with the support of the conservative, Right National Bolshevik sector in the Party, cultivated by Stalin through 'Lenin's call' for new national cadres that had preserved a link with the essence of the people and a feeling for the state. Stalin took absolute advantage of the fruits borne by Trotsky's and Lenin's acceptance of the *Smenovekhovtsy*, but was wise enough, in doing so, to annihilate his enemies with their own weapons. At every step in Stalin's career, one can detect this unspoken but perpetually contemplated conception — the conception of 'Right National Bolshevism.' It is as though Ustrialov was the one to give expression to Stalin's thoughts, his Harbin confessor... Stalin without Ustrialov is simply inconceivable.

And it is no accident that the sacking of Zinoviev's 'opposition' was perceived by contemporaries as a total victory of Ustrialov's ideas.

Agurskii also sees Stalin's sympathies toward the rightist version of National Bolshevism in the latter's warm relations with Bulgakov and, in particular, his exaltation at Bulgakov's openly National Bolshevist play The Days of the Turbins [Дни Турбиных]; Stalin had seen this play an estimated fifteen times. At the play's conclusion, the White officer Myshlaevskii argues to his comrades that they must switch over to the Bolshevik side:

> Myshlaevskii: I'm for the Bolsheviks, but only insofar as they are against the Communists... At least I'll know that I'm serving in the Russian army. The people aren't with us. The people are against us.
> Studzinskii: ...We had our Russia — a great state [держава]!
> Myshlaevskii: And we shall have it in the future! In the future!

This passage contains the quintessence of Right National Bolshevist thought.

Agurskii further underlines how it was Stalin who welcomed the 'Sergiian' line of Orthodoxy, which had reached a compromise with the Soviet regime, and yet rejected the restorationist 'Christian socialism' which appealed much more to the 'Left National Bolsheviks.' The definition of restorationism common to that epoch was rather curious — 'the church's Trotskyism.' There were also two possibilities in relation to the Church's collaboration with the Bolsheviks — the 'revolutionary church' of the restorationists, who strove to grasp and comprehend, to 'Christianize mystical nihilism,' or a strategic compromise on the part of official Orthodoxy; in the case of the latter, we can perceive undertones of such an approach before the Metropolitan (and later Patriarch) Sergius took on the position of Patriarch Tikhon after his release from prison.

The Jewish Factor

Agurskii analyzes the Jewish problem in the context of Bolshevism in a totally unexpected manner. From his point of view, the mass participation of Jews in the revolution can be explained not so much by their enmity toward Orthodox Russia, a revenge for the 'pale of settlement,' or by their rootlessness and Western cosmopolitanism, as it can be explained by a particular eschatological, messianic inclination characteristic of some varieties of sectarian Judaism (Hassidic or Sabbataist), widely disseminated among Eastern European Jews. It was precisely the likeness of apocalyptic fanaticism, the religious nature they shared with representatives of Russian sectarianism and the gnosticism of the intelligentsia, which determined the Jewish role in the Bolshevik movement. Moreover, Agurskii emphasizes that many Jewish Bolsheviks felt themselves to be passionate Great Russian nationalists, for whom the October Revolution had annihilated any remaining impediments preventing them from total integration with the Russian people. The majority of them were either baptized and assimilated or were otherwise distinguished by their specific mystical predilections and belonged to esoteric Kabbalistic groups.

Of course, this description can by no means account for all Jews. Zinoviev, Kamenev, and almost the whole of the 'Petersburg Group' were authentic Jewish Westernizers who had adopted communism solely on a socially rational and dogmatic basis. The imperial [великодержавный] National Bolshevism of some Jews (Lezhnev, Tan-Bogoraz, Kerdetsev, Pilnyak, and even the early Trotsky who, by the way, harbored an active interest in Freemasonry and had been a member of the 'Grand Orient' lodge) sharply clashed with the Russophobia of others. But even with the Russian Bolsheviks, this dichotomy finds a reflection in the opposition between Stalin's new Russian leaders (Molotov, Voroshilov, Kirov, etc.) and Russophobic Great Russians such as Bukharin.

National Bolshevism versus National Communism

Agurskii elucidates an important terminological distinction between the two abovementioned terms. By 'National Bolshevism,' he means the Great Russian, Eurasianist variant which stood for the unification of all lands that had previously fallen within the Russian Empire into a single, centralized socialist state—the USSR. Among the Bolshevik leaders, this position is unilaterally associated with the figure of Joseph Stalin.

In its turn, 'National Communism' refers to the separatist tendencies of the national outer territories of Russia that had striven to use the October Revolution as a means of achieving national independence. Represented among the strongest of National-Communist tendencies were the independence movements of the Tatars (Sultan-Galiev) and the Georgian and Ukrainian communists (Skrypnik). They (fairly) believed that the Bolsheviks' imperialist inclinations were too dominant, that Ustrialov's formulation of National Bolshevism was pregnant with promises of a new 'Moscow diktat.' It is telling that the most active opponents of separatist National Communism were representatives of those same nations, but who professed the Soviet principle of 'unfractured unity [единонеделимчество]' and, more specifically, National Bolshevism. It was for this reason that Stalin and Ordzhonikidze fought such a death struggle with Georgian separatism. Only in the Ukraine was the pro-Moscow party headed by a majority of ethnic Great Russians, as well as assimilated Jews.

This moment is of the utmost importance, as it shows with crystalline focus the fundamental difference between the simple adaptation of communist ideas to a concrete national context (National Communism) and a special, universalist line of thought, exclusively bound to Russian eschatology, messianic and pan-human, integrative and open to all Eurasian peoples. Thusly does National Bolshevism reveal itself as a super-ethnic, imperial, and universal reality. This is its principal moment.

A Parallel Ideology

Agurskii attributes National Bolshevism to several other authors — Marietta Shaginyan, Maksimilian Voloshin, Osip Mandelshtam, Andrei Platonov, the Futurist Rodchenko, Vladimir Mayakovsky, O. Khvolson, M. Prishvin, A. Akhmatova, M. Tsvetaeva, N. Tikhonov, N. Nikitin, Ya. Livshits, K. Chukovsky, etc. If one analyzes Soviet literature with a careful eye — right up to Sholokhov, whom Agurskii fails to name — one finds that, almost in its entirety, it contains a plethora of National Bolshevist thought; it is practically impossible to find pure 'socialist realism' within Soviet culture, with the exception of the most 'conventional' works that have borne the stamp of 'culture' in a strictly strategic sense.

We should pay especially close attention to the figure of Marietta Shaginyan, who has become a classic of Soviet literature. In both her art and her intellectual evolution, multiple substantive aspects of National Bolshevism coalesce into a whole.

Firstly, she was an assimilated and Russified Armenian — a fact which is perfectly compatible with Agurskii's understanding of the phenomenon of great socialist statehood [социалистической великодержавности], whose greatest proponents were more often than not assimilated foreigners — Georgians, Jews, Armenians, etc. If, in the western territories (Ukraine), the most active centralists and promoters of Moscow power in the Party had been Jews, then in the Caucasus (Azerbaijan and Georgia), it was the Armenians who played such an active role. And so Shaginyan's adoption of National Bolshevism is quite telling.

Secondly, before the revolution, Shaginyan had been an active participant in the Religious-Philosophical Circle of Dmitrii Merezhkovsky and Zinaida Gippius, where she was acquainted with a gnostic worldview in which she took great interest. She began her spiritual journey like any typical representative of the 'new religious consciousness.' Shaginyan was one of the first to accept the October Revolution, having evaluated it along mystical lines. She discerned in the revolution "the roots of some new Slavic-Bolshevik consciousness.' After the revolution, she progressed even farther on her gnostic path — like the gnostic Cainites, she began to interpret the negative personae of the 'Old Testament' (Ham, Cain, Esau, etc.) as carriers of the true spirit and as forerunners of Christ, the enemy of the evil 'Demiurge-usurper.' Her intellectual gnosticism was a direct analogue of the sectarian peasant gnosticism of Kliuev or Esenin.

Thirdly, Shaginyan — like both Andrei Platonov and the scholar Vladimir Vernadskii — was a devotee of the doctrine of Nikolai Fedorov relating to the 'resurrection of the dead,' which is one of the classic themes of operative occultism.[25] This theurgic principle of

25 For A. Dugin's study on this topic, see "Le complot ideologique du cosmisme russe [The Ideological Conspiracy of Russian Cosmism]" in *Politica Hermetica*, No. 6 (Paris, 1992).

Fedorov's thought inspired many Eurasianists, particularly of the 'left' variety — Karsavin, Savitskii, and the publishers of the Parisian journal *L'Eurasie* [Eurasia] (Tsvetaeva's husband, Efron, etc.). Fedorov's heterodox (from an Orthodox perspective) but nationalist and anti-Western doctrine was the ideological lens through which the 'right-wing' conservative mystics were able to approach and adopt communism.

And fourthly, in her fiction, Shaginyan attempted to create a 'new proletarian mythology,' the many moments of which served as typical models of conspirological consciousness, characteristic of traditional mystical or occultic thinking.

Taken as a whole, the fate of Marietta Shaginyan represents the archetypal National Bolshevist evolution. In this sense, her figure is paradigmatic for Soviet National Bolshevism in general.

Agurskii's analysis creates such an impressive picture of Soviet society in its deepest mythological strata that it leaves one with the feeling of being in a parallel world, where all the tired external dogma, the lame utilitarianism, and the cruel banality of official Soviet history is resolved in a deep, rich reality, full of metaphysical intuitions and magical occurrences. It is this 'second reality' of Sovietism — from its first sources unto its final days — that provides the whole with meaning, fulness, and hermeneutic clarity. This is a vivifying reality, paradoxical, passionate, and deep, in distinction from the dry statistical data, the censored historical summaries, or the shrill criticisms of the dissidents, who are just as tedious as Soviet historians in their cataloguing of facts (only these facts, instead of bearing a triumphal, optimistic tone, are drenched in an atmosphere of tragedy and cruelty).

Mikhail Agurskii is not merely a historian with an original schema. He is a fateful man for Russia. And the symbolism of his trajectory is revealed in the fact that he died not in Jerusalem, not in America, but in Moscow, the Third Rome[26], where he had traveled to attend

26 *The Third Rome* is the title of the complete English-language version of his book.

the 'Congress of Compatriots [Конгресс Соотечественников].' The date of his death — 21 August 1991 — is no less symbolic. This was the final day of the Great Soviet Empire, the final moment during which National Bolshevism ruled the expanses of Eurasian territory.[27]

L'age d'argent ou l'age mordoré?[28]

("The Red-Brown Shade of the Silver Age")

A Known Unknown

There are thousands of studies devoted to the culture, and especially the poetry, of the Russian Silver Age. It would seem doubtful that anyone could reveal something new about it. The theme, moreover, has been exploited so actively and for so long that it has become banal and has begun automatically to put one in a state of desperation, longing, and boredom. The names of Blok, Gumilev, Akhmatova, Tsvetaeva, Gippius, Briusov, Severyanin, Kuzmin, Sologub, Merezhkovskii, Kliuev, Ivanov, Esenin, Radlova, Khlebnikov, Bely, and Mandelshtam have been worn thin, and any appeal to them is received either as a gesture of pseudo-cultural kitsch or as an unintelligible and (more rarely) specialized academicism (in the event that we are speaking of a serious and documented study).

However, in reality, everything is much more complicated. Today, the fact is that there is not a single adequate methodology — neither

27 Article first written in 1996, first published in 1996 in the journal *Elements* [Элементы] (No. 8 — Dossier "National Bolshevism").

28 "The Silver Age or the Red-Brown Age?"; this is a play on words: in French, the expression 'Silver Age' sounds like 'The Age of Money'; and the word 'mordoré' refers to a noble, kingly hue that is red-brown with a golden tint. Jean Parvulesco writes about this in his *Order of the Red-Brown Unicorn* [*L'Ordre de Licorne Mordoré*].

in Russian culturology, nor in Russian literary studies — that would allow one to analyze the entire pleiad of colossally famous Silver-Age authors and their works, the whole cultural and spiritual context of that epoch, even in the crudest approximation.

Why?

During the Soviet period, the ill-considered strictures of ideological censorship simply could not have provided the basis for an adequate evaluation. This much is obvious. Because of this, Soviet culturology and its fundamental assumptions can hardly be taken seriously for our purposes. But, in addition, the majority of art and literary scholars developed their ideas in precisely this environment, and it is unlikely that they can extricate themselves from these entrenched cliches and models in any short span of time. Inertia in education and habituated modes of thinking are rooted out only with difficulty. Even if one were to turn everything on its head and analyze everything through a positive lens which had previously been understood negatively, it would nonetheless be difficult to rid oneself of those original assumptions; after all, such an inversion would still take place in the same evaluative system of coordinates and would be inadmissible in our case.

At the transitory, 'reconstructive [перестроечном]' stage, everything seemed quite simple — the rejection of ideological prohibitions and the revelation of dissident motifs in the culture of the Silver Age was presented as an adequate background for an explanation and understanding of the phenomenon. But, actually, the republished works of these authors and the mass of historiographical material related to them were not a new discovery in the full sense of the word. True discovery implies comprehension and, at that time, such comprehension was fatally lacking. There was not only a lack resulting from the abovementioned limitations of contemporary post-Soviet culturology, entrenched in late-Soviet cliches. The main reason lies much deeper, and is utterly ideological in nature.

The fact that Silver Age culture was not inscribed into the norms of Sovietism is obvious and requires no proof—entire tomes have been written about persecutions (both physical and moral) waged against its principal figures. But there yet remains one most important consideration. But there is yet another factor which is of the greatest importance. *This culture, likewise, could in no way be inscribed into the norms of Western liberalism, which have now become the ersatz ideology of contemporary Russia.*[29]

In order to elucidate this thesis, we must first make a slight digression.

There are two authors whose works are fundamental to an understanding of the questions we have posed. Both (though to varying degrees) occupy positions of liberal ideology. Both are emigrants from Jewish families. Both are brilliant connoisseurs of Russian history and Russian culture. We are speaking here of Mikhail Agurskii and Aleksandr Etkind.

Mikhail Agurskii: A Definition of National Bolshevism

Agurskii was a dissident historian who had emigrated to Israel in the 1970s. Along with Solzhenitsyn and Shafarevich, he participated in the collection *From Beneath the Slabs* [Из-под глыб]. But the primary work of his life was the book *The Third Rome*, a part of which came out in Russian, published in Paris as a separate text under the heading *The Ideology of National Bolshevism*. At the current time[30], this work of Agurskii's is considered a classic and the best point of reference for a

29 [Translator's note]: This statement refers to the Russia of 1997 and, at the time of this translation (February 2022–January 2023), mostly no longer applies, save for an increasingly alienated group of liberal figures belonging to Russia's current intelligentsia.

30 [Translator's note]: Again, 1997.

study of the topic, both in academic circles and among political theorists. Unlike the books written by Yanov and Laker, Agurskii's study stands apart due to its magnificent objectivity, argumentation, and subtle feeling for that which is complex and paradoxical.

His fundamental thesis can be reduced to the following.

The division of Russian society which had appeared in the nineteenth century in the guise of the Slavophiles and the Westernizers was not as unilateral as many take it to be. Both camps — on the right and the left — contained an entire spectrum of shared values, organizational principles, and orientations. The Slavophiles and, later, the philosophers of the 'new religious consciousness' (beginning with Soloviev) were not as reactionary as their forebears and frequently stood apart through their radicalism and social non-conformism, which was completely untraditional for the classical right wing. On the other hand, the 'Russian Westernizers — from Chaadaev, through Herzen, and up to the Bolsheviks and the socialists — were a far cry from classical cosmopolitans and internationalists; rather, they developed their ideas within the framework of a left-wing nationalism, the most striking example of which can be found in the populist movement [народничество] and, afterward, in that of the Social-Revolutionaries. Bakunin, Herzen, Lavrov, Mikhailovskii, and many other early social-democrats are more appropriately called national-revolutionaries than classical liberal Westernizers; in this sense, they come close to the Slavophiles. These latter, in their turn, took a critical view of the post-Petrine monarchy and hailed the archaic world of the commune, the pre-schismatic Holy Rus', and propounded an ideal of society founded on justice and social solidarity. Both groups advocated for a certain paradoxical 'Russian paradise,' simultaneously national and universal (messianic). Their hatred of capitalism, their love of the simple folk, their faith in Russia's messianic destiny brough the right and the left together on the level of ideas, giving birth to concepts that would later, in the twentieth century, be gathered under the mantle of 'National Bolshevism.'

The Silver Age was the direct descendant of this 'right-left' national-progressivist orientation, which enables us to understand the complex and entangled ideological fates of most cultural and political figures of the time. The entire National Bolshevist, conservative-revolutionary field of ideas, intuitions, themes, and theories created a living core of Revolution. The Bolsheviks were only one offshoot of this mighty tree. Having gained total power, they found themselves in the position of the sole descendants of these tendencies, having been funneled into a new Soviet reality through those who came to the Bolsheviks both from the right (specialists, military officers, civil functionaries) and from the non-Marxist left (anarchists, Social-Revolutionaries, Mensheviks, etc.).[31]

The meaning of Agurskii's astounding discovery consists in the fact that Russian political history, beginning with Aleksandr I (if not from the schism itself), did not develop through the dualistic logic of 'conservatism-progressivism' (as it did in the West). Instead, both society and the intelligentsia, fascinated by the Russian mystery, the Russian paradox, torturously sought some unexpected synthesis that would reveal a fantastic perspective, would return the Golden Age as something simultaneously super-contemporary and super-archaic.

The Russian type, predating National Bolshevism proper, is a person (a folk, a commune, a church) in search of lost sacrality. The sharp

---

31 [Translator's note]: In the 1997 edition of *Templars of the Proletariat*, the following segment is removed: "Such an evolution received its conceptual formation in works by Nikolai Ustrialov and in the publications of the Left National Bolsheviks, which are now forgotten, but were vastly influential in their day and popularized the principles of National Bolshevism. In the artistic cross-section of this conservative-revolutionary, National Bolshevist movement, we find 'Scythianism,' the literary 'fellow travellers,' Imaginism, and Futurism; later, these trends became the foundation of Soviet culture."

pain of this loss forms the backbone of this type's whole psychology and ideology. It is precisely for this reason that what would, at first glance, appear to be a strange transition on the part of the Russian intelligentsia from Marxism to Orthodoxy and back was so easy to justify. This was analyzed and experienced not as a change from black to white, but as a search within the framework of a single, intuitively grasped (but inexpressibly national-revolutionary) position which desperately wanted to appear from the depths of the national unconscious into the daylight of concrete social reality.

We note that there also exists a contrary type at the opposite pole of this phenomenon — a person of the establishment, a conformist carrier of the system. This person was incarnated in the externally Orthodox and conservative nobleman (the civil servant) with a European education, but who was utterly separate from the life of the simple folk. As a result, conservative types such as these were entirely open to the ideas of market transformation and bourgeois reforms. Ultimately, there were right-wing and left-wing elements at this conformist pole, but they were of an evolutionary, instead of a revolutionary, bent — representatives of limp patriotism mixed with frequent trips to the West. They bore attributes of the landed gentry and tolerated the advent of the merchant class along with the establishment of bourgeois social relations. On the psychological level, we are dealing here with a type that is absolutely deaf to sacrality, satisfied in his profane milieu, who corresponds wholesale to that day's type belonging to the general European culture.

It is precisely between these poles — the national-revolutionary pole (often wearing the mask of internationalism) and the national-conservative pole (obscuring within itself an authentic cosmopolitanism) — that the force lines of secret resistance passed through, even if the most active participants of ideological discussions and political movements hid this truth at every turn.

According to Agurskii, the October Revolution represents the unequivocal victory of the national-revolutionary layer of Russian society, although, naturally, not every component of its previous stages and formations found a place there. The Marxist dogma, taken as the sole yardstick and without alternative, did much to harm the living and creative development of foundational and, frequently, the most interesting tendencies of this general direction.

In this light, National Bolshevism becomes a certain common denominator of the forces in Russian culture and politics which were fanatically engaged in a search for the sacred, and which, like the medieval gnostics, did not establish the external, hollow forms of a pseudo-religious, pseudo-spiritual conformism. This search for lost sacrality also explains the sympathy shared among the revolutionaries, intellectuals, and poets of the Silver Age for heresies, the ideas of the Old Believers, and the life of the people which had preserved several aspects of ancient culture, where all elements of being were recognized as sacred and not just cathedrals and icons. For the educated class, this overflowed into their searches into Sophiology or the 'new religious consciousness' (Soloviev, Merezhkovskii, father Sergius Bulgakov, Berdiaev, Bely, Blok, etc.); for those emerging from a peasant milieu, this tendency expressed itself in sectarianism, heresy, revolt (Esenin, Kliuev, Karpov, Klychkov, etc.). But both worlds were intimately connected and were animated by a single 'National Bolshevist' pathos.

In their broad features, these are the theses of Mikhail Agurskii from which he derives his non-contradictory interpretation of the last stages of Soviet history. He speaks of a time when — already after the destruction the a living and polyphonic element that preceded the Revolution — the same paradigms continued to function in a new form and on another level, explaining the logical contradictions and absurdity of the period.[32]

Aleksandr Etkind: Four Particularities of the Russian Intellectual

In total independence and by other means, another most interesting student of this period came to similar conclusions: Aleksandr Etkind. Previously, he had specialized in the Russian psychoanalysis that had emerged at the beginning of the century.

In his book *Sodom and Psyche: Essays on the Intellectual History of the Silver Age*, he describes assiduously and with high cleverness the 'shadowed' moments in the biographies of certain dominant figures of the Silver Age. These moments are not 'shadowed' as in shameful, but in their strangeness, inscrutability, unknowability, or political 'incorrectness.'

Etkind's conclusion is extremely interesting — that the majority of this epoch's major figures were literally possessed by four incessantly repeating motifs, which Etkind himself glancingly attributes to a single form of psychic deviance (which is already of less importance to us).

The first motif is the cyclical problem of sex. Practically none of the representatives of the Silver Age take a banal approach to this problem, and instead are constantly gravitating toward radical and often perverse situations. These situations are quite varied — the *ménage à trois* (some classic examples of which are the relationship

32 [Translator's note]: In an earlier version of this text, Dugin ends this section as follows: "Agurskii concludes that, for 74 years, the country had been living not under Bolshevism, but under National Bolshevism, though, at some point, even the leaders had ceased to clearly perceive it. It is striking that Agurskii himself died on the 21st of August, 1991, in Moscow, where he had traveled from Tel-Aviv to attend the 'Congress of Compatriots.' The death of this magnificent historian, who had devoted his entire life to these careful and scrupulous studies, coincided precisely with the end of the National Bolshevist Empire."

between Pauline Viardot and Ivan Turgenev; the Merezhkovsky-Gippius-Filosofov triangle; the triangle between Lilya and Osip Brik and Vladimir Mayakovsky; the relationship between Bely and Blok's wife, Mendeleeva, etc.), homoeroticism (Kuzmin, Briusov, Tsvetaeva, Radlova, Akhmatova), orgies and the ritual gatherings at the home of Vyacheslav Ivanov (in which sectarians took part), female dominance [женопоклонничество], masochism, and an obsession with virginity on the part of Vladimir Soloviev's disciples, Rozanov's theology of sex, Gumilev's sado-masochistic motifs, Esenin's pan-eroticism, etc. Even if we discard a certain reductive psychoanalytic interpretation, it is utterly obvious that sex constitutes the central axis of the Silver Age. And by this, we do not refer simply to sex as such, but to its deep, metaphysical dimension, which so interested the poets and thinkers of this epoch; we refer here to a penetrating intuition of its sacred content, its mysterious message that calls for interpretation, revelation, realization. It is rather facile to think of all this as mere 'deviance.' Rather, a question is being posed about the spiritual status of 'norms' — a question of sex, seen as a drama, as the most important moment of spiritual and national history.

The second motif is a fascination with political extremism. The majority of the Silver Age's figures supported revolutionary and socialist forces without the slightest of caveats. It was not only the Bolsheviks whom they supported, who only became the true masters of the situation following the revolution of October 1917 (and who did not, after all, achieve that supremacy immediately). The Social-Revolutionaries, the populists, and the anarchists became the natural political milieu toward which the representatives of the Silver Age gravitated. Everyone dreamed of a revolution [переворот], an uprising, a revolt. Even those who rejected the Bolsheviks often turned their backs on those threatening to fracture the Revolution and claiming the right to sole authority. Their social radicalism was not motivated by conformism, myopia, irresponsibility, or abstractionism. It was the intrinsic characteristic of the entire Silver Age.

The third motif is nationalism. Each Silver Age figure regarded it in a particular way. For some, it took the form of Judophobia and a sympathy for the Black Hundreds (Khlebnikov, Kliuev, Esenin, Karpov, etc.); for others, it took on a softer, more cultured visage. Etkind introduces an episode during which Blok himself expressed his rather radical antisemitic theses. However, the essence of this nationalism is not to be found in antisemitism or chauvinism. We find it instead in an obsession with Russia, an inexhaustible love for the land, the people, the national fate, its history, its paradox — for all things Russian, considered in a global, metaphysical dimension. All were caught up in a mania of Russia.

The fourth motif is mysticism, extreme religiosity, esotericism. This feature, too, is universal for all representatives of the Silver Age. Its forms might have been diverse — ranging from a plunge into the dogma of Orthodoxy to heresies, occultism (Bely's Steinerism), neo-paganism, or a nationalist Satanism (Briusov). And, in this question as with those preceding it, the norm was nothing other than extremity — not the surface-level religion of the pedestrian and not the pragmatic atheism of the European profaner, but a passionate, burning faith in the strength and reality of the beyond [потустороннего], a fanatical immersion in the problems of the soul, death, and the mystical meaning of events. It is no coincidence that Rasputin was of such vibrant interest to them, along with the *Khlysty*, the *Skoptsy*, and other nationalist sectarians.

To summarize, the four motifs are a honed eroticism, political extremism, nationalism, and esotericism. Such is the portrait of the typical Silver Age figure (common to both the genius and the mediocrity, the superlatively famous and the forgotten) which Etkind paints. And it is with unmarred logic that he transitions from there to the

Bolsheviks, whose psychological type turns out to be surprisingly close to what has been described above. The only difference in the case of the latter is that these motifs are more arid and are oriented toward political praxis and social realization. We recall Chernyshevsky — the literary Bolshevik Rakhmetov performs yogic exercises, takes an interest in the Kabbalistic texts of the late Isaac Newton, and is reminiscent of an initiate. Vera Pavlovna practices polyandry and is obsessed with prophetic dreams. We also note the historical Bolsheviks. Trotsky was a member of the 'Grand Orient' Masonic lodge, the author of a monograph on mystical symbolism which he wrote in exile and lost during his ramblings in the underground. Bogdanov was a pupil of the cosmist mystic Fedorov and dreamed of achieving physical immortality through scientific means via infusions of the blood (just after the revolution, Bogdanov was appointed director of the Institute of Blood Transfusion and died as a result of an experiment that he had carried out on himself). Bonch-Bruyevich was a specialist in the study of sects and published a sectarian journal called *New Dawn* [Новая Заря] (note the similarity it bears to the famous magical organization known as the Golden Dawn) with the aim of attracting people of that persuasion to Bolshevism. Kollontai was famous for her adherence to extreme forms of unfettered erotic experiments.[33]

But ultimately, the Silver Age — as an epoch dominated by theoreticians — came to an end. In its wake arose the harsh weekdays during which the 'sacred society' entered a phase of active construction as the 'new society.' Planning and industrialization could not fail to append parodic features to the realization of a national, mystical, erotic, and political utopia.

---

33 [Translator's note]: Not included in the 1997 *Templars*: "And finally, Lenin himself, in supporting Bonch-Bruyevich's Protestant line, gave his assent to social experimentation with orgiastic sex and welcomed both the *Smenovekhovtsy* and the National Bolsheviks (Ustrialov, Kliuchnikov, etc.)."

But the spiritual, psychological, and typological likeness to be found here is apparent.

Eternal Paradigm

Etkind voices interesting notions about the link between the Silver Age and the Golden Age (the age of Aleksandr). Here, he evinces the same pivotal motifs; it is merely the form and terminology that change between the two epochs. The problem of sex can already be clearly discerned in the work of Pushkin and Lermontov, while in the final Golden-Age generation of Dostoevsky and Chernyshevsky, it comes to occupy an almost central importance. The typical Russian model of political extremism is represented by the Decembrists, with their palette of political utopias, each of which—whether imagined by Muraviev, Pestel, or the 'Northern Society'—was saturated in a nationalist subtext. At the same time there came a flourishing of mysticism—the Biblical Society, Prince Golitsyn, the 'Zion Herald'; in addition, the *Skoptsy* and *Khlysty* rose in influence to the highest peaks of society (Tatarinova's esoteric salon, the chamberlain-*Skopets* Elenskii, the reemergence of Freemasonry, etc.).

The 'National Bolshevist' Silver Age simply received the baton, passed down from the previous period of the Alexandrine epoch. And, once more, a certain general type emerges: the Russian intellectual, the nationalist revolutionary, the paradoxical radical, the artist, the politician, the conspirator, the mystic, and (to all profane outward appearances) the deviant. We might also add the 'madman.'

Even if, between the reign of Aleksandr I and Nikolai II, there passed a period of relative quietude and external profanity, the line that extended through this gloomy age of repressions and capitalist reforms (which were, without exception, repulsive to the Russian soul of national-revolution) remained uninterrupted. Whether the Slavophiles, the followers of Petrashev, the populists, or the anarchists, the most brilliant Russian geniuses joined these ranks; they were attracted by the conspiracy, the political extremism, the fanatical spiritual search, the conjunction of populism and aristocracy, the cruelty and compassion, the pain and the hate... All of Russian culture, with the exception of the romances and the servile beacons of the official press, was saturated with a single spirit, a unified will, a general passion. Beyond it, all that remained was the boredom of routine, submission, bureaucracy, French governesses and provincial balls.[34]

A Different Line of Descendants

And so, we have arrived at a paradox: the Silver Age, which was the cultural banner of the late-Soviet intelligentsia, preparing the way, morally and ideologically, for Perestroika, has revealed itself to be utterly incompatible—if we look the truth in the eyes—with those Western, liberal norms that have been so fervently upheld as the supreme system of values in contemporary Russian society. In some sense, this political upheaval has outstripped any ruptures found in culture (the Russian intelligentsia continues to praise proto-Bolshevik culture, while in the political arena, Western liberal-cosmopolitan watchwords have already openly reigned for some time).

Under Gorbachev, the discourse revolved around pluralism within a socialist framework and (to some degree) a nationalist one—if only because Russia's social trajectory in the twentieth century had not been entirely besmirched—and, therefore, appeals to the Silver Age were more than justified. The logic was constructed as follows: the circle of Silver Age authors was oriented, as a whole, toward socialism; but the narrow thinking of dogmatic Marxists and the alienation resulting from the Soviet system (Stalinism) led to the sacrifice of the Revolution's spiritual leaders, just as, later, the first pleiad of

34 [Translator's note]: Originally, this sentence concluded with the names "Ostrovskii and Chekhov."

revolutionary practitioners had been annihilated by their successors. But when our society made its leap toward a radical, unadulterated liberalism after the Western model (1991–1996), the whole culturological picture was distorted until it became unrecognizable. From that time, a strange situation unfolded — the Silver Age fell from the grace of 'political correctness' (swiftly and in its entirety) under the aegis of the liberals; but there was neither time, nor the brains required to reflect on the fact, or to theoretically prepare for this step. And so a paradox opens up: the rightful heirs of the Silver Age would appear to be the ideologues of the current patriotic opposition — the 'red-browns.' After all, on the level of paradigmatic worldview, it is the 'red-browns' and no others who trace a direct line of continuity from the conceptual formula, common throughout the Silver Age, of the Russian Conservative Revolution, which unites versions of socialism and nationalism of a decidedly unorthodox and paradoxical sort.[35]

However, a vast group of intellectuals, who have attached themselves to the notion that the Silver Age was the manifestation of free liberal thought and the democratic impulse, will feel obliged somehow to react to the fact that the founders and activists of that era, as Etkind

35 [Translator's note]: Here, in the 1997 *Templars*, Dugin has redacted the following paragraph: "Of course, it would be inadmissible to compare the level of genius present at the beginning of this century to the level of creativity found in our contemporary patriots. But that is not what is at issue. Rather, we are concerned here with a continuity of a conceptual, paradigmatic kind, which, in a sense, has yet to reach its full potential. One doubts that the patriots, themselves, are aware of the force they represent. This connection relates solely to an orientation toward the third-position, innovation, and Eurasianism, the preliminary outlines of which can be found in issues of *Day* [*День*], *Limonka* [*Лимонка*], and *Elements* [*Элементы*]. At the same time, many who find themselves in this camp because of 'temperament' belong to a completely different lineage — the banal, conservative, bureaucratic, conformist line of both the communist and monarchic Romanov regimes."

and Agurskii show, were the most natural forerunners of red-brown ideology, understood in its broadest sense.[36]

Will There Be a Bronze Age?

The periodization of Russian culture takes on quite a rigid structure: there is, first, the Golden Age of Aleksandr I, Pushkin, and so on. Further, with Nikolai I, we see the beginnings of reaction and stagnation. Afterward, there is a thaw, leading to the Silver Age. 'Pushkinism' arrives. Then, once more, there is a period of stagnation — a fugue. Now the stagnation has clearly come to an end. The phase of the Bronze Age approaches. But it is as though nothing presages the fact. All around, there is degeneration and despair, stupidity, piggishness, and dissolution. Mediocrity saturates everyone and everything.

But the Bronze Age, according to Hesiod, is the age of heroes. Not heroes assigned to any mission, chosen and prepared, but willful characters who have risen up against Fate without any pretense for doing so. Heroes, in distinction from gods, do not enjoy the guarantee of immortality. They rip it out of the clutches of battle. And, in the course of the attempt, they can easily fail. The penance in such an event is monstrous (let us not forget Prometheus's kidney).

The Bronze Age could also not happen. It all depends on the will and presence, in the territory of Rus', of a particular, definite type, who

36 [Translation note]: Here, the following paragraph has also been cut: "And so, the democratically inclined intellectuals, refusing to abandon their cultural pretensions, now face a task of the greatest complexity: either they defenestrate their idols and take their last decisive steps toward the West, assimilating into the liberal system (here we should disregard the usual 'red' Sartre and 'brown' Heidegger, the 'New Left' and Buñuel, anything anti-liberal, far-left, or non-conformist which makes up a fundamental component of what we now are strictly describing as Western culture), or they reevaluate their naive and seemingly externally imposed liberal-democratic aggression, generously garnished with Russophobia, and they accept National Bolshevism (perhaps in some new, watered-down variant)."

is required immediately — today. He is actual, not spontaneous or artificial. If this type does appear, the Bronze Age has a chance of taking place. If not, then a non-Russian banality and the primitivism of consumer society will finally swallow a great nation and a great people.[37]

The paradigm of a potential Bronze Age is nonetheless plain to see already today: this is a new version of the very same National Bolshevism which served as the seed for both the Golden and Silver Ages. This is a necessary condition — *sine qua non*.[38]

But the arrival of heroes is not written in the spirals of history. It is only a possibility, a free choice, a potential uprising, the freedom to love one's land and one's people in extremity, madly, excessively, passionately.[39]

---

37 [Translator's note]: 1997 redaction: "But there's nothing you can do in the latter case."

38 [Translator's note]: 1997 redaction: "One may not suppose that the impotent patriots of the masses will conflagrate and give birth to genius from out of their scant midst. This is out of the question. It is also highly unlikely (though not off the table) that a fraction of the more talented 'democrats,' having fallen accidentally into these ranks, will stumble and rethink their positions. It is most likely that we will need to await a new generation. Having had their fill of foul overseas surrogates and American vulgarity, Russians will sooner or later explode into outrage. They will pull themselves together. They will remember what is theirs, will attempt to understand and affirm it anew.

39 [Translator's note]: 1997 redaction: "Radical erotic experience. Social extremism. A spiritual bonding with the nation throughout history, ages, epochs. An irresistible pull toward spiritual abysses and mysterious worlds. The search for the sacred. A war declared on the profane. National Bolshevism forever"; this programmatic article was written in 1996, first published during the same year.

Да.
Charles Yodis

PART III

A GENERAL THEORY OF REBELLION

The Subject without Limits

Crossing the Threshold

Whenever we wish to define the phenomenon of aggression, more often than not, we make an appeal to its emotional, psychological, and sentimental characteristics, turning our attention away (as is always the case in the modern world) from its deepest metaphysical aspects. In the vein of humanist tradition, a resolutely negative relation to aggression, considered to belong either to modern extermination or (more realistically) to minimalization, came together all by itself. But no matter what, aggression is so closely tied to human nature that it gives a constant reminder of itself—both in daily life (quotidian psychology), and in the political reality of war, conflict, collisions. We shall attempt to make sense of aggression, avoiding all of the usual stereotypes—those of pacifism, those which make apologies for it via *épatage*, those employing psychoanalysis, and those of a socially deterministic kind.

As a phenomenon, we can define aggression as a 'violent crossing of the threshold.' It is precisely in this meaning that we find its essential quality, recognizable in common conflicts, criminal acts, and mass military clashes. The criminal violently crosses the threshold of social ethics, the moral, physical, or economic integrity of another person or the collective. This is aggression. The army violently crosses the threshold of an enemy state, or the opponent's defensive lines. This is also aggression. Finally, ideologues, in fracturing the restive stereotypes of thought, violently cross the threshold of mental clichés. And this, too, is aggression.

But only social or strictly human existence is filled with diverse forms of threshold, the violation of which gives birth to a plethora of aggressions. The structure of all reality is founded on precisely these various thresholds, separating each thing and each modality from all others. The threshold makes every thing what it is in itself, manifesting within itself distinction, differentiation from other objects. In the broadest sense, aggression can take on a cosmic, universal dimension, emerging through the violent intervention of one into the world of another. The animal and vegetable kingdoms abound with examples of aggression, where the existence of one or another being is sometimes upheld at the expense of violence applied to others, instantiating a vortex of transformations, assimilations, and adaptations of the universal environment and the beings which populate it.

Consequently, aggression must be something universal and inseparable from the very foundations of reality.

Vae victis[1]

There are two aspects latent in the violent transcendence of thresholds: first, there is the conditionally negative; second, the conditionally

1 [Translator's note]: Lat.: "Woe to the vanquished" or "woe to the conquered."

positive. The subject of aggression (i.e., the being who partakes in aggressive encroachment upon another, the object of aggression), strives for the sake of such an action to expand his own thresholds or boundaries, to strengthen, perfect, and fulfill his own nature. The cunning beast, depriving its prey of life, sates its own hunger, supports its own existence, acquiring resources necessary to its organism. Military aggression widens territories and multiplies the wealth of the winning side; even in a drunken fistfight, the victor bolsters faith in himself and receives moral satisfaction. In aggression, the subject's positive expansion, the widening of his sphere of possibility, is realized.

But the object which undergoes the aggression, the consumed or pummeled victim, the defeated people, on the contrary, as a result of the violation of their threshold (a ubiquitous part of the process), has only lost that which it had before the aggressive event; it experiences a constriction of its sphere of possibility. The object becomes the payment for the other's success, the scapegoat. The fact of aggression turns it into nothing above an object, whereas before the encroachment, it may have enjoyed the illusion of subjectivity and have wielded aggression against other beings, objects, and peoples. This is the negative aspect of the 'violent crossing of thresholds.'

In both proto-humanist and non-humanist (traditional) civilizations, which exist even today, both aspects of aggression were seen as an organic whole, as two mutual supplementary elements, built into the foundational structure of the cosmos. The Chinese symbol of the Yin-Yang is a perfect example of this fatal dualism. The subject therein is presented as the white portion of the circle, while the object is represented by the black portion. In the symbolism of sex, the former is identified with the masculine principle (Yang), and the latter with the feminine (Yin). From this source flows the universal 'legitimation' of aggression, characteristic of the traditional world, where to no one does it occur to artificially oppose man to the fundamental forces of reality. Of course, subtler civilizations have introduced plenty of nuance into the laws of aggression when it comes to the social, setting barbarian mores in sharp relief against themselves. However, even in these cases, the right to 'violently cross thresholds' is preserved, even if in a sublimated form; this right to aggression was upheld both with regard to war and to individual repression, the functions of which were assumed by special traditional organizations — the prototypes of our modern-day police. The feats of conquerors, warlords, and destroyers have been hailed in legends and epics, all of them united, without exception, in the formula '*vae victis*!'

Tradition's Legitimation of Aggression

What is the metaphysical justification of aggression for traditional civilization, if not an immediate observance of natural law?

The fact is that Tradition has perceived the existence of thresholds and boundaries as an expression of paucity in the cosmos in relation to its Reason, which was thought to be something Absolute, Singular, and lying in the beyond of all limits. To strive for the expansion of one's existence, for a 'violation of thresholds' (in Latin, *transcendere*: to 'transcend') was seen as a profound impulse of movement toward the Godly, an echo of longing for the Absolute, embedded in the world and its beings. Naturally, one could refer to metaphysical and ascetic practices as the pure form of aggression; these are practices in which the initiates strove to violate all boundaries, to maximally absolutize their internal 'I,' submitting to aggression not exterior objects, but reality as a whole. On the way to Godhood, the aggressive impulse is maximally concentrated, as the Godly causes a dissolution of all borders and boundaries which constitute the essence of the ungodly, the immanent. It is from this source that we derive the word 'Satan,' which roughly translates to 'impediment,' i.e. a 'boundary,' understood as something negative.

Progressing from this idea, it is no difficult matter to take the next step and clarify the mechanism of the so-called 'demonization of the adversary,' so frequently encountered in traditional legends, epics, and religious doctrines. That which serves as an impediment on the way to expanding the people, the state, religion, the more narrow society of people and, finally, of the individual person — that which limits his will to totalization, the expansion of being — automatically falls under the sign of 'Satan' and takes on the quality of a theological negative; in turn, aggression is legitimated at the highest level. Through such a 'demonization of the adversary' or of the sacrifice, the people attain their objectivization, their deliverance from subjectivity, their escape beyond the brackets of generic, social, or religious solidarity. Iran against Turan, Achaeans against the Trojans, Judaeans against the goyim, Muslims against the infidels, Æsir against Vanir, the gods against the titans, and sometimes even women (Amazonians) against men — these are various paradigms of dualism, born from an original impulse toward aggression; they abound in the most ancient chronicles, religious codices, poetic legends, and so on.

By vindicating their camp, traditional peoples were, in fact, vindicating something more — the very principle of aggression, the primordial will to 'violently cross the threshold,' a striving to totalize one's subjectivity (regardless of how it may take shape — through nationality, religion, or clanhood).

Anti-Aggression

The modern world has seen a total rupture with centuries of tradition, which has entirely inverted the mental and social structure of modern humanity in comparison with the long millennia of the past. The Enlightenment, humanism, rationalism, and other 'progressive' tendencies' have promoted a system of interpretations and values which totally contradict the fundaments of traditional society. It goes without saying that, in this case, the principle of aggression (perhaps more so than any other principle) has been affected.

The European Enlightenment cultivated in people a one-sided view of aggression — a view taken exclusively from the perspective of the victim. The bright side, founded on a will toward the Absolute, totality, the extreme expansion of the subject into the sphere of the Godly, ceased to be understood in its concrete, ontologically rooted sense, and was thus identified as an archaic vestige, atavism, inertial barbarism, the temporary and principally correctible flaw of civilization. Having lost its metaphysical legitimacy, aggression came to be represented as an illegitimate violation of that which had been declared the highest value — the human individual, society, the living being. From this source springs the entire line of 'natural rights' that began in the thought of Rousseau. If existential expansion soon ceased to be metaphysically justified, the victim promoted his pretensions to 'total security,' i.e. to an artificial guarantee against aggression, raised up to the highest ethical imperative. Aggression, from that point, was effectively illegal. It is with this idea in particular that the whole 'democratic' juridical predilection, forbidding war propaganda, is connected.

If it has become possible to change the cultural and social arrangements of society, then changing the basic tendencies of the cosmos and of human beings has naturally been impossible for everyone. Therefore, aggression has not disappeared, neither from the stage of history and everyday life, nor from nature. It has merely come to be seen as an evil, as something which, from time to time, temporarily erupts, and as the unfounded pretense of one limited being to utilize another. Because the totalizing process of the subject was taken beyond its brackets, aggression came to be regarded as a purely quantitative procurement, a multiplication of external objects, a blunt and vulgar egoism struggling fatally for its own life. And so all aggression gradually began its reduction into the purely economic sphere, while its appearance in other areas was censured by 'public opinion.' From that point on, 'total security' and 'human rights' were guaranteed by an application of aggression in the sphere of abstract material templates — money, capital.

The Metaphysical Genesis of Terrorism

In proportion to the expansion of Western thought, capitalist globalism, and the liberal system, a commensurate discreditation of aggression and its manifestations followed. This effect took place on the political, cultural, and ideological levels. Civilization, entirely founded as it was on the exclusive defense of the victim's interests, worked toward a steady purge of those institutions, structures, and models of behavior which had been organically preserved in human society from the time of the traditional, 'pre-humanist' order. Inscribed in this tendency are the movements of pacifism, female emancipation, weakening of the state apparatus, and the ideology of 'human rights'; in other words, that which gives an ideological façade to modern-day liberalism, which has become the sociopolitical model dominating the planet.

At its final stage, this process has resulted in the total illegality of all forms of aggression, whether it be of the everyday variety, political, or aesthetic, while boundaries have become something sacred. On the heels of this development, another phenomenon appeared — the tendency of 'non-violently overcoming the threshold,' globalization, the 'soft' mixing of all objects, people, and beings into a melting pot of sorts — into One World. After the phase of inviolable boundaries came the phase of stripping boundaries, but this time the point was not to expand and totalize the subject and aggressor, but to consolidate victims into a single, purely objective space. The ultimate form of such an ideology is the model known as 'soft ideology,' in which the idea is to mix the most diverse components whenever they are deprived of a sharply expressed aggressive origin or subjectivity.

Historically, as the first signs of 'soft ideology' were appearing (i.e. at the end of the 1960s and beginning of the 1970s), a coinciding phenomenon emerged: modern terrorism. Of course, terrorism existed beforehand, but until a certain moment it remained a rather marginal phenomenon, in which the most intensive aspects of aggression in the face of the system's unshakeable wall were concentrated. Modern terrorism, however, is entirely distinct from the radical politics of the revolutionaries of the nineteenth and early twentieth centuries, as it has a tendency to mutate away from extreme politics and pragmatism toward a certain self-sufficient phenomenon — an ideology in itself. The representatives of societies founded on soft ideology gradually broadened the concept of 'terrorism,' including within it all phenomena that have begun to reassess the basic aspects of their doctrine. To put it differently, terrorism became synonymous with aggression in its most general metaphysical sense.

All those components of contemporary reality which have proved incompatible with norms tied to the 'world society of victims' have slowly but surely gravitated toward the terroristic pole. Political parties which present themselves as an alternative to the liberal system, religious movements, even entire peoples have moved into the sector of 'terrorism,' forced there by the inflating model of the West.

Terrorism has increasingly become the last refuge of the subject who desires totalization in his world — a world that has outlawed such a desire. It is no surprise that an independent doctrine of aggression has begun to coalesce — a doctrine of pure terror, going beyond the narrower interests of party, nation, or religion.

The First Line

The phenomenon of pure terror is the last word in the history of aggression and the liberal struggle with it. The time of 'terror along strictly party lines' has come to a close. More and more people have come to realize the pragmatic value of belonging to a concrete party when it comes to a personal existential choice. Moreover, it is becoming clearer that classical ideologies are defenseless in the face of the all-consuming and omnipotent soft ideology of globalism.

The eruption of May 1968 led to a despondent and toothless series of recuperative reforms, to a caricature of social-democracy. The Palestinian Intifada ended in a conspiratorial compromise between Arafat and Tel-Aviv. As a result of the collapse of the Soviet system, the decaying hold-outs of the guerilla movements in Latin America were abandoned to the whims of fate. Right-wing terrorism had been dealt with much earlier. There presided a naked defeat, doctrinal and ideological, of all 'enemies of the Open Society.'

But despite any surrogates offered by the proponents of soft ideology (the eccentric and purely visual aggression of youth fashion, the endless television serials with bloodied corpses on full display, relaxed censorship of sadomasochistic productions, etc.), a special type of person has been preserved, from whom aggression cannot be wrung, who experiences an incessant, torturous desire to 'totalize the subject,' to exit beyond all boundaries into the sphere of transcendence. It is precisely this sort of person that has begun laying the foundation of a new ideology—a universal ideology, beyond the aged clichés that have outlived their usefulness.

In 1994 in Italy, a book by Enrico Galmozzi was released called *The Subject Without Limits* [*Il soggetto senza limite*]. Its author is a founder of the far-left terrorist organization known as 'The First Line [Prima Linea],' which rivaled the famous 'Red Brigades.' It is extremely telling that a book written by the leftist extremist and anarcho-communist Galmozzi is dedicated to D'Annunzio, a founder of Italy's fascist party, partisan of the aristocracy, and, in general, a person traditionally associated with the far-right flank of politics. Enrico Galmozzi magnificently interprets the phenomenon of D'Annunzio from an existential point of view and introduces the most interesting parallels with details relating to anarchism and even to Lenin. Most importantly, he does not read D'Annunzio 'from the left,' but seeks a single, universal criterion which can unite people of a common metaphysical type, beyond the vagaries of ideological disagreement. The formula which Galmozzi discovers in naming his book is so successful that it could serve as the universal slogan for all who oppose the 'soft concentration camp' of modern globalism.

The Subject Without Limits is a pure manifestation of the metaphysical meaning of aggression. It is a shockingly precise slogan which expresses the deep nature of Pure Terror.

From now on, all will depend solely on the ability of 'solitary people' to bid farewell to their former ideological illusions, having perceived the metaphysical necessity and intractability of a restructured social field — not within the scale of 'left' and 'right,' but according to the following criterion: 'friends of aggression' versus 'enemies of aggression.'

And who's to say that this will not in turn provoke a globalist integration of object-people — victims — into a unified, planetary liberal society, a Unified Absolute Object, in response to the appearance of the latest face of world history — the Absolute Subject, the Subject Without Limits, who will commit the final act of the eschatological drama?[2]

Der Arbeiter (On Ernst Jünger)

Ernst Jünger is the most illustrious author among the German modernists; his literature and political fate is the classical symbol of everything avant-garde, living, and non-conformist in twentieth-century European culture. A participant in and witness of two world wars, one

2 Article written in 1995, first published in 1995 in the journal *Elements* [Элементы] (No. 7 — Dossier "Terrorism").

of the main theoreticians of the German Conservative Revolution in the 1920s and 30s, the inspiration for National Socialism, a dissident 'from the right' after Hitler's rise to power, disgraced under Nazi totalitarianism and submitted, despite the fact, to ostracism by the victors during the period of 'denazification,' someone who was able, in the depth of his thought and talent, to overcome the preconceptions of the 'democrats' — Jünger is rightfully judged today as the emblem of the twentieth century, the voice of feelings belonging not only to the 'lost generation,' but to the 'lost century,' full of a passionate, dramatic struggle for the final sacred throes of national life against the suffocating profanity of universal, technocratic modernity.

Jünger authored several novels, essays, and stories. He was many-sided, complex, sometimes even self-contradictory and paradoxical. But the main theme of his art was and remains the 'Worker' — a central, almost metaphysical character who, either explicitly or latently, makes his presence felt in all of the author's works. It is not by accident that his most famous and conceptual book, which he edited and rewrote over the course of his entire life, is called *The Worker* [*Der Arbeiter*].

The 'Worker' is the central type of all those political, artistic, intellectual, and philosophical movements which, despite their variety, were united in the concept of 'Conservative Revolution.' The 'Worker' is the main character of this Revolution, its subject, its existential and aesthetic core. We are speaking here of a certain kind of modern man who, through an extreme critical experience of profane reality, sunk into the very heart of the soulless technocratic mechanism, the iron innards of total war or hellish industrial labor, in the center of the nihilism so characteristic of the twentieth century, observes within himself a secret buttress which leads him beyond 'nothingness' toward the elements of a spontaneously awakened inner sacrality. Through an intoxication of 'modernity,' Jünger's 'Worker' attains the gleaming immobility of the Pole, the crystalline cold of objectivity in which both Tradition and the Spirit appear, but not as something old or ancient — as something Eternal, an eternal return to the timeless Source. The 'Worker' is neither a conservative nor a progressive. He is neither a defender of the old nor an apologist for the new. He is the Third Hero, the Third Imperial Figure (as Niekisch would have it), the new Titan in whom, through an extreme concentration of modernism, in its most poisonous and traumatic forms, through the chaos of industry and the war front, a certain transcendent dimension opens up that mobilizes him toward a metaphysical, existential feat.

The 'Worker' is represented by the people of the trenches and factories, the 'asphalt nomads,' deprived of any inheritance in technocratic civilization, answering the call of a spread-eagle reality and accumulating in their souls special energies which will allow for a great uprising; this uprising will be as cruel and objective as the aggression meted out by the bourgeois-industrial environment.

Ernst Jünger created the politico-ideological concept of 'total mobilization,' which became the theoretical and philosophical basis for many conservative-revolutionary movements.

'Total mobilization' refers to the necessity of a nation's universal awakening for the sake of building a new civilization, in the center of which the Heroes and Titans are revered; it is these figures which carry the flame of National Revolution, born in an act of will from the abysses of social alienation.

But, in Jünger's conception, the total mobilization of the masses, the nation, and the folk is based upon a certain unique existential experience without which the Revolution will either be reduced to materialist degeneration or will be 'recuperated' by the inertial Pharisee-conservatives. And so, the existential dimension takes priority in Jünger's art, providing an entire gallery of images depicting the 'third hero' (as in the novels *Storm of Steel, The Adventurous Heart*, *On the Marble Cliffs*, *The Forest Passage*, and *Heliopolis*), as he walks the path of inner Revolution, studying the most extreme forms which carry the greatest risk — war, mysticism, narcotics, eroticism, and borderline psychological states. Nietzsche's formula, in which he states that "that which doesn't kill me makes me stronger," is Ernst Jünger's credo in both literature and life. Like his heroes, he calmly sips champagne in Paris amidst exploding bombs and panicked human droves. Author and literary hero combined, Jünger passes the terrible twentieth century in 'mobilization' and 'labor' as a prophet, calm and convinced by his limitless pain as he tells of the Titan in its process of birth, of the coming maker of Gods.

Jünger reached the age of 100 in 1995. But time holds no sway over his crystalline reason and blinding talent. Recently, in a letter addressed to Christopher Gérard, editor of the Belgian journal *Antaios*, Jünger wrote: "*The twenty-first century will be the age of Titans, and the twenty-second will be the age of Gods.*"

These words contain a brief résumé of modernity's greatest writer, the 'worker' and hero Ernst Jünger.[3]

Guy Debord Is Dead: The Spectacle Continues

On 30 November 1994, at the age of 62, Guy Debord committed suicide. His name has long been a myth. The Situationist International (established by him at a conference in Cosio di Arroscia on 27 July 1957 and over which he presided for many years) has gone down in history as one of the most radical political orientations ever known. Crowds both feared and worshiped him. He was one of the authors of and main inspirations for the unsuccessful European revolutions of 1968. He died from a lack of escape and an awareness of the total

3 Article written in 1995, first published in 1995 in the journal *Tomorrow* [Завтра].

defeat suffered by non-conformism in the West, accompanied by the total triumph of the System.

Charlie Chaplin Unmasked

In the happy epoch of the early 1950s, when the avant-gardist Michel Murr, disguised as a Dominican monk, gave a lengthy, super-radical Nietzschean sermon during Easter week at the Notre Dame cathedral, when the 'Atelier of Experimental Art,' in exhibiting the works of a certain 'Congo' and having received positive reviews from avant-garde critics declared that the artist had in fact been a chimpanzee, a young genius by the name of Guy Debord made his explosive entrance into the non-conformist universe; he was deep, radical, and ruthless. He bested all with his energy, courage, and talent, as well as with his ability to drink great amounts of alcohol. As Debord himself would later write, "All I ever did in life was read and drink. I might have read a lot, but I drank far more. I wrote less than other people concerned with writing, but I drank more than those who concerned themselves with drink."

Debord's first scandalous act was a ferocious attack launched against Charlie Chaplin on the occasion of the latter's arrival to Europe in 1952. Debord dubbed this snot-nosed comic of humanism "the swindler of feelings and the blackmailer of suffering." His thrown gauntlet was punctuated with the words: "Go home, Mister Chaplin!" In this occurrence, we can already see the basic trajectory of the future situationist—a hatred of the bourgeois surrogates of mass culture, especially when they are marked by a false progressivism and a Pharisee humanism. Debord's position can be essentially reduced to a struggle against the right and an unmasking of the left. In other words, he wanted radical revolt against the System and its cunning totalitarianism, masked as 'democracy.' It only makes sense that more committed leftists denounced Debord, fearing his lack of compromise and overwhelming consequence. Eventually, Debord himself would formulate his irreplicable criticism of the 'avant-garde':

> At early stages, one of the characteristic traits of the developed bourgeoisie is a recognition of the principle of freedom for intellectual or artistic works. The next stage constitutes a struggle with these works. Finally, the bourgeoisie adapts these works to its own interests. The bourgeoisie has no choice but to support a critical feeling within a small group of people — a spirit of free inquiry — but only on the condition that these efforts will be concentrated into a narrowly limited sphere and that these criticisms will be diligently compartmented from society as a whole [...]. The people who have distinguished themselves in the sphere of non-conformism are accepted as individuals by the System, but only at the cost of disavowing any global application of their ideas and with the agreement that their activity will be strictly limited to the most fragmentary social niches. It is precisely for this reason that the term 'avant-garde,' which so lends itself to bourgeois manipulation, should in itself raise suspicion and laughter.

Revolt against the 'Society of the Spectacle'

Guy Debord's primary work, which has now become a modern classic, is his *Society of the Spectacle.* In this book, he mercilessly condemns modernity, the 'epoch of lonely crowds.' "*Just as leisure is defined by the fact that it is not work, the spectacle is defined by the fact that it is not life.*" The modern world, as a consequence, is reduced to isolation, representation, and death. Instead of any unifying life experience, it is the laws of the image which reign supreme, flickering pictures which merely represent reality. Debord, building off of Fromm, observes that the social degradation of the liberal System has spent a considerably long time in its final stages. At first, 'to be' was changed into 'to have.' And by now, even 'to have' has disappeared, transformed into 'to appear.'

At first, the bourgeois world subordinated nature to its industrial laws; then, it subordinated culture to itself. The spectacle has annihilated history. "*The end of history provides a sigh of relief to all existing authorities.*"

Having suppressed in man and society a taste for the real, replacing states and experience with 'representations,' the System has worked out the newest method of exploitation and enslavement. Before, it had separated people into classes, then it used force to drive people into the factories and jails, and now it has shackled them to their television sets. In doing so, it has once and for all won a victory over Life.

> The relentless accumulation of images gives the viewer the impression that everything is permitted, but simultaneously impresses him with an assurance that nothing is possible. You can look, but you can't touch. The modern world becomes a museum, where the very passivity of its visitors becomes its chief security guard.

To define the essence of the society of the spectacle in such a way is nothing short of genius. Was it not an epiphany, a clear gaze into the depths of this terrible truth, which drove revolting Russians in October 1993 to attempt such a hopeless storming of the Ostankino tower, that highest symbol of the System's absolute lie? Perhaps in that moment, those participating in the uprising intuitively manifested the testaments of Debord: "One should seek the formula for '*détournement* [rerouting/hijacking]' not in books, but in concrete experience. One must diverge from the prescribed trajectory in broad daylight so that nothing reminds one of wakefulness. Striking encounters, unexpected obstacles, grandiose betrayals, risky enchantments — these will more than suffice for this revolutionary, tragic search for the Grail of Revolution, which no one asked for."

A New March on the Ostankino Tower

After the collapse of the 1968 revolution, Guy Debord paid far less attention to his International and, in 1972, it dissolved on its own.

From time to time, Debord would still publish articles and shoot the occasional film, but the bitterness he had imbibed as a result of his defeat was too deep. Even his uncompromising criticisms had been swallowed effortlessly by the System; his main work had become a canonized classic to which everyone made reference, while few took the time to read it. The expression 'Society of Spectacle,' which had been so loaded and terrible in the mouth of Guy Debord himself, had become a commonplace in the political lexicon, having lost its revolutionary, non-conformist, unmasking charge.

Debord was then marginalized, isolated, and 'recuperated.' The Situationists vanished, and only a handful of 'anarchists from the right' and European followers of Evola (in particular, Philippe Baillet) made an admittedly unsuccessful attempt to reinstate a certain relevancy to his ideas. But the West continued further down the path of spectacle, moreso than we could even imagine.

Never before has death ruled the world so absolutely and with such horrifying obviousness as it does today in the liberal world. Guy Debord's suicide is the final flourish written in the blood of a *living person* at the command of the Society of the Spectacle. It may be that he was the last person remaining in the West who could end *himself* [покончить с *собой*] since no one there possesses an authentic 'I' anymore.

Chirac's election as the president of France, the success of 'Proctor and Gamble,' Madonna's final tour, Henri Bernard-Levi's work on a new advertisement text for the bourgeois Yves Saint Laurent, the hollow cyborg smile of Naomi Campbell, democratically confected in a test tube filled with sperm from representatives of all four human races… Even more time has passed since the unnoticed death of the great Witness…

The Beast hefts its television body, crawling morosely toward the oblivious, agonized, faltering East.

But all the same… All the same, we must rise again and again and march on Ostankino tower. Both the living and the dead. Together with Guy Debord. This malevolent television tower is the phallus of Satan, constantly birthing the poisonous hypnosis of the 'Society of the Spectacle.' Having exploded it, we will castrate the very demon of violence which hides behind the decrepit masks of the System's marionettes.

Sooner or later, the endless spectacle will come to an end. Only then will we have our revenge, and it will be merciless.[4]

The Threshold of Freedom

If we reevaluate the usual ideological clichés and develop a new Revolutionary Theory (or a General Theory of Revolt), we will have no choice but to appeal to both the far-right and the far-left, to nationalism (traditionalism) and socialism (communism). The political component will be taken from the right and the economic component from the left. This is the meaning of National Bolshevism, Conservative Revolution, the Third Way. Through this lens, our main ideological enemy is liberalism or liberal democracy, in which the abovementioned proportions are reversed: their politics are of the left and their economics are of the right. In some sense, liberalism has become synonymous with our absolute ideological, political, and spiritual opponent.

Indeed, this is the case. But when we use the word 'liberalism,' which is derived from the Latin 'libertas'—'freedom'—we run the risk of reaching false conclusions and negating Freedom itself. And that is far from our cause.

Liberalism in no way suggests complete individual freedom; all it does is guarantee the individual's economic freedom. Liberal

4 Article written in 1996, first published in 1996 in the journal *Limonka* [Лимонка].

philosophy whole-heartedly negates any extra-rational, super-individual elements in a person's being, as it considers these things to be an illusion, a vestige, a fiction. And so, liberalism can only operate with a rationalistic individual form, with that '*homo economicus*' — economic man — which is driven by nothing other than an egotistic desire for wealth, enjoyment, comfort, property. All other strata of the human personality are considered secondary and inessential.

Such a human model deliberately limits a person's fundamental freedom, which is his defining trait — the freedom to be what one desires. This desire is laid in the foundation of man as a being which overcomes obstacles, which is granted the invaluable gift of exiting the framework of its concrete limitations, and doing so in accordance with its own will. The economic freedom of the 'Open Society' is something opposed to true spiritual freedom; liberalism views the human being as something fixed, completed, and concerned with nothing but the optimization of his conditions for existence, instead of with the willful transformation of his concrete nature. Liberalism practically refuses man his existential dignity, equating him with a 'thinking monster,' with an absolutized ego placed at the center of everything.

Man can realize his spiritual dignity only through a willed definition of the self. There are two paths toward such a realization, both of which depend on one's human predilection. The first path, in Hinduism, is known as *Devayajna* — the 'path of the gods.' Here, spiritual freedom is realized through acquiring the supreme 'I,' a personal 'deification' in which one is transformed into a Superman. This is the path inwards. The second path — *Pitriyajna*, 'the path of ancestors' — is a voluntary melding with an organic human collective, social group, nation, race, clan, or family. In this latter case, the individual overcomes his limitations by identifying himself with a new collective being, a society in which he dissolves and for the sake of which he lives and dies.

The degree to which this realization, this broadening of the individual horizon, is accomplished is the degree to which the very concept of 'freedom' is altered. At a certain point, man begins to apply this definition to that supreme reality with which he is constantly identified. This can be most easily observed in the example of the 'path of ancestors,' for which the majority of people are destined (whereas the 'path of the gods' is a matter belonging to the chosen minority, the elite). The man of society, the man of Tradition, perceives his individual freedom through the freedom of his family, his kin, his tribe, his class, his nation.

Belonging to the group, in which such a person sees his true 'I,' is comprehended and experienced in such full degree that, for the sake of the freedom of the organic collective, he will consciously adopt a stringent discipline, will deny himself any superfluous individual possibilities, and will even go to his death to preserve his society's freedom.

This moment lays the foundation of patriotism, nationalism, service to social ideas, etc. In this case, it is entirely just to affirm that a person cannot be free as long as the people, the society to which he belongs and of which he is a part is unfree.

When it comes to the 'path of the gods,' freedom contains an even more absolute and super-individual meaning, suggestive of an exit beyond the boundaries that the cosmic environment sets around an incarnate being. This is the ideal of 'exiting the cosmos,' the becoming of the Absolute. Hindus call those who have completed this path *Jivanmukta* — 'freed during life.' For this category of the elect, there are no obstacles, either in life or beyond the grave; they are garbed in the brilliance of pre-eternal glory, and their freedom is discovered to be an attribute of divinity.

There are, of course, intermediate forms of realized freedom that are associated with the phenomenon of 'heroism.' A hero is a person who has combined the 'path of the gods' with the 'path of ancestors.'

He achieves impossible feats which reveal his superhuman qualities, but in the name of other people, in the name of the society, the nation, the state, the class. This is neither an ascetic nor a volunteer, but a lone revolutionary who has abandoned the conventions of everyday humanity while preserving an organic link with the society from which he has emerged and for whose benefit he offers up his life. This is also an authentic, inalienable, light-bearing [светоносной], and sacrificial path of freedom.

It is clear that liberalism bears not the slightest relation to this way of life. Liberalism dismisses ascetics as unfortunates, collectivists as weaklings who require 'mutual aid [круговой поруке]'; it portrays heroes as dangerous maniacs and terrorists. Having marked their banners with the word 'freedom,' as in the Orwellian anti-utopia, liberals treat it in such a way that authentic freedom is excluded from the very definition. In yoking everyone with the obligation to be alone through individualism and rationalized egoism, liberals simultaneously excise everything ideal, spiritual, and sacrificial in man — everything that elevates the individual beyond existential 'thrownness' (Heidegger's *Geworfenheit*).

The threshold of freedom is bound up with the very mystery of the human species. No one can guarantee us this freedom externally, neither liberals nor their opponents.

This is the dynamic trajectory of our fate; it is only in acting that we prove our worth, only in overcoming, in sacrifice, in heroism, in aggressive idealism do we become something valuable. "Man is an arrow cast toward the Superman." This definition given by Nietzsche is the most concise elucidation of the anti-liberal, anti-capitalist, anti-democratic doctrine.

There is no excuse for following the lead of our enemies, who make such artificial attempts to spin us as champions of 'totalitarianism,' 'boot lickers [держиморд],' apologists of 'police terror' and 'militarization of everyday life.' Our goal is freedom: the nation's freedom from the Atlanticist yoke, labor's freedom from the shackles of capital, the freedom of genius from the dictatorship of the rank-and-file idiot. We call for the freedom to be something more than human, which is to be absolutely human, true to that mysterious testament which divinity has laid in the very center of our souls as a mission; we are called to realize this divine mission, either in life or in death. But this freedom is incompatible with the claustrophobic cells of the 'consumer society,' of the 'Open Society' of fur traders who wish to insure themselves against everything ideal, pure, sacrificial, and materially unmotivated.

Therefore, the Uprising is inevitable.[5]

5 Article written in 1995, first published in 1995 in the journal *Limonka* [Лимонка].

CY

PART IV

MUSTARD SEED

Templars of the Proletariat

Everyone participates in our Russian politics: engineers, the intelligentsia, bureaucrats, bums, schizophrenics, women, spies, and plenty of other types. It may be said with absolute certainty that, in this arena, there is only one class for whom there are no representatives — the workers. Accepting on faith the Marxist demagoguery, the rabid partocrats of Perestroika have, for some reason, inculcated the following dogma in the consciousness of the masses: the workers were the class hegemon for the entire duration of the Soviet period and now they must be banished from the political realm, forgotten, marginalized. Western society, too, which so many Russian politicians earnestly try to copy, has dealt successfully with the working class, having swept it off of the political stage. Once the domination of capital has become total and capitalism has transitioned from its industrial phase to an information-based postindustrial society, the basic figure of the Laborer, the Manufacturer, the Creator of all objective reality within human being is almost completely defaced before the glimmering of computer screens and the false lights of advertising.

The workers have disappeared from our lives. They've gone off somewhere, turned into something else. The labor of the worker in the epoch of management and know-how has been devalued.

Blackened, crude, oil-stained men, with their coveralls and their iron instruments, have been dissolved into social non-being.

But this is nothing more than an optical illusion, an exquisitely fabricated social mirage. They are attempting to convince us that every thing that surrounds us has sprung directly from money itself, as well as from their limitless power; they want us to think that intelligent machines, subservient to the almighty white-collar technocrat, have produced them.

Nothing of the sort has occurred. As before, in the bowels of factories, hundreds of thousands of living organisms swarm, transforming crude materials into comprehensible forms. As before, idealists in the guts of the earth are chiseling through the thick of inert substance with their jackhammers, violating the deathly, passive comfort of the mineral kingdom. The black blood of the subterranean veins sprays up into the faces of oil rig surgeons. Block-shouldered giants with brick faces roll up the burning steel.

The Worker, the Laborer, has gone nowhere in fact. He has simply retreated once more to the underground. Betrayed by a degenerated Soviet socialism, cinched in the suffocating noose of cunning capital, whose domination today has become not only a formal and external fact, but an absolute and internal one, the Worker gazes grimly upon a petrifying reality, greedily built up around him by scoundrels of every stripe, nation, and class. Having changed from a slave of the Party functionary to a slave of the 'New Russian,' he is degraded and crushed as he was before — more so even than before. Chased into the dark underground of society, intoxicated by surrogate cyber emotions and ubiquitous pseudo-erotica, he rattles his narrow cage, tapping the energy of his agony in order to turn the cogs of a terrible machine with a computer screen for its façade, which would collapse without him like a pyramid of crumbling sand.

The pure world of the 'New Masters' forces the Titan into an embryonic state, throwing him only the most paltry scraps. "Here's a half-liter of 'Kremlin' vodka for you, hegemon!"

But can it really be that all mystical aspirations associated with the liberation of Labor have shamefully collapsed, gnawed upon by the fat worm of Soviet experiment? Is it so that suspicions of identity between the Working Subject and the Object, shaking the foundations of being, have turned out to be merely silly moral metaphors obscuring a prosaic will to power for the next band of greedy and imperious apparatchiks?

No, it cannot be. The Deputy Council's pitiful dissolution, as well as that of its rotten leaders, represents nothing more than a pause, a syncope in the terrible awakening of the Titan. The working class has yet to fulfill its historical mission. It has yet to say its final word. It has yet to complete its Revolution.

Ours is the day of parasites. These parasites are both old and new, domestic and foreign. They are people who use and appropriate that which they have not created. Centrists sell out the radicals; directors of venture firms sell out their subordinates; heads of state sell out the riches of their great nations; the journalists of the mass media sell out their conscience. In the midst of the garbage pit are squeals and panting, shots fired from around corners, and blood-chilling lies.

Today's Russian Worker looks gloomily upon this chaos from the deep bottom of being. He is sharp-cornered and concrete, catching upon things like a mechanism, and hesitant, as if in deep thought. He does not believe now, or ever will he believe, in the social demagogues wearing their 'rose-colored' glasses. Again with this scum? No, that is quite enough. The final account will also be swift for the 'capitalists.' Only the stout, passionately despairing strength of a growing nationalism can reach these fundamental, unhurried people. But whenever talk arises of a 'royal house,' 'the reinstatement of noble privileges,' banners, Cossacks, or 'national enterprise,' it is the patriots, too, who come up against a despondent indifference: the 'Mummers.'

Early every morning, at the rising of the sun (no one besides these people have remembered the sun for a long while), they crawl out of the cages that are their apartments, away from fat, stupid wives and snot-nosed piglets [корытников], moving at a measured pace into the concrete wombs of Industry. They do this in order — with great difficulty and without inspiration — to wage a diligent, rhythmic, unceasing cosmic battle with matter; they strive with a matter that is unyielding, raw, rough, *noxious*. The grim workers know that the evil demon of matter has taken a thin and fragile Life, the Sun Maiden, prisoner. This is the form stolen by the crude usurper of material. One may only save this Life by means of a feat, of a terrible, merciless, and decisive war against the sedimental ice of reality.

The Titans have waged a battle for centuries and millennia against entropy in the Universe. The working class. The working brotherhood. The Order of the Worker.

Having consumed Dionysus at some point in the course of these long millennia, they themselves have become saturated with his flesh. And so, they themselves have come to love the sacred intoxication of the resurrected Iacchus.

Somewhere above them, clueless of the subterranean drama, naïve or dishonest 'aristocrats,' intellectuals, and merchants make cynical use of the fruits of this bloody battle. They have no intercourse with Matter, freed from it by the voluntary sacrifice of the *Templars of the Proletariat*. They scarf down and desacralize the trophies prised with a terrible flourish from the clutches of Outer Darkness by the underground knights.

But this paralysis will not persist for long. The workers are steeling their minds and spirits. No one makes any guarantees of longevity to the scum which rages through today's Russian politics. Of course, the eyes of the proletariat are compelled toward the Earth, the eternal opponent and enemy.

Sooner or later, though, the proletariat will look up… and will strike its final blow. It will fracture the corpse-matte finish of the computer's eye socket, the shimmering display window of the bank, the wry face of the overseer.

The proletariat will awaken. It will rise. It will kill. Neither the police nor the counterfeits of the socialist parties will be able to hold it back.

Its business with history is unfinished. The Demiurge yet breathes. The Soul of the World still weeps. Her tears birth a reverberant roar in the black conscience of the Creator. This is a call. This is the factory blowhorn. This is the sounding of Angelic Trumpets.

They — the blacksmiths of Tartarus — are once more making their proletarian Revolution. A True Revolution. The Final Revolution.[1]

The Royal Labor of the Peasant

[ЦАРСКИЙ КРЕСТЬЯНСКИЙ ТРУД]

The peasant is the most important figure of the Indo-European tradition. The cultivation of grain-bearing plants and especially wheat was seen by our forebears as a sacred activity, a special cosmic liturgy. It is no accident that bread of all things became the earthly substance chosen by the Savior for the transubstantiation of His Holy Flesh.

It is also no accident that God himself, in the evangelical texts, is likened to a sower (i.e. a peasant, a sacred figure of humanity). From time immemorial, the peasant's labor has been called 'noble.' In sacred society, a discrete ethics of labor had yet to come into existence, and

1 Article written in 1994, first published in 1994 in the journal *Limonka* [Лимонка].

the concept 'noble' was in no sense applied metaphorically. The fact is that, during sacred Indo-European rites, the tsar' himself carried out a ritual sowing of the earth. And in a symbolic sense, the labor of the peasant can be called 'royal [царским]' in every sense of the word.

With his liturgical activity, the peasant supplemented the fullness of the tripartite hierarchy of ancient Aryan society. The priests struggled with spiritual darkness, with ignorance; the warriors and the tsar' struggled with darkness of the soul, physically incarnated as enemies; and the peasants struggled with material darkness, the forces of the earth, the soil. This triple darkness with which the Aryans strived was often symbolized as a *Serpent*. The Serpent was a trivalent symbol of ignorance (for priests), enmity (for warriors), and the untamed earth (for peasants). Precisely on this basis, the act of plowing was understood as a symbolic battle with the Serpent, as well as a sacred marriage of Earth and Sky, the latter being represented by the peasant himself with his plow. It is from this relation that we receive the ancient equivalence of the words 'to plow [пахать]' and 'to bellow/shout [орать],' formed from a root which also refers to 'light [свет],' 'shining [сияние],' etc. In accordance with the degree to which traditional society has degraded, when the priest's estate has gradually lost the meaning of doctrines and rituals entrusted to it, when the warriors have soiled themselves with passions and hedonistic pleasures, only the peasants, the serpent slayers, have preserved the legends and myths in their purity, alluding to that time when Indo-European society was at its spiritual zenith. Therefore, in Russia it has been none other than the peasantry that has preserved the old ways and faith, the convictions and rites of antiquity, full of the highest meaning for him who understands the laws of the sacred Aryan cosmos.

The traditional being of the peasant has passed not only into the very center of nature, but into the center of a special, enlightened nature, shot through with the rays of Logos. The inhabitant of the village has never been a 'primitive' (or uncivil) 'Wildman,' as the arrogant gentry culture of the last decades of tsarist Rus' perceived him. That which, upon first glance, may have appeared to be his archaism and ignorance was in fact a sign of his deep rootedness in the sacred archetypes, a phenomenon of the highest super-rational knowledge, which had at one time during the golden age been the axis of collective being for a complete sacral civilization. Behind the irrationality of the peasants, their wisdom has been hiding; behind their laziness — their contemplativeness; behind their unhurriedness in worldly affairs — an unfaltering ascesis. The peasant has not lived in a world of skepticism and critical cleverness, but in a world of ancient symbols and signs, in a living, brilliant space where Earth and Sky, Sun and Moon, Day and Night, Summer and Winter revealed themselves as living realities of a tense cosmic drama. Peasant life has been full of signs and legends, guided by a certain sacred rhythm, and this has given the highest liturgical meaning to their existence.

It was the peasantry, and not the Westernized Russian nobility, which carried within itself the last remnants of the ancient solar civilization, Sacred Rus'. Peasants in Russia have spent many centuries in a deprecated state. The shame of serfdom, the exploitation of waxing capitalism, and finally, the second-class status they experienced in the nominally proletarian Soviet state — these are all stages of the Russian peasant's long path of martyrdom. Despoiled, yoked, and pressed into military service through various means — by the promoters of urban culture — the peasants have borne their cross with immeasurable calm and obedience, safeguarding for some higher eschatological aim that sacred Aryan legend which has furnished the essence of his being. The harsh, yearly struggle for bread, for the harvest, was a physical aspect of labor's cosmic liturgy, repeating itself endlessly despite all oppression, persecution, torture, and suffering.

On the strength of what hope, of what faith, have generations of Russian peasants lived?

Clearly, they secretly knew, instructed by the changing of seasons from winter to spring, that a Restoration and Renaissance would at some point arrive and that the great solar Tradition of the radiant Slavs would once more ignite into Kupalo's brilliant flame. Indeed, only with the peasants (and by no means the caricatured nobility, to say nothing of the former Party nomenclature) do we find (even today) the remains of an ancient knowledge, echoes of Tradition in its authentic, living form. And only by starting from this third Aryan caste can we make a theoretical beginning of reviving the social hierarchy of the true Russian society.

Just as, in Russian fairy tales, the Third Son, the youngest son Ivan the Fool [Иван-дурак] (equivalent to the third, peasant caste) often becomes the savior and benefactor of the two remaining brothers, so, when it comes to reinstating the Russian sacred tradition, we should appeal first and foremost to the peasants, who have preserved within themselves to this very day more authentically royal [царских] elements than the degraded descendants of the very tsarist dynasty. The True Tsar, the Emperor of the Great Russian Land, must be an authentic ploughman if he is to know the raw, acrid taste of the life-giving Slavic soil.

Soviet socialism's disdain for the spirit and for religion, its atheism and hatred for history — it was this fact and no other which became the chief misfortune of Russian Bolshevism and led ultimately to its death — were manifested for the communists in their explicit hatred of the peasantry. The majority of orthodox Marxists unilaterally saw the peasants as a reactionary class (in this surmise, they were correct). A lack of Orthodox Christianity and a disdain for the peasants were the most negative features of Soviet socialism. The new Russian socialism must in no wise repeat these fatal missteps. The new socialism must be emphatically Christian and peasant-oriented, these two terms being not only historically, but even etymologically proximate.[2]

From a different perspective, nationalist movements must rally to realistic positions and somewhat temper their passion for tsarism. In the matter of a national renaissance, one must not be guided by the degenerated models of a once sacred social and spiritual order. For several centuries prior to the rise of the Bolsheviks, the monarchic regime in Russia had become a caricature, a parody — not in its principles and declarations, but in practice, it's concrete reality.

The peasant, peasantry, husbandry — these are the mystical guidelines of the New Russia. They are not only the providers of material nourishment, but the secret preservers of the ancient tradition, in whom a profound knowledge of the structure of the Aryan cosmos is imprinted.

Therefore, ideologically, politically, and metaphysically, the type of the Russian Peasant must come to occupy the center of revolutionary doctrine for those people who sincerely strive to resurrect Tradition in its full stature. Only in this way can we win a victory over the World Serpent, the Serpent of the West, splitting its reptilian skull with the peasant's plough as the Indra once did.[3]

---

2 [Translator's note]: The Russian word for 'peasant [крестьянин, *krest'yanin*]' indeed bears immediate etymological ties to the word for 'Christian [христианин, *khristianin*].'

3 Article written in 1994, first published in 1994 in the journal *Limonka* [Лимонка].

Our Motherland Is Death[4]

The stepfather of a close friend of mine, a passionate anti-Soviet dissident, died just before the end of the SOVDEP[5], literally on the eve of Gorby's rise to power. In his final agonies, he repeated the following words in a tone of horror: "It (i.e. the SOVDEP) will persist for eternity… It will never end… No one can change anything…"

---

4 [Translator's note]: 'РОДИНА-СМЕРТЬ' — this chapter title is derived from a song of the same name by Egor Letov and his band Civil Defense [Гражданская Оборона]; the name of the band, when contracted, spells the word 'ГрОб,' which translates to 'coffin.' Egor Letov was a founding member of the National Bolshevik Party. The song's lyrics are as follows:

He who is quickest is right
He who is blackest is alive
He who remains is holy
Is this really how it has to be? Is this how we'll live?

It's useless trying to love without causing pain
It's hopeless trying not to do evil
Gradually remembering yourself in a dream,
Awakening in reminiscences

Death — there's plenty of room for those who are dead
Death — there's plenty of room for those who are alive
This is a meeting place for those who've wandered
Barefoot in diamond fields of rye
Our motherland is death,
Our motherland is death…
That which does not involve death is a lie
He who doesn't know will continue to live
He who finds out will take a knife in the back
Is this really how it has to be? Is this how we'll live?

5 [Translator's note]: The contracted term 'SOVDEP' [Совдеп; the Council of Deputies], refers to the status of the Russian Soviet Federative Socialist Republic [RSFSR] after 1918 as a federation of different 'councils' or 'soviets.' In both the émigré press and in popular parlance among domestic dissidents, 'SOVDEP' became a pejorative used to refer to either the RSFSR or the USSR.

Literally just a few years hence from that reality which the dying man described with the word 'eternity,' in its every sense — after all, he was born, had lived, and had died in it — not a trace of that world survives. In his book *Socialism as a Phenomenon of World Culture*, Igor Shafarevich introduces the example of the dynasty of Chinese usurpers who came to power for only a couple years but heralded their era and undertook to rewrite history in such a way as to justify their future thousand-year reign in advance.

There are many things which seem to us unshakeable, absolute, eternal, and stonily immobile; but all it takes is a slight breeze and they disappear, dissolve, dissipate like a ghost or a fog. In this regard, psychoanalysis employs the concept of the 'complex,' i.e., an autohypnosis of personality which transforms a meaningless detail or incidental experience into an insuperable psychological barrier that makes a person's existence an unending nightmare.

Today, there are no longer any Brezhnevian chimeras passing themselves off as guardians of eternity: the slogans, party committees, portraits, KGB agents, and the OVIRs[6] have disappeared. And that disappearance happened quickly, like a stroke of lightning. That which had seemed without end had collapsed in a single moment; the massive thrones and solid careers turned out to be fragile — a ripple on the surface of the water.

But human consciousness is set up in such a way that it is compelled to submit to hypnosis, erecting idols to whom it imparts a fictive immortality, even if the sorrowful fate of their ancestors has been grimly sealed right before their very eyes.

---

6 [Translator's note]: 'ОВИР [Отдел виз и регистраций]' — i.e. the 'Department of Visas and Registrations' — was a part of the Soviet Ministry of Internal Affairs which kept track of foreign nationals in the USSR while regulating (and usually denying) any travel of Soviet citizens beyond its borders.

And now, in the empty place left behind, a new mass mental illness is formulating itself, fabricated from complexes — the very picture of disease. Instead of the Party caste, the 'rich' have appeared, and their power now already appears to be absolute and invulnerable. In politics, everything is divided between a few of the cleverest characters. The same holds for culture, where a new official class has coalesced which evinces a clan-based solidarity no less insular than that of Brezhnev's time and which admits no random members into its ranks.

It would appear now to be just like it was during the period of Stagnation [застоя], that the social magma is hardening and losing its last traces of plasticity. The cycling of elites has been practically stopped before it could even seriously begin. Every spot, even those in the second-rate gallery, is allotted. All zones of influence, election districts, and privatized industrial sectors are spoken for.

Yes, it would appear to be so, but this is an illusion. This is hypnosis — a complex. And complexes, as is well known, are not an external matter, but an internal one. It is not the happenstance aggressor who makes a slave of a man, but the man himself. No one at any time can ever debase a hero — neither the zone, nor the SOVDEP, nor the concentration camp, nor liberalism. The hero is a simple, healthy man who has liquidated his complexes, as a result of which the spells of an endless procession of Little Zacheses (who've now formed a professional council [профсоюз]) no longer have any effect on him. They all only exist as a result of our voluntary castration, our autohypnosis. We are so frightened of death that we would prefer to die without thinking about it, without encountering it, without throwing the gauntlet down before it.

And we therefore betray our own dignity and entrust our fate to the System, which is founded on a mutually responsible coalition of mediocrities, idiots, and bastards. We, ourselves, give birth to the illusion whose insuperability we later lament.

In actual fact, the System's power is built upon a complete fiction, a vulgar deceit, a thief's primitive sleight-of-hand. It takes as its foundation the weakness of the little man — an unwillingness to die 'here and now' — and blows it up to gigantic proportions. In traditional society, this problem was easily solved through initiation rites. A person would undergo initiatic death and, after the fact, would observe that behind one form of existence there follows another; consequently, death is but an episode, a syncope, a transition. If after such an initiation that person were to submit himself to certain definite norms, then he did so only on the conscious basis of their spiritual justification, and not for fear of losing his own hide. Initiation is that which separates man from animal. With the loss of initiation, people were changed into inferior, shivering sheep. They accepted the System and began to believe in its miserable myths. Pseudo-values and pseudo-authorities appeared on the scene. The ephemeral and accidental came to be regarded as eternal. And, by the same token, spirit, mind, and depth were discredited as something marginal, ineffective, excessive.

We live in a world that totters on the precipice of collapse. It is just about to dissolve. Our society is constructed on ideas and principles for which no one has paid any price, which no one has washed in his blood, and which have never been pried from anyone's fingers in mortal battle. We have passively relinquished one ideology and have just as passively garnered the various fragments of other ideologies, which frequently contradict each other. We are governed by utter idiots, and these are the same idiots who lead the opposition — the second echelon, clutching at power. The last sparks of heroism that characterized the brief period of authentic struggle occurring between 1991 and 1993 have finally gone out. There is not even enough fire to ignite the most flaming hearts. The moss of the swamp has consumed everything. And once more it would seem that there is no end in sight… while, in reality, we stand at the very edge of the next turning.

The true elite which is to replace this whole irreal farce must grow from the regions of death. One contemporary poet (Roman Neumoev) strangely declared death to be his 'Motherland [родиной].' Death dissolves the complexes of fear, lays bare the rays of the real; like fallen leaves, the televisions, banks, stock exchanges, government analysts, and sowers of Kremlin intrigue — the entire paranoid panopticon that so arrogantly tries to pass itself off as reality — will disappear into non-being.

In those 'dismantlings [разборках]' nearest at hand, the normal people will not find their portion. The greedy crowds have already apportioned even the scraps among themselves. But this filth is soon to vanish.

We must live and act as though this phase were already finished, 'here and now.' We must behave as though we have already died and the pure horizons of spiritual reality, drenched in heavenly rays of thought and bedeviled from below by sanguine tongues of cosmic passion, are already before us.

We require a *New Party*. A Party of Death. A party of total verticality. A Party of God, the Russian analog to the 'Hezbollah,' which acts in accord with utterly alternative laws and contemplates utterly different vistas. For the System, death is indeed the end. For the normal man, it is only the beginning.

Geidar Dzhemal' once related to me the following historical episode: at the end of the war, an Italian general from the Salo Republic, sending his people toward certain death, admonished them with the words, "Do you really think you'll live forever?"

This is an incredible argument. The majority of people, despite all logic, continue to live as though they are immortal. But the feeling of justice requires from us that we help humanity to dispel this delusion.

It is our Motherland which requires this of us — the Motherland of Death.[7]

The Reign of the Crowned and Conquering Infants

The child was the symbol of Divinity long before the arrival of our Savior Jesus Christ. Tradition regarded children as special beings, directly linked with the mystery of the universal soul. The Chinese descried the future on the basis of naïve couplets sung by children in one or another province of the Celestial Empire. The esoteric Heraclitus saw the child at play as the highest symbol of the free and flaming spirit. Ceremonial operative magic came with an obligation to let young children participate in the rituals — black mages, inverting the sacred symbolism, demeaned children while white mages, on the contrary, treated them as oracles and guides between the world of men and the world of the gods. (For the same reason, the black mass could only be presided over by he who had been, in accordance with all rules, ordained as a Christian priest.) In every instance, in sacred civilization, the child was considered an almost supernatural being, equal to priests and seers. But it was, naturally, in the Christian world that reverence for the child reached its peak, where adherents bowed down to the very incarnation of the God-Word [Богу-Слову], represented in the image of the infant.

Why a child? After all, this is an incomplete, helpless, uneducated, and chaotic being which, both inside and out, constitutes a parody of a fully grown man. Why would a child possess such important meaning for Tradition, being identified with the Highest Principle?

---

7 Article written in 1994, first published in 1994 in the journal *Limonka* [Лимонка].

The answer to this question provides us with the full depth of difference between the world of Tradition and the world of the profane, between the sacred civilization of antiquity and the degrading, utilitarian civilization of modernity.

The point is that, within these two realities (the traditional and the modern), there reign two mutually exclusive, opposing super-ideologies, which from their very sources determine every permutation of their practical manifestations. According to Tradition, the possible is superior to the actual, truth is superior to usefulness, the idea is superior to its manifestation, the archetypal is superior to its reflection. The modern world is founded on an entirely contradictory approach. Here, the actual is placed above the possible, utility — above truth, and the concrete and factual is master of the ideal. Modernity is grounded in the spirit of skepsis; it trusts in nothing but the material fact. But since facts result from interpretations, modern man must easily come to ignore facts themselves if they should alarm his narrow, godless, complex-ridden, unsteady consciousness.

The child is the manifestation of the Possible. This small person retains his connections with the world of the soul from which he has only recently floated in order to appear in a material wrapping. He is woven from a whole gamut of possibilities which still co-exist within him simultaneously and uncompromised, without conflict or contradiction. This child is the grain seed of the lost Golden Age, a spark of paradise. In this regard, he carries within himself not only the potential to become an adult, the spectre of multiple choices for the coming form. Inside him, we can clearly observe the traces of something else: the traces of an invisible world, a luminous reality, from which he distances himself in a degree commensurate with his maturation. This unearthly world of children's eyes is a nearly physical phenomenon; here, the beyond pours out into our world, bearing some subtle knowledge, pointing the way down special paths, leading not from the possible to the actual but from the actual into the depths of the possible. There is a certain something in the child that evinces a vast superiority to adults; it is the breath of eternity, the glimmer of immortality…

The child stands above sex. More accurately, the child stands above sex in the sense of its separative quality, the strict separation of erotic roles. He is androgynous. He experiences love with all of his being, as a universal pole, in which the rays of spiritual happiness converge. And, in like measure, this love permeates the world that is near him, independently of the animation or inanimation of objects, of the sexes and ages of those surrounding him. It is no coincidence that, in alchemy — a science which affirms that all objects (to include minerals) have a soul and that all beings are secretly androgynous — the crowning moment of the work marked by the color red, *rubedo*, is depicted as a child at play. This is the magical possibility of transformation, enlightenment, salvation through super-sexual androgyne Love, the magic of the Golden Embryo [Золотого Зародыша][8], of the mysterious point at the center of the universal circle.

The Philosopher's Stone, the child at play — *Puer Ludens* — is Possibility which never becomes actuality, but instead dissolves actuality in the solar rays of an absolute Love which knows neither boundaries nor distances. In the center of Tradition stands the infant, the child. And the highest, the most ultimate of traditions — Christianity — sets at the foundation of its doctrine the divine Christmas, the incarnation of the Son, that small, gentle being in a Bethlehem manger who has brought salvation to a Universe which had gone savage, immersed as it was in toxic nightmares.

The modern world is based on a total negation of Tradition. It only recognizes the possible when it becomes actual, *a posteriori*. The axis

8 [Translator's note]: this term can be variously rendered as 'Golden Embryo,' 'Golden Germ,' or 'Golden Bud.'

of our society is the adult human, capable of regular labor, the payment of taxes, the earning of money, and of voting. The very notion of man is stamped from this template. Childhood is considered preparation for adult life, which is why so much attention is paid to education, upbringing. The most fundamental attention is concentrated upon the speed and efficacity with which a youth is made to resemble an adult.

This is called 'acceleration,' quickened development. It goes without saying that the profane world sees this as a positive process since the transformation of a child into an adult is regarded as a form of elevation, an improvement of character and social status. But in becoming an adult, children lose not only their subtle connection with invisible worlds, with luminous regions of creation, but they also gradually lose the possibility to choose — to become this or that, to take one or another path. As time goes on, they come away from the lush paradisiac fulness of gracious love and arrive at a strictly limited, fragmented individuality, defined sexual, professional, social, and economic lines. They are changed into a certain alienated, predetermined, and harshly limited atom, practically stripped of all freedoms and doomed to an interminable future of physical and social degradation. Ultimately, they are relegated to a dull, mechanical disappearance. The youth once had the possibility of becoming whomever he might choose. Moreover, he could have chosen the narrowest and most tortuous path — the path which leads to immortality, verticality, the worlds of the spirit, where the laws of eternal youth and eternal Spring rule. This possibility is latent not only in specific children, but in all children without exception, in the very state of childhood, which is greater than individuality and the concreteness of human personality. With age, possibilities narrow, one's choices become increasingly hemmed in, the soul is crammed into a cage of socio-sexual specialization and forms into a restricted shape that is subject to destruction. The breath of the beyond goes quiet. At a certain moment, we are no longer dealing with a living being but with a programmed, easily anticipated socio-erotic machine, totally lacking in interest and extremely unfree. Through money, work, the police, the television, and the bed, this adult being is defined and governed more easily than a computer might be.

Everything actual and concrete is easily calculated. Only pure possibility slips away from the cold, deathly world of rationality and social manipulation. Beginning in kindergarten and grade school, children begin their submission to spiritual genocide, internalizing false laws and unjustifiable taboos, shearing down the mass of their souls to conform to a despicable, ungodly form known as the modern adult. The children run away from their classroom desks and false lessons to clean the machines, passing through a murderous radiation cloud of money's poisons. By the age of twelve, these are already finished adults — hopelessly cynical idiots without dreams or visions, without subtle premonitions or a wise faith in miracles, without pure love or a carefully cultivated taste for the magic of dreams.

The modern world is predicated on the crushing of childhood, on the moral repression of children, who are denied their most fundamental generic rights — especially the primary right: that of attention, respect, one's own free being, protected from the whims of adults. Children are more valuable than adults. They are smarter, purer, nobler, and more dignified. From the spiritual point of view, they are even older.

It is children who must govern a normal state and a normal society — crowned and conquering infants or, at the very least, those whose souls are most childish — seers, wisemen, saints, prophets. These, like children, are the ones who hold a pure belief in the universe of miracles and who retain their connection with the spiritual world that precedes birth.

If we wish to live in a normal civilization, all proportions must be immediately inverted. Adults, in the highest academic institutions, must study myths and fairytales, pass exams on miracles and visions, become attuned to unforeseen associations and imperatives given by a limitless and many-sided love. Labor must become the consequence of an effusion of the joyous, creative forces of the soul, an amusing game, easy, compelling, selfless, and free.[9]

Today, Hesiod's words about a fourth Iron Age in which infants will be born with greyed temples are almost literally coming true.

The modern world is an apocalyptic spectacle; in this world, even children resemble bureaucrats, while their toys are perfect, miniaturized mock-ups of the adult's accoutrements — computers, cars, domestic appliances… The heroes of modern fairy tales — whether children or animals — imitate adults like peas in a pod: aggressive bandits, teenage mutant ninja turtles eating globalist slices of pizza in innumerable quantities, the dull, greedy pawnbroker Scrooge, the typical grown-up Anglo-Saxon mongrel, and everything else in the genre. Today's children are anti-children. Their temples are greying, their glances are hollow, their interests are materialistic, and their calculations are cynical. What is to be done? It's the Iron Age, the Fourth Turning. The extremum of degeneracy.

But along with this, here and there, one can occasionally glimpse in children's eyes a strange, solar joy. The secret order of little ones knows something that is hardly conceivable for the revolutionaries who are on in their years.

It is as though the rays of the Golden Crown are punching through the current twilight… as if the emissaries of the Crowned and Conquering Infant, disseminated among more average kids, are preparing for some unutterable conspiracy that will divert the march

9 [Translator's note]: 1997 redaction: "But to bring this about, there must be a revolution, after which the people with childlike consciousness, childlike naivete, and childlike wisdom must be set in power…"

of history, shake the tired ways of the world, unfetter the eschatological uprising of Love…

Despite whatever evidence to the contrary, there are some faint intimations that *Puer Ludens* is returning; and following with it comes the Golden Age, the rule of children, the Great Restoration.[10]

Under the Banner of the Goddess

The historian Johann Bachofen brilliantly showed in his work *Maternal Right* [*Mutterrecht*] that our current patriarchal civilization, founded on the primacy of the man, was preceded by a different civilization — the civilization of women. At some moment, man was able to carry out a revolution against the 'Maternal Right' and, from that moment forward, the social psychology of the most disparate peoples and civilizations was founded on the lordship of men. Woman has been assigned a socially supportive role; she has been expelled from the public sphere and bound to domestic space, family life, housekeeping. In some sense, she has been reduced to the status of a pet or a servant.

The Judaic tradition refers to woman as a "bodily organ of man that has been given autonomy." The semitic peoples and Abrahamic faiths (Judaism, Islam) have come to significant and radical conclusions relating to the patriarchal structure of society. But even in Indo-European traditions, feminine mythology almost always has something to do with holdovers from more ancient historical strata, while the active pantheon is ruled by masculine divinity.

Nonetheless, alongside the 'diurnal' social order and the official ideologies (religions), deeper levels and subliminal motifs rooted in a period of 'Maternal Right' have been preserved in the Indo-European psyche. In epochs of spiritual tumult, social cataclysm, and a heightened

10 Article written in 1994, first published in 1994 in the journal *Limonka* [Лимонка].

strain within the Aryan soul, the thematics of the Sacred Woman, the White Lady, the *Weiße Frau*, emerges with striking regularity. The vestal virgin of Rome and the Thracian witch, the cults of Aphrodite and Cybele, the sacred gnostic femininity of the early Christian Church and veneration of the Holy Mother of God [Пресвятой Богородице], the courtly tradition of the Middle Ages and the Lutheran protest against priestly celibacy in the Catholic Church — these are all traces of a departed primal myth in which the main active figure was the Woman, the Goddess, the Mother, and the Wife, who filled the cosmic elements with her bright presence.

The loss of matriarchy was a catastrophe for the world of Tradition. Reverence for the supreme beginning as feminine suggested the originary divinity not just of the world as a structure, but also of the world as material, substance. All reality was understood as a fabric of metamorphoses, where there is no death but transformation, dynamic trajectories of an abundant life that pummels its way through all boundaries. Man was swathed in Woman, who acted both within and without him, who served and inspired him, who was simultaneously his *thought* and his *flesh*. The golden-haired goddess of Heaven and Earth, the pure Freya, the mother of gods and heroes, she infused everyday life and the cult, contemplation and action, art and creation with her presence. The masculine beginning was not opposed to the feminine, nor was it subordinated to it. The masculine remained like a Fish in water, preserving its concentration in the ubiquitous elements of the Thought of Woman, the Wisdom of Woman. The Hindu Tantra, the gnostic myth of Sophia, and the Kabbalistic idea of the Shekhinah — the female presence of Divinity — are all motifs which refer to the most ancient epochs of Aryan matriarchy.

The rise of patriarchy was not a victory for men. It was their defeat, as the enslavement of woman coincided with the degeneration of man himself, who subordinated to his rational, discrete consciousness (which had become self-sufficient) those spheres of being that had previously been enclosed by authentic intuition. The Thought of Woman was reduced to the level of a woman's body. Spirit and matter, having once been identical in the luminous synthesis of the Goddess and her presence, were divorced and came into conflict. Man affirmed his formal logic, his fields of causality. The world was separated from its Cause; the two sexes were divided by a wall; An idea emerged of linear time — the product of the absolutization of the masculine mentality, torn away from feminine intuition and enclosing the entire cycle.

At the same time, woman, too, degenerated. Brought down to the lowly rung of her instrumental functions, driven into the carceral boundaries of the kitchen and the family yard, she began to lose her spiritual majesty, directing her intuition toward the earthly, gradually exacting her revenge on man through hysteria, a thirst for acquisition, and a deliberate, emphasized stupidity which irritates the rational monster of the patriarchal age. It is only in the role of the harlot that woman has preserved her sacral dignity, denigrated and mocked by male pragmatism, contempt, social shame, and the economic subtext. This is the Fallen Sophia, the Shekhinah in exile.

The epoch of revolutions has restored the hope for a Restoration. The Valkyries and passionaries of uprisings, social struggle, and revolutionary terror have advanced to the proscenium of history. It would seem that the age of the victorious Elektra is just beginning. The roll played by women in both communism and Nazism was massive. They understood the anti-rational underpinning of these doctrines and were penetrated by the spirit of the Great Return, which brimmed with these superficially modern, but deeply eschatological ideas. However, in the bosom of Nazism and communism, the matriarchal tendencies did not dominate. Along with worshippers of the feminine such as Ludwig Klages and Herman Wirth (the founder of the Ahnenerbe [Ancestral Heritage]), with priestesses of the Germanic cult — the beautiful Mathilde Ludendorff and Martha Kunzel — there was the masculinist line of the idiotic Rosenberg, the philosophy-by-rote of Baeumler, and the conservative theories of the 'three Ks (Kueche, Kinder, and Kirche).' The same state of affairs held with the Soviets: beginning with free love, the universal orgiastic ecstasy of Revolution [Переворота] — with the likes of Vera Zasulich, Larisa Reisner, and the practitioner of sexual magic Alexandra Kollontai — everything ended up in a state of Stalinist moralism and the vulgarized erotics of the late SOVDEP.

The feminist movement was originally associated with neo-paganism and occult organizations; it bore a marked 'anti-semitic' (and simultaneously anti-bourgeois) character. Afterward, it degenerated into a liberal caricature, where instead of a luminous transformation of the world, women desired the mere freedom of becoming identical with that repulsive apparatus which is the modern man.

National Bolshevism is the last revolutionary doctrine in history. It absorbs into itself all previous anti-system, non-conformist ideologies, which are resolved into a general intellectual and practical synthesis. The concreteness of economic and social requirements flows without contradiction into the highest spheres of metaphysics. Myth is deciphered through action — not through rationalization. Therefore, the awakening of the Sleeping Beauty, the cosmic Maiden, the White Lady, the restoration of the Nordic, Hyperborean matriarchy, the tantric triumph of the Shakti, the pronouncement of that great formula of the Hindu saints, "I am She" (which is identical to the precept of the Sohravardi "I am the Sun [ana-l-shams]") — all of these things comprise our sacred work, the task of our Revolution. This is the national, messianic work of Russia — the work of socialism.[11]

11 Article written in 1995, first published in 1995 in the journal *Limonka* [Лимонка].

I Swear by the Declining Day

"Verily! Man Is in a State of Loss"

The belief in progress is a pure fiction. A vestige of the optimistic eighteenth century. Not one religion teaches progress. On the contrary, they all posit that humanity is moving down the path of degeneracy, fallenness, and sin. Everything is moving from the Golden to the Iron Age. The 'surahs' of the Qur'an, which the ingenious Geidar Dzemal' loves to quote, are spoken as follows: "*I swear by the declining day: verily! Man is in a state of loss.*"

It was not only sacred doctrines which understood the loss of man. Already in the twentieth century, certain superficially modern ideologies bore an implicit relationship to cyclical time, complemented by an implication of degradation, the remedy to which would be none other than the arrival of a new Golden Age. The most brilliant of these ideologies were National Socialism and Bolshevism. The bourgeois capitalist regime was established as the limit of degeneration, against which the red and brown romantics mobilized the glimmering perspectives of the New World, the reinstated Golden Age. The active pessimism of the radicals directed the will of the masses toward the achievement of two goals: the annihilation of degenerate (dilapidated [ветхого]) humanity and the creation of a principally new paradisiac civilization. The purges and bloodlettings of the Bolsheviks and Nazis had a mystical subtext. This was no excess of sadism, cruelty, or anti-humanity. Simply put, it was obvious to the elites: "Verily! Man is in a state of loss!" The declining day hastens inexorably toward midnight. But in the womb of gloom, a New Dawn has already begun to shine. The New World. The Great Noon of the prophet Nietzsche.

Communism. Paradise on earth.

In the Struggle against 'Progress'

One finds in the word 'progress' a concentrated doctrine of 'the worldly prince,' the liberal 'anti-Christ' of consumer society. The Fall is presented as a rise, illness as health, crisis as flourishing, pathology as the norm, monsters as humans, reptilian scum as the bastion of morality.

It is only logical that the representatives of all religions and traditions should be against 'progress.' This is the right, conservative flank. It is the Fascists and Conservative Revolutionaries who come out against 'progress,' the builders of the New Middle-Ages. For them, 'progress' is materialism, the triumph of the 'mercantile,' cosmopolitan mentality. And the greatest paradox is that authentic communists, too, battle with 'progress,' initially opposing the instrumental, manipulative improvement of conditions for workers in capitalist countries (the snare of the anti-Christ) to the romantic, mystical perspective of 'class struggle' until the last drop of blood — the dawn of Revolution.

That "man is in a state of loss" goes without saying for the Christian, the Muslim, the Buddhist, the Fascist, the Bolshevik. One must overcome 'Man.' The New Man must replace the old one, whose historical mission has been fulfilled. This is not progress, but revolution. It is not a gradual improvement (which is actually a gradual degeneration), but a radical change of all conditions, systems, proportions, and parameters.

The unified front must be composed of Traditionalists and Revolutionaries. There is one enemy, one method, one goal. This is the Flaming and the New… luxuriant gardens of a newfound paradise after the grinding of a bloody battle, which has twisted the hollow carcass of humanity inside-out…

The Taste of Wormwood

Defeats are accumulating. Religions are being perverted; they are forgetting their own core. Society flouts tradition. Questions of the spirit now hold interest only for bespectacled academics. Priests are obediently blessing the banks. Mullahs are haggling for real estate. Lamas are struggling for ecology.

The Fascists have all been pummeled, scattered, and squeezed out of society.

They listen glumly to their marches, hiding in their crevices.

The grandiose construction of the Soviets has collapsed. The party elites went to shit; the vulgarized masses went to sleep; the slothful Cheka went out of their heads. Only the simple women with their frying pans are left to wave their Pioneers' kerchiefs at Anpilov's rallies.[12] This is all that remains of a great experiment…

The declining day has swallowed everyone who remained true to the inescapable dawn, even at the most stifling hour of night. Each trump card of 'spiritual warfare [брани духовной]' (the defeat of Tradition), struggles for the nation (the collapse of Fascist regimes), and the class struggle (the fall of the global socialist bloc) has been meticulously played to no avail. Not a single doctrine aimed against the inexorable logic of bourgeois degeneracy, against 'progress,' against the 'anti-Christ,' retains its effectivity or adequacy. The 'state of loss' in the human condition has consumed even that which was originally aimed at eliminating and overcoming it.

The material factors have finally subordinated people's souls. The nations have been dispersed into a cosmopolitan mixture. Capital has beaten Labor, having made the latter into a marionette, its own instrument.

12 [Translator's note]: Viktor Ivanovich Anpilov (b. 1945; d. 2018) was a hardline communist politician and trade unionist who held large demonstrations and rallies after the fall of the Soviet Union.

Our defeat is total. Our values have crumbled into dust. Our textbooks and classic literature provoke nothing beyond an ignorant shrug of the shoulders, even among ourselves. We have been surmounted by 'progress,' sacked by the 'anti-Christ,' sold at the clearing house… We've been corralled into one giant, shared ghetto, where the Christian brushes elbows with socialists and the Muslim wins his millimeter of living space from the Fascist, who is eaten up by persecution mania.

This is the general taste of wormwood, the taste of total defeat.

Is all lost?

What Is to Be Done?

Of course, we could throw up our hands and lament the inevitability of the cyclical laws.

Midnight is midnight. But this would amount to nothing more or less than *betrayal.* In our passivity, somnambulance, and distraction, it is as if we are saying: "All of our forbears have fallen for nought. The rivers of blood poured from the veins of friend and foe have done so for no other reason than to gratify the demon of fate, the Moloch of history, the gluttonous automaton of degradation." It is also folly for each faction to stick stubbornly to its guns. If something doesn't work, doesn't yield results, then it is stupidity to plug one's ears and bury one's head in the sand. One cannot change the fact of defeat through autohypnosis.

Only one path remains to us. There is only one way out, one possibility left.

The modern world has pushed all of those ideas, forces, and qualities which once ruled civilization to the periphery, the underground, the toxic waste zones. The saint and the creator, the genius and the martyr, the prophet and the visionary, the conqueror and the emperor are huddled together in the basements of modernity. And on the surface, the rulers are the usurers of loss, the loan sharks of degeneracy, the manipulators of gravitational forces which have placed their saddles on the backs of human cattle, the eschatological microbes of the end times. But *all* of the disenfranchised, those deprived of their inheritance, the outcasts, the denigrated, and the downtrodden must — have an obligation to — gather for the final act.

Those accursed of all colors, political convictions, castes, orientations, sexes, nationalities, confessions and interpretations, dislocations in the world of 'progress' and liberal values, the runaways and veterans of every lost war in history — we are all smeared in the stain of the same task: Uprising.

We must have a Revolution, united and indivisible, like Love, like the Motherland, like the Church, like Death. Only the common denominator of Negation will save us. We must negate those who occupy the center. And all there is at the center is the 'diminishing man'... Camouflaged by millions of policemen and bank accounts, we find the pitiful Little Zaches — that naked, rickety deformity who only has ghosts of thoughts and prostheses of feelings. All we must do is blow the covering of illusions off of him, and we shall see before us a pathetic clump of mucus...

It is so, so easy to do this — to grab the anti-Christ by his protruding lip...

But in order to do this, we must first melt everything that opposes the modern world and 'progress' into a single ingot. There can be no monopoly on the truth in our catacombs.

No theological arguments. No doctrinal discussions. The *Pistis Sophia*, the Qur'an, the apocrypha, the Gospels, *Das Kapital*, and *Mein Kampf* are all equally valid and true. There must not be any fractions or sects in our struggle. We have all equally been despoiled and denounced. We have a common enemy. The time has come to create a party of a novel type. This must be a religious, nationalistic, Bolshevist, occult, subversive party. It must be beyond the boundaries of all dividing lines.

The Act of Uprising is what will make us brothers. Only through this will we understand each other. Only in doing so can we test our doctrine.

From now on, only that which unites the ununitable can be our theory. That theory will test its truth through an explosion of desperate resistance.

Despite everything, we hoist the banner of War over the last holdout bunker. Its color is least like the bleached sheet of surrender. On our banner, all of the colors of lives that have been lived, thoughts thought through, and burned-out passions have coalesced. We bear on the face of our banner the symbols of all religions and orders.

Dull bipeds of cosmic midnight, regardless of everything, we will absolutely defeat you!

I swear by the declining day.[13]

The Gnostic

The time is coming to reveal the truth in its entirety, to lay bare the spiritual essence of that which groveling pedestrians call 'political extremism.' We have spent enough time confusing them, changing the register of our political sympathies and the paint coat of our heroes, transitioning from the 'right' to the 'left' and back again. This has all been nothing more than an intellectual and artistic preparation, a sort of ideological warm-up.

We have frightened and tempted both the extreme right and the extreme left; now both have lost their points of orientation and been knocked off the beaten path. This is a wonderful development. As the

13 Article written in 1995, first published in 1995 in the journal *Limonka* [Лимонка].

great Evgenii Golovin loved to say: "He who walks against the day should not fear the night." There is no greater feeling than when the soil falls away from under your feet. This is the first sensation of flight. It's a feeling that kills cretins and tempers angels.

Who are we, actually? Whose terrible visage is becoming all the clearer behind the paradoxical, radical politics that bears this frightening name 'National Bolshevism?' Today, we can answer the question without need for equivocation or tendentious definitions. But, before we can do so, we must take a brief excursion into the history of spirit.

There have always been two sorts of spirituality in humankind, two paths — the 'right-hand path' and the 'left-hand path.' The first is characterized by a positive relationship to the surrounding world; on this path, we observe harmony, equilibrium, goodness, and peace. Here, all evil is the exception, a local diversion from the norm, something inessential, transient, lacking a deep transcendent cause. The 'right-hand path' is also called the 'path of milk.' It does not bring any special suffering to men; it preserves them from radical experiences, leads them away from any immersion in the torture, the nightmare of being. This is a false path. It leads one into sleep. Those who walk this path never reach any destination of worth...

The second path, the 'left-hand path,' sees everything in the reverse perspective. Instead of milky goodness, it delivers black suffering; instead of silent peace, it brings the tormenting, fiery drama of fractured being. This is the 'path of wine.' It is destructive, horrific; anger and rage reign here. On this path, all of reality is perceived as hell, as ontological exile, as torture, as a plunge into the heart of some unthinkable catastrophe which has its origins in the very heights of the cosmos. If, in the case of the first path, everything seems good, then everything on the second path seems to be evil. This path is monstrously difficult, but is the sole path to truth. Missteps are all too easy when walking it — and it is even easier to disappear entirely. This path provides no guarantees. It tempts no one. But only this path is correct.

Whoever takes it will find glory and immortality. Whoever holds out is victorious and receives a reward greater than being.

The one who walks along the 'left-hand path' knows that his imprisonment will eventually come to an end. The dungeon of matter will implode, transforming into a heavenly city. The chain of initiates is passionately preparing the desired moment, the instant of the End, the triumph of total liberation.

The two paths are not two different religious traditions. Both paths exist in every religion, every creed, every church. There are no external differences among them. They are concerned with the most intimate sides of man, his secret essence. No one chooses one path over the other. It is the path which chooses the man, as a sacrifice, as a servant, as an instrument, as a weapon.

The 'left-hand path' is called 'gnosis' — 'knowledge.' It is every bit as bitter as knowledge; it gives birth to just as much grief and tragedy. At one time in antiquity, when humanity still afforded a decisive meaning to spiritual things, the gnostics formulated their theories on the level of philosophy, doctrine, cosmological mysteries, and on the level of the cult. Then people gradually degenerated, ceased to pay attention to the sphere of thought, and immersed themselves in the world of physiology, the search for individual comfort, the routine of daily life [быт]. But the gnostics did not disappear. They transferred their debate to the level of things that were comprehensible to the modern pedestrian. Some of them shouted the slogans of 'social justice,' worked out theories of class struggle and communism. The 'Mystery of Sophia' became 'class consciousness,' 'struggle against the evil Demiurge, the creator of the cursed world'; everything took on the character of a social battle. Threads of ancient knowledge were drawn toward Marx, Nechaev, Lenin, Stalin, Mao, Che Guevara… The wine of socialist revolution, the joy of revolting against the forces of fate, the sacred berserker passion of destroying all that is black for the sake of securing a new, utopian World [нездешнего Света]...

Others, in opposing the everyday, sought out the mysterious energies of the race, the thrumming of blood. Against miscegenation and degeneration, they propounded the laws of purity and a new sacrality, a return to the Golden Age, the Great Return. Nietzsche, Heidegger, Evola, Hitler, and Mussolini clothed their gnostic will in nationalist, racial doctrines.

It is rightly said that the communists didn't have much to do with the workers and that the same held for Hitler with respect to the Germans. But this was in no way the result of cynicism. Both sides were obsessed with a much deeper, more ancient, and more absolute striving — the general gnostic spirit, mystery, and the terrible light of the 'left-hand path.' So what about these workers, these Aryans?... What matters is something else entirely.

Between the 'reds' and the 'blacks,' the 'whites' and the 'browns,' it was creative personalities that launched into spiritual quests, all called toward the 'left-hand path,' the path of gnosis. Tied up in a flurry of political doctrines, fallen into extremities, in no state to express the metaphysical contours of their obsession, artists from Shakespeare to Artaud, from Michelangelo to Eemans, from the troubadours to Breton, were suckled on the secret wine of suffering, greedily drinking in the heteroclite fragments of a terrible doctrine in the midst of society, passions, sects, and occult brotherhoods, which deprived them of the ability to smile. The Templars, Dante, Lautréamont... None of them ever smiled once in their lives. This is a sign that they were specially chosen — a trace of the monstrous experience common to all travelers of the 'left-hand path.'

The gnostic regards our world with his heavy gaze — with the very same gaze as that of his predecessors, the links of an ancient chain composed of those chosen by Horror.

A repulsive picture presents itself to his gaze. He sees a West that has lost its mind in a consumerist psychosis, an East that has grown despicable in its retardation and pathetic obeisance, and a drowned planet lying on a murky bottom.

> In submarine forests, the mad dash becomes useless and one's gestures are restrained... (Evgenii Golovin)

But the gnostic does not abandon his business. Not now, not tomorrow, not ever. And there is every reason still to celebrate quietly to oneself. Have we really not been telling the naïve optimists of the 'right-hand path' where their unbounded ontological trust will lead them? Have we really not been foretelling the degeneration of their creative instinct into that grotesque parody which passes itself off as modern conservatives who make peace with everything that disgusted their more sympathetic (but no less disingenuous) predecessors a couple millennia ago? They did not listen to us...

Now is the time to simply let them blame themselves and read 'new age' books or pamphlets on marketing.

We have forgiven no one, forgotten nothing. We haven't deceived anyone with a superficial shift in social decorations and political actors. We have a long memory and very long arms. Our tradition is very cruel.

Ours are the labyrinths of being, the spirals of thought, the whirlpools of wrath...[14]

---

14 Article written in 1995, first published in 1995 in the journal *Limonka* [Лимонка].

PART V

GUARDIANS OF THE THRESHOLD

The Solar Dogs of Russia

Terminus

The State is surrounded by a Border. It is this border which describes the State. It determines the State in the capacity of its limits. Everything is, thanks to its boundaries. After all, it is precisely boundaries which separate a thing from other things. From this follows the most important meaning of the concept 'boundary,' not only in the sense of international law, defense doctrine, or the structure of the armed forces, but also for philosophy as such. The boundary is not just an instrument of philosophy, but its essence, since the highest philosophical concept — transcendence — means, when translated from the Latin, "that which lies beyond the boundary."

The boundary expresses externally that which lies within while, simultaneously, delimiting the essence of a thing as it collides with other things. The boundary is something sacred. The ancient Greeks had a special god — Terminus; this was the god of the limit and the boundary. He was not simply a deity who watched over borders, but a border-deity as such. This was a certain special, sacred conception which played a central role in the worldviews of ancient Indo-European peoples.

There is also an important concept in magic known as the 'guardian of the threshold.' This is a special being who inhabits the intersection of two worlds: our world and the world of the beyond, the world of crude matter and the world of subtle matter, the world of the living and the world of the dead, the world of waking and the world of dreams. This being is the very same ancient Terminus with a slightly altered visage.

The hierarchy of 'guardians of the threshold' is assiduously described in the tradition of tantric Tibetan Buddhism. In this system, they are illustrated in the form of the 'dakini,' horrifying feminine beings belonging to the retinue of Kali or Tara. They throw themselves upon a person the moment he arrives at a new level of being — whenever certain rituals are completed (especially the ritual of 'Chöd'), when traveling through desolate places, immediately following death, etc.

The 'guardians of the threshold' are there to ensure that things and people remain themselves and that their internal 'I' is preserved unmolested and constant. And as soon as someone crosses the line, they are immediately present. One can say the same when it comes to the philosophical side of things. A thing exists by way of its concept, a certain linguistic and meaningful aura which does not allow it to dissolve in the chaos of unstructured, irrational reality. The boundary is tied to reason, to its mysterious nature. Reason, as a strictly human and, in the highest sense, divine quality, reveals itself through the institution of boundaries, definitions, and determinations of the essence of things and phenomena.

And so, the boundary is the foundation of thought, the manifestation of the divine origin. God himself is unbounded, 'transcendent,' but he observes his divinity precisely through the absence of boundaries, which He imposes on being in order to distinguish Himself from that which is not him and to 'be known' by the not-him, if only partially.

If all conforms to this idea, then the boundaries of the state and those who defend them should be set apart with a special symbolism, should fulfill their sacred mission which far supersedes the purely utilitarian, administrative, and strategic military functions.

Border guards are not simply a part of the larger armed forces; rather, they are a special, sacred group. These are the modern adepts of the most ancient cult of the god Terminus.

Expansion: From Tribe to Empire

The boundary indicates not quantity, but quality. The greater its expanse, its sweep, the more universal and self-sufficient is its concept. Therefore, in accordance with the degree to which the concept is expanded (definitions, enclosures of space via limitation), it captures an ever-growing number of particular aspects. In other words, everything that is included in the concept is grasped by reason as a part, while earlier it may have erroneously been perceived as some kind of whole. The expansion of the boundary of things and concepts is a dynamic process in which a unified essence unfolds itself, visually demonstrating that universal which was initially present in the form of two (or more) distinct things. The concept of 'beast' includes in itself tigers, hares, mice, turkeys, elephants, and so on. But 'beasthood [звериность, зверскость]' unmasks its universality by capturing all forms and variations of living beings, which themselves transition in this process from a particular to a universal form.

The same holds for states. A tribe or clan has its territorial, cultural, and linguistic boundaries among others. These boundaries widen, expanding into the concepts of the 'people [народ],' the 'nation,' the 'state.' And finally, the highest form of the state arrives as Empire. The boundaries of the Empire are gigantic; they include the greatest possible number of natural human formations. The Empire has enough room for tribes, clans, cultures, religions, nations, ethnicities, and even, in some cases, semblances of independent states (provinces, dominions, etc.).

The Empire, in its capacity as a state structure, is the highest category that can be compared to the more sacred and all-encompassing gnoseological concepts such as 'God,' 'Truth [Истина],' the 'Good [Благо].' This is why the concept of the 'Holy Empire' is so perennial and steadfast.

The sacrality of Empire flows from the *quality* of its boundaries, which must offer a certain absolute, universal message [весть], a certain global mission that establishes the essence of the imperial state as having both historical and national commonality. For this reason, the boundaries of the Empire are directly linked to its foundational theological orientation. The Roman Empire and its boundaries carried within themselves a single meaning; the Empire of Alexander the Great carried another; the Arab Caliphate — a third; Byzantium — a fourth; Rus' — a fifth. The quality, too, of these boundaries — maritime, river, dry land, mountain, steppe, desert — depended on the axial mission of the Empire. It is as though the highest idea of Empire splashed out into the landscape and the structure of the boundaries themselves. The study of the transition from land borders to maritime borders allows us to trace the dynamics of the spiritual and social development of society and even sometimes to explain its most important religious, cultural, and economic transformations.

Only after the unification of all lands into a unitarian state did England regard herself as an Island, changing her religion, moving over to a maritime form of existence, and laying the foundations of capitalism and industrialization.[1]

The movement from clan to Empire is not a political, but a spiritual process, which is only reflected in earthly reality. As borders expand and different landscapes, civilizations, religions, and ethnicities are incorporated into a unified geopolitical space, a certain new, more universal Idea that had previously hidden under the kaleidoscopic multiplicity comes to reveal itself.

Templars of the Great Wall

In traditional civilization, on the basis of a direct link between the sacred meaning of Empire and her boundaries, militarized ranks of border guards and warriors formed, called to preserve the far-flung limits of the state. This connection is most clearly made in the knightly order of the Temple — the Templars — who were warrior monks, carriers of a special, universal knowledge. This esoteric knowledge consisted in the mystery of general proportions which could unite the different regions of the feudal, medieval West, including the lands of the Near-East. In the symbolism of the Templar order, one meets not only with the most ancient pre-Christian motifs connected with the sacred geography of Europe, but also with doctrines culled from esoteric Islam, particularly from Sufism and Shiism. It is no accident that the overwhelming majority of Templar commanderies were located near megalithic monuments dating back to civilizations of much earlier epochs. The Order of the Temple united North and South, the past and the future. The Templars fulfilled an important role by protecting the secrets of a unified West. At one and the same time, their understanding of Islam opened up the possibility of a truly imperial expansion beyond the bounds of Europe, toward the south and south-east.

---

1 See: Carl Schmitt, "Tension Between Land and Sea" in *Elements* [*Элементы*], No. 8, 1996.

Increasing their esoteric competency, the members of the Order potentially paved the way to expanding the State, the Western Roman Empire. And so, along with the annihilation of the Order at the hands of Philip the Fair (IV), the hope of a United Europe disappeared forever. The line of the Ghibellines and Staufens lost to the Guelphs, the Vatican, and fractured national states such as the centralized and absolutist France.

The Templars and their analogs in other civilizations were a shield which kept the lower forces of hell, the Gogs and Magogs of the Bible, from penetrating into the Empire. They defended the sacred civilization from the torrents of decay and illness. It was for none other than this reason that Alexander the Great strove to build his 'iron wall.' The same symbolism can be found in the origins of the Great Wall of China, as well in the ancient fortifications on the northern frontier of the Roman Empire. When the Order of border guards dissolves, the fundaments of imperial unity are undermined, the forces of chaos penetrate a civilization, a collapse begins, and a new Babylonian confusion of tongues takes place. The death of the Empire is a catastrophe for the order responsible for defending the borders (both in the physical and magical senses).

An excellent illustration of the magical nature of border service can be found in the film *The Desert of the Tartars*. Here, a mysterious, purely male collective (*Männerbund*) of border guards awaits an attack from the enemy, an imagined enemy, the belief in whom is seen by the guards themselves as a prolonged collective mania. They perish one by one from internal stress. Only the last one of them, beleaguered by premonitions and visions, receives his reward: he has the luxury of participating in a true miracle when the imagined enemies become a reality and their wild hordes indeed converged on the almost undefended fortress which has lost most of its people.

The last templar stands against a horde of Gogs and Magogs.

The Doghead [*Cynocephalos*]

The Soviet Empire was an empire in the full sense of the word. It was united by a shared universal idea—the idea of Socialism, in which the original Russian will to Truth and Justice were incarnated.[2] The archetypal mysticism of boundaries was entirely analogous to the traditional understanding of the role of the Templars, the guardians of the threshold. The Soviet period was filled from the very beginning with a deep esotericism which, by the way, was rarely expressed in a rational, open, or finished manner.

In order to discern the traces of the templarian element in the conceptions of the USSR border guards, we shall turn to a more banal association—"the border guard and his faithful dog." A dog is not merely an instrument used to defend the state's borders. It is something more—a symbol.

In Tradition, the symbolism of the dog is intimately connected with the idea of the boundary in its broadest understanding, to include its metaphysical component. The dog defends the home, located on the rim of inside and outside. This animal is the incarnation of the 'guardian of the threshold,' an occult personage whose mission it is to preserve the identity of the thing. But together with this, the dog symbolized *movement* across boundaries and, therefore, accompanied, in shamanic rituals, the soul of the deceased into worlds beyond. To put it another way, the dog is the animal incarnation of the god Terminus—the god-boundary.

This is where we derive the most ancient myth of the origination of men from dogs. The Mongols and Turks have a saying that the forefathers of their tribes were 'yellow dogs.' The same legend was preserved by several North American Indians. The hero of the Celts'

2 [Translator's note]: 1997 redaction: "The Soviet era was a legitimate continuation of the Russian and the Orthodox, but more universal, more global."

national epic is Cú Chulainn, whose name means 'Culann's dog.' Even in Christianity, the dog is a sacred symbol. Dante's *veltro* [hound] refers to the mysterious herald of the Second Coming as well as the "Ghibelline emperor" (and, yet again, we have a connection with Empire!). And the monks of the Catholic order of Saint Dominicus deciphered their name, 'Dominicans,' as 'Domini canes' — 'dogs of God.' The same sense yet again is found with the Egyptian cynocephaloids, deities with canine heads — particularly Anubis, the 'guide of the dead.' From this source, we also get the Greek Cerberus.

This symbolism provides us with the following picture: the border guard (modern analog of the Templar) is not just the master of his dog, of whom he makes use, but in the spiritual perspective, he himself becomes a projection of the Sacred Dog, the incarnation of Anubis, the *cynocephalos*, the 'yellow dog.' Animal and man switch places in a way. Human individuality retreats in the face of the highest magical function. Personality dissolves in the mystery of the boundary.

It is not the eagle, but the Dog's Head which must be seen as an emblem of the border guards, the stamp of a neo-Templarian division. And this, in its turn, brings us to a recollection of the symbolic attributes of Ivan the Terrible's 'oprichniks'...

Requiem

The Fall of the Empire is not only a sociopolitical catastrophe. It is a spiritual catastrophe. Together with the reduction in borders comes the collapse of the organic idea which animated the state. A blow is struck against the highest philosophical spheres. The parts are losing their comprehension of belonging to the whole; they are falling away from the life-giving center, withering and degenerating. The collapse of boundaries is the fall of concepts and ideas, a mental turbidity. This is blood and the mixture of tongues. This is a deep catastrophe for that sacred figure which is called the border guard. The forces of hell are penetrating the nations; the thief is clambering into the house; strife and stupefaction are descending upon peoples. The dog-headed god Terminus is losing consciousness, departing from us. The chaos of spiritual night swallows the people.

The Empire is good itself, incarnated within immense, ever-expanding boundaries. The end of the Empire is evil itself, appearing in the form of broken boundaries. This betrayal is both national and governmental, but these categories do not exhaust its reality. The warriors who have fallen at the border, Templars of the Soviet Idea, are betrayed by their own descendants. But their magical action is initially tied with the sacrament of thought. The disintegration of boundaries gradually provokes a greater and greater crisis in philosophy. The chaos of the Gogs and Magogs penetrates reason. Idiots come to power in the country.

The bastion of the spirit is falling.

The doors of hell are open. Hordes of enemies are crawling into the cracks that have been made in the Great Wall…

Everything is lost.

But those cast away and sold off, the lonely and forgotten, the last border guards of the Empire, carry on their duties at remote outposts.

They are the lost islets of Order amid an ocean of chaos. From now on, they are the senseless preservers of those remains which once truly composed a Great Wall.

They are left forgotten in their semi-demolished guard booths, like Baudelaire's sailors. But for now, like the dog of Saint Dominicus, they continue to unleash fiery tongues of wrath from their lungs. They are tracer bullets fired into a light which has become darkness.

This is the 'flaming air,' about which Ernst Jünger once wrote:

> The flaming air is what the soul needs in order to suffocate. This air forces one to die, day and night, in total isolation. In that hour, when youth feels that its soul is just beginning to spread its wings, it is absolutely necessary

> that its gaze turn away from those mansards, away from those shops and bakeries; it must sense that there, far below, on the boundary of the unknown, in No-Man's Land, there is someone who does not sleep as he guards the banner, and that there is a guard who stands at the farthest outpost.

Dead or alive, with a dog's head or a human's, asleep or awake, our people [наши] stand at the bleeding edge of our boundary. They are the last people who think of everyone. They are the guards of a sold-out Idea. Preservers of No-Man's Land. Watchmen of the farthest outposts.

In their veins beats the pulse of the world, our Russia, which will be resurrected on that great Judgment Day, which is so sweet and so close.[3]

Pentagram

> My friends made a gift of a squid,
> And with drunken eyes trained on the bar,
> I hacked off each limb in excess —
> I'm a madman for five-pointed star[4]
>
> — Evgenii Golovin

The symbolism of the swastika, adopted as a fundamental sign by the Nazis, has been interpreted by several authors. The swastika denotes a pole, a center, an immobile point of eternity. This is well-known, and on the basis this analysis of the swastika's symbolism, both the opponents of National Socialism and its partisans have constructed their

3 Article written in 1995, first published in 1996.

4 "Друзья подарили мне спрута,
И глядя сквозь пьяный угар,
Я лишние щупальца срезал —
I'm a madman for five-pointed star."

theories about its mystical orientation. Though strange to say, there are almost no analogous studies of the symbolism of the 'red star,' the fundamental sign of Bolshevism. It could be that the external atheistic and materialistic dogmatism of the communists is repellent to esotericists. In actual fact, however, this star deserves no less attention than the swastika, and its connection with the mystical essence of communism is as instructive as in the case of National Socialism.

Stella Maris

In Tradition, the star refers to sacred multiplicity, which, in theological terms, can be called 'the angelic host.' In ancient Hebrew, the terms 'host,' 'angelic host,' and 'star' were frequently condensed into the concept of 'zaba,' from which came the commonly used name of God in the 'Old Testament'—'Elohim Zabaoth,' i.e. 'Commander [of the heavenly] Army' or 'Lord of the Stars.'[5]

The stars are multifarious personifications of divine light. If the sun and the moon are merely two heavenly luminaries, as two archetypes of the two sexes, the two universal poles of the cosmos, then the innumerable multiplicity of stars symbolizes the plethora of living beings who populate the world, like scattered particles of matter within the transcendent fullness of the Source.

In some sense, the star is the soul of man, his luminous, heavenly root, his higher 'I.' This connection was made between stars and men in the Chinese tradition, in which it was explicitly believed that a man's death (the death of a great man, at least) was accompanied by the falling of a star. The same idea serves as the foundation for the magical concept of the 'individual soul' as an 'astral substance,' a 'sidereal body.' In modern occultism, harkening back (even if in a distorted form) to

5 Here, we should pay attention to the fact that, strictly speaking, only the two words together, 'Elohim Zabaoth,' create this meaning; 'Zabaoth' by itself merely refers to 'hosts' or 'stars.'

the ancient Rosicrucian tradition, one speaks of the 'astral plane,' i.e. the internal reality of the soul, crafted from stellar light. In Islamic esotericism, as well as in the thought of Paracelsus, we encounter the theory that people come into the world through orifices in the heavenly firmament which we perceive as stars and that, also through these orifices, people depart from the material cosmos. In the course of this process, the angelic 'I' of man is wrapped in a more resilient, semi-material substance which serves as an intermediate instantiation between this 'I' and the corporeal body. In alchemy, the same 'sidereal' reality is known as 'mercury,' and its symbol is also the star. Moreover, all Hermetic tradition, going back to the Egyptian Hermes Trismegistus (as a mythological foundation) and the Greek Hermes (as a messenger god, conductor god, and interceptor between heaven and earth), assiduously studies precisely this 'subtle plane' which is connected with stars and their invisible 'matter.'

The modern alchemical author Eugène Canseliet, student of the legendary Fulcanelli, noticed that the alchemists often made use of the symbolism of the 'sea star.' He saw in this a laconic résumé of the whole of hermetic cosmology. The fact is that 'mercury' is that intermediate space located between the world of material forms and bodies and the sphere of 'Principles,' pure Light. This 'mercury' is also known as 'water of the philosophers' or the 'alchemical sea.' At the bottom of this 'sea' is the sea star, a concentrated double of the higher 'I,' which shines above the surface of the water. The 'sea star' — 'stella maris' — is the lower pole of the soul; its upper pole is the real heavenly luminary which gives birth through its rays to the subaquatic human being at the sea floor. The unification of these two stars into one is the meaning of the Hermetic path and the 'transformation of the philosophers' black magnesium' into the 'red powder.'

Two Faces of the 'Morning Star'

In Tradition, there is an even more centralized personification of the star — the Star *par excellence.* This is the figure of the 'third heavenly light,' which is compared with the sun and the moon. It is the morning star [денница], known in Latin as 'Lucifer.' The Greeks associated this star with the goddess of Love, Aphrodite, Venus. The ancient Germans saw it as identical to the golden-haired Freya, the *paredros* (co-regent) of Odin and the mother of the Aryans. This star held a double meaning, like any female personage of traditional mythology. Venus appears on the horizon twice in the course of twenty-four hours — immediately before sunrise and immediately after sunset. It is as though she anticipates the trajectory of the divine luminary and illuminates the beings of the universe that stand in its mysterious course. As the morning star, Venus is positive. As the evening star, she bears within herself the sorrow of nocturnal gloom. But, importantly, this is one and the same star, one and the same being which fulfills two opposed functions. The theme of the 'fallen angel' that had been the first among the heavenly hierarchy reflects this sacred meaning in its theological dimension. This is where we get an identity between Judaism's 'fallen angel' and Rome's 'Lucifer.' The role of Eve, the first woman, in the fall of original sin also bears a direct relationship to this idea. The 'morning star' is most often depicted as a female deity, the goddess of Love and Eros. The biblical Apocalypse, moreover, uses the term 'morning star' in a positive manner. As Christ himself says, "[H]e that overcometh, and keepeth my works unto the end, […to him will] I give the morning star."[6] And so, a unilaterally negative interpretation of this theme is clearly inadequate to any understanding of it. There is yet another star

6 [Translator's note]: Revelation 2:26–28. In Dugin's rendering of this passage, he quotes Jesus as saying, "I will give the morning star to the victorious [Побеждающему дам звезду утренюю]," which is not necessarily a distortion of the original passage, but is, at the very least, a significant abridgment of it.

important to Christianity — the star of Bethlehem, which is the sign that the Savior of the World is born. This star of the wise men [magi] is a proclamation that the arrival of the divine child is accompanied by the coming Resurrection of the world.

The morning-evening star is a general archetype for any star, any soul. In each man, in his very depths, there exist two beginnings — the solar center of the heart and the snake of sucking darkness which twines around it. In either instance one finds a vertiginous vector of falling as well as a will to restore the dignity of light. Therefore, these star-souls, these 'sea stars,' have the most direct relationship conceivable to the symbolism of the 'morning star.' For this reason, the soul is often depicted in the form of a woman, a Wife. Strictly speaking, when it comes to 'venereal diseases,' one would do better to refer to maladies not of a sexual, corporeal type, but to those of a mental type.

Venus (Lucifer) is simultaneously double and singular; she is functionally double and substantially single. The same state pertains to both people and their souls, which latter are cast from the rays of mysterious nocturnal radiance.

Baron Tschoudy's Book

The star — particularly the 'flaming star' — is a symbol most characteristic of Freemasonry. The famous Mason Tschoudy used precisely this title for his exhaustive, encyclopedic work. As can be readily understood from what I have introduced above, this image must be related to some kind of intermediate, bifurcated reality, located between the corporeal and the heavenly. And so it is: the five-pointed star of Freemasonry is the identifying sign of the second degree of initiation — the 'Fellow Craft' or 'companion.' This degree signifies that one is more than a mere 'pupil,' but less than a 'master.' It is the 'astral' degree. It is interesting to note that, even in orthodox (i.e. strictly male) Freemasonry, to say nothing of the 'Egyptian' or mixed rites, this second degree and one's initiation into it has preserved the traces of a long-forgotten symbolism connected to the feminine. In Ariosophic lodges, reformed in accordance with Germanic mythology, initiation into the second degree was unambiguously associated with the mystery of marriage, an emphatically erotic ritual.

The flaming star is a person who has comprehended and realized his luminous nature but has yet to reach the immobile center of the heavens. This marks the halfway point of the path, an earthly paradise intermediating between material ignorance and the heavenly realm which lies beyond the firmament. The star symbolizes an immense spiritual achievement, but does not yet guarantee one's joyous completion of the path toward the Absolute. One has not yet ruled out the possibility of falling. But not even this dismaying perspective can deprive the initiate of a special internal quality which dramatically distinguishes him from the profane. The man who has learned the mystery of the 'sea star,' even if he has not managed to float to the surface, will never return to his irretrievably lost ignorance. It is for this reason that some dark sects use the symbolism of the star as their chief sign — especially in the form of the inverted pentagram.

But it would not do to simplify the meaning of this sign, even if it does not point us toward the higher aspects of spiritual realization. Occultists are frequently inclined to banalize the meaning of this first stage of the 'working,' while the Masons themselves sometimes fail to understand the degree to which a deep disquietude should accompany those rituals which are everywhere seen as exotic gestures or moral allegories. The Man-Star, the 'fellow craft,' the 'companion' — this is a 'new humanity,' an unconditional elite that has turned back from the corporeal inertia of profanity and has ascended from the hell of everyday, peripheral existence. These are the 'last' who have become the 'first.' A total realization of the initiatic possibilities of this esoteric plan should give man nothing more or less than 'immortality,' i.e. a continuity of consciousness independent of whether the person exists in a body or without one. In life, this state is most often felt through one's ability to maintain complete consciousness during dreams, which doubles as a lucid awareness of the oneiric fabric, hidden for the usual waking man under the mantle of material. Taking this double structure as our point of departure, it is easy to understand the doubled meaning of such an 'immortality,' capable both of positive traits (the saints) and of degeneration into vampirism.

The star is not the center in an absolute sense, but in a relative one. On the level of the earth, it is associated with the Center of the World.

Nordic Matriarchy

Now we will take a momentary detour from the esoteric. Herman Wirth gave a surprising interpretation of the symbolism of the five-pointed star. He brought attention to the fact that, in German folk language, the pentagram is known as the 'witch's paw' or 'Drudenfuss.' Wirth claims that 'Drude' (i.e. witch) is a distortion of the word 'Thrud' which was used during in the epoch of the Skalds to denote the mother of the god Thor. Almost nothing is known of this goddess. Wirth suggests that her meaning is practically exhausted in the image of the pentagram — a sacred symbol of the calendar referring to the winter solstice, the New Year, Yule. Basing his ideas on the theory of man's polar origins, which Wirth so deftly developed in his works, he puts forth the hypothesis that this pentagram, five-pointed star, or its symbolic equivalent (the palm or the sole of the foot), served as a hieroglyph denoting the year (the six-pointed rune Haglaz) but missing its bottom member pointing to the south, where the sun is in the midst of winter's polar night. The absence of this member is an allusion to the fact that, in those climes and at that time of year, the sun fails to rise at all. And this being the case, the symbol becomes a synonym for the

Arctic, the polar ur-motherland, the ancient city of 'Vara,' written of in the Avesta as a place that lay in the far North.

In this symbolic chain of identifications between the pentagram, the pole, the Arctic, the Indo-European peoples, the symbolism of the hand (and the foot), the sacred centrality of the middle of winter (the New Year), and the female deity, the fundamental idea of Wirth's entire theory is manifest. He argued that humanity, at the dawn of its history, inhabited the pole; that its sociopolitical structure was matriarchal (the cult of the White Goddess); that writing and literacy developed from signs of the calendar which, in turn, are metaphysical and geometrical forms that can be observed in the course of the full polar year; that the symbolism of all religions and traditions all hail from a single originary source pertaining to a phonetic, hieroglyphic, and conceptual nature.

This all was incarnated for Wirth in the symbol of the five-pointed star and the swastika, as well as in the raised hand. It is very telling that Herman Wirth was the founder of the Ahnenerbe under Hitler (though he was driven from his position under pressure from Rosenberg, promoter of Aryan patriarchy), but that he simultaneously sympathized with communism in the belief that the epoch of patriarchy as the suppression of the original Nordic sacrality of the White Lady ended in 1917, thanks to the successful Bolshevik revolution!

The star coincided with the swastika as a symbol of the Pole, the high Nord.

"Comrade, Believe Me — She Will Ascend..."

How did the star become the symbol of Bolshevism? History tells us that this is formally the work of Trotsky, who, having been a member of the 'Grand Orient' Masonic lodge and the author of an extensive monograph (which he lost during his revolutionary adventures) on Freemasonry, deliberately applied this emblem to the Bolsheviks, providing an excellent statement with regard to their esoteric meaning. But despite what anyone may suggest, this could not have been the personal initiative of a single man, since the meaning of the symbol and the spiritual subtext of far left movements were closely linked long before Trotsky and Lenin. When one reads the history of French socialism, one begins to feel as though this is an encyclopedic recounting of occultism up to that time. And likewise, the description of esoteric organizations in Europe during the nineteenth century creates the impression that this entirely milieu was driven by political radicalism. One encounters the same repeating names: Blanqui, Cabet, Yarker, Leroux, Mackenzie, Éliphas Lévi, Fabre d'Olivet, Fourier, etc. Freemasonry and political utopia walk hand-in-hand. These are the Rosicrucians and Hermetists, recasting the lead of the body into the gold of the spirit, bolstered by Marxist ideas of transforming the proletariat into the philosopher's stone of social revolution and the attainment of the 'red powder' of communism.

This is reintegration, the 'new humanity,' 'earthly paradise,' man as an intercessor between heaven and earth, the initiate who has replaced abstract dogmas of deism with the vital experience of personal spiritual realization. Revolutionary humanism flows from initiatic doctrines, and the traces of these doctrines are preserved in the signs, language, emblems, coincidences, and perpetual repetitions of the same plots, rituals, and gestures.

The pentagram has more to say about the essence of Bolshevism and revolutionary socialism than all historical materials relating to the various congresses, schisms, betrayals, and fractions that occurred. Bolshevism is the idea of the 'New Man,' the man-star who rises through an effort of will above the darkness of unconsciousness. Neither the degenerate aristocracy nor the clerical Pharisees were the primary enemies of the Bolsheviks. Bourgeois profanity, the reign of quantity and money—this is what the communists revolted against.

The proletariat is the symbol of the philosophers' *prima materia.* As Sophia says in the Psalms of David, "I am black, but comely…"[7] This is that '*chose vile*,' that vile thing which, for the alchemists, was more precious than golden ingots.

Red stars ignite above the Kremlin, center of the Third Rome, the Third International. This is the image of the center of the world — the pole.

Under the sign of the star, the socialist state expands, new cities arise, aviators ascend into the air, Stalin's polar explorers plow through the ice, detachments of the NKVD leave on a trek to Tibet. The palm, sign of the White Goddess, which is encountered in the most ancient cave paintings, glimmers with gold — like the Revolutionary Restoration of 'cave communism'; like the most ancient testament — on the fiery banners of the Bolsheviks.

Pushkin, having written those famous words to his Masonic brother in praise of the Pentagram, wrote a prophecy which later came to pass.[8]

---

7 [Translator's note]: This quotation, rendered by Dugin in the Russian as 'Я черна, но я прекрасна,' is not actually found in the Psalms of David, but rather in Solomon's song of songs (Song of Solomon 1:5). Obviously, Sophia is not directly referenced in either book, but Dugin is clearly reading this passage through a sophiological lens.

8 Article written in 1997, first published in 1997 in the journal *Elements* [Элементы] (No. 8 — Dossier 'National Bolshevism') under the pseudonym 'Leonid Okhotin.'

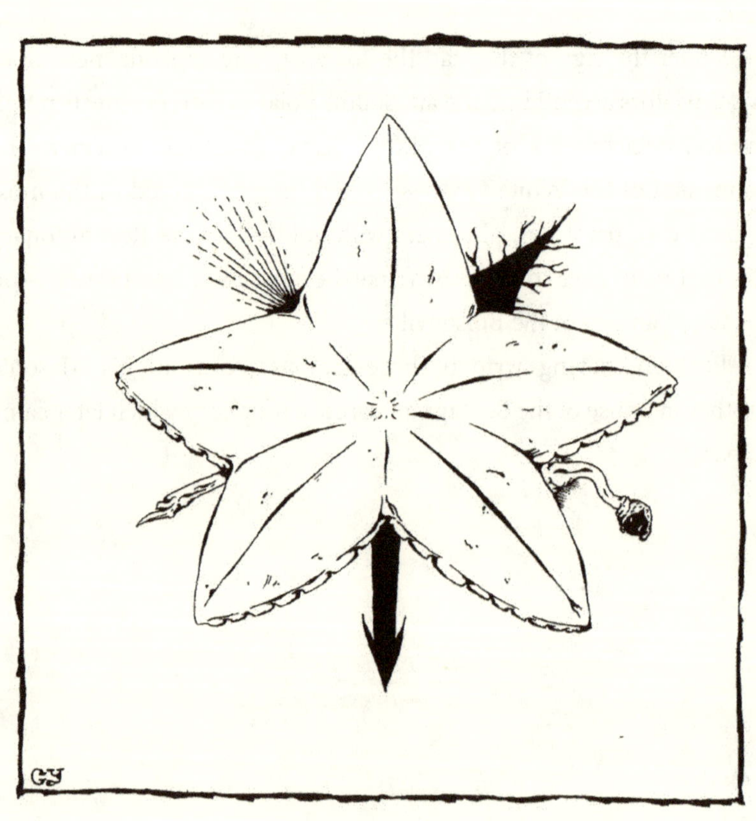
GY

PART VI

CHAOS MAGIC

The Man with a Falcon's Beak

(An Essay on Aleister Crowley)

The Crashing Waves of Cefalù

Entire generations have already grown up on rock music, psychedelia, punk, rave, and techno. It is easy to reproduce the melodies that have been played thousands, tens of thousands of times. It is more difficult to do so in words. Of all the rock fans in the world, only one in a hundred knows English. Even less of them can make sense of the words in the songs… And when it comes to the deep underbelly of rock culture in its broader sense, the strange mystical theories undergirding it, the unsettling, mysterious personae who stand at the very foundations of the genre—only rare initiates know of these things.

On the cover of the Beatles' *Sergeant Pepper's Lonely Hearts Club Band*, among other figures respected by the group, one can spy a certain person with a heavy gaze and a massive face. A 'supreme stranger.' A dark individual. Jimmy Page, his disciple and fanatic, bought the man's estate not far from Loch Ness. This person's ideas inspired the Rolling Stones as they wrote their album *Their Satanic Majesties;* this was after they had befriended the strange film director Kenneth Anger and had begun to dress themselves in SS uniforms. This man was the adopted spiritual teacher of Arthur Brown, Sting, David Bowie... But his absolute cult in radical music begins with Genesis P. Orridge of Psychic TV and Throbbing Gristle. A few hundred groups generated by this scene known as 'dark wave' or 'industrial music' made the study of this mysterious man a crucial component of their art. The sound of his voice has been mixed in and sampled; his books have been transposed onto the medium of music; his rituals have been performed on stage. A CD has even recently been released containing a recording of waves crashing upon a shore not far from Cefalù — the place where this person at one time lived and founded his Rabelaisian, tantric abbey called 'Thelema.'

The initiated are already aware of whom I speak... of the Beast, that very great Beast (*To Mega Therion*).

The Perverted Initiate

Edward Alexander (Aleister) Crowley was born on 12 October 1875 in Lymington (Warwickshire), England, into the family of a Protestant preacher belonging to the sect of the 'Plymouth Brethren.' From early childhood, he witnessed the ascetic fanaticism of his father, the sermons, the mortification of flesh, the religious exaltation. The Puritan suppression of all bodily desires was the primary motif of his upbringing. This extremism (this resounding 'no' against the erotic), so characteristic of Anglo-Saxon culture, would later become its opposite — 'yes to all forms of erotic experience.' It is worth remembering that pornography appeared in precisely those countries where social taboos against the sexual sphere were the strongest.

At Cambridge University, Crowley crossed paths with a small group of aesthetes and occultists who were inspired by decadence, Wilde, and Ruskin. Here, the youth, rich, talented, exquisite in his tastes, and known for his subtle beauty became an idol. Despite his marriage to Rose Kelly, he neither limited the company he kept, nor the innumerable lovers who were his sexual accessories. He traveled extensively, conquered the highest peaks of the world, visited Egypt, Russia, Scandinavia, France, and Mexico. His was the life of a dandy, an intellectual, an alpinist, a mystic, a poet, a seeker of adventure. In 1896, in a Stockholm hotel, Crowley underwent his first epiphany. He felt that he was being called upon a solemn magical path. In short order, he encountered the occult organization which would facilitate his entrance into this path and would arm him with secret knowledge. This was the 'Golden Dawn in the Outer,' the most mysterious and powerful organization of Western magic of that age. The order had admitted into its ranks such famous figures as William Yeats (a Nobel laureate), Maud Gonne (the inspirer of the Irish Republican Army), Constance Wilde (widow of Oscar Wilde), the actress Florence Farr (the muse of George Bernard Shaw), and Moina Bergson (sister of the famous philosopher Henri Bergson and the wife of the Golden Dawn's leader, Samuel Mathers).

In the Order, Crowley learned about the initiatic use of narcotics, special magical rituals and practices, the mysterious doctrines of the Kabbalah, Rosicrucianism, Yoga, alchemy, and operative magic. At his estate, Boleskine, on the shores of Loch Ness, he conducted secret experiments in summoning the 'angel preserver.' His most complicated experiment took six months to prepare, but it ultimately came to nothing. Only a few years later, in Mexico, and under strange circumstances was he able to spontaneously encounter the phenomenon (and it would leave an indelible mark on Crowley's life).

In 1904, during a trip to Cairo, Crowley received a special revelation. A terrible 'preterhuman being'—the 'demon Aiwass'—chose him to be the bearer of a new knowledge and the herald of a new age, a new æon, the 'Æon of Horus.' From that point on, Crowley understood himself to be 'the Beast 666,' which is described in the Book of Revelation and whose initiatic name is rendered as 'To Mega Therion' or 'The Great Beast.'

From then on, right up to his death in 1947, Aleister Crowley carried out a most important mission — the dissemination of his doctrine. Its most important source was the famous *Book of the Law*, which was dictated by Aiwass. The first of the laws is, "Do what thou wilt shall be the whole of the law.' After this, Crowley did not do much to change his habits. Externally, all remained as it had been before: he continued to engage in occult practice, unhindered sexual copulations of all varieties, literary opuses, narcotics, poetry, alpinism, ironic spectacles conjured up to scare the profane, and contact with the powerful of the world. But all of this activity had been illuminated by a certain disquieting light, penetrated with a special meaning. 'The Beast 666' was not merely a man. He was the head of the initiatic organization known as Astrum Argentum, to which belonged, according to Crowley, the 'invisible brethren' who control human history by means of the occult orders of the past. Crowley would send *The Book of the Law* to Hitler, Lenin, and Churchill, and would introduce it to Trotsky. His agents and pupils were active in the most diverse fields: Captain John Fuller, an adept of his, was an occultist and the chief English strategist in the matter of tank operations — a man of the conservative milieu; Martha Küntzel, a passionate National Socialist, was the handler of Hitler and his circle; Walter Duranty, the only Western journalist favored by Stalin, was active in Moscow. Crowley was situated in the middle of a world conspiracy, weaving the web of the new æon. Women, narcotics, magical operations, political intrigues — all of these followed the teacher of 'Therion' until the end of his life. Many of those who got close to him lost their minds. The majority of his former wives and some of his lovers, after parting with him, would immediately land in a psychiatric clinic. His black doctrine and horrific practices terrified not only the profane, but even occultists. Given that he was, for a certain time, a bearer of the highest Masonic degrees, Crowley was gradually driven from every corner; the 'brothers' feared his doctrines and shrank away from his moral reputation. The Second World War and its horrors caused the Western press to forget about this strange man, whose name was practically never stricken from the list of 'Scandal.'

His death occurred almost unnoticed on 1 December 1947, the result of bronchitis and a weak heart that gave out in his 72nd year. During that period (starting from the birth of Crowley) the point of spring equinox shifted precisely one degree. It was an astrologically unimpeachable death.

The Science of the Beast

The doctrine of Aleister Crowley in its broad strokes goes something as follows.

Civilization develops in accordance with certain cycles, each of which defines a religious and cultural level of humanity. Every cycle lasts approximately 2,000 years, which coincides with the transition of one of the twelve constellations of the Zodiac into a new sector. Contemporary humanity is living at the tail end of the 'Æon of Osiris,' which is characterized the 'archetype of the dying and resurrecting god.' This 'æon' or cycle is determined by patriarchal ethics and a perception of divinity as something abstract and moral. The law of this cycle requires that man be ascetic and deny his own will. But this is now all coming to an end. The next cycle — the 'Æon of Horus' (the son of Osiris) — draws near. In this next period, there will be a different religion and a different culture, founded on a new ethics. Then, the 'deity' will be inside of man ("Each man and woman is a star," as one of Crowley's most important laws states), instead of beyond him. As a result, there will be no limitations, and a reign of total liberty will commence. Crowley considered himself to be the 'prohet of the Æon of Horus,' and believed that he would inform humanity of the coming changes. In his letters written to Duranty in Moscow, he insisted on the idea of Stalin's rise to power in the Soviet Union as a form of celebration, that this would occur "in honor of the people, who had demolished the cathedrals of the god of the previous æon and had hoisted the symbol of the five-pointed star of magic above their most sacred shrine — the Kremlin."

There exists a special period between the two æons — the 'storm of equinoxes.' This will be an epoch in which chaos, anarchy, revolutions, wars, and catastrophes reign supreme. These waves of horror are indispensable in order to wash away the remnants of the old order and to clear a place for the new one. According to Crowley's doctrine, the 'storm of equinoxes' is a positive moment which those who serve the 'Æon of Horus' should welcome, hasten, and utilize. Therefore, Crowley himself supported all 'cataclysmic' tendencies in politics — communism, Nazism, anarchism, and extreme nationalism of a liberational character (particularly Irish nationalism). Moreover, at the origins of these movements, one finds other secret organizations that were often quite open and legal, so that the path toward realizing the political projects of the master of Therion was rather simple — all it took was to convince a few occultists of his esoteric veracity and his influence on politics was guaranteed. Along with this, Crowley highly valued modern art as a method of realizing the 'storm of equinoxes.' Rebellious, stripped of boundaries and aesthetic principles, extremely individualistic and anarchistic, it bore within itself, according to Crowley, all the seeds of the current civilization's demise. This art awakened perversions, the magic of fascinating insanity, and the ephemerality of destructive narcissism.

Many people count Crowley a 'Satanist,' and his appeals to the Apocalypse give ground to these claims. However, things are slightly more complicated. Crowley himself believed that the Book of

Revelation was a truly prophetic text which described the end of his cycle with perfect accuracy, but he also evaluated the book from the very positions of Christianity (i.e. the religion which, in his opinion, was destined to vanish along with the end of the 'Æon of Osiris'). Consequently, he came to the conclusion that the negative figures of the Apocalypse are not all that negative if one perceives them from the vantage point of a new, different æon. When one does this, the Whore of Babylon and the Beast transform into the prophet and his female hypostasis and cease to be mere, pitiful 'Satanists.' It should be noted that, from a non-Christian perspective (whether that be pagan, Hindu, etc.), this approach to decoding the Apocalypse could very well be justified. Crowley persisted in his occult milieu, far from Christianity, the enchanted East, and Hermeticism; this milieu saw nothing particularly 'diabolical' in Crowley up to that time. Even the Traditionalist Julius Evola (whose ideas were remote from Christianity) found Crowley's 'Satanism' to be nothing more than the épatage of an esotericist who had taken the 'left-hand path.'

The 'Æon of Horus,' as Crowley describes it in his *Book of the Law*, is reminiscent not only of the occult utopias of the Theosophists and their contemporary devotees of the 'New Age,' but also of the future envisioned by Hitler and certain socialists. Esotericism, culture, avant-garde art, psychedelics, and radical politics were tightly interwoven into the personality of Aleister Crowley. In some sense, he could be called the symbol of the twentieth century. Mystic and rebel. Revolutionary and politician. Dandy and alpinist. Astrologist and psychoanalyst. Sexual pervert and practitioner of the Tantra. Religious fanatic and cynical sceptic. Mystifier, actor, fame seeker, and cultivator of secret knowledge. Drug addict and healer.

Beast.

A Cruel and Bloody Bird

There is a mistaken point of view according to which the youth counterculture that emerged in the West during the 1960s under the aegis of rock music is pure liberal leftism, humanism, anti-totalitarianism, and softness. Against this background, the fascist armbands of Led Zeppelin or the Rolling Stones during their Crowley period and, later, the swastikas of the first punks arrived like thunder amidst a clear blue sky. Along with the 'dark wave' of Psychic TV, Throbbing Gristle, Sol Invictus, Coil, Death in June, Current 93, Monte Cazzazza, Boyd Rice, Allerseelen et al., 'fascism' (or to be more precise, 'Nazi-Satanism') had already openly engulfed the radical youth of the day. As a matter of fact, the black pathos inherent in this scene is not so different from the revolt of the early hippies. It is just that, at this stage, commensurate with the hippies' 'revolution from the left,' there came an equal 'revolution from the right.' The Crowleyan design is above the exigencies of party or doctrine. All doctrines are good which demolish the system, the old Æon of Osiris, the remains of its former might that find expression in Anglo-Saxon morals, the police system, and the dictatorship of bureaucracy.

Previously, the influence of Crowley's doctrine had been peripheral. Now it had become explicit. John Balance of the band Coil has the following to say about it:

> Personally, I believe in the coming of the age of Horus, the age of Thelema. But I also believe that chaos, changes, tumult, and maelstroms must come first. A chaotic period of transition. A cruel and bloody bird. The final cycle of the system of the Aztecs and the Kali-Yuga of the Hindus is just on the precipice of ending. It's no surprise that we are beginning to see clear signs of the end. I think that we — both as the band Coil and as individuals — should actively participate in this. We need to strive for chaos and

> confusion, to help annihilate the old order so that a path toward the new æon will open up.[1]

It is the very same ethos, by the way, which underpins the currently trendy 'chaos-parties,' a spawn of the modern Crowleyan movement with an explicit Nazi-Satanist ideology. In distinction from the usual pin-headed neo-Nazis and reactionaries, who are loyal to the System, these latter Nazi-Satanists entirely lack any anti-communist sentiment or hatred for other revolutionary ideologies.

One can encounter followers of Aleister Crowley in the most diverse groups and movements. The free love of the hippies is also a sign of tantric Crowleyism, as is the idea of a higher race of initiated masters — "The slaves shall serve and suffer," as it is written in *The Book of the Law*. Homoeroticism, narcotics, intensive operative magic, avant-garde music, super-perverted eroto-comatose antics, the phosphorescent portrait of insanity, political extremism — these are all precisely laid out, systematized, concentrated, and predetermined in Aleister Crowley's doctrine of Thelema.

---

1 [Translator's note]: The interview from which Dugin draws this excerpt appears to have taken place in 1985 for a zine called *The Feverish*. The interview itself is titled "A Letter-Interview with John Balance (Coil)" [https://brainwashed.com/common/htdocs/publications/coil-1985-the-feverish-4.pdf]. Because Dugin's translation alters some of John Balance's wording and slightly condenses his meaning, I am reproducing the original English text here:

"I personally believe that the age of Horus — of Thelema — will occur. But that in between will be chaos — change and turmoil. A state of confusional transition. A violent & bloody Bird. The descriptions afforded by *The Book of the Law* are not peaceful and idyllic — but ridden — hard and ruthless. One can go into the ancient theories about the cycles of the ages, etc. But it is true that both the Age of Kali and the last age — the final cycle of the Aztec System — are calculated about now. So no wonder, the signs are beginning to manifest themselves. I think that [we, as Coil and as individuals, should] attempt to relate to all of this — and you can't help but be wholly involved — one should attempt to generate chaos and confusion — [help] bring down the old order in order to speed on the advent of the New."

Like it or not, we all live under his sign, under his watch, under his commandments. Anyone who is even in the slightest affected by the terrifying spirit of the modern world is put in some relation to his ideas. "Ignorance of the law is no excuse."

A bloody and cruel bird.

A falcon.

The Egyptian symbol of Horus.[2]

Absolute Beginners

David Bowie, the Initiate

David Bowie is famous as a musician and actor; few know that he is also a member of an initiatic organization that promotes the principles of the 'left-hand path' and 'thelemism.' And so, it comes as no surprise that his songs, videos, and aesthetic projects possess an occult dimension.

His song 'Absolute Beginners' represents the typical model of his multi-layered message, in which emotionality and manifest psychological aesthetics obscure an esoteric core.

A Counterfeit

The words 'Absolute Beginner' come together into a phrase of total logical contradiction. This which is absolute does not 'begin,' since the truly absolute has neither beginning nor end; it neither emerges nor disappears. And, alternatively, that which has a beginning is essentially not absolute but, quite to the contrary, something relative. This is the phrase's philosophical aspect.

2 Article written in 1995 for the journal *Om*, first published in 1997.

There is also a contradiction on the purely everyday level: we see this in our contemporaries' attempt to 'start from the beginning,' in their tepid and inexpressive protest against their own degeneration, aging, and growing senility against the background of a rapidly petrifying society where no one can withstand the entropy any longer and doesn't even try to; such an endeavor is doubtful to the highest degree. In accordance with Hesiod, children are being born with grey temples and immediately come scrambling out of their cradles to wash their cars and open bank accounts. These are all the signs of the end of the Iron Age. What sort of 'new beginning' could one even hope to countenance in this state of affairs, much less an absolute one?

Bowie himself, despite his inventiveness and talent, can hardly pretend to know an alternative. His fascination lies precisely in his image as a decadent, a pervert absorbed in a sort of manic narcissism, an aged, melancholic, Anglo-Saxon reprobate; but in no way can he legitimately be seen as a hero or bringer of the 'new.' He has no relationship either with the 'absolute' or with any 'beginning.' Rather, all he has to offer is the soporific exoticism of decay, the aroma of rotting flesh enclosed in globalist gadgets.

The Absolute Beginner is a concept derived by David Bowie from an arsenal of deep gnostic doctrines. It has exuded a pretty good song and a rather odd video.

The Doctrine of the Star

The Absolute Beginning, which does not and cannot exist, is nonetheless the axis of a forbidden, heroic knowledge, passed down along a secret chain. Through a banal, static picture of metaphysics — below, the changeable and relative, above, the unchanging absolute — a special, paradoxical will shared among a few initiates has affirmed (at great risk to life and mind) a vertiginous, captivating perspective. There is a certain something that cleaves logical and religious dualism. It is the

Eternal Beginning, the mysterious Ray which is 'closed' on one side and 'open' on the other. In this ray, all the great proportions and correspondences of the three worlds lose their meaning. The high and the low switch places; an impossible, unthinkable wedding of Heaven and Hell occur which Blake so ingeniously foresaw.

This is called the 'Doctrine of the Star.'

Thelemites, followers of Francois Rabelais and the Englishman Crowley (it is precisely from these sources that Bowie drew the concept of his song, being himself a member of the 'Ordo Templi Orientis'), believe that "every man and every woman is a star." The incarnation of finitude and relativity, a clearly unfortunate species that has ended its history with the most total, inconceivable vulgarity [пошлостью] that is the World Bank and the World Market, an obvious biological counterfeit wearing the proud and pure mask of an angelic being — this is man. However, from a different (thelemic) point of view, this man carries within himself a 'star,' which glares with a frigid ray. Through the godless mess of his pathetic little soul streaks a strange, impossible, vertiginous light.

This is the light of the Absolute Beginning — that which cannot be.

Black Rays

The soil crumbles away beneath one's feet. The values of tradition have degenerated and been profaned to such a degree that one has no capacity to resist the limp nihilism that remains in their place. Conservatism and progress have proven to be nothing more than the two faces of this very same degeneration. All that remains of a once chaotic history is hunger, lust, and the police. All signs indicate that we are as far as we can be from the Beginning, both the old one and the new one. All passion is lost.

What do the 'Thelemites' mean — whose troubling ideas are entirely foreign to the optimism of the New Age and the pensioners of Theosophy—when they affirm within *everyone* the paradoxical possibility of a 'star,' a 'new beginning?' Of course, we do not speak in this instance of some vulgar 'transformation,' 'enlightenment,' or 'attainment of truth.' Look: on the faces of these 'neophytes' of every religion and cult, you see a haunted gaze, flashes of holy stupidity, a strange gesticulation of internal bodies that are clearly in ill health… They withdraw, trembling and hissing, in no way having transformed or conceived of something new.

The black ray of the thelemic star slips along a different trajectory. It is not fixed from without; it is not enveloped by the usual environment. It causes deliberate fright and repulsion, garbed (provocatively) in the vestments of antinomianism. It swiftly abandons those who want to turn its transformative intuition into a system. It is not subject to institutionalization. But it sparkles, absolutely and eternally, in its æonic rhythm, spurning the will of cycles and the condensing masses of dark epochs. It decides its own forms and elects the bodies in which it will manifest, rushing into them without meaning or purpose. Its decisions are willful and unprovoked, independent of merit, honor, or acts. It is indifferent to 'moral standing' and cares nothing for one's success in breathing exercises.

The Absolute Beginning is without sex, age, profession, or post. It is a razor of crystal awakening that rips through a curtain of atoms sewn together by the spirit of a midwit.

A Trusty Alternative

The question is, in fact, central: the idea of 'no future' is not simply the cheap thesis of a grotesque youth movement which has, by now, finally croaked. The thesis of the 'End of History,' as developed by Francis Fukuyama, is in essence the same thing, but cast in more optimistic, milquetoast terms. Exhaustion is the fundamental discovery of post-modernity. The triumph of simulation is a moribund joy. The cunning predators of the electronic lie have raped reality so entirely that they will finally end their social manipulation in the company of mad machines. In the final calculation, all fantastic literature of the nineteenth century has become a technical banality in the twentieth, and the same relation holds between the twentieth and twenty-first centuries. This is especially the case when we consider that the majority of major fantasts (from Jules Verne to H. P. Lovecraft) were members of powerful esoteric organizations and actively participated in providing civilization with a deliberate, predetermined façade.

None of the fantasts or futurologists of the 'New Beginning' were prophets. Their prognoses are horrific: the more distant the future, the more monstrous it appears. And man dashes headlong into a narcissism which can save him from nothing, under the ragged mantles of obviously false and non-reassuring formulas. Bankers and newscasters hover over the ruins like painted-up vultures. They are the dead necromancers of corpses. To believe in telemyths is to turn into an idiot; not to believe is to lose your mind from loneliness (everyone around you continues to believe). No star in sight.

The Soviet system looked coldly and bluntly upon the desperate attempt by the 'new left' to develop an alternative ideological version of the bourgeois order by means of a modernization (and reevaluation) of traditional anti-capitalist doctrines. The comfortable apparatchiks spit on the desperate bid of non-conformists to make their great leap toward a positive project. Having then already recognized the imminent collapse of the SOVDEP, the 'new left' appealed to esotericism, gnosticism, and other disciplines that were not compatible with the orthodox left.

The 'new right' developed along a comparable trajectory, rejecting chauvinism, xenophobia, and the market-mindedness of the 'old right'; the 'new right' had discovered for itself the values of revolution and socialism. But both of these 'new' sectors — both the right and the left — were accused by the SOVDEP partocrats (who would go on after the fall of the USSR to rebrand as 'democrats' and CPRF[3] members) of 'nihilism,' while the latter went tumbling headlong with their well-fed bodies into the fetid rot of 'reforms' and national betrayal. Once again, the true nihilists, as they had done a thousand times before in history, had accused those who strove to overcome nihilism of the very thing they were struggling against.

The outcome was sorrowful. Without the help of Moscow, the smart and honorable, but impotent 'newcomers' were crushed by the System (Foucault, Deleuze, and Debord each met their end in suicide while the rest either died of natural causes or vanished into obscure oblivion); yet others were corrupted into 'thought police' (Bernard-Henri Lévy, Glucksmann, Habermas, and other bastards). Without the fanatic spirit of flaming rebellion, Moscow herself slipped down into the snares of the World Government.

In all, there is no Beginning, no hint, no chance. In the best-case scenario, as the pessimists of the intelligentsia are hoping, the coming catastrophe will go over smoothly, like euthanasia. What, in principle, could all of the 'democratic' and 'patriotic' publications have against Marcuse's 'one-dimensional man?' Like the 'people [народ]' at the beginning of Nietzsche's *Zarathustra* who craved the arrival of the 'last men,' all sectors of our society would most gladly end up at the 'one-dimensional man' who governs a 'coalition government.'

---

3 [Translator's note]: CPRF [КПРФ]: The Communist Party of the Russian Federation [Коммунистическая Партия Российской Федерации]. When Boris Yeltsin was sworn in as president of the newly formed Russian Federation, he held a referendum which resulted in the outlawing of the Communist Party of the Soviet Union (CPSU) [Коммунистическая Партия Советского Союза (КПСС)]. Almost immediately afterward, former CPSU members reformed their party as the CPRF, which allowed them to function legally in the new country.

And, meanwhile, the former youth (who are now well past thirty) would listen to Bowie's songs while sipping on their Heinekens.

An End to the Illusion

There is neither an alternative nor a New Beginning to be had. There is nothing outside (counterfeits surround us). There is nothing inside (the forces of the soul have frozen over). And nonetheless, the grapes of wrath are ripening; networks of conspiracy are weaving themselves together — the world conspiracy against the loathsome present.

This is the conspiracy of the Star. At any age, in any place, in any state, at any time, in any situation, in any pose — "every man and woman" can *begin*, can discover the Absolute Beginning and penetrate him or herself with the black Ray that has no end, that passes through cycles and epochs in spite of all logic, of all external determinism, of the whole causal system. Any impulse to life, any passionate rush, any piercing state of being can suddenly cross the threshold if it becomes an excessive, unbridled, transcendent idea. Greed and generosity, asceticism and hedonism, jealousy and faithfulness, hatred and gentleness, illness and satiation can become an Absolute Beginning, a terrible, thunderous accord of the New Revolution, single and indivisible, right and left, external and internal.

But one must now allow a new collapse to occur after arriving at the peak. The intensity must only increase; beyond each culmination, there must be an even greater one; the white heat of individuality must ignite the external world with the flame of rebellion — that rebellion which (according to Sartre) constitutes the sole force which saves man from loneliness.

The Absolute Beginning does not depend on objectivity. It has no conception of 'early' or 'late,' 'here' or 'there.' All the better if there is "nothing much to offer, nothing much to take…"

The end of the cycle is ultimately the end of an illusion, as Guénon wrote.

Bowie's song, accompanying one's reading of *The Book of the Law* and the bitter bite of absinthe, which Crowley referred to as the only initiatic substance among alcoholic beverages (the 'green goddess'), is the unexpected reeling of an erotic coma, the wonderful fanaticism of an extremist political cell, a shadow accidentally cast which resembles a Celtic cross...

The Absolute Beginning is only as far away as your outstretched (left) hand.[4]

Liapunov Time

The newest studies in physics, which prioritize research pertaining to 'strong states of disequilibrium' and chaotic systems, make use of a certain technical term — 'Liapunov Time.' The term refers to the period during which a certain process (physical, mechanical, quantum, or even biological) exceeds the limits of exact (or probable) predictability and enters a chaotic regime. In other words, the process's trajectory is subject to strict regularity only up to a specific moment in real time. Beyond the limit of this moment, 'normal' time ends and the paradox of 'Liapunov Time' (or, more specifically, 'positive Liapunov Time') begins. This kind of time possesses curious characteristics. Unlike the usual physio-mechanics of normal time, which is seen in classical physics as a principally invertible magnitude (this is to say that time is nothing other than a static axis which expands three-dimensional space into the fourth dimension; see the academic model of Einstein), 'Liapunov Time' flows irreversibly, in one direction, and therefore does

4 Article written in 1996, first published in 1996 in the *Independent Gazette* [Независимая Газета], reproduced in 1997 in the journal *Elements* [Элементы] (No. 8 — Dossier 'National Bolshevism').

not consist of a permanently assigned trajectory (in four-dimensional space), but of 'moments,' i.e. utterly unforeseeable movements that are willful, accidental, and non-periodic. Processes which flow into 'Liapunov Time' are described as 'chaotic,' in distinction from processes unfolding in the classical, mechanical structure.

This principle can be illustrated through the following, mundane example. Imagine that three people are sitting down to drink at a bar. Up until a certain moment, their behavior is rather predictable: they'll discuss their acquaintances, friends, life problems, sports, women, and politics. Gradually, as their intoxication heightens, a certain aspect of 'noise [шумы]' will begin to creep into the conversation (this is the term employed in modern physics to describe superfluous obstructions that appear as a process unfolds). This 'noise' can be expressed when the inebriated drinkers repeat separate passages of speech several times, as a result of which the situation becomes agitated, arguments and conflicts erupt, the atmosphere thickens. At some point, the scene reaches a stage of bifurcation (this is a key term in the 'catastrophe theory' of the famous physicist René Thom). When this occurs, the behavioral logic of the drunken company as a whole and of its individually taken participants can randomly move along one of two equally possible trajectories. For example, two of the men might doze off, while the third heads home; or one of them might lunge at another one with his fists raised as the third tries to break them up; or all three of them go stumbling out into the street and start a fistfight with passersby, taking offense at some negligible detail; or they all could peacefully go their separate ways and guiltily crawl home to their families.

At the moment when they are first sitting down to drink, the endgame of their drunken lark is yet unknown. Until a certain point, this session of drinking is subject to a limited set of psychological parameters which vary depending on the cultural and intellectual level of the drinkers. But, despite whatever preconceived notions these individuals may hold, if the drunkenness develops progressively, a moment of bifurcation will sooner or later occur and the group will imperceptibly fall into 'Liapunov Time,' in which all proportions are blurred together, in which the least detail can provoke an incommensurate reaction, in which no act is entirely predictable or motivated by a causal series.

But the most interesting thing about 'Liapunov Time' is that it is not quite a period of complete disorder in which all developments are totally random. Rather, it is something in between a structured system and the absence of system. Fragments of the trajectory are preserved; the drunken behavior is subordinated to blocks of logically and psychologically determined links. Chaos has its own special, paradoxical system which is known as the 'physics of unintegrated processes' or the 'system of fractal attractors.' As a result, 'Liapunov Time' belongs to a specifically paradoxical dimension, but one that is more flexible and more broadly understood than the determinism of 'reducible systems' (i.e., the usual classical or quantum trajectories). Some modern physicists — Ilya Prigozhin, in particular — believe that processes which flow into 'positive Liapunov Time' are the key to the mystery of life. In this intermediate state, *between* strict structure and the total absence of all structure, models and events, that which is given and that which is spontaneous, we experience this combination as 'life.'

Purely logical, rational models, as shown by Kant, are incapable of 'grasping' the thing in itself, the essence of reality, which remains always inaccessible and noumenal. The 'noumenon' itself observes complete silence. Only in chaotic worlds, in the flow of 'Liapunov Time,' is the mysterious transition from silence to language, existence to non-existence, the irrational to the rational, completed.

Though striking they may be, the ideas of Prigozhin and other theorists of 'irreducible processes' strictly coincide with the traditional doctrines of alchemy, whose practitioners believe that the 'philosophers' stone' must be sought in the 'corpuscle of ancient chaos,' which the creator disdained at the moment of creation! This is the 'magnesium of the philosophers,' 'our Cybele,' 'our Latona.'

'Liapunov Time' is an important concept on two isomorphic levels — that of individual spiritual realization and of social transformation. For the personality which seeks its true center, the priority in 'Liapunov Time' is the cultivation of borderline states between a fresh diurnal consciousness and a nocturnal (alcoholic, narcotic, etc.) faint. Only on this borderline can one grasp the magical, spectral point at which individual existence is brought into proximity with super-individual realities — both of an infracorporeal and purely angelic order. Here lies the essence of the initiatic mechanism. 'Liapunov Time' is a phase of 'initiatic death.' He who gains control over this 'isthmus [перешейком]' goes beyond the boundary of the fatal dualism of life and death. On the social level, we find an analogical picture. Every regime, social order, and economico-political formation is subject to strictly determined laws that are manifested within the structure of power, in its ideology and internal norms. But social energy, like any other form of energy that exists in the corporeal universe, is unilaterally murderous; it 'facilitates entropy.' Therefore, any given power or social formation will only function logically and predictably for a certain limited portion of time. Once a certain moment is reached, 'Liapunov Time' takes over. Just as in the case with the drunken company, once a society has passed a certain borderline, it will begin to act unpredictably, chaotically. That which is peripheral will grow to gigantic proportions while that which was previously central will disperse to the periphery.

There is no doubt that, in the case of the USSR, 'Liapunov Time' began in 1985. The current president[5] (and notice, he was 'unpredictable') is a typical example of the type of 'particle' one encounters in a

5 [Translator's note]: In 1997, Dugin is naturally referring to President Boris Yeltsin.

chaotic system. Before our very eyes, from the 'dissipated remains' of the late, degenerated socialism, a new liberal system is being born. But even this new system is aging, decaying; the entropy within it is amplifying at a horrific rate; it is becoming strikingly reminiscent, down to the smallest details, of the last phases of Soviet society. It is not off the table that our liberal cycle will be short-lived, since some systems are incapable of life on principle (in the context of particular conditions).

There is yet another important point to consider: the collapse phase of Sovietism occurred in an atmosphere of complete *intellectual* passivity on the part of the chief active forces of society. There was no social organism that could have 'grasped' the fundamental content of social 'Liapunov Time' in our situation, who could have laid this invaluable knowledge into the fundament of a new social order. The most interesting detail of the collapse would appear to be that everyone slept through it. But initiatic death is substantially different from everyday death in that it continues to allow for a level of consciousness (maintained in a special state). Chaos must not only be survived, but made sense of. If this doesn't happen, the chaos will inescapably recur. Yet another catastrophe, another phase of social earthquakes, another accord to take a 'dissipative leap [диссипативного скачка]' will emerge. Moreover, this will repeat in an accelerating rhythm until some social formation appears which does not take responsibility for working scientifically and practically with dangerous, alluring chaotic structures.

The current 'stability' and 'resilience' is even more deceptive and ghostly than during the final days of the SOVDEP (and a return to the past is generally unrealistic).

Today, our society is the same ethereal mirage as before, dubiously buttressed by the same self-assured idiocy of the contemporary Philistine. But *we* know that 'Liapunov Time' is *our* time. And so our hands reach for… (no, not for what you're thinking) the books of Poincaré, Kolmogorov, Stengers, Thom, Prigozhin, Capra, Nikolis, Mandelbrot, and other authors of interest.

Besides the inheritance of the 'new right' and the 'new left,' we add to our universal doctrine of Revolution the theories of the 'new physicists.'[6]

De Sitter's Universe

Fundamental physics is an enthralling science. At our current stage of history, during which the previous self-assuredness and arrogant obscurantism of the positivists has vanished without a trace, it is a pure pleasure to wind through the new hypotheses from the position of integral traditionalism.

Let us analyze the newest cosmogonic hypothesis of Ilya Prigozhin (who, by the way, was awarded the Nobel Prize for his discoveries in the realm of chemistry). Afterward, we will compare his ideas with a traditionalist view of cosmogony and initiation.

According to Prigozhin, the initial state which preceded the emergence of our universe can be described as a vacuum or 'Minkowski Space,' i.e., a geometrical space in which (unlike in real cosmic space) there are no distortions. But, as the newest studies in physics have shown, in a vacuum, there can and do exist several various fields. Diverging from Stephen Hawking's 'Big Bang' theory, which explains the birth of material by way of some singular cataclysm that destroyed the balanced state of the vacuum once and for all, Prigozhin propounds a different version. From his point of view, material appeared as a result of 'vacuum fluctuations,' which his to say anomalous phenomena in the field states of Minkowski Space (or Minkowski's Universe). It follows from this that the emergence of the Universe was

6 Article written in 1996, first published in 1996 in the journal *Limonka* [Лимонка].

not a singular, one-time event, but a certain constantly extant potential in Minkowski Space.

We make here the immediate caveat that this entire problem, though it is stated in a way that is totally foreign to traditional metaphysics, is in fact like two peas in a pod with the traditional doctrines of creationism and manifestationism. Creationists, partisans of a singular Creation, are followers of Abrahamic religion. Their analogues in the sphere of contemporary physics are Hawking and other proponents of the 'Big Bang.' Prigozhin, on the other hand — a theoretician of chaos — has affinities with the manifestationists, who affirm the theory of 'permanent creation,' characteristic of Indo-European traditions. But the most interesting is yet ahead.

Fluctuations in the vacuum lead to the birth of the progenitor particle [первочастицы]. Taking into consideration concepts that were developed on the basis of quantum mechanics, we know that the idea of a 'particle' or 'atom' is not precise and shares the same level of plausibility as the idea of a 'wave.' And so, a fluctuation in a vacuum that gives birth to material is not an irreversible and one-time transition between non-existence and existence. It is, rather, an extremely imbalanced state connected with the dual image of both material and vacuum. The particle is more like material and the wave is more like a vacuum. Logical extrapolation then leads to an explanation of small black holes and cosmic background (relic) radiation. The appearance of a progenitor particle of inconceivable density from out of the 'silence' of Minkowski Space, where nothing happens and there are no impediments to geometric purity, inaugurates the 'Planck era.' This 'Planck era' persists for a very brief time. But, in that time, it is a sheer horror. The unfathomably dense material, like an anomaly called upon to sully the geometric order of Minkowski's Universe, evinces itself in a radical environment that is alien to all previous parameters. If, from the perspective of waves, this material is somehow related to the vacuum and its fields, then it is emergent like a particle. This theme recalls the gnostic myth of the evil demiurge who, having been born in the luminous pleroma, clamped the shackles of decay upon the heavenly archetypes. The Planck era is a monstrous era. It gave birth to the most infernal processes that he universe has to offer. But it only persisted for a short while (in its pure form).

Afterward, a new epoch arrives. The newborn, super-condensed mass begins exponentially to expand. Chaos bursts out of the Planck era like a fountain. This is de Sitter's Universe. This is no longer the Planck era, in which everything exists in a super-condensed form. Now we are dealing with a semblance of structure, but something that is not yet identical to our Einsteinian Universe. The particles flee from one another with untamed speed. All processes are 'sensitive to their original conditions' and are 'unintegrated.' It is as though there is one unending resonance, one ongoing division toward zero. It is a catastrophe: a field of real chaos, mediating between structure and the nightmare of the Planck era. De Sitter's Universe interests us most of all, and we shall return to it as soon as we conclude our general description of the cosmogonic process.

De Sitter's Universe, worlds of chaos, is also discontinuous, but is much more expanded than the Planck era. When these chaotic processes finally calm down, the whole system of the Universe strives once more toward the equilibrium of Minkowski Space, with the sole exception this time that everything is packed with matter that is gradually disappearing, dissipating, departing by way of an entropic process into non-being (according to the second law of thermodynamics). In our Universe, the law of E=mc2 is already in effect. But this is already of less interest to us. On the whole, this is the Universe of Isaac Newton in which the laws of mechanics are valid. This is almost Minkowski Space, but distorted by dissipated and vanishing material, which simply is not and creates a kind of anomaly.

The two realms of modern physics have clashed in such a way that the Newtonian Universe is still not the entire Universe and that rational laws do not cover the entire reality of physics. From rationalism and creationism (renewed and expanded though they may have been by Einstein and the first stages in the development of quantum mechanics), scientists were forced to turn their gaze toward different spheres. An intensive study began into astrophysics and the atomic and subatomic levels. In physics, the magnitudes of the ultra-small and ultra-large drove scientists toward an unexpected problem. It turns out that the Newtonian Universe is a demiurgic parody of the angelic Minkowski Space—that it exists only on a mesolevel as seen from the human perspective. Beyond this cutoff, other more ancient laws continue to exist. To put it succinctly, de Sitter's Universe has not conclusively disappeared. In this universe, the process of demiurgic usurpation is still evident, while the ancient chaos continues to dominate. Black holes and photons, radiation of an absolutely black body, and other epiphenomena of the early stages of cosmic history bear the stamp of a most important cosmogonic process. They connect us with the horrific Planck era and, through it, with Minkowski Space itself and its pure, dignified state, free from the encroachments of the Newtonian imitation and its counterfeit spawn.

Now we must ask the following question: how does initiation differ from the commonplace of religious dogma? We will explain this with an example of fundamental physics. Religion has something in common with a certain spiritual analogue of the Newtonian cosmos. Here, all affirmations bear a striking resemblance to the truth, are eternally close to it, but are nonetheless every so slightly different from it. This gap is quantitatively negligible, but qualitatively absolute (see Guénon's book *The Metaphysical Principles of the Infinitesimal Calculus*). This gap is equal to the presence of material which distorts proportions. Religion despises material and, in doing so, remains forever in the inescapable labyrinth of approximation. Initiation takes a radically different path. Here, it is the gap which contains primary meaning. In order to strive for the Absolute, one must reject compromise. One must descend into hell, immerse oneself in chaos. This is tantamount to a dive into de Sitter's Universe. Here, the initiate grasps the essence of material, the meaning of the distorting approximation, the root of evil which is discovered in its full scale. Only by way of this traumatic experience can one exit beyond the limits of material and, in doing so, exit radically and with no way of returning. This is the great ideal of Liberation. This path is extremely dangerous but unavoidable.

It is thanks to de Sitter's Universe that Newton's mechanical world can live. Life is a chaotic process. On one hand, it is deeper and more demonic than the strict laws of geometrical science. But, on the other hand, it reveals the abyss of the lie on which reality is based. Prigozhin (like another author that interests us, Fritjof Capra) has a correct view of the source of life that populates these worlds. It is all quite as he suggests. But pulsing, senseless life is not good in and of itself; it only has value as a call, as a path to its own overcoming, as a paradoxical road to Ultra-life. De Sitter's Universe is the goal for Satanists, whereas for gnostics it is a means. *Mokṣa*, a great liberation, is our primary task. In the end, knowledge of evil is not evil itself. If there were never a fall, there would never be salvation; this is a *Felix Culpa*. Eve did the right thing. Eve is life. Feminine chaos, pregnant with the Absolute, bearing horror, insanity, and something besides, is more valuable than anything known by the old gods of the Law.

Creationism and the ratio are inescapable. Their correctness is repulsive…

Fractal attractors, resonances, bifurcated fields…

The universal solvent of de Sitter's Universe is interested in us.[7]

---

7 Article written in 1996, first published in 1996 in the journal *Limonka* [Лимонка].

The Fascists Arrive at Midnight

Eloquent Fear in the Face of the Brown

We ought to ask a question which, despite its relevance when taken as a whole, is for some entirely strange reason never posed. Why is everyone afraid of 'Fascism' (both in Russia and in the rest of the world)? Why exactly is this word the most commonly used term in the political, cultural, and everyday lexicon, especially when there hasn't been an adequate and fully comprehended political and ideological Fascism since 1945 and, if there has been, then it has only been a marginal phenomenon deserving of no greater attention from the public than any society of lepidopterists or stamp collectors?

This couldn't just be an accident. We would serve ourselves well to dissect the freight of meaning contained in this expression as it is used today. By 'Fascism,' we clearly do not mean a concrete political phenomenon, but rather our deep-seated, secret fear, which brings the nationalist, the liberal, the communist, and the democrat together. This fear does not possess a political or ideological nature; within it, we find the expression of some more general, more profound feeling which is equally imbedded in all people irrespective of their political orientation. This 'magical Fascism' that hounds our unconscious is so obviously different from the political, concrete 'Fascism' of history that, if we were ever to get the chance to speak with a concrete neo-Nazi belonging to some marginal youth movement, we would experience no other feeling that disenchantment — "Is that it? No, this is no Fascist at all!"

In that case, what is it that we really fear? Who is a real 'Fascist' and what is real 'Fascism,' not in its historical guise, but from a psychological, or even psychiatric perspective?

Human Humanity

Fascism undoubtedly coincides in the average consciousness with Absolute Evil, and this commonly-held understanding, independent of political orientation, shows that this identification is a universal fact. But what, today, could unite a people (even through a negative criterion), so varied in terms of culture, social interests, religious creed, and ideology?

Only one thing can accomplish this — a sense of general belonging to 'humankind,' a vague and existentially basic humanism found on the right and the left, at the extremes and in the center. Humanism is the last anchor preserving the relative balance of a civilization that is torn both internally and externally by political and ideological conflicts; humanism is what holds civilization fast in the face of the global crisis of culture, ecology, and society. If one were to remove this unconscious humanist element in the current, strictly secular, strictly human humanity, society would immediately succumb to an abyss of insanity, fanaticism, hysterics, breakdowns, and suicides. Modern man, with all of his cynicism, practicality, pragmatism, individualism, and agnosticism, nonetheless believes in the sanctity of his final fetish — 'the human factor,' the 'human fact' which, while neither bad nor good in itself, is the universal platform of human existence.

Naturally, such a 'human humanity' inspires fear of possible catastrophes, i.e. that this last bastion, this 'unconscious' humanism can have its legs knocked out from under it. There are two ways this might happen — one threat would come from without, the other from within. The sense of external danger, the obsessive syndrome of thinking about 'the end,' has made itself felt through two potent discourses: 'ecology' and 'pacifism.' This is a position from which one foresees the approach of a threat to 'human humanity' from outside; either the surrounding environment, 'extra-human' or 'inhuman' in essence, will shatter the illusion of human self-sufficiency and will explode the human sense of security, or the 'evil warhawks' will set off a military conflict that annihilates humanity. This last psychological factor was the basis for the 'stress' politics of Western anti-communism during the decades leading up to Perestroika[8]).

But the internal path toward annihilating 'human humanity' is far more important for our purposes. It is precisely this internal rupture which is understood today as 'Fascism' on the unconscious level. Some clinical 'anti-fascists' have even suggested a special term—'psychofascism.' And this term, despite its apparent awkwardness, eloquently demonstrates how the fear of 'Fascism' possesses a consummately psychic, psychiatric nature. And so, 'Fascism' is the internal threat to the humanized subconscious of modern man, the premonition of its possible collapse as it exists today.

De Sade's Whip and Dagger

The term 'Fascism' is often associated with another term, 'sadism,' which is no coincidence. Practically every main character in de Sade's novels is an incarnate crystal image of that which the 'humanist' subconscious fears most of all; de Sade ingeniously perceived the total future dissemination of this subconscious back in the seventeenth century. His main characters are people who, in answering the call of liberal ideology which took the principle of maximum individual freedom as its cornerstone, drive these tendencies to their logical limit; here, they burst and destroy the limitations of 'individuality' that had been preserved in 'democratic' and 'enlightened' society as an inheritance from 'dark,' 'illiberal' times, a 'vestige of theocracy, statism, and moralism.' The political ideas of de Sade, clearly and rationally laid out in his *Philosophy in the Boudoir*, constitute the mathematical application of

8 [Translator's note]: 'Perestroika [Перестройка]' was a Soviet policy set in place by Mikhail Gorbachev in 1985 which promised to radically 'restructure' the Soviet government and Soviet society in general, allowing for liberal reforms of the socialist system.

liberal dogmas to the most intimate sides of human life, in association with erotic complexes, deep-seated inhibitions, and vegetative psychological reactions (all of this described in the language of 'black humor' which distinguishes de Sade's works). De Sade struggles neither with 'humanism' nor with the 'psychology of humanism' that follows from it, but rather follows the humanist line to its logical conclusion without stopping halfway as did his naïve and optimistic contemporaries, who were enraptured by the ideas of 'liberalism' and 'humanism.' De Sade represents the inner limit of society's movement toward the liberal model, and it is no accident that the West was only able to understand his ideas by the beginning of the twentieth century, when de Sade's prophetic gift revealed itself to its full extent in all its truth — when his texts yielded ecstasy to the likes of Kierkegaard, Nietzsche, Bakunin, Freud, the Surrealists, etc. But, in line with liberal, 'republican' principles, de Sade paints such a horrifying picture of unending crime and perversion that the liberals themselves can hardly recognize this pure distillation of their ideal society.

Why is this? It can only be ascribed to the fact that the liberal consciousness is incapable of encompassing the entire ideological space of its own position, and its 'preconceptions' prevent it from legalizing the full breadth of criminal and perverted versions which they would prefer to 'recognize' and 'accept' in a gradual, sequential manner. De Sade proposed the legalization of theft (which was practically accomplished with the advent of capitalism, which takes theft for a foundation). He considered the permission of all forms of sexual perversion to be unavoidable, putting homosexuality in the prime position (modern liberal society bears this out). He insisted on discontinuing the death penalty, even for the most horrific crimes (the struggle for such a law has been crowned with success in many developed nations).

The only aspect which prevents de Sade from becoming a true architect and classic of modern liberalism is that complex which, in psychology, was named after him — 'sadism.' Liberals and 'humanists' find this aspect more unpalatable than any other, for it is precisely sadism which has placed a stumbling block before de Sade's integration into the pantheon of supreme liberal ideologues.

The fact is that the assiduous and extremely honest de Sade, going all the way in his negation of traditional societal values — from his disavowal of church and monarchy to his denigration of the state, morality, and ethics — encountered a metaphysical problem of grave importance: who exactly will be the subject of freedom, won as a result of a diligent and total annihilation of the 'old' world? Maurice Blanchot correctly notes in his book about de Sade that, whenever one of his characters falters along the path toward increasingly horrific and destructive crimes, he himself gradually becomes the victim of a still more diligent 'liberal.' Nietzsche spoke of the same situation in his parable of the 'pale criminal': "The pale criminal leaned down; he had murdered, but what's more, he had also stolen."

For Nietzsche, 'theft' is a degradation of pure crime, committed in a direct act of unmotivated murder. In committing such an act, the subject of liberation ceases for de Sade to be a mere common man and becomes a special, 'detached,' heroic man who not only clearly comprehends the fact that one man's liberty can only be increased at the expense of another (which moderate liberals never admit), but who also strives to bring his personal liberty to its maximum and to reduce the liberties of everyone around him to their minimum. It is precisely this 'sadist' type created by de Sade which slowly came to haunt the collective unconscious of modern man.

Why? Because the appearance of such a character is not a coincidence, but an *inescapable* consequence of the humanist 'development' of humanity on the way to liberalism and enlightenment! This sadistic subject is implicitly present in the 'humanist subconscious' of people who have been deprived of the sacred coordinates of traditional civilization. He is the 'dark double' in whom humanity's collective tab of freedom and 'humanity' is gradually run up. Squirming at the bottom of the 'human' subconscious of humanity are the ghostly heroes of *Justine* and *Juliette*. With the whip and the dagger, they menace those who have come to a cowardly halt on the path to humanity's 'liberation.'

Do we not recognize a familiar specter in de Sade and his characters? Do his heroes not exude the panic-inducing aroma of a 'Fascism' — not the concrete Fascism of history, but the 'psychic,' notorious, and frightening 'psychofascism?'

They're Here

The liberal subconscious of modern man contains its own death sentence, its own negation, its own demise. At the extreme edge of his soul's dark energies lives a terrible being — the 'magical Fascist,' a ghost in the flesh, a character from the pages of the Marquis de Sade that has burst into one's apartment… In Orwell's *1984*, there is a very important scene which bears witness to his rather deep understanding of the laws of human psychology: in the final and most terrifying torture room in which Winston Smith finds himself, he encounters the thing he has feared more than anything else throughout the course of his life, in dreams, reveries, and manic visions. The rats begin to gnaw at his face. If modern society, or to put it more broadly, modern humanity is so horrified by the 'Fascist,' and if this figure corresponds to a certain layer of the 'collective unconscious' at the lowest possible depth, then this 'Fascist' will undoubtedly appear. Of course, he will not do so in the form of a political movement resembling the Italian or German precedents. Historical Fascism and Nazism have almost nothing in common with the 'psychic Fascism' which poses such a grave internal threat to humanity today. The new 'Fascism' will emerge in accordance with a different logic, on the basis of different laws. Most likely, it will be much more horrific than its predecessors, since it will be qualitatively *different*. It will emerge not as a salvation from liberalism (as the former version of Fascism attempted to achieve), but as a punishment for liberalism; and it will be born not without, but within liberal society. The new 'Fascism' will appear as the final destination of liberal history, as its inevitable end. But because humanity has now practically identified its fate with 'humanism' and 'liberalism,' one has every reason to suppose that this even will serve simultaneously as the end of humanity.

The 'Fascist' is an internal concept. He who does not understand the necessity of taking upon himself the full brunt of the nightmare belonging to the world of de Sade's characters — he who cannot accept the tragic and wild mission of the 'sadist' — will inevitably become the 'victim.' The laws of this genre are cruel — as cruel as the results of liberal reforms are in practice. Of course, one can already analyze several 'Fascist' and 'sadistic' traits inherent to today's radical liberals, themselves. But in comparison with true 'sadists,' these traits represent only the first steps of the 'humanist' kindergarten. It is doubtful whether the liberals can find the strength within themselves to approach the ideal of Saint-Fons, Maldoror, or the Superman. Their humanism remains too 'lukewarm' (neither hot nor cold) for such a leap to occur. And so they remain the 'victims.'

If all of this is so, then Fascism will arrive for them in the role of executioner. It will not appear at the political meetings and congresses of nationalists; we will not encounter any 'psychofascists,' any terrible heroes of the modern subconscious, in the midst of the criminal authorities. Beyond collectivist ideologies and banal criminality, they don their black masks at the midnight hour, arm themselves with sharp knives and leather whips, and will silently hover down the dark streets in search of a victim. They will appear unexpectedly and suddenly as black nocturnal ghosts, called up by our irreducible terror, our psychosis. They are anonymous and without number. They torment and torture us in unending post-Perestroika nightmares. They are slowly rising to power — but not the political, compromising, limited sort. They are rising to an absolute power, based on the total dominion of the 'sadist' over the cowardly, trembling masses of damned victims and 'anti-fascists.'

In and of themselves, Fascists are neither evil nor cruel. Their violence is cold and unemotional, almost ritualistic. In our fear, our involvement in the liberal norms of modern isolation, we ourselves are provoking their mysterious nocturnal visitation. This is a silent visitation, absent of all threats or political demands. "Every empty nut wants to be cracked open." It is this cracking with which the 'Fascist' concerns himself, this horrifying personage at the dusk of liberal civilization who has now secured his terrible physical birth into our world.

Everyone who believed in 'human dignity' and 'human liberty' in a secularized world without Tradition or the sacred will pay a dear fee — both for himself and for his forebears.

The Fascists have reached the city. They are everywhere. They are in us.

Their razors are sharp. They will not refuse the 'sovereignty' presented to them, but we will pay them for the burden and tragedy of it. The Fascists will arrive. Undoubtedly. And they will begin their tortures, not stopping until they can read the first sign of understanding in our eyes that we see which reality we are in and what we ought to have done about it. If our eyes remain the same as they are now, the foreboding ghosts of civilizational midnight will excuse themselves of any responsibility for this sorrowful outcome.

Sooner or later, this arrogant faith in naïve humanity and its 'happy ending' will be upended in the sad and horrific epilogue of the 'vanity of virtue.'

Do you remember what happened in the end with Justine?[9]

---

9 Article written in 1994, first published in 1994 in the journal *Moscow Pravda* [Московская Правда] (in the supplement *The New View* [Новый Взгляд]).

The Aquatic Regime

To Become a King

In magical practice, the principle of Water corresponds to the first stage of internal realization. This operation is frequently referred to by the hermetic term 'dissolution,' i.e. the effect of water on solid objects. In order to understand the Aquatic Regime, we will briefly review the magical understanding of the world. From the viewpoint of magical theory, man does not presently occupy the place that was originally assigned to him by the laws of Being. According to his original principle, man was created as the central figure at his level of existence, destined to rule as a king on this plane — the plane of Earth (It is for this reason that the magical doctrines make such indispensable appeals to royal symbols). But, in practice, things are otherwise — man is not the subject of the fixed, material world, but an object that is submitted to the influence of surrounding forces, whether human or natural, social or political.

Therefore, the 'physical world,' with which man concerned himself in the beginning, having turned onto the path of magical realization, is now something 'wicked' and 'inimical' that calls for a radical transformation. The structures and laws of this world, fixed within principles of nature and social codices (if they should soon confirm the status quo in which the mage's position is decentered), belong to the logic of destruction, dissolution, erasure. This is all so that, later, beyond the point of 'false crystallization,' the mage-subject can created a different world, a different Earth, structured on the principle of the centrality of the initiate. It is precisely in pursuit of this task — the dissolution of the 'false crystallization' — that the Aquatic Regime serves its solvent purpose. It is obvious that the average beginning practitioner of magic has no means by which to act directly on the material world which surrounds him; he has none of the instruments required to 'become a king,' to trample the laws of nature and reorganize sociopolitical reality according to his own prerogatives. Attempts to find a material 'universal solvent' through material means — even though such searches have been attempted in the past and will evidently be attempted in the future (such as the search for the 'universal weapon') — will, in an overwhelming majority of cases, yield no serious effect. What's more, such a dependence on the material world can only distance the mage from his realization. This is to say that, on his path to 'dissolution,' the mage must look for other, immaterial means. The simplest and most acceptable of these means is to be found in the 'world of dreams.'

The Dream Personality

When one is immersed in the 'world of dreams,' when one is 'drowned' in it, this serves as the first phase of the magical 'dissolution' of reality. At this stage, the most various means are employed in order to provoke the deformation of the external world for the practitioner, whether they be narcotic hallucinogens or simply alcohol.[10] Sometimes, diligent exercises in 'lucid sleep' yield a comparable result. The general meaning of this operation is to be found in the constant 'straightening' of one's perception of the external world, blurring its material, objective, and social connections. In the dream state, man exists in a world of 'liquid images' which emanate directly from his own psychological organism — the dependence of the 'external' on the 'internal is entirely obvious to the psyche. The mage who is working in the Aquatic Regime should perceive the 'waking state' along these precise lines. One must 'stretch' the boundaries of surrounding objects and beings, assuming the possibility of an indefinitely broad change

10 Aleister Crowley believed, by the way, that the value of alcohol is extremely limited and that narcotics are far more preferable. The only exception to this rule, in his estimation, was 'absinthe,' to which he referred as the 'Green Goddess.'

in all surrounding objects — in quality, quantity, and form. The water of the mages — the 'universal solvent' of the unending dream — must abolish the 'separateness' of things, both from each other and from the being of the mage himself. Say, for example, that you are looking out of a window into the street. In the Terrestrial Regime, in a normal state of consciousness, all possible combinations of scenes unfolding beyond the window are strictly limited and determined in advance. But if you look out the window in the Aquatic Regime, you might see something that would change an average person into a rabid lunatic. Multiple suns, gigantic black statues that slowly drift above the roofs of the highest buildings, bright red figures with amorphous contours sliding along the walls… The Aquatic Regime is a sort of artificial and voluntary insanity; the only difference between this state and true madness consists in the fact that the practicing mage still preserves a distance in relation to the 'liberated' subtle world, keeping one foot out of the paranormal situation and maintaining an internal irony and detachment. Like the average man of everyday life, it is rather easy to learn how to separate the primary from the secondary — and therefore to count the majority of events and things as nothing but the usual trivialities — in the Aquatic Regime, the mage quickly develops a quotidian relationship to the plastic transformations of miraculous forms. As a rule, nothing that occurs in the subtle world takes precedence over the menial occurrences of the ordinary world.

Who Are We? Where Are We?

For the mage, crossing into the Aquatic Regime is not a goal in itself, but an acclimation to 'fluid [текучей]' reality; it is generally the first preparatory step required in order to work in this element. But what is more important than anything else in this process is that the practitioner dissolves his assigned natural and social surroundings, that he quits the prison walls that physically and socially define his fixed and objective place in fixed and objective reality. Of course, in the Aquatic Regime, the mage is still quite far from becoming a subject, a 'king of things'; but at the same time, he has ceased to be a slave to things. The Aquatic Regime blurs his previous confidence in his 'I.' At this stage, the novice mage often asks himself an odd question: "Who am I?" In other instances, he asks, "Am I this? Am I that?"[11] The first variant (Who am I?) is, undoubtedly, the preferable one, since attempts to determine one's mystical name (e.g., "I am Agrippa von Nettesheim" or "I am an incarnation of Buddha") only lead to a false crystallization and often end in a banal mental illness ("I am Napoleon"). But in any case, the mage rids himself of the shackles of determination and becomes an 'unknown,' 'altered' magnitude, for himself first and foremost. During this period of magical work, it is best to change one's environment, one's usual surroundings. It is important that people and things do not impose on the practitioner as a person who has long been known to them. If this proves impracticable, the mage must simulate his own 'mental illness' (a 'mask of the possessed') for the benefit of his habitual surroundings — whether it be drug addiction, alcoholism, or split personality. Only then will the surrounding world admit and acknowledge the practitioner's 'lawful right to strangeness.'

Further development of the Aquatic Regime must be oriented toward fortifying oneself in the 'fluid world,' making oneself at home there, fixing the 'psycho-aquatic' element onto a horizontal plane; this plane's qualitative principles should become as obvious to the mage as the qualitative boundaries that define the 'crude,' material plane. If the 'dream personality' is as well-formed, discreet, and mobile in

11 Theories of reincarnation are based precisely on the exploitation of this magical state of the 'dissolute I.' But in the theories, there is an attempt to replace the authentic, spontaneous, and kingly fixation on the magical triumph of acquiring a Name with an appeal to history and the past (is there a past in the world of Water?), to psychological elements of the dead and 'stray influences' that have been preserved on the subtle plane.

relation to the psychic landscape as the human body is in relation to physical reality, and if this personality can exhaustively master all the rules and mechanisms of the 'subtle' level (as a child gradually masters the mechanisms of the grown-up world), he my consider the Aquatic Regime to be entirely his own. Then, the mage will have been born and have grown up in the 'aquatic' spaces of the beyond. The limit and end of the Aquatic Regime is the 'acquisition of the Name,' which the mage will learn and comprehend on the subtle plane. The 'Name' is a qualitative evaluation of the 'dream personality,' the 'race,' 'caste,' and 'social position' of the mage in the world of dreams. Strictly speaking, the mage's terminal fixation on his 'I' on the subtle plane is his 'coronation' and ascent into the center of things. Having liberated himself from the chains of materiality, the mage now belongs to a level whose sanction is indispensable in order for any phenomenon to appear in the material world — both that of nature and of society. The power endowed to the practitioner by this tamed, mastered world of dreams is humongous. The knowledge which he gains by realizing the Aquatic Regime is invaluable. The only obstacle that remains before the mage in the material world is the subtle impulse of other mages like himself who have 'awakened' beyond the 'crude' plane. If the mage cannot manifest something in the sphere of solid objects and embodied beings, it is due to the counter-action of another person who has passed through the Aquatic Regime. Like clashes with like. But it is important to note that the counter-active will does not always emanate from a human mage. Besides 'dream personalities,' the subtle world is populated beings only known to the devil. Nonetheless, the mage will learn to orient himself in the Aquatic Regime and to swiftly uncover his invisible rivals.

The Joys of the Liquid Body

The Aquatic Regime is intimately connected with the feminine beginning, synonymous with the aquatic element by its very nature.

Therefore, the majority of magical practices pertaining to the Aquatic Regime abound with elements of erotic symbolism and appeal to sexual energies. Erotic drunkenness is yet another means of magical intoxication practiced by mages. Naturally, we are speaking of the psychic, subtle feminine presence which is not necessarily associated with a physical woman, and is even sometimes most palpable in her absence. The mage, dissolving into the 'dream,' enters the sphere of incessant ecstatic arousal, an uninterrupted erotic rapture comparable only to the culmination of a sexual copulation. The mage's being becomes a 'body of delights.' The Aquatic Regime can be thought of as an unending wedding night in which two are merged into one, dragging after themselves the totality of the objects surrounding them as they give way to voluptuous exultation. In the first half of his 'dissolution,' the mage merges with the feminine erotic type; he comprehends the fullness of subtle energies as torrents of external pleasure. Afterward, as he nears the mystery of the 'Name,' he begins to take control of these energies, coming to the realization that they are manifestations of his own subtle nature. In parallel with this, his erotic state moves into a masculine, organized state. Instead of melting together with the waves of the subtle world, he now derives the greatest satisfaction from their distinction, their submission, their taming, and, finally, their fixedness. At the very limits, the 'dissolved' becomes the 'dissolver,' the 'solvent,' and changes from the one who perceives the erotic torrent into the very source of this torrent; he becomes the center of sexual, psychic arousal of the subtle elements. Here, the Aquatic Regime itself ends as the Feminine Regime. From this point forward, the potent but dangerous forces of the subtle world serve the 'operator' as dedicated and passionate concubines in the court of King Solomon. In accordance with this will, the 'women' of the subtle world now dissolve the material boundaries, revealing to the mage an open path to regal dignity.

The Profession of Being

In the Aquatic Regime, the mage masters a special profession which consists not in doing, but it *being*. When one is attached not only to the results of action (which generally results in a mage's complete disqualification), but to action as a pure end in its own right, he comes up against a horrible obstacle on the path to 'dissolution.' A mage does not work. He just is. His sole occupation is involution. But, since there is no space inside, this is a path of immobility, *in situ*. Only a vision of water, of aquatic elements, aquatic beings and objects is to be found there. Talismans, evocations, rites, and rituals are only external attributes employed in order to dislocate consciousness from its established position. None of this is obligatory. It is something else entirely when a human being can't do anything at all. And so, compelled through necessity, the mage must sometimes concern himself with definite things. But in that case, he chooses something deliberately strange, externally senseless, and deprived of all content. When man floats in the sea, he usually just floats. When he makes love — he is simply making love. In the Aquatic Regime, the mage simply 'dissolves.' The 'Name' is either acquired without effort or is not acquired at all.

The Path of Water is meant for special beings who are, in principle, dissatisfied with the very quality of external reality. If someone accepts this reality in its entirety, he is lost with regard to magic. Magic will be closed to him. The majority of people have no interest in the problem of being. Just as with animals, being for them is not subject to question; it is an obvious, tangible thing. It is just the opposite with the mage. He experiences profound suffering in the world of material and social 'eggshells.' He wants to escape this world and go to the center of things, where the mystical axis of being passes through. It for this precise reason that he mage takes no particular risks when he approaches the practice of the Aquatic Regime. For him, there is no other option — otherwise, the 'eggshells' and phantoms of quotidian reality with brutally murder him. For the curious and incautious average man, tormented by complexes, the path of dissolution is equally as safe since this type cannot go very far along the secret paths of magic; the average man has the animal instinct of self-preservation (like most people). For him, magic is not dangerous — it is simply inaccessible. Even charlatans and buffoons with pretension to magic will only end up adding a little variety to their dull material reality and nothing more. When the Aquatic Regime ends, another regime comes to take its place. But only he who has attained the 'Name' is capable of understanding it.[12]

12 Article written in 1994, first published in 1994 in the journal *Elements* [Элементы] (No. 6 — Dossier 'Eroticism'), written under the alias 'Alexander Sternberg.'

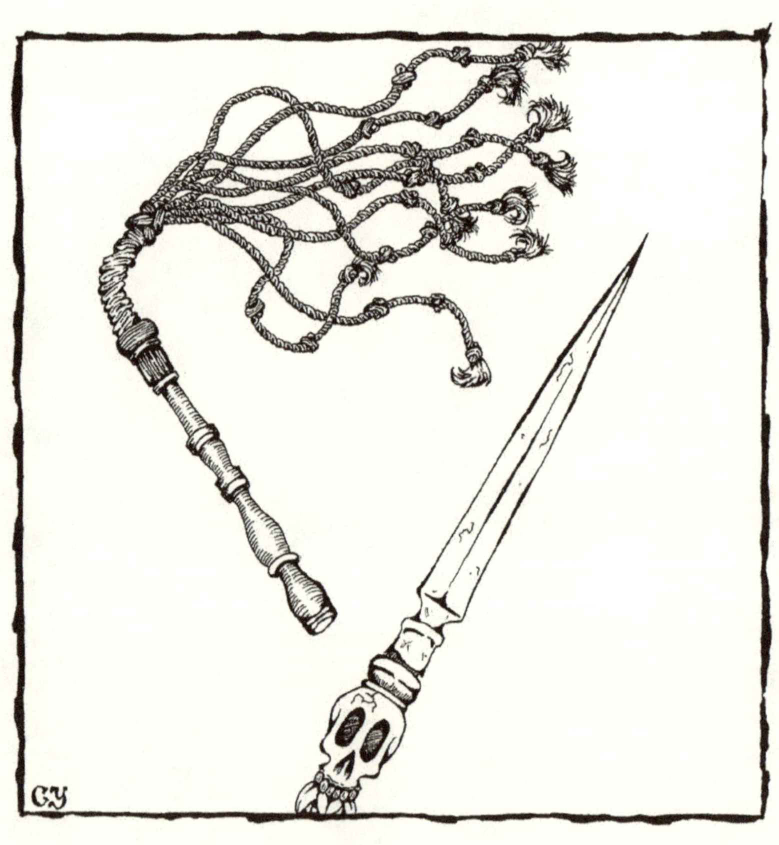
CY

PART VII

THE KINGDOM OF SATURN

(From Beneath the Black Cloak)

The Star of the Invisible Empire

(on Jean Parvulesco)

Profession — Visionary

Jean Parvulesco is a living mystery of European literature. He is a mystic, poet, novelist, literary critic, connoisseur of political intrigue, revolutionary, friend, and confidant to many European celebrities of the second half of the twentieth century (from Ezra Pound and Julius Evola to Raymond Abellio and Arno Breker). His true personality remains a riddle. As a Romanian who fled to the West in the 1940s, he became one of the most brilliant Francophone stylists in modern prose and poetry. But no matter how various his works, ranging from tantric treatises and complex occult novels to the biographies of his great friends (in particular, his *Red Sun of Raymond Abellio*), his current calling is as a 'visionary.' That is to say, he is a direct and inspired contemplator of the spiritual realms, which reveal themselves to the chosen from behind the flat, grim appearances of the profane modern world.

In this sense, Parvulesco has no commonality with the vulgar representatives of the modern neo-mysticism which is today so widespread, serving as a sort of instrumental compensation for the informational-technotronic routine of everyday life. Parvulesco's visions are grim and tragic; he has no allusions about the hellish, infernal world of modernity (in this sense, he is a Traditionalist). The infantile optimism of the Theosophists, occultists, and the pseudonymous 'conservatives' of the New Age could not be more foreign to him. But unlike many Traditionalists of an 'academic' temperament, he does not limit himself to skeptical lamentations about the 'crisis of the modern world' or to insubstantial, marginal surmises of material civilization at the end of the Kali-Yuga. The texts of Jean Parvulesco are filled with the Sacred, which speaks directly through them on the oneiric, almost prophetic level of a strange revelation; these are 'visitations,' descending from the highest spheres and penetrating a magical blockade of dark energies which fill today's world of collective and cosmic psyches. Parvulesco is an authentic visionary, doctrinally prepared and of an adequate depth to avoid taking the first phantoms of subtle reality who cross his path for 'messengers of light.' But at the same time, he strains his intuition to the breaking point in a dangerous 'journey inward,' to the 'center of the Black Lake' which exists in the modern soul, unafraid to pass beyond the bounds of fixed rational dogmas (it is this fearlessness which results in the multi-storeyed paradoxes that fill his books).

Parvulesco's message can be defined as follows. The Sacred has hidden itself from the daytime reality of the modern world, and it is entirely obvious that we now live in the End of Days. But this Sacred has not vanished (after all, it is incapable of vanishing on principle, given that it is eternal), but has transitioned to the nocturnal, invisible plane, from which it is now ready to collapse into the physical human cosmos during the apocalyptic instant of history's apogee — at a point when the world, having forgotten its spiritual nature and having sworn off of it, will be forced to collide with sacrality at the cruel moment of Revelation.

For now, this has yet to occur, and humanity sleeps peacefully in its dark, material illusions. Only the chosen, visionaries, members of secret brotherhoods and the Apocalyptic Order are awake, secretly preparing the way for the coming Final Hour, the 'Heavenly Kingdom,' the Great Empire of the End.

Jean Parvulesco does not consider himself a *litterateur*, but a herald of an Invisible Empire (this is the title of his latest book — *The Star of the Invisible Empire*); he sees himself as a 'speaker' belonging to an occult Parliament, composed of the planetary elite of the 'awakened.' His personality is doubled, trebled, and quadrupled in the characters of his novels, where the author, his doppelgangers, his occult doubles, real historical personalities, shades from the beyond, the shells of 'outer darkness,' 'demons with names, and secret agents serving occult intelligence services all play an active role. Parvulesco reveals an entire parallel world and not just the scenography of individual fantasies or memories. The inhabitants of his texts are chillingly realistic; his unusual (often black) humor sometimes spans across the sacred relics of religion, dogmas and canons out of which a mysterious internal essence is awakened, deprived of the dull fetishistic veneration which is so lethal to the soul. Following the prescriptions of the Tantras, Parvulesco animates language, makes it operative. And, for this reason, his texts are something more than literature. These are magical incantations and scandalous unmaskings, a provocation of events and a prophecy of their meaning; this is an immersion in the Ocean of Interiority, the subterranean tunnels of the Hidden, an advance into the terrifying empire of that which exists *inside* each of us. Parvulesco is sometimes just as terrifying as any true genius: he studies us from within with diligence and science, sometimes crossing in his experiments a well-known boundary. He is a visionary and an anatomist.

In the Beginning There Was Conspiracy

Parvulesco's Invisible Empire boils. It is saturated with energies, high-voltage currents, illuminations, shades, threatening discharges, and lightning-quick materializations. In this universe, identity constantly changes names and masks, dissolving in a current of luminous doctrines, immersed in the invisible concreteness of the psyche. This is a spiral-shaped nation of the occult, whose capital lies in the abyss of metaphysics, religious formulae, and mystical doctrine and whose periphery borders with our quotidian world — with its politics, culture, advertisements... The connection between the capital of Parvulesco's Empire and normal reality is brought about by certain 'agents,' both human and inhuman, who often stray from the difficult path of fulfilling their mission onto secondary branches of the Great Prophetic Spiral and fall into the occult traps of the Anti-World — the reality of the Dark Cloak which carries out its uninterrupted, eternal struggle with the worlds of Light. There, in the transitory space between the Heaven of Spirit and the Earth of Man, the threads of horrific conspiracies are spun, doubled through other counter-conspiracies, weaving in and out of each other, exchanging agents and information until they reach human civilization; it at this latter point that they manifest into political, religious, and economical intrigues, putsches, sabotage, and ideological conflicts. In this way, Parvulesco explains not only the usual human history with the help of conspiracy theories, but shows how reality, itself, is conspiratorial from top to bottom. Take the following characteristic example: an angel appears to a believer; who is he — a messenger of light or a vile chimera? Only the complex and esoteric science of 'discerning spirits' can help the Christian unveil the mysterious true nature of this being, which hails from a subtle world.

After a fashion, this is an unveiling of the conspiracy of spiritual forces. Parvulesco extends the science of 'discerning spirits' to all levels of reality—from metaphysics to geopolitics and economics.

As Parvulesco writes, "In the beginning there was Conspiracy." More accurately, there were two immediate conspiracies—the Conspiracy of the Forces of Being versus the Conspiracy of the Forces of Non-Being. Later, after duplicating and spilling over into the transitory world, becoming subject to diffractions and disintegrating into thousands of rays, the threads of conspiracy penetrated the Universe, divided into two hosts of angels and spirits, religions and peoples, elites and masses. The agents of Light and the agents of Darkness have filled both invisible worlds and human societies.

It is to this Conspiracy that the secret sources of all material and immaterial events are attributed; even natural phenomena are governed by the Conspiracy—a conspiracy of the elemental spirits. And so, making an exception of Parvulesco's specific flavor of irony, it is precisely within this framework that all major traditions belonging to sacred civilization understood the world.

But, for the visionary Parvulesco, *everything remains as it was before* and, if the mystical component has ceased to be perceived by the masses, it nonetheless remains the fundamental criterion in all decisions made by the hidden elite; in reality, these shadowed echelons rule the modern world, controlling it through this magical worldview.

However, we now must ask: what is the quality of this hidden elite?

Parvulesco gives an answer that is simultaneously clear and paradoxical: *the elite is two-sided.* The secret agents of Being and Non-Being are present in all crucial spheres related to ruling the modern world, governing every process of civilization. From the interference of the two energetic vectors underlying the two occult networks comes the fabric of actual, concrete history. Generals and terrorists, spies and poets, presidents and occultists, church fathers and heresiarchs, ascetics and mafiosi, Masons and naturalists, prostitutes and holy fools, salon artists and leaders of the workers' movement, archeologists and counterfeiters — these are nothing more than obedient actors in a fraught, conspiratorial drama. And who knows just what social identification obscures an even higher initiate? It is often the case that a crook or a pauper turn out to be the curators of the President or the Pope while military commanders or bankers prove to be nothing but marionettes of the salon poet, behind whose grotesque and fantastical persona one uncovers the cold-blooded master and architect of a cruel political history.

Against Demons and Democracy

The Star of the Invisible Empire is the most recent and among the most important novels of Parvulesco. Within its pages, the threads of his previous books convene in one place. Here, he describes our approach to the final resolution of that transcendental meta-history and serves as its chronicler. Here is his résumé. Across the planet, and particularly in France and Portugal (as well as Peru and Mexico), magic 'acupunctural' zones of the occult West, the agents of Non-Being have constructed the *black pyramids* — physical and super-physical objects meant to provide demonic energies, hordes of Gogs and Magogs, with a direct path by which to invade the world. This apocalyptic project is given a secret name, 'the Aquarius Project.' This is because, in correspondence to astrological symbolism, the 'Age of Aquarius' is soon to arrive, bringing with it not joy and harmony (as the 'agents of Non-Being' strive to assure humanity), but disintegration, rot, chaos, and death — a 'dissolution in the lower waters.' The hero of *The Star of the Invisible Empire,* Tony d'Entremont, describes his prophetic vision of the advent of the 'Age of Aquarius' as follows:

> With Lovecraft, I see a swarm of repulsive, gigantic masses, moving in unending waves, encroaching upon the last remaining crystal structures resisting the spiritual elites; in the ecstatic impotence of my hallucinatory awakening, I contemplate the sparkling black foam — the foam of black decay, the terror-inducing stench of democracy, and the horrifying apparatuses of these convulsing corpses who, painted up like filthy whores with their false smiles, with the smiles of Californian beaches which all European anti-Fascists share, with smiles of mannequin sluts beaming from shining storefront windows (this is how I would describe it), they prepare our final defeat, leading us somewhere that we ourselves don't know or, more precisely, that we know all too well. And in leading us there, they relish in sucking out our bone marrow; this is the hallucinatory lead cloak of Human Rights, that vomitous, fecal excretion of Hell. But, in saying such things, I offend Hell.

The servants of 'Aquarius,' opening a road into the human world for the black 'eggshells' of outer darkness, attempt to elevate their unnatural arrival into a good, a salvation, a limit of evolution that hides its essence — *Vomitto Negro* (the Black Vomit) — beneath the political and spiritualist slogan of the New Age or the New World Order.

But against the conspiracy of Aquarius, in which is concentrated the entire, horrific, 'metagalactic' potential of the agents of Non-Being, seeking their final incarnation in the 'New World Order' — representatives of a secret Western order known as Atlantis Magna wage their struggle. Woman, known under the mystical name of Licorne Mordoré (the 'Red-Brown Unicorn'), plays a special role in this order's rituals. In physical reality, she bears the name Jane Darlington. However, this woman's true essence extends, in principle, beyond the frame of individuality. More accurately, she serves a certain sacral function, determined among all women in the order, whose personal and everyday relationships with one another reflect the ontological hierarchy of being itself (one of them corresponds to the spirit, another to the soul, and a third to the body). The men of the Order, to include Tony d'Entremont, possess an individuality that, in a strict sense, is just as tenuous: the deaths and adulteries which abound in this novel illustrate the strictly functional essence of the main characters; the ritual death sustained by one among them only activates the conspirological behaviors of another. And their wives, in their unfaithfulness, demonstrate that they remain faithful in essence *to one and the same being.*

And so, Atlantis Magna weaves a continental network for the struggle with the conspiracy of Aquarius. On the highest transcendental level, what is at stake here is the ritual tantric realization of an eschatological Phenomenon connected with the arrival of the Consoler along with the arrival of the Wife. Only on this level can the builders of the 'black pyramids' be bested. The preparation and organization of the secret ritual of the 'red circle' serves as the novel's fundamental plot. The members of Atlantis Magna, on their way to completing this procedure, undergo symbolic travels, analyze mystical texts, seek out the true reasons for political transformations, study strange aspects in the history of certain ancient European peoples, decipher esoteric ideas (appearing as an information leak in the usual boulevard press), experience amorous and erotic connections, are subjected to assassination attempts, become the victims of assassination and torture; but this is all a concrete flesh of entertainment—almost a detective novel. It is nonetheless an uninterrupted interpretation and refinement of the mutually connected visionary reality of the Final Event of History, the appearance of the Great Eurasian Empire of the End, the *Regnum Sacrum* or *Imperium Sacrum,* whose accents are discernable in all aspects of the modern world.

On the level of political conspiracy, the novel's heroes are active and decisive. Their spiritual resistance to the New Age, to neo-spiritualism, for whose representatives (from Alice Ann Bailey to Pierre Teilhard de Chardin and Sathya Sai Baba) Tony d'Entremont suggests that the Order build an "occult super-Auschwitz and super-Maidanek," projected onto a political resistance against the 'New World Order,'

Americanism, and liberalism. This forces the 'agents of Non-Being' to form networks for the planetary conspiracy with the participation of all political forces that oppose globalism. Palestinian terrorists, underground groups of European neo-Nazis, Social Revolutionaries and members of the 'Red Brigades,' descendants of aristocrats who loathe 'democracy' and who secretly desire the end of the liberal epoch, members of the Italian Mafia, Gaullists and Francoists, revolutionaries of the Third World, shamans from America and Asia, communist leaders, German bankers — all of them become participants in a geopolitical project aimed at reviving the final Eurasian Empire. Diplomatic devices, trips abroad, confidential discussions, and information gathering furnish the political aspect of the conspiracy of the 'agents of Non-Being,' providing a specific plot line to the novel that rests on the characters' occult conversations and prolonged esoteric monologues.

Parvulesco's novel is structured not along the lines of Traditionalist logic — of a completed narrative. It is quite characteristic of him that he ends the novel in the middle of a word on page 533. The entire preceding content will have brought the reader face-to-face with the eschatological climax of an occult war, but... it is here that the literary world ends and true reality begins.

The majority of characters in the novel are historical figures, some of whom have died and some of whom who have yet to do so. The books and texts cited in the course of narration actually exist. Many episodes and retold legends are also authentic (even though many are not).

One idiosyncratic detail in Parvulesco's writing is the inclusion, in parentheses, of birth and death dates for the majority of names that are mentioned. After reading *The Star of the Invisible Empire*, a foreseeable question arises: what exactly have we just read? A novel? A fiction? A fantasy? Surrealist literature?

Or perhaps we've just read an esoteric tract?

Or maybe we have been reading an authentic revelation of the true subtext that lies beneath modern history, seen from the position of its metaphysical fulness, in its entire scale, beyond the hallucinations which are, in essence, banal notions that are incapable of explaining anything and are extremely far from the truth?

In a unique dedication which adorns the copy he gifted to me, Jean Parvulesco himself calls his novel the "most secret and most dangerous initiatic novel, in which Absolute Love brandishes its final weapon against Absolute Power and lays the occult foundations for the future of the Great Eurasian Empire of the End, which will become identical with the Heavenly Kingdom, the *Regnum Sanctum*."

His novel is nothing more and nothing less than this.

Shiva, Red and Brown

In one of our shared conversations, in which I was explaining the meaning of the term '*nashi* (ours)' in Russian political culture, Jean Parvulesco grew very animated and showed me a place in one of his early novels (from the mid-1970s) where, through providence, he had employed the same term, and in a strikingly similar sense. For him, '*nashi*' referred to members of the 'conspiracy of Being,' a secret network of influencing agents who were united by a common occult task which lay beyond political differences; these agents resisted profane, cosmopolitan civilization that had been established across the planet. Moreover, my Italian friends sent me a copy of one of Parvulesco's essays from the end of the 1960s in which he wrote of 'Eurasianism' — the geopolitical project of creating a Continental Bloc; he wrote about the necessity of a Russian-German union (a renewal of the Molotov-Ribbentrop Pact) and even the necessity of reconciling the red and brown forces into a unified, revolutionary, anti-globalist front. How strange were the texts of this shocking man which found their popularity only in their capacity as literary works and which provoked a condescending smile from the 'academic' Traditionalists. His books, with an almost prophetic clairvoyance, describe over the course of several years that which has become a political fact only in the most recent days, even in remote Russia...

This all leads to rather troubling thoughts regarding this ingenious author's true nature. Who are you, after all, Mr. Parvulesco? Is he the commander of Altavilla?

No matter who he is, he is undoubtedly 'red and brown,' if only because all of his sympathies fall on the side of a mysterious feminine figure who, in certain actually extant initiatic societies, is known as the 'Red-Brown Unicorn,' the *Licorne Mordoré*. But here we should note that the French word '*mordoré*' more precisely refers to 'red-and-brown-with-gold' or 'with golden accents.' Besides the squeamish and disparaging term 'red-brown,' which has long been used as a label to describe the most interesting political forces in Russia, there is also a regal, tsarist inflection to this color — as the final eschatological coronation of the great continental Eurasian Revolution with Alchemical Gold; it is '*nashi* [ours],' the clear yet secret 'agents of Being,' who are today preparing and manifesting this revolution.

There is yet another character of sacred tradition to which this color is attributed. We are speaking here of the god Shiva, titled liturgically as 'the terrible' and 'the red-brown.' The character of this god is elementally proximate to our [*nashi*] current red-browns.

Yes, this element is terrible and destructive in its external guise.

But it is precisely the terrible red-brown Shiva who serves as preserver of the mystery of Eternity, which opens up in all of its fulness at the End of Time, negating, with its 'terrible' appearance, the beginning of the Age of Aquarius.

The red-brown Shiva is the protector of the sacred tradition of Love, the Tantra. He watches over the very same Tantra to which one of Jean Parvulesco's first books is dedicated — *The Merciful Crown of the Tantra.*

The agents of the internal Continent are awakening. We can already regard the appearance of the magical Star, heralding the imminent transformation of the Internal into the External, in the night sky of our miserable civilization. This is the Star of the Invisible Empire, an Empire in the name of Jean Parvulesco.

Orion, or the Conspiracy of Heroes

(Cesare della Riviera)

An Open Entrance into the Closed Text of Della Riviera

A book of Cesare della Riviera by the name of The Magical World of the Heroes was published in 1605. Later, already in the twentieth century, Julius Evola reissued it together with his own commentary, insisting that precisely this hermetic tract contained the most lucid and comprehensible explanation of the principles of spiritual alchemy, the hermetic art. However, in his review of the book, René Guénon noted that this work of della Riviera was nowhere near as transparent as Evola claimed.

Truly, The Magical World of the Heroes is highly enigmatic — firstly, because of its literary form and, secondly, because the things and words with which the author operates are in themselves something extremely mysterious, incomprehensible, and without equivalent in concrete reality.

But perhaps the difficulties of understanding that accompany the theme of the book result from the fact that the very 'principle of heroism' — the figure of the Hero — is rather remote from the sphere which surrounds us. It may be that, for true heroes, this difficult text is crystal clear and requires no further decipherment.

A book that is crystalline and as transparent as ice…

The Cosmogony of Ice

In books by Evola dedicated to the most disparate Traditionalist and political problems, he always makes an appeal to the principle of Cold. The theme of Cold erupts first here, then there, despite whether the author is discoursing about the Tantra or the existential position of the 'solitary man,' whether about Zen Buddhism or the mysteries of knights in medieval Europe, whether he is analyzing modern art or compiling autobiographical notes. 'Cold' and 'distance' are perhaps the two most commonly encountered words in the 'Black Baron's' lexicon.

The hero must be *cold* by definition. If he does not separate himself from those around him, if he does not freeze within himself the warm energies of everyday humanity, he will not be on the level required in order to accomplish the Impossible (i.e., where the hero does that which makes him a hero). The hero must depart from people. But beyond the threshold of social comforts, the penetrating winds of objective reality, cruel and extra-human, whip and bluster. Earth and minerals rise up against the vegetal and animal worlds. Aggressive vegetation eats away at minerals while wild beasts mercilessly trample the stubborn grasses.

The elements lying without society known nothing of condescension. The world, all on its own, is a triumphal feast of matter, whose lowest surface is melded with slabs of abyssal cosmic ice. The hero is cold because he is objective—because he accepts and runs with the world's baton of spontaneous force, crazed and malevolent.

The character of all historical heroes—from Hercules to Hitler—was identical: they were deeply *natural*, elemental types, unfathomably cold and distanced from social compromise. They were the bearers of the abyss of Objectivity.

In his strange, hermetic manner, Cesare della Riviera traces the word 'Angel [Angelo]' as follows:

> Angelo = Antico GELO [Angel = Ancient Ice]

This has to do with another phase of the heroic feat — not a retreat to objectivity, but an exit beyond its boundaries, beyond the border of the 'icy firmament.'

There is much in alchemy and the Kabbala related to the mystery of the 'icy firmament.' This is a border which separates the 'lower waters' of life from the 'upper waters' of Spirit. Della Riviera's phrase possesses a strict theological meaning: in quitting the sphere of the soul's life, the hero becomes a crystal shard of ice in the glass sea of the Spirit — a gleaming angel on whom the heavenly throne of the tsar' is anchored. Andersen's Snow Queen forces the young boy Kai to craft the secret angelic word *Ewigkeit* out of pieces of ice, but the warm forces of the Earth ('Gerda' in old German means 'Earth') send the unsuccessful hero back to his paltry and inescapable everyday world [быту]. Instead of an angel, he becomes a rosy-cheeked Scandinavian burgher with his eternal beer and sausages.

The Cold signifies both a corpse and an initiate. The bodies of yogis become frozen to the degree that the sacred serpentine energy has been awakened within them; the higher the Kundalini climbs, the more lifeless the yogi's corresponding body parts become; finally, the initiate turns into a statue of ice, an axis of spiritual permanence.

Every hero is obliged to travel to the pole, to the heart of midnight. There, he learns to love that dark and incomprehensible substance which the alchemists call 'our Earth,' or 'the magnesium of the philosophers.' The urn which contains the ashes of Baron Evola is buried in the thickened depths of an alpine glacier, at the peak of Monte Rosa.

This mountain may have been named in honor of the sacred beloved of the undying Friedrich Hohenstaufen. *La Rosa di Soria*—The Polar Rose.

Travels of the Polar Nymph

Siliani, a mysterious alchemist of the nineteenth century whose pseudonym was established only with the help of Pierre Dujolle, 'Magathon' (a friend of Fulcanelli's), and the mysterious Valois, wrote about how his heroic travels to the 'magical world of the heroes' began with a strange visit from the 'nymph of the polar star'...

Where are its footprints?

They lead inward, into the ground, where a fantastic material known as the 'sulfuric acid of philosophers' lies hidden. *Visitabis interiora terrae rectificando invenies occultum lapidem.* The stone is completely black like a soul wrapped in a 'diametrically opposed spirit'—the '*antimimon pneuma*' of the gnostics.

From this point—from the blackness of personal non-definition, from the indifference of the 'I' which slips away from all names, the magical feat begins. If the hero does not question that which appears to be his essence, he is doomed. Even divine parents are unable to provide an answer to the problem of the I's emergence.

The Secret of the Celestial Dragon

The search for the nymph is associated with the problem of determining the authentic polar star. The heavenly axis, like the 'retreating Atalanta,' moves in a circle.

At some point, the subtle creation was hidden in the fur of Ursa Major, not far from Arcturus. Now, she calls herself 'Shemol.' In 12,000 years, she will say of herself, "I am Vega." But what is the Axis, around which the dance of millennia is danced?

There is a black dot in the northern sky. The dragon wraps around it, coaxing the attentive gazer, offering the doubtful fruits of knowledge.

The polar nymph gave Siliani the key to victory over the Dragon. The Hermetics believe this to refer to the ur-mother — the dragon of the heavens, the true north of the ecliptic. It guards the boreal heart of black distances, like a spiral etched around an absent center.

A Second of Betelgeuse

Orion is the most mysterious of constellations. Time hides behind his right shoulder. He is the main hero of the subterranean (and not only subterranean!) world. In Arabic, 'Betelgeuse' translates to 'the hero's shoulder.' Precisely this shoulder preserves the mystery of that book which Fulcanelli initially gave to Canseliet before taking it back and forbidding him from publishing it. The book was *Finis Gloria Mundi*, the *third* book of the adept. When the milk of the Maiden touches upon the muscular shoulder of the 'black god,' and he himself loses his arms to the merciless blades of the executioners, a universal fire arrives, and the sphere turns around. The sky falls. As we all know, it is made of stone.

The heroes mysteriously prepare horrific cataclysms for society. Society, in turn, calms itself with the idea that it has banished these heroes from history. But where is the fine line between the library and the nuclear testing grounds, between the darkened meditation corner and carpet-bombing runs?

There are reports that the agents of Betelgeuse, the denizens of the 'magical world of the heroes' masked as civil workers, have reached the heating plant of power.

Their brains are filled with nothing but the cruelty of celestial correspondences and precessional cycles. The nuclear bonfire of the northern hemisphere is their path to Olympus — it is the bonfire of Hercules.

Aside from his external mission, Evola had a secret, inner one…

The Forest of Rambouillet

"The forest of Rambouillet is a forest of blood." These are the words which Jean Parvulesco hypnotically repeats in his novel. At one moment, they contain the white stag with a slit throat; at another moment, they enclose the corpse of a woman stripped bare, evincing an identical wound. This is the magical forest in which Dante once wandered — the 'Forest of Philosophers.' On one engraving depicting the 'Emerald Tablet' of Hermes Trismegistus, a man with a stag's head is handing the moon to Eve. Later, if Parvulesco's word is to be believed, they meet in the garden of Rambouillet.

An unhappy rendezvous.

"One day, Apollo will return. And, this time, it will be forever." Such were the last prophetic words of the Pythia of Delphi in the fourth century after the Birth of Christ.

Venus Victrix[1]

Two Surrogates from One Traditional Science

Modern astronomy has one extremely negative trait: it appeals to pure pragmatism, is almost entirely exhausted in the compilation and interpretation of horoscopes. As a result, the more substantive aspects of the science, which in antiquity possessed an absolutely traditional character (in the Guénonian sense) and was an element of a broader cosmological doctrine, falls completely out of view. In ancient times, all traditional cosmology was primarily understood in connection with an even greater general sphere — Metaphysics.

1 [Translator's note]: Lat.: "Venus the Victress."

In the process of civilization's desacralization, cosmology gradually lost its connection to Metaphysics. This moment is very clearly evident in late-Egyptian civilization, where problems of a strictly metaphysical sort completely disappeared, having ceded the ground to cosmic magic. But, nonetheless, such cosmic magic, even though it contained quite doubtful aspects, was an authentic traditional science. It remained so in the framework of a strictly Christian civilization, in a complex of sacred sciences brought together under 'hermeticism.' Astrology was one of the components of this hermeticism.

Later, on the eve of the New Age, a double process took place. Traditional sciences — in this case, astrology — were divided into two categories. From one end, the rationalistic, positivistic side of science changed into astronomy (though the ancients treated 'astronomy' and 'astrology' as synonyms). Astronomy came strictly to occupy the physical side of cosmic phenomena; it was concerned with the corporeal level of heavenly bodies and their movements. Observing a rigor of rationalistic methods, astronomists disregarded the 'subtle' plane of creation, which made their conclusions and affirmations inaccurate, despite the external exactitude of their calculations.

The other half of a science that had been torn in twain became the purview of fortune-tellers, charlatans, and lunatics who were incapable of the intellectual interpretations and conclusions of the rationalist astronomists, and who departed into the realm of fantasies, strained ideas, and voluntarism — in a word, 'obscureville [темнилово].' But, from a different point of view, this occult tendency managed to preserve certain elements of authentic, traditional astrology — themes, horoscopes, the foundations of mythological interpretation. However, in doing so, they lost sight of the most important keys and the mystery of proportions which, in antiquity, joined studies of the material world with those of the subtle one. Strictly speaking, this second piece of traditional astrology is what is known as 'astrology' in the contemporary sense.

After this occult stage of degeneration, there followed another, even more dubious one. Astrology, in its applied state, fell to an already profane reality along with weather prognoses and statistics. And this is not to say that astrological prognoses do not come true — that is besides the point. Weather prognoses rarely correspond with the truth. At issue here is that this occult parody of traditional science had become even more degraded and deformed, moving over into the latitude of secular publications and television screens. The most spiritual, subtle part of the ancient science came to be used for increasingly utilitarian and primitive purposes, as opposed to academic astronomy, which at least preserved its status as a hard science. And so, the spiritual (in a distorted, fragmentary form) became even lower than the material and physical. This should be a lesson to the neo-spiritualists who feel around with their tepid brains for the great foundations of Tradition, which for them is incomprehensible and inaccessible. In our time, to be an astrologist is a greater shame than to be a thimblerigger [напёрсточником] or an embezzler [казнокрад].

One Abnormal Planet

But our original desire was by no means to speak of this, but of Venus.

There is a concept known as the North Pole of the ecliptic. This point in the sky, to which not a single star corresponds, lies somewhere in the constellation of the Dragon. The North Pole of the ecliptic differs from the polar star since the axis of our planet declines 23.6 degrees from the perpendicular of the plane of rotation. Moreover, in accordance with the precession of equinox, the polar star (or, more accurately, the Earth's polar star) describes, in the course of 25,920 years, a complete circle. It is important to note here that the Northern Pole of the ecliptic is only northern when regarded from Earth. This means that we are speaking of a center around which a projection of the Earth's pole is oscillating in the firmament. Along with this, if one examines the entire solar system as a circle whose center is the sun, then the North Pole of the ecliptic also serves as a point of perpendicular intersection for the sun and the heavenly arch [небесного свода]; as such, it is the point which lies at the center of the polar star's precessional revolution in the northern hemisphere.

Here, we encounter an interesting moment: is the North Pole of the ecliptic a relative category (i.e., a convention) founded on the geocentric position, or is it something more universal? If, for the Earth, the problem of what is north and what is south cannot be definitively decided, then it is less obvious for other planets. In this case, we can take the direction of planetary revolution as a common metric and, if it coincides with the revolutionary direction of Earth, then we can recognize Earth's north pole as applicable to the rest of the solar system.

Now we have uncovered an extremely interesting picture. Astronomy tells us that all planets in the solar system, with the exception of one, turn in the same direction — that in which the Earth turns. In other words, it can be confidently concluded that terrestrial north is north for the majority of the other planets, as well as for the sun itself. This also means that the North Pole of the ecliptic is the true, objective northern pole of the heavens.

This is the north pole of a circle in whose heart lies our beloved flaming star. Our Father. *Pater ejus est sol.*[2]

There is only one planet not subject to this logic. Only for it alone are all proportions inverted — the north is not north, and the south is not south. Clearly, such an anomaly must reflect the peculiar quality of this planet, its special status and nature. And this is where the most interesting part begins.

2 [Translator's note]: Lat.: "His father is the sun."

Among the five traditional planets known to the ancients (Saturn, Jupiter, Mars, Venus, and Mercury), only Venus was associated with a feminine deity. The Romans referred to Venus as 'Lucifer,' the 'morning star'; and later, in the Christian tradition, this figure was identified with the devil. This is no coincidence. The impression begins to emerge that Venus is a planet in reverse—not only different, but sexually, qualitatively, mythologically opposite. She is in a symmetrical relationship not only with Mars—her symbolic partner in relation to the sun[3]—but to all masculine planets in general, even if only on the basis of her sexual sign as a mythological character and the physical sign of the antipode.

We have arrived at an important conclusion. The names of mythological personages, given as they were to one or another planet in the ancient astrological systems, took certain physical qualities of theirs into account which could not have been known to ancient humanity on a scientific level. The system of identifications between physical and mythological realities was based on a knowledge which preceded both subjective worldview constructions and an objective, physical picture

---

3 We remind the reader that distinction in the positions of Venus and Mercury in the spheres of traditional astrology and in astronomical reality is connected to the fact that the speed at which Mercury revolves around the sun is greater than that of Venus; the ancients directly associated this revolutionary speed with distance from the sun. The greater the speed, the closer the planet was. From this speed-bound perspective, Venus is symmetrical with Mars while, in astronomy, Mars is symmetrical with Mercury. It is curious that the Greeks ascribed androgenous characteristics to Hermes (Mercury). Among all the masculine planets, Mercury is the closest to the feminine beginning, though he remains male.

There is yet another important detail: taking the asymmetry between speed of revolution and proximity to the sun, it follows to analyze the possibility of the interchangeability of the zodiacal houses of Venus and Mercury. And here we reach an fascinating perspective: Gemini and Virgo more accurately correspond to Venus, as myths relating to twins very often bear some relation to Venus while she, herself, is the Virgin to a much greater degree than the feminine-masculine Hermes. Is there not an astrological subtext to the myth of Hermaphrodites, the duel-sexed child born of Hermes (Mercury) and Aphrodite (Venus)?

of the cosmos, while at the same time bringing them together. The planets and stars received their names not on the basis of any external, coincidental correspondences, voluntarist decisions, or complex calculations, but as a manifestation of a special gnoseological complex with a non-human origin which reflected the internal reality of these things as it manifested itself in their physical, bodily constitutions.

'Pre-Adamites' in Antarctica

In various mythological systems, there is one curious narrative connected with the emergence of humanity, or at least that of a certain part of humanity. This narrative describes how people came from Aphrodite, or the Germanic Freya. It is difficult to place the original source of this myth. But the details are as follows.

Firstly, from an astrological perspective, the origin of people (or human souls) on Venus is almost a tautology, since Venus is the only feminine planet among the five traditional spheres, and since, in the subtle constitution of the human being (irrespective of sex), the feminine element is always present. It is no coincidence that, even in the profane world, the astrological sign of Venus represents woman and all that is associated with her.

Through this lens, we are all, in some sense, 'children of Venus.'

Secondly, there exists a legend (exceedingly contentious from a historical standpoint, but surprisingly curious from the position of mythology) of the Chronicles of Ura-Linda, in which it is said that the progenitor of the 'white race,' the Frisians, the Indo-Europeans, was the goddess Freya, the wife of Odin, whose planet was considered to be Venus. In this regard, the old self-applied title of the Slavic tribe known as the 'Veneti' or 'Venedi,' which was preserved in the Finno-Ugric languages as 'Vene' (the word for Russians), is of extreme interest.

Thirdly, one of the chief deities among the natives of Central America is Quetzalcoatl, the 'feathered serpent.' He is seen as the creator of humans and the founder of the capital of the Toltecs — the city of Tollan, which is often associated with the capital of Hyperborea — Thule. The color of Quetzalcoatl is green, as is that of Venus. He, himself, is interpreted to be the spirit of the planet Venus, which formed the basis of a special five-month calendar that observed not a solar year, but 'venereal' years (five venereal years correspond to approximately eight solar years). Just like Venus, Quetzalcoatl is associated with doubleness, dualism.

The second sex, the doubled appearance of the morning-evening star on the horizon, the inverted rotational orientation…

All of these threads somehow converge in a strange theory of the origination of people on the planet Venus. Of course, this immediately summons associations with 'Luciferianism.' Very often, this Luciferianism is tied to a strictly Hyperborean theme, the theme of the north pole and of that country which, according to legend (the Greek, the Iranian, and the Vedic), was located in the far north. It is not impossible that this legend speaks of some parallel line of anthropogenesis associated with a special type of humanity and reflected mythologically in the biblical narrative of angels coming to Earth to mate with humans, with the 'daughters of man.'

This entire thematic complex is circumscribed by the idea of the 'pre-Adamites,' i.e., people who came before Adam. There is a surah in the Qur'an which speaks of them. This narrative underwent a strange development in the movement of Aryosophy, upon whose fragments a later Nazi mysticism was based. The story goes that the 'pre-Adamites' or the 'Luciferites' — the children of Freya — were the Nordic predecessors of the Aryan race. In the course of their migration to the south, they commingled with the 'Adamites,' the 'autochthonics' of the planet Earth. It is from this mixture that all peoples were born. And the purest Adamites (at least in the ideological sense) were preserved in the form of the Semitic race and its religions (Judaism, Islam), while the fragments of the 'pre-Adamic' worldview, belonging to the 'children of Venus,' were easily uncovered in Indo-European mythology.

For this line of humanity, the North Pole of the ecliptic is not the black heart of the Dragon, but something to the contrary. And now it is already entirely clear from whence came the theory of mystical Antarctica in neo-occult mythology. The expeditions of Admiral Dönitz[4] to the land of Queen Maud… Hollow Earth and the voyages of the most authoritative neo-Nazi mystic Miguel Serrano… The strange battle in Antarctic waters between the American battle group of Admiral Byrd[5] and unidentified underwater craft… The alarming motifs of Edgar Allan Poe in his *Narrative of Arthur Gordon Pym* and of Howard Phillips Lovecraft in his novella *At the Mountains of Madness*… The delirious 'revelations' of H. R. Martin about the existence of a secret Siegfrid, the occult leader of the coming Fourth Reich, in Antarctica… Add to this the Nazis' keen interest in the problem of the American Indians (German authors with clear nationalist sympathies such as Karl May introduced to adventure fiction images of the 'good Indian' and the 'evil pale-face' — images thereafter taken up by Soviet film and, more particularly, that of the German Democratic Republic; For the Anglo-Saxons and French, on the contrary, Indians were most often depicted as 'filthy bastards'), translation of Indian dialects in light of the 'Hyperborean theory,' carried out by the Ahnenerbe's founder Herman Wirth in his book *The Accession of Mankind* [*Der Aufgang der Menschheit*], and the expeditions of Hans Hörbiger and his pupils to the Peruvian temples (i.e., the 'trace of Quetzalcoatl')… The colony of 'Dignidad,' currently existing in the south of Chile, consisting only

4 [Translator's note]: In the Russian, Dönitz is rendered as 'Denitsa [Деница],' in response to which Dugin writes in a supplementary note, "A funny coincidence — the German Dönitz and the Russian 'morning star [dennitsa/денница].'"

5 What are we to make of the following message, sent by Admiral Byrd via telegraph: "The pole lies between us and our enemies"? What enemies?

of Germans and holding stewardship of an island called 'New Order' which lies close to Antarctica… The obsessive theme of the 'Thing' which has been so frequently evoked in the latest fantasy films, in which Antarctica becomes once more the epicenter of an invasion of anti-matter onto earth…

As Evgenii Golovin once wrote:

> In the distance of the zodiac, like a malevolent lesbian,
> Anarctica lay outspread…[6]

It is quite the curious ensemble of harrowing narratives, which are connected to the green star born from the foam.

Astrology against Astrology

Venus is only an example chosen at random of the correspondence of astrology to adjacent topics — of an astronomical, mythological, symbolic character. Venus, brought to bear on such an approach, suddenly extinguishes every banal horoscope, down-to-earth (and therefore untrue) interpretation, and dim-witted neo-spiritualist exercise with her terrifying light. The only interesting orientation left with regard to astrology is the tendency, practically absent today, of returning to the metaphysical bases of this sacred science, to a new observation of its deep, lost meaning. If the planet Venus is connected with such meaningful themes, if the threads of such overwhelming mysteries all converge in her symbolism, then it is a shame to interpret the presence of her influence in horoscopes as an 'indication of quick infatuation with prospects of marriage, passion, a pleasant time, etc.' What talk can there be of a pleasant time when enclosed by the Antarctic ice, embraced by Luciferic beings from the subterranean bases of the Fourth Reich?! Venus is the patron goddess of Love, but hers is an initiatic,

---

6 "В дали от зодиака как злая лесбиянка
Раскинулась нагая Антарктида…"

tantric, eroto-comatose, realizational Love. This planet (her spirit, her 'I') turns idiots into swine, as happened to Circe.

The other planets—some of which have been endowed with names which are entirely incorrect—harbor mysteries no less wild and abysses no less horrific.

The Indian Shukra, the Arab Zukhra, the Greek Aphrodite, the Toltec Quetzalcoatl, the Roman Lucifer—these are all representatives of a revolutionary reality which by turns frightens and attracts, which is sadistically cruel and filled with an unencountered bliss. The goddess, her presence, her sacrament, her mad and suffering descendants, lost in labyrinths of degeneracy…

The cosmic underground, the alternative pole, the scheme by which the terrestrial globe inverts its poles like a water clock (*klepsydra*). The Typus Mundi of a mysterious alchemical text, deciphered by Eugène Canseliet…

Astrology against astrology. The explosive reality of a blinding revelation against its dull and servile profanation at the hands of occult businessmen and aging ladies with shattered psyches…

In the final calculation, the North Pole of the ecliptic is the spawn of only the masculine planets. It is the fruit of their conspiracy. But, before patriarchy, a more ancient and sacred civilization existed—the era of Mothers. For this reason, in some languages (to include German), the sun takes the feminine gender: *die Sonne*. Might not this be an encoded indication that the true ecliptic pole of the sun's highest 'I' lies on the other side of the firmament's sphere?

Somewhere in the neighborhood of the Southern Cross… If this is so, then it is our task to bring things back to a just state. And then we shall see *Venus Victrix* in all her impossible, blinding brilliance—the Bronze Virgin who does not fit into the Universe, crowned with a diadem of ice and awash with the rays of the feminine sun. The sun is her clothing, her attire, her golden brocade. The distance from the reddish-green copper to philosophical gold is but a hand's breadth. One need only whitewash the face of Latona and tear all books to shreds — a child's amusement.

And Russians ought to think seriously about their origins… Who is the mother of us children? Could it be her?

Lunar Gold

(Charles Baudelaire)

"Andromaque, je pense a vous"[7]

With these words, Charles Baudelaire begins his poem "The Swan [Le Cygne]." Evgenii Golovin, ingenious authority on the art of the 'cursed poets [*poètes maudits*],' pointed to the fact that the majesty of Baudelaire can already be seen in his appeal to Andromache with the reverent '*vous*.' From the very start of these verses, one detects a vibration of *distance*, which is the meaning of the entire poem. This is the distance between the poet and the Widow, the symbol of Absolute Sorrow. Simultaneously, this is a distance between the Widow herself and the lost fulness of her marriage with the hero of Troy. Apollo, the Hyperborean god, was the patron of Troy. With the victory of the Achaeans came a triumph of the banal. The sacking of Troy was an affirmation of great distance and the beginning of a paradox. Aphrodite was more magnificent than Hera and more refined than Pallas, even if the resultant cost was the demise of a great city… The descendants of Troy, outcasts and wanderers, would later found Rome. And they would have their revenge. The *Iliad* is unfinished. The royal purple of Rome managed to write further tomes, but this imperial purple was fed on misery, a sharp pang of loss, penury, deprivation. Romulus and

7 [Translator's note]: Fr.: "Andromache, I think of you."

Remus, the unhappy foundlings, arose from beneath the tits of a beast to conquer the universe.

Andromache, once the wife of a most glorious husband, was given up to the whims of a petty Achaean tyrant. She was Pistis Sophia, having fallen into the abyss of matter from the æon of light; she was the exiled Shekhinah, deprived of the King's attentions. For Baudelaire, the thought of Andromache provoked another remembrance — the remembrance of the swan. The proud white bird, having escaped the cage of a cheap menagerie, dragging its wings through the filth and dust, found itself desperately breathing in the dust of a dried stream bed and declining its delicate, snow-white neck.

> Water, when will you gush forth?
> When will you come crashing down, lightning?[8]

The heavens are hollow and grim. Only the smoke from a Parisian train station livens their indifferent chill. Perhaps the disgraced, cursed, paradisiac bird has beseeched God himself…

> I think of the negress, gaunt and pthisical,
> Stomping in the muck and seeking with haggard eye
> Behind the immense wall of fog
> The absent coconut trees of superb Africa…[9]

Andromache, the White Widow — White like the swan who has escaped from the menagerie but is, nonetheless, doomed — becomes the Black Woman, to whom those mysterious, prophetic Biblical words allude:

---

8 [Translator's note]: Fr.: "Eau, quand donc pleuvras-tu? quand tonneras-tu, foudre?"

9 [Translator's note]: Fr.: "Je pense à la négresse, amaigrie et phtisique
Piétinant dans la boue, et cherchant, l'oeil hagard,
Les cocotiers absents de la superbe Afrique
Derrière la muraille immense du brouillard…"

"I am black, but comely."[10] Africa is the black motherland. Kémi[11], the black earth, the royal art… In another place, Baudelaire writes: "For you, I change gold to lead."[12] All of moon-eyed and fog-covered Europe is transformed into luxuriant Africa. Some commentators are of the conviction that Baudelaire here is alluding to his dark-skinned lover. Who can say whether the earthly woman and the great alchemical principle melded as one in his absolute consciousness?

In the first posthumous publication of *The Flowers of Evil*, Théophile Gautier wrote that Baudelaire belonged to those people who have a complex way of thinking, and who, later, in either a text or a conversation, strive to simplify their thoughts so as to make them understandable. (Such an undertaking is not always successful.) On the contrary, the majority of people think through banality, but sometimes, in an attempt to seem intelligent, purposely convolute their constructions. Maybe Baudelaire's 'negress' is both a symbol and a concrete, living actress at the same time. Or maybe she is even something in addition to that — the "secret messenger from the star Betelgeuse," for example, as Jean Parvulesco might say.

The 'cursed poets' were magically attracted to poverty, misery, damnation, and privation. Nerval's "El Desdichado" and his "Christ Among the Olive Trees [Le Christ aux oliviers]" serve as a mystical manifesto for all of the 'cursed' ones. I was especially struck by the demise of Nerval — he hung himself out in the street toward morning, just as the fresh sunrise was beginning monstrously to decant itself into the sky. Baudelaire's swan, too, slipped its menagerie prison at

10 [Translator's note]: See previous note pertaining to this quotation on p. 183.

11 [Translator's note]: A francophone equivalent of the Egyptian for "Black," This is likely an allusion to the famous Pan-Africanist Kémi Séba, who is in alignment geopolitically with Dugin's neo-Eurasianist vision, and with whom the Russian philosopher held talks in Moscow in 2017.

12 [Translator's note]: "Par toi je change l'or en fer"; This verse can be found in Baudelaire's "Alchemy of Sorrow [Alchimie de la douleur]."

sunrise — "At the hour when Labor awakens under the heavens cold and clear."[13] For those who have learned the mystery of distance, the morning is often unbearable. The royal children were previously hidden in a cellar, while the Hermetics forewarned that it is forbidden to expose the material of the philosopher's stone to the rays of the sun — otherwise, the Great Work will be disrupted. When the ray of the pseudo-dawn of the decrepit, untransformed world falls upon the 'Aquitaine prince,' whose tower is 'abolished,'[14] he suffers like a Transylvanian vampire.

The logic of poetry is the inverse of everyday logic. He who is saved from the storm and reaches shore loses the game, along with everything else. The 'sufferer of defeat' is a true loser. The Poet, like Shiva, having drunk the poison of Halahala at the bottom of the world ocean, is spellbound by the lowest point of Being. He perceives in it a salvific mystery. The Bottom of Evil provides the poet with a model for the ontological dimension, a taste of metaphysical distance, an attainment of proportions. Banal beings fear the Bottom. They do whatever necessary to avoid it. But the Bottom compromises them from within until it finally consumes their souls. There is not a single saint who would pass over the temptations of Hell. There is not one saved soul who would not seek knowledge of the sacraments of sin. The 'upright [добропорядочные]' are beyond salvation and poetry. They are but a historical entourage, cardboard decoration…

> I think of sailors, forgotten on an island…[15]

---

13 [Translator's note]: Fr.: "à l'heure où sous les cieux
Froids et clairs le Travail s'éveille."

14 [Translator's note]: Gérard de Nerval, "El Desdichado": "Le Prince d'Aquitaine à la Tour abolie."

15 [Translator's note]: Fr.: "Je pense aux matelots oubliés dans une île."

That is, he thinks of hard-hearted people who inspire no sympathy; of dumb and cynical crooks, marked by scars and pocks... But the 'forgotten sailors on the island' are transforming. If they were to peacefully sail on their ships, their pathetic souls would not change the mighty and senseless path of Fate by even a hair's breadth. However, they have simply been forgotten on one of many islands. Maybe the captain concluded that they had been ripped to shreds by wild beasts, or that someone had simply stranded them there as retribution for an attempted robbery or mutiny... Maybe they had crashed upon a reef. No matter the scenario, they have been 'forgotten.'

Hopeless, known to no one, discarded, senseless in both the past and the future, nameless and unloved, 'accursed,' they enter directly into the central gates of Being — a path preordained even for the chosen.

The distance which separates them from the Great Earth is absolute. They are in the center of Hell. At night, the angels look into their pupils, dilated with terror, and are frightened to see that they cannot see their reflections therein...

> I think of sailors, forgotten on an island,
> Of the captives, of the vanquished!... Of many others, too![16]

To be spurned, held captive, defeated, forgotten — this is a great reward which he Spirit gives to 'those who belong to it [своим].' Like the Templars, Dante never smiled.

Some have said that this is because he spent time in Hell. Guénon balked at this, suggesting instead that, to the contrary, he did not smile because he spent time in the Heavens and that, from then on, whenever his eyes fell upon the ground, he was offended beyond measure. Lautréamont's 'Maldoror' was also incapable of smiling. And so, he grabbed a finely honed knife and cut open the corners of his mouth.

16 [Translator's note]: Fr.: "[...] Aux captifs, aux vaincus!... à bien d'autres encor!"

Looking at himself in the mirror, he found that the attempted artificial smile had been a failure...

To smile is to sin against the Spirit. He who smiles does not think of Andromache. He who does not think of Andromache is forever blotted out of the secret book of Light.

And, in turn, he will be forgotten by the destitute, the nobodies, the eternal inhabitants of filthy hospitals, gloomy cells, cruel dens, undignified squats, dumps, and basements... These will sit as terrible jurors in the Final Judgment.

> I think... of many others, too...

But who are these 'others?' With whom does the great Baudelaire concern himself?

Are we to understand that he speaks only of new categories of the reviled, whom he had previously forgotten to list?

Or maybe the thought of Andromache drove him to some precipice, beyond which begins an encounter with the 'inexpressible ones'—those whose suffering is so great that the very utterance of their name would destroy the delicate world surrounding us?

They say that, during his last days, Francis of Assisi beheld the most horrifying image of the world—a crucified and sobbing Cherub, hanging over a hill sitting upon a grey cloud. And what figure did the half-strangled Gérard de Nerval in his final moment?

Against the backdrop of the true dawn, someone's shadow rose before his gaze... There was nothing hopeful in it...

The Americans imprisoned their compatriot and greatest poet, Ezra Pound, in a cell. He was jailed for the fact that, like Blake, it was obvious to him that money and riches are the most horrific evil, and that poverty, justice, and purity are the greatest good.

"The roosters still sing at dawn in Medinaceli"[17]—these are the words inscribed upon the sole monument in the world erected to Pound, located in the Spanish province of Soria. All of the world's disenfranchised come here on a mystical pilgrimage. What do they feel standing there, in that simple Spanish village, where no one knows in whose honor the Italian prince Ivancici and Chilean Nazi Miguel Serrano erected this strange stone?

It was erected in honor of poverty and simplicity, insignificance, doom… The great and ingenious are connected by mysterious knots to the minor and simplistic. This is the anointment of universal Sorrow, the sole and indivisible Sorrow of the 'night in Gethsemane.'

In Hinduism, all avatars of Vishnu concluded their incarnation—so full of heroic feats—with an immense, inhuman *toska*[18]… Rama despaired [тосковал] instead of rejoicing at his attainment of Sita, whom he derided out of annoyance; Krishna wandered in solitude amid rotten tropical jungle until he died of *toska*… In the Garden of Gethsemane, Jesus endured something inexpressible, of which perhaps only Nerval could have conceived.

> Tout est mort, j'ai parcouru les mondes…[19]

There is an ancient legend about the first Saint, Hazrat, who was once a friend of God, himself. But, one day, he asked God: "Why does Hell exist, and why is it that not all of the universe, which You have created, is magnificent?" God whispered an answer in his ear which did not please him. Hazrat asked his question once more. God answered once

---

17 [Translator's note]: Span.: "Aún cantan los gallos al amanecer en Medinaceli."

18 [Translator's note]: The Russian 'тоска' cannot be accurately rendered in a single English word. It refers simultaneously to an inescapable resignation, an oppressive fatal awareness, a paralysis, and an existential boredom which goes beyond the pettiness of French '*ennui*.'

19 [Translator's note]: Fr.: "All is dead, I've toured the worlds…"; Gérard de Nerval, "Christ in the Garden of Gethsemane [Le Christ aux oliviers]."

more. After the third time, Hazrat grabbed his sword and exclaimed: “You do not know the answer! I shall do battle with you!”

God’s friend went to the side of the disenfranchised, the accursed, the ‘sufferers of defeat’; to the side of ‘emaciated orphans that wither like flowers’; to the side of Andromache, Hector, Troy. He took a stand against Zeus. He had every reason to do so.

Hounds

(Lautréamont)

> By the light of the moon, nearby the sea, in the isolated places of the countryside, we see how, plunged in bitter reflections, everything takes on a yellow, indecisive, fantastic form. The shadow of the trees, sometimes quickly, sometimes lazily runs, coming and going in various forms, flattening itself and cleaving to the ground. In times when I was carried aloft on the wings of youth, I would be made to dream things which seemed strange to me: now I am accustomed to them. The wind moans its languorous notes through the leaves, and the owl sings its grave lament, which causes the hairs of the listener to stand on end.[20]

Thus resonates the malevolent intonation of the eighth fragment in the first “Song of Maldoror.” As a whole, this fragment shocks one with ideal, inhuman finality: opening up before us is the profound worldview of Lautréamont, that ‘great unknown’ of world literature.

---

20 [Translator’s note]: Fr.: “Au clair de la lune, près de la mer, dans les endroits isolés de la campagne, l’on voit, plongé dans d’amères réflexions, toutes les choses revêtir des formes jaunes, indécises, fantastiques. L’ombre des arbres, tantôt vite, tantôt lentement, court, vient, revient, par diverses formes, en s’aplatissant, en se collant contre la terre. Dans le temps, lorsque j’étais emporté sur les ailes de la jeunesse, cela me faisait rêver, me paraissait étrange ; maintenant, j’y suis habitué. Le vent gémit à travers les feuilles ses notes langoureuses, et le hibou chante sa grave complainte, qui fait dresser les cheveux à ceux qui l’entendent.” Comte de Lautréamont, *The Songs of Maldoror* [*Les Chants de Maldoror*], Song I, stanza viii.

There are a few basic versions of the Lautréamont legend. He was discovered in the early twentieth century by the French Surrealists, who acknowledged him as their forebear. There exists the vulgar opinion that he was severely mentally ill, while other literary scholars read his texts as parodies of romanticism and the gothic novel, or as lightweight exercises in black humor.

However, none of these surmises bring us even remotely close to an understanding of Lautréamont, who remains a malicious enigma, having enchanted more than one generation of those seeking radical answers and unorthodox questions. Let us look more closely at the above excerpted fragment from the first "Song of Maldoror," draw nearer to its author — this 'child of Montevideo,' half-man and half-demon, in whom the extreme cruelty of de Sade, the 'Satanism' of Baudelaire, the blinding brilliance of Rimbaud, and the despair of Nerval are intertwined.

It is already obvious that, in the above-mentioned entourage, something terrible is bound to occur — some sort of monstrous, impossible event, whose nearness casts a shadow of paranoia on an alarming, dusk-cloaked landscape of hallucinations. (When reading Lautréamont's descriptions of nature, one feels that he is witnessing some psychedelic vision, more reminiscent of computerized graphics than any rectilinear observation of the external world; one forms the impression that these landscapes were written in a place having nothing in common with the images depicted.)

Who shall now appear at this macabre scene? A vampire? A murderer? The blonde beast Maldoror? A perverted hag with a bloodied blade? A monster?

No. This time, it will be *hounds.*

> Then the dogs, rendered insane, break their chains, escape from their remote farms; they run here and there throughout the countryside, a prey to madness.[21]

It would seem that nothing could have presaged such an abrupt turn of events; the beginning suggested an insidious, evaporating evil — not this inexplicable lightning strike of canine hysteria. But the fact remains: the text turns upon these mad hounds, having lost their dogged minds without reason, meaninglessly, just because, all of a sudden. And all of this against the backdrop of malevolent shades and the light of the moon.

Hounds are sign-beings that allude to a spontaneous awakening, terrible forces without reflection or psychological endowment. They tear into the fabric of the text despite the wishes of its author. It would seem that the phrase, "Then the dogs [...] break their chains," has pounced upon Lautréamont without warning, from somewhere outside of him. It is possible that he had been planning to write some other macabre thing, to immerse himself in other contemplations of nightmare. But the hounds — who are these hounds? — insisted upon themselves, trampling upon the author's will. "They are merely images, this is merely text," our everyday consciousness attempts to whisper to us, already clearly aware that it has collided with something unusual and terrifying that departs from the boundaries of literature, psychology, and the conventional language of mental constructions; the everyday consciousness collides with the crude, three-dimensional, corporeal reality of Lautréamont's hounds.

21 [Translator's note]: Fr.: "Alors, les chiens, rendus furieux, brisent leurs chaînes, s'échappent des fermes lointaines ; ils courent dans la campagne, çà et là, en proie à la folie."

> Suddenly, they come to a halt and glance around on all sides with a fierce disquietude, eyes crazed.[22]

After such a tableau, there can be no doubt remaining that these beings—these hounds—have only just made their appearance in the world; they behave not as rabid animals, but as beings that have suddenly, in a manner which they themselves completely did not expect, found themselves in a three-dimensional space, utterly unlike that to which they are used. This has caused the 'fierce disquietude' of their 'crazed eyes.' Then arrives a time of strange mystery, of a special ritual in which the newly born, uncontainable horror incarnates a hymn to its own eternality.

> [A]nd, just like elephants in a desert on the brink of death, they cast a final glance at the sky, raise their trunk in despair, lowering their inert ears as the dogs lower their inert ears [an anatomical specificity—A.D.], raise their head, inflate their terrible neck, and [...].[23]

What do they begin to do now?

> [A]nd, one after another, begin to howl [...].[24]

Then follows a series of metaphors pertaining to their howling which may serve as a paradigm for describing the indescribable.

> [A]nd, one after another, begin to howl
> Like an infant crying out of hunger,
> Like a cat with a wounded belly lying atop a roof,
> Like a woman in her birth labors,

---

22 [Translator's note]: Fr.: "Tout à coup, ils s'arrêtent, regardent de tous les côtés avec une inquiétude farouche, l'œil en feu."

23 [Translator's note]: Fr.: "[E]t, de même que les éléphants, avant de mourir, jettent dans le désert un dernier regard au ciel, élevant désespérément leur trompe, laissant leurs oreilles inertes, de même les chiens laissent leurs oreilles inertes, élèvent la tête, gonflent le cou terrible, et [...]."

24 [Translator's note]: Fr.: "[E]t se mettent à aboyer, tour à tour [...]."

> Like a dying man stricken with plague in the hospital,
> Like a young girl who sings a sublime air [...].[25]

This metaphorical series puts us in a special relation to our perception of sound: the gentle voice of a woman and the squeals of a cat with shredded intestines or the dry, roughened moans of a dying man are aligned only for the being who possesses an extremely *alien* psychological constitution, entirely opposed to the nervous system and emotions of the common man.

Even rationally undeveloped toddlers can differentiate the positive and negative orders of sound—despite their cultural or ethnic particularities. This is to suggest that the author has entered a world of ethereal hounds, where different laws and correspondences rule the day. Now it is clear to us just *how* the hounds are howling. (Is it clear?) But at what are they howling?

> [A]gainst the stars in the north, against the stars in the east, against the stars in the south, against the stars in the west [...].[26]

We direct the reader's attention to the sequential nature of these cardinal directions—first, the north, then the east, then the south, then the west. This cross of orientations corresponds to the polar, annual movement of the sun in a counter-clockwise direction. This indicates the left-turning swastika.

---

25 [Translator's note]: Fr.: "[E]t se mettent à aboyer, tour à tour, soit comme un enfant qui crie de faim, soit comme un chat blessé au ventre au-dessus d'un toit, soit comme une femme qui va enfanter, soit comme un moribond atteint de la peste à l'hôpital, soit comme une jeune fille qui chante un air sublime [...]."

26 [Translator's note]: Fr.: "[C]ontre les étoiles au nord, contre les étoiles à l'est, contre les étoiles au sud, contre les étoiles à l'ouest [...]."

> [A]gainst the moon; against the mountains, so like giant rocks in the distance, reclining in obscurity [...].[27]

(How unprecedented and avant-garde to compare mountains to rocks!)

> [A]gainst the cold air which they inhale into their full lungs, which rends the interiors of their nostrils, red, burning;
> Against the silence of the night;
> Against the owls, whose oblique flight razes the tip of their nose as they carry off a rat or a frog in their beak, living nourishment, fresh for their young;
> Against the hares who disappear in the wink of an eye;
> Against the thief who takes off on his galloping horse after having committed a crime;
> Against the serpents, stirring the briars which cause their skin to tremble and their teeth to rasp;
> Against their [the dogs'] own howling, which gives them a fear of themselves [...].[28]

This is a very important detail: the dogs howl at their own howls, fear their own fear, go insane from insanity. In Lautréamont's world of absolute aggression, there is no starting point which, as a result of the literary process, would be dialectically reflected in that which follows. In this lies his essential, radical distinction from the Surrealists, who started with the norm and proceeded from there into insanity.

---

27 [Translator's note]: Fr.: "[C]ontre la lune ; contre les montagnes, semblables au loin à des roches géantes, gisantes dans l'obscurité [...]."

28 [Translator's note]: Fr.: "[C]ontre l'air froid qu'ils aspirent à pleins poumons, qui rend l'intérieur de leur narine, rouge, brûlant ; contre le silence de la nuit ; contre les chouettes, dont le vol oblique leur rase le museau, emportant un rat ou une grenouille dans le bec, nourriture vivante, douce pour les petits ; contre les lièvres, qui disparaissent en un clin d'œil ; contre le voleur, qui s'enfuit au galop de son cheval après avoir commis un crime ; contre les serpents, remuant les bruyères, qui leur font trembler la peau, grincer les dents ; contre leurs propres aboiements, qui leur font peur à eux-mêmes [...]."

Lautréamont starts from insanity and moves further into it. This is a special kind of dialectic, accessible only to hounds. Hounds who howl…

> …against the toads whom they mangle with a jerk of the jaw (why have they come so far away from the swamp?) […].[29]

Lautréamont's note, placed in parentheses, bears witness to his condescension and concern for simple-minded readers, who have ventured too far (from the swamp) in search of meaning.

> [A]gainst the trees whose leaves, gently rocked, amount to mysteries which they [the dogs] cannot comprehend, which they wish to uncover with their fixed, intelligent eyes […].[30]

Here, yet again, is a direct allusion to the emergent character of the hounds, who have arrived from nowhere and have found themselves in full possession of their minds and in a psychic equilibrium with a world penetrated by insanity and the necessity of objects.

> [A]gainst the spiders, suspended amid their long legs, who climb the trees to save themselves […].[31]

More likely, the spiders have managed to weave a web for themselves between the dogs' paws while the latter have been gazing at the trees, attempting to understand them.

Obviously, this moment has drawn on for quite a long time — maybe several days.

---

29 [Translator's note]: Fr.: "…contre les crapauds, qu'ils broient d'un coup sec de mâchoire (pourquoi se sont-ils éloignés du marais ?) […]."

30 [Translator's note]: Fr.: "[C]ontre les arbres, dont les feuilles, mollement bercées, sont autant de mystères qu'ils ne comprennent pas, qu'ils veulent découvrir avec leurs yeux fixes, intelligents […]."

31 [Translator's note]: Fr.: "[C]ontre les araignées, suspendues entre leurs longues pattes, qui grimpent sur les arbres pour se sauver […]."

> [A]gainst the crows who have failed to find something to eat during their journey, and who return to their lodging on fatigued wing;
> Against the rocks on the shore;
> Against the fires which appear at the masts of invisible ships;
> Against the deaf sound of waves;
> Against the great fish who, swimming past, reveal their black backs before sinking into the abyss;
> And against the man who makes them [the dogs] his slaves [...].[32]

The description of their howls is finished. Like a magnetized arrow, the aggressive insanity of the hounds has passed through the many sectors of a delirious landscape, snatching inflamed scraps of reality from either non-being or the everyday. Emptiness and the myriad beings who fill it have been scrutinized by the careful eyes of these mad animals, up until the extreme limit: "against the man who makes them his slaves." This is a crystalline expression of metaphysical misanthropy, a hatred of man, serving as the central line of Lautréamont's missive. Man is a wrapping for delirium [бреда]. Both within and without him, a metaphysical hell bubbles and froths, full of inscrutable hints and cutting fear. But man — the enslaver of the hounds — has found a way to hide himself, to run away from the howl of reality. He has convinced himself of his safety. He has made a caricature of thought, life, spirit, and death.

More than once, Maldoror senses the threat of having passed through life for nothing. Sooner or later the hounds will revolt. Shortly afterward in this fragment, a phrase of homicidal notes begins clearly to sound.

32 [Translator's note]: Fr.: "[C]ontre les corbeaux, qui n'ont pas trouvé de quoi manger pendant la journée, et qui s'en reviennent au gîte l'aile fatiguée ; contre les rochers du rivage ; contre les feux, qui paraissent aux mâts des navires invisibles ; contre le bruit sourd des vagues ; contre les grands poissons, qui, nageant, montrent leur dos noir, puis s'enfoncent dans l'abîme ; et contre l'homme qui les rend esclaves [...]."

> After this, they once more set about running through the countryside, leaping with their bloody paws over the ditches, the paths, the fields, the grass, and the stone escarpments. One would say that they have attained a rage, seeking a vast pond to appease their thirst. Their prolonged screams frighten nature. Woe to the lingering voyager! The friends of the cemeteries will throw themselves upon him, will tear him to shreds, will eat him with mouths from which blood falls; for they do not have rotten teeth. The savage animals, not daring to approach and take part in this repast of flesh, run away as far as the eye can see, trembling.[33]

This textbook passage masterfully paints the picture of what will happen to man and humanity if they do not immediately change their relationship to the hounds (to Lautréamont's hounds; it is already obvious that we are speaking here of something entirely distinct from the 'domestic pets' known as dogs).

> After a few hours, the dogs, exhausted from running here and there, nearly dead, tongues hanging from their mouths, rush toward each other, not knowing what they do, and tear each other to a thousand shreds with an incredible rapidity.[34]

That's it. The infernal liturgy has ended. The hounds, having appeared from the life-bearing darkness of non-existence, having done everything they could, have disappeared. Thus passes a bout of the falling

---

33 [Translator's note]: Fr.: "Après quoi, ils se mettent de nouveau à courir la campagne, en sautant, de leurs pattes sanglantes par dessus les fossés, les chemins, les champs, les herbes et les pierres escarpées. On les dirait atteints de la rage, cherchant un vaste étang pour apaiser leur soif. Leurs hurlements prolongés épouvantent la nature. Malheur au voyageur attardé ! Les amis des cimetières se jetteront sur lui, le déchireront, le mangeront avec leur bouche d'où tombe du sang ; car, ils n'ont pas les dents gâtées. Les animaux sauvages, n'osant pas s'approcher pour prendre part au repas de chair, s'enfuient à perte de vue, tremblants."

34 [Translator's note]: Fr.: "Après quelques heures, les chiens, harassés de courir ça et là, presque morts, la langue en dehors de la bouche, se précipitent les uns sur les autres, sans savoir ce qu'ils font, et se déchirent en mille lambeaux, avec une rapidité incroyable."

sickness, the reeling of hallucinogens, the squirming threads of life in the tissues of a walking corpse. The hounds have eaten one another. There was no other way out for them. Otherwise, Lautréamont would have nowhere to put them. They had already chewed through their chains at the beginning of the text.

The cycle of aggression is complete. Further, we read an interpretation, by Lautréamont himself, of the metaphysical meaning of that which has occurred.

> They do not behave this way out of cruelty. One day, my mother said to me with glassy eyes, 'Whenever you are lying in bed and you hear the howling of dogs in the countryside, hide under your blanket; do not turn in derision at what they do: they have an insatiable thirst for infinity—like you, like me, like all other humans—for a figure tall and pale. As for me, I will allow you to stand before the window and contemplate this spectacle, which is quite sublime.' From that time on, I have abided by the death wish. Like the dogs, I feel a need for infinity… I cannot, I cannot satisfy this need! I am the son of a man and a woman, from what I've been told. This astonishes me… I had thought myself to be something more! Besides, what do I care from whence I come? If it were up to me, I would rather have been the son of a female shark, whose hunger is a friend of tempests, and of the tiger, whose cruelty is renowned: I wouldn't be that vicious.[35]

35 [Translator's note]: Fr.: "Ils n'agissent pas ainsi par cruauté. Un jour, avec des yeux vitreux, ma mère me dit : « Lorsque tu seras dans ton lit, que tu entendras les aboiements des chiens dans la campagne, cache-toi dans ta couverture, ne tourne pas en dérision ce qu'ils font : ils ont soif insatiable de l'infini, comme toi, comme moi, comme le reste des humains, à la figure pâle et longue. Même, je te permets de te mettre devant la fenêtre pour contempler ce spectacle, qui est assez sublime. » Depuis ce temps, je respecte le vœu de la morte. Moi, comme les chiens, j'éprouve le besoin de l'infini… Je ne puis, je ne puis contenter ce besoin ! Je suis fils de l'homme et de la femme, d'après ce qu'on m'a dit. Ça m'étonne… je croyais être davantage ! Au reste, que m'importe d'où je viens ? Moi, si cela avait pu dépendre de ma volonté, j'aurais voulu être plutôt le fils de la femelle du requin, dont la faim est amie des tempêtes, et du tigre, à la cruauté reconnue : je ne serais pas si méchant."

The thirst for infinity. This is a basic impulse, a current of high strain that illumines and dumbfounds the accidental beings of a nightmarish world. Seldomly. Like lightning. Like a sudden gash from a razor.

The riddle of the hounds has been elucidated. Something greater than their being has shifted about inside of them, giving off an aura of cold and casting them into a mad whirlpool of universal annihilation. The hounds are the thoughts of Shiva, the Bloody One, the red-brown — of the eternal, hidden, omnipresent Shiva.

Maldoror had a wonderful mother. Foregoing the pedagogical instinct, in the end she decided to explain the meaning of infinity [бесконечности] to her child and permitted him to observe the homicide and subsequent collective suicide of the hounds. She cultivated in him a "respect for the death wish" and a "need for infinity." The suggestion somehow makes itself that this surprising woman harkens back to Kali, Shiva's wife. After all, only this Lady is more terrifying than the shark who feeds on the corpses of shipwrecks.

Further on, Lautréamont describes Maldoror's existence in a cave.

> From time to time, when my neck can no longer turn in the same direction, when it stops to turn to the other side, I suddenly gaze at the horizon, looking over the rare gaps left in the thick brush which covers the entrance [of the cave]: I see nothing! Nothing… save the country fields that dance in whirlwinds along with the trees and the long files of birds that traverse the air. This troubles my blood and my brain… Who is it that strikes me over the head with an iron rod like a hammer striking an anvil?[36]

36 [Translator's note]: Fr.: "De moment en moment, lorsque mon col ne peut plus continuer de tourner dans un même sens, qu'il s'arrête, pour se remettre à tourner dans un sens opposé, je regarde subitement l'horizon, à travers les rares interstices laissés par les broussailles épaisses qui recouvrent l'entrée : je ne vois rien ! Rien… si ce ne sont les campagnes qui dansent en tourbillons avec les arbres et avec les longues files d'oiseaux qui traversent les airs. Cela me trouble le sang et le cerveau… Qui donc, sur la tête, me donne des coups de barre de fer, comme un marteau frappant l'enclume ?"

Nothing. Sooner or later, he who thirsts for infinity arrives at Nothing, at its taste, its absolute, final element. In actuality, these fields and trees do not exist. They have long departed, along with the hounds that have torn themselves to shreds. The hounds have dragged the trees away with them, into the vortex of eternity, having turned the landscape inside-out.

The strike of the hammer cannot kill, just as the pure air, full of morning ozone, cannot revive.

Nothing.

Rien, cette écume…[37]

37 "Nothing, this foam…" (Mallarmé); [Translator's note]: This is the beginning of Mallarmé's poem "Greetings [Salut]." The word *écume* can also be translated as 'scum.'

PART VIII

THE GUEST FROM WITHIN

Russian Вещь[1]

Russia is a country of dreams. Her borders are blurred; her landscapes are befogged; Russian peoples' faces do not stick in one's memory. Language is based on intonations and associations, on some mysterious current of the unspoken and irrational, which bleeds through everyday words and phrases. Within the mystery of the Russian language is the mystery of Russia.

One day, the ingenious Evgenii Golovin pointed, with shocking precision, to the existence of a certain layer in the Russian language, which is located between speech and silence. These are not yet words, but are also no longer their absence. This is a mysterious world of dream sounds, strange vibrations which precede phrases, propositions, and affirmations. One cannot call them thoughts.

During the conversation, Golovin presented a phrase of Yuri Mamleev's from his epochal novel *Shatuny* as an example: "Fyodor

1 [Translator's note]: As Dugin further expands on below, the Russian word *veshch'* [вещь], nominally rendered as 'thing' in English, possesses its own specifically Russian meaning, grounded in the roots of the language.

dug a way over to the Fomichevs."[2] Here, this intermediate layer, this elemental fabric of the Russian dream can be felt in all of its almost carnal swollenness. "Something is squirming inside of something else in order to get somewhere." One indefinite term operates within another in order to reach a third. This is neither psychoanalysis, nor madness, nor banal idiocy.

It is just that, in the basements of the national soul, something nameless is twisting, curling away from the light, rejecting any incarnation into a form, which would already be intelligible, firmly grounded, and falser.

Martinez de Pasqually, founder of the mystical doctrine of 'Martinism,' which so greatly influenced the European (and Russian) mystics of the eighteenth and nineteenth centuries, developed a special, mysterious concept which he called '*Chose*.'[3]

According to Pasqually, an encounter with such a reality serves as a crowning moment of spiritual experience, the ultimate result of the most complex theurgical and magical operations. Of course, one could translate the French word '*chose*' to its Russian analogue '*veshch*' [вещь],' but things are not so simple. The Russian '*veshch*" derives etymologically from the verb '*vedat*' [ведать],' i.e. 'to know.' Therefore, '*veshch*'', in the Russian language, does not refer to an object in itself, but to the fact that it is known, that it is familiar — it refers to thought and information relating to the thing. '*Veshch*" is that which is known to man (or non-man [нечеловеку]). '*Chose*' is something different: the dark side of the object, slipping away from reason's regard. '*Chose*' is more closely related to a state of semi-speech and semi-silence. It is

2 [Translator's note]: "Фёдор рыл ход к Фомичевым." In Mamleev's novel, the main character — Fyodor Sonnov — digs a tunnel through the ceiling of his sister's basement into the floor of the Fomichevs' side of the house; the Sonnovs and Fomichevs live in the same village house, which is partitioned down the middle.

3 [Translator's note]: Fr.: 'Thing.'

an illumination brought about by an irrational presence more akin to a living darkness.

Dreams are born when the eyelids are closed. Russians live in this way. In part, they see what is, while also seeing what is not. A slight inebriation, unexpected coincidences, obscure forebodings... How much more intense this all is than the rational actions, banal goals, and miserly enjoyments of a flesh desiccated by the tedium of waking life! Russians live in constant anticipation of the '*Chose*.' This is all quite near and comprehensible to us.

The pricking gloom of our content, the soft fabric of our mental underground, the blanched spots of our native twilight...

"Fyodor is digging a way over to the Fomichevs." The context of this missive, unsusceptible to interpretation, is an almost physical expression of Pasqually's '*Chose*.' And there is nothing clearer than this for our great folk, dreaming their prophetic dream.

It is no coincidence that Joseph de Maistre, famed French Martinist and thinker of the extreme right, settled in Russia and named his principal work *Evenings in Saint-Petersburg* (as an aside, he was Chaadaev's mentor, who brilliantly intuited the full abnormality of Russian life, even if he was incapable of transitioning from a bewilderment at it to a love for it—perhaps due to his horror before the pure elementality of the '*Chose*'). It is also no coincidence that Saint-Yves d'Alveydre, another great esotericist, was enamored with the Russian people, married a Russian wife, and often said that "these people have mysticism in their blood—they require no instruction.' It was here that Doctor Papus was drawn, together with his teacher, Maître Philippe.

And the founder of Theosophy—Madame Blavatskaya—was a total Russian hysteric. It is unimportant *what* occultists concretely say or how they rationalize their experience. It is their systems as such that are their most interesting feature. Of much greater hilarity is that unique taste of madness and dreamy lunacy that is ubiquitous in their writings. Whatever ramblings they may have produced with regard to the astral plane or the chakras, "Fyodor is digging a way over to the Fomichevs" through their brains; in the warm blackness of their souls swarms something disturbed. It is that which is in all of us.

There is a 'Russian trace' in all esoteric doctrines. It is so for a reason. Dreams are born in our territory, within the bounds of Russia. Our nation is responsible for them, just as the dwarves are responsible for the treasures of the Rhine, and the fairies of Monmur for the Holy Grail. The Russian language is an unending mantra. Its context strangles any message with its solidity; events are dissolved in its background; mirrored analogies rupture any logical discourse. The Russian language is the mother of all languages, because it is not a language, but the possibility of language. There is no affirmation in it which does not carry its own rebuttal, auto-irony, a message of absolute opposition. This is the case not only in our literature, but also in our newspaper columns and officially issued government statements.

"Eighteen hostages died as a result of the operation" (from the Chechen casualty reports).[4]

What does this mean? Perhaps all five hundred of them died; perhaps it was a mistake (or deliberate disinformation) and no more than five perished. Maybe they were not hostages, but undercover agents, or even the combatants themselves. Maybe nothing happened at all. Maybe something horrific happened on an incomparably greater scale of carnage. Maybe the people who died just happened to be there. Maybe death doesn't exist in general and, in its place, there are only smooth transitions from one dream to another… Maybe, on the contrary, life does not exist and we have all been dead for a long time. Nothing surprises Russians. They wink inwardly, in their souls, scratch themselves, and pour out another shot.

4 [Translator's note]: At the time of this book's publication, the First Chechen War (December 9, 1994—August 31, 1996) had just concluded.

The '*Chose*' is more important than any word or message. It presses on one from within and saturates all with its intoxicating juices. Like blind gods — angelic idiots — the '*Chose*' swarms in our national unconscious.

Other peoples could not withstand what we do — not for even a few days, to say nothing of centuries.

The Russia of dreams — draped in interrogative snow[5] and bright, suffocating *toska*[6] — is higher than reason and paranoia, filth and shamelessness, time and its end.

Motherland.

Dark Is the Water

(On Yuri Mamleev's *Shatuny*)

> In Schein, you include all the riches of the world,
> and yet you deny its very objectivity!
>
> — V. I. Lenin
> (on Hegel in the *Philosophical Notebooks*)

Yuri Vital'evich Mamleev[7] is not quite a writer; one's tongue does not rise to call his works 'literature.' But neither is he a philosopher. He is

5 [Translator's note]: Appropriately, this phrase — '*в вопросительных снегах*' — is untranslatable from the original Russian, as it plays on the phonetics of the Russian term for 'question mark' — '*вопросительный знак*.' The final word of 'question mark (*voprositel'nyi znak*)' bears an assonance with the phrase 'in the snows (*v snegakh*).'

6 [Translator's note]: See note on p. 255 for the untranslatability of the word '*тоска* [*toska*].'

7 [Translator's note]: Yuri Vital'evich Mamleev (b. 11 Dec 1931 — d. 25 Oct 2015): founding member of the esoteric underground group known as the 'Yuzhinskii Circle' (named after Yuzhinskii Lane [Южинский переулок] in Moscow, where members would meet to discuss questions of metaphysics and read their writings

somewhere in between, where artistry spits upon style, and speculation knows nothing of rigor. But is this not the state of all Russian literature? It has always been too smart for *belles-lettres*, but too disheveled for the likes of a philosophical tract… Nothing that falls outside of this category — Nabokov, for example — can be said to be too terribly interesting, too terribly Russian. By definition, the Russian text must possess a certain sloppiness (due to its fulness of feelings and intuitions), confusion, depth, a chuckling laughter [похохатывание][8] that spills over into a fit of weeping, and a special clairvoyance, tinctured with *toska*. The concept flings itself into the elemental roughage and attains a certain abnormal being, citizenship, and place in the unique universe of Russian letters. Of course, it is not just anyone who ends up there — in these letters, the world of our national intellect. Beyond any shadow of a doubt, Mamleev is one of Russia's *litterateurs*.

Unknown Monsters of the 1960s

In his novel *Shatuny*[9], Mamleev formulated a myth from which no one is spared. It is an incantation (chilling in its corporeality) of a

---

to each other); emigrated from the Soviet Union in 1973, making a brief stop in Wien, Austria, before spending nearly a decade (1974–1983) in New York as a professor at Cornell University, and the following decade (1983–1993) in Paris; Though he had already left before Dugin was initiated into the Yuzhinskii Circle in the late 1970s, Mamleev's metaphysical doctrine and 'literary' texts were of fundamental importance to the former's intellectual development; Dugin would finally meet Mamleev upon the latter's return to Russia in 1993; from that year until his death in 2015, Mamleev would explicitly formulate his 'literary' method, terming it 'Metaphysical Realism' and forming a 'club' around it.

8 [Translator's note]: One of the most important motifs in Mamleev's writings is 'chuckling laughter [хохот],' which is associated in his 'literary' system with demonic knowledge and states of transition between the 'here / this side [посюстstation]' and the 'beyond / that side [потустороне].'

9 [Translator's note]: Considered by many to be Mamleev's most fundamentally important work, *Shatuny* tells the fractured stories of Fyodor Sonnov (a 'contemplative killer') and a gallery of other backwards village folk and

remote and guessed-at meaning which has broken through to us and calls us toward something which we are utterly incapable of grasping. In *Shatuny*, neither the images, nor the words (to say nothing of the plot) are of any importance. This is a novel which contains a certain presence that cannot be identified with any one thing. *Something* is buried therein. Something that has nothing to do with novels. It is as though what you hold in your hands is not a book, but an empty space, a black, impish vortex that can suck large objects into itself. *Shatuny* is the secret seed of the 1960s. There was also a hierarchy in the non-comformist underground. The outermost layer was composed of minor officials and figures of the intelligentsia who were of a liberal persuasion, but did not part ways with the system. These people were generally of little interest, feeding as they did on scraps and brown-nosing whomever they could. Farther down were the political *antisovietchiks* (who cleaved both to the left and the right—let us not forget that these were both Westernizers and Slavophiles; for every Sakharov there was a Shafarevich, and for every Bukovskii, an Osipov)[10] and the bohemians of the art scene. These types were outside

urbanite 'metaphysicians,' who all, in one way or another, are consumed by notions of death, parallel worlds, planes of subtle matter, the unknown, the 'beyond,' and—most significantly—the supreme 'I,' around which all other realities and quasi-realities revolve. Written in the early 1960s, during the heyday of the Yuzhinskii Circle, *Shatuny* became a notorious, even dreaded relic of the Moscow underground, which may have been the inspiration, along with the writings of Venedikt Erofeev, for all underground movements (specifically, Moscow Conceptualism) that were to follow in its wake.

10 [Translator's note]: Andrei Dmitrievich Sakharov (b. 21 May 1921 – d. 14 Dec 1989): Soviet physicist; one of the creators of the first Soviet hydrogen bomb; Social figure and political dissident with left-liberal leanings; recipient of the Nobel Prize in 1975.

Igor Rostislavovich Shafarevich (b. 3 Jun 1923 – d. 19 Feb 2017): Soviet and Russian mathematician; longtime professor and correspondent in the Academy of Sciences; right-leaning dissident often wrongly discredited by his enemies as an 'anti-semite' for formulating the phenomenon known as 'Russophobia' (a hatred of Russians both in the liberal West and among domestic parties;

of mainstream society, under observation by the authorities, but were nonetheless in an intermediate state; they read bad samizdat publications and snatched whatever crumbs they could from the next circle deeper from them. In the central circle of the so-called 'schizoids,' Yuri Vital'evich Mamleev himself held court at his apartment on Yuzhinskii Lane, along with a few 'supreme unknowns'—the 'metaphysicals.' It is about these last that the novel *Shatuny* is written. It is a realistic narrative (accompanied by the naïve desire to impart a beauty of style) about that which was an everyday affair for the inhabitants of the innermost circle.

"Pigs vomit when they see me," says Lautréamont's Maldoror. Mamleev's world provoked approximately the same natural reaction on the part of those of the outer circles who approached him unprepared. Legend has it that, during one of Mamleev's readings the 1960s, a lady from the 'outside,' having accidentally traipsed in, acted in accord with the pigs. Her knight-in-shining-armor, a little red-faced engineer who had become enraged, shouted something like the following at Mamleev: "What kind of writer are you?! You're not even worthy of kissing my boots..." At this, Yuri Vital'evich grinned and said, "That's where you're wrong—I am worthy," after which he crawled under the table to defend his honor...

Shafarevich claimed that a considerable contingent of Jews, Russian and otherwise, were responsible for promoting Russophobic ideas, but took care to add the caveat that ethnic Russians were just as capable of being Russophobes).

Vladimir Konstantinovich Bukovskii (b. 30 Dec 1942 – d. 27 Oct 2019): author and publicist known for his dissidence during the Soviet era; authored several books criticizing the Soviet Union and the Russian Federation from a liberal point of view.

Valentin Osipovich Osipov (b. 10 Jul 1932 – d. 11 Dec 2020): Soviet and Russian author, journalist, and publisher; an active publisher throughout the late Soviet period and until his death in Russia, he was associated with a more conservative politics.

If one is to believe the magnificent Russian philosopher Skovoroda[11], then "one must everywhere see double" — "everything is doubled." From the dust of forms, another side reveals itself. If one immerses oneself into this other side, the world of dust itself — the everyday world — will appear in an entirely new light (or a new darkness). *Shatuny* is the development of such a theurgic realism as it applies to our spiritual situation.

Mamleev the 'Criminal'

When I was taken to the Lubyanka[12] in 1983, after the KGB had confiscated Mamleev's archive (which had been entrusted to me by one of the 'supreme unknowns' and, to this day, has never been returned), the following threat of a question was posed to me: "Is there not a social subtext behind Mamleev's literature?" At that time, it seemed to me that there was a subtext, if only a highly peripheral one, since it was practically impossible to live immersed in *Shatuny* and watch Brezhnevian television at the same time. It was some kind of profound death sentence for the system... True, the novel glowed through the cracks, but the already unstable, tongue-tied SOVDEP was a pitiful object for the destructive effects of *Mamleevshchina.*[13] It was necessary to widen one's sights, to think of the foundations of the modern world and, perhaps, of humanity as a whole. This terrible problematic, as it was seen by the 'metaphysicals,' had already taken on universal proporitons...

11 [Translator's note]: Grigorii Savvich Skovoroda (b. 22 Nov/3 Dec 1722 – d. 29 Oct/9 Nov 1794): a philosopher of the Russian Empire (considered by many to have been the first properly Russian philosopher) of Cossack origins.

12 [Translator's note]: The headquarters of what was then the KGB (currently the FSB) on Lubyanka Square in Moscow.

13 [Translator's note]: '*Мамлеевщина*'; in Russian, when the suffix -shchina is appended to a last name, it is a reference to the set of ideas and actions with which that name is (usually notoriously) associated.

Now, *Shatuny* has been published openly and on several occasions as its own standalone book. Mamleev himself will sometimes make an appearance on the television screen with his cat in his lap, serenely waving his hand. He has returned from emigration and become a member of the PEN club[14] — if he had a will to, he could probably sit down with a minister of state… But were I in the shoes of the current authorities, I would ban every single one of this author's works, and I would have even ampler grounds for doing so than the KGB of Brezhnev's 'stagnation.' Just read what is written there:

> Having shoved the young man against a tree, Fyodor dug around in his stomach with a knife, as if to find and kill something there that was still alive, but unknown. Then he laid the murder victim down on God's grass [Божию травку] and dragged him a little out of the way into a glade.

This is on the first page — things only become amplified from here. With great care, we can observe a number of overtones which backhandedly, dramatically distinguish the Mamleevan text from the all too common '*chernukha*.'[15] Behind his visible obscurantism[16], one can

---

14 [Translator's note]: The PEN club is an international organization, founded in 1921 in London, which exists to defend the freedoms and rights of writers all over the world; there are over 100 autonomous chapters of PEN club, corresponding to their respective countries. The Russian chapter of the PEN club was founded in 1989 amid the liberalizing reforms of Perestroika, and came to be one of the premier writers' organizations in the Russian Federation after the Soviet collapse.

15 [Translator's note]: '*Чернуха*.' A cultural phenomenon that reached prevalence during the last years of the Soviet Union; afterward, during the tumult of the 'wild nineties,' it became a ubiquitous feature of everyday life. Derived etymologically from the Russian word for 'black,' *chernukha* is the practice of 'blackening' (in a derogatory sense) or exposing the 'blackness' inherent in Russian reality; in films and novels, this frequently took the form of narratives that depicted people falling into depravity and despair; themes of extreme violence, murder, madness, and prostitution were common.

16 [Translator's note]: Dugin here is using the term 'obscurantism [мракобесие]' — one of the fundamental motifs of Mamleev's textual system. In

clearly detect some kind of hidden freight, a sort of unimaginably important meaning, a chilling verity... One recalls Savinkov, the author and terrorist (famously having penned *Pale Horse*), or Jean Ray, the black fantast and real-life graverobber.

A compelling St. Petersburg *litterateur* by the name of Kushev, in a clever analysis of Dostoevsky titled "730 Steps," demonstrated that Fyodor Mikhailovich himself was the one who murdered the old pawnbroker. It is just as clear that Mamleev is somehow complicit in that which he describes.

But murder is not the most important thing, even though the protagonist of Shatuny, Fyodor Sonnov, is nothing short of a murderer; Mamleev specifies that he is not just any garden-variety murderer, but a *metaphysical* one.

Wanderer in *Nichts*[17]

And now we return to Skovoroda and his bifurcation of things. There is a reason he is considered to be the first true Russian philosopher.

Whom does Fyodor seek to kill?

If there are two sides to every thing, and if the second side can somehow be grasped, then anything belonging to a negative category can transition into the positive. And, likewise, the usual, the ordinary can become doubtful, unproven, problematic. It is this which oppresses all of Mamleev's characters. This is the key to every '*shatun*.'[18] Fyodor

---

Shatuny, this term describes a violent rejection of the rational laws of the secular, modern world. It is worth noting that, though the term has a centuries-long history in the Russian language, it can be interpreted through a vulgar literalist lens to imply some relationship with demons and darkness; it is highly likely that Mamleev is playing on this second potential reading of the word.

17 [Translator's note]: Germ.: 'Nothing.'

18 [Translator's note]: Yet another word for which no readymade English equivalent exists, a '*shatun* [*шатун*]' is a bear that has risen amid its winter hibernation. It is not awake, however; rather, it is in a somnambulant, trance-like state,

Sonnov practically incarnates the deep thought of Skovoroda in the most direct and unsubtle manner: if the life of the soul is greater than that of the body, then the moment of murder becomes strictly gnoseological, a magical point at which something from the beyond appears before one's eyes. Fyodor strives to use the departing soul of every new victim as a tramcar into the beyond, as an elevator which might carry him away to a world that is truer than the airless shades of earth. This is the Russian folk, pregnant with metaphysical revolt, carnally and greedily hungering after *pleroma*. In rending flesh and bone, he is liberating the sacred content within it. In transgressing, he sacrificially smears himself over the horizontal plane, so that the vertical can come. Horrifying and cumbersome, turgid in his thoughts and impossible to encompass around the elbows, he carries his tormenting, burdensome contemplation of the Other [Ином] through the ages.

Fyodor the murderer does not, in fact, murder anyone. He exerts himself in thought, strains to comprehend himself, the thrum of his Russian blood, spellbound in its mission, bewitched in its awakening, betrothed to the final mystery. Fyodor bears witness to that which does not fit inside of him, which presses at all of us from within.

> 'You bring a great joy to people, Fedya,' he thought, remembering Ipatievna's words as 'he wandered up to a bench. Either in the air or in his imagination, the images of his murder victims were carried aloft; they became his guardian angels.

And, truly, it is a 'great joy' that he brings. It is the epiphany of freedom from elsewhere.

---

liable to attack any man or creature that crosses its path. In Mamleev's novel, the word takes on a metaphysical meaning, referring to characters who are neither entirely in the material world, nor entirely in the 'beyond,' but are stumbling ('*shatun*' derives etymologically from the verb '*shatat'sya* [*шататься*]'—'to stumble') about the world in a half-dreaming metaphysical fugue, also liable to maul or maim anyone they can at the slightest disturbance or whim (as in the case of Fyodor Sonnov).

All other folk characters in *Shatuny*—the *Skoptsy*, idiots, holy fools, Klavunya, bound to the raw earth, the auto-cannibal Peten'ka, Lida and Pasha Fomichev, the Russian tantrists—are merely the entourage of the 'metaphysical killer'; they represent a spectrum of not so radical experience which is fueled, however, by a valid impulse. Petya, in eating himself—first his zits and blemishes, and then his own blood and meat—is a particularly expressive figure. Thus is a being pulled into itself, to the other side of things. The pragmatic Hindus call this the 'practice of the turtle.' This act gets closer than any other to the essence of Fyodor, the Wanderer in *Nichts*.

The Russian Metaphysical Elite

Fyodor stands in for the folk. He understands everything concretely. He thinks with his hands, his belly, his body. In *Shatuny*, there is yet another pole—the 'metaphysicals.'

These intellectuals introduce a theoretical basis to the enlivening folk practice of obscurantism [мракобесие]. In this realm, Mamleev has painted his characters in more individualized, recognizable tones. The super-solipsist Izvitskii falls in love with his own 'I' as with an embodied woman, or with something even more fleshly.

We recognize in him the obvious traits of one ingenious poet and mystic. Izvitskii is an aesthetic extremist of the 'I' religion. This is a special esoteric doctrine, according to which one may access the other side of things, endlessly refining one's subjective beginning. One may slip along a strand into a mirrored world by means of a self-obliviating love of the self. It is an operatively magical narcissism, in which the original turns to stone while the aqueous reflection acquires a particular, inexpressibly full life. It is a mode of being within the subaquatic forests.

Anna Barskaya is the alter-ego of one very famous personage in Moscow. Before his unwise departure abroad (what this Russian author — so deep he evokes a squeal — must have forgotten in dull America no one, including the man himself, can say), Yuri Vital'evich referred to her as his 'spiritual daughter.' She was the maddest and most entrancing woman of the schizoid 1960s — the 'Mother of the Russian Revolution.' The wife of one of the greatest non-conformist artists — a man known for having dropped a dose of narcotics so equestrian that all of California's hippies together would have died from it — she attempted to bring the 'metaphysical' to the outermost circles of the underground. Bereft of Mamleev and having lost the tight scale of the 1960s in the later SOVDEP, Anna Barskaya could only comment on the past and tie on some drinks with the artists. Often, in front of her apartment in Fili, the drunken Zverev would be lying on a rug. (It was said that he possessed a piece of paper from some ministry confirming that he was a national treasure and, therefore, was not to be sent to the drunk tank.)

Professor Khristoforov — he who transforms into a 'chicken-corpse [куро-труп] — is Mamleev's satire of those belonging to the 'outer' circles of the underground who had taken an interest in the 'metaphysicals' and had been taken aback by the questions they posed. Having placed a set of despicably comprehensible old books between themselves and the metaphysical reality of Russia, they were reduced to a savagery between the horror of thought and the blessed idiocy and serenity of the Brezhnev era. During Perestroika, they became the premier authority of the intelligentsia. Mamleev's 'chicken-corpse' is the 'architect of Perestroika.'

And, finally, the main character is Anatolii Yur'evich Padov. We clearly find several autobiographical traits in him. He is the intellectual double of the folkish Fyodor and represents the Russian metaphysical elite. This elite, in the course of our history, is as indestructible as our folk, inspired as it is by a strange spirit. Plunged into its own depths, frequently indistinguishable from the click-beetles passing through as they take over the foreground, the elite has existed from century to century—in secret societies, under the vaults of imperial libraries, in radical movements of opposition, at the center of conspiracies, in some province buried in the snow, but most often in Moscow.

This is the true aristocracy. The living prototype of Izvitskii once told me the story of how, in the Lenin Library, he had stumbled upon a most rare and enigmatic tract by the alchemist Sendivogius[19] titled *On Salt*; it contained notes from a nineteenth-century reader (in the old orthography) that read: "Everyone in Russia is a fool. Only I am smart." And there was an addendum which read: "If you read this tract by Sendivogius the son, you will attain the stone." Padov is among the 'smart' ones.

> One day in late fall, as the wind ripped about and swept the leaves, creating voids in space, a sober young man in a worn suit lay in a ditch near a lonely suburban interstate and quietly moaned. This was Anatolii Padov.

Padov moans because of his mind, because of the extreme clarity of the metaphysical problem that has been given to the Russian consciousness without any supplemental instruments: directly, cruelly, and mercifully. "Abyss calls upon abyss."[20] These words in the Psalms have served as the motto of a certain mysterious alchemical order. This is the formula of true thought. The abyss of an indefinite, given, visible world that is unrolled, non-empty, crushing, raises a terrible question in one's consciousness concerning the other side of reality. The other side is not a palatable, primitive, Catholic scheme in which heaven

---

19 [Translator's note]: Michael Sendivogius (1566–1636) was a Polish alchemist, philosopher, and medical doctor who is credited, among other things, with having been among the first to detect oxygen as a discrete substance in the earth's atmosphere.

20 [Translator's note]: Psalm 41:8: "Abyss calls upon abyss, with the voice of your floodgate. All your heights and your waves have passed over me."

and hell are like a *rayok*[21] and the people are like little wheels. Within the all-encompassing Russian scale is a limitless Russia: mysterious, terrifying, native. It consumes man, stretches his consciousness to the extent of its limitless boundaries, and all for the sake of raising a question about the *Other* [*Ином*] — that reverse side which is even greater, stranger, and more mysterious than our sacred country, itself. It is life and death, the 'I' and something more than the 'I,' a depth and a bottomlessness which reduces depth to the shallows. It is a whirlpool of contemplation, a rapture of imperceptible blindness, a darkness of inadmissible intuition.

Here, one starts to howl.

The Girl Who Reads Mamleev

No matter what should happen, or what twist of fate should come, Mamleev and his *Shatuny* are something hidden, beyond the confines of profanation — something meant for only a few. Glancing at my current luxuriant copy, I think back nostalgically on the xeroxed, un-embossed tomes in their green hand-made bindings (which was done to make them inconspicuous to the special services: a naïve trick); In the opening years of the last decade[22], there were no more than fifty copies of Mamleev's works in circulation. Of course, it wouldn't be the worst thing if those dense inhabitants of the 'outer circles,' having accidentally bought a copy of Mamleev's novel out of ignorance, were to behave as the pigs of Lautréamont which I have referenced above. I am afraid that we can no longer expect such a pure reaction. Those cynical contemporary readers, who have been acclimated to things

21 [Translator's note]: The '*Rayok* [*Раёк*]' (literally: 'little heaven') was a Russian form of folk theater, delivered in an enclosed cart with magnifying lenses on one end where viewers looked in; inside of the enclosure, the 'rayoshnik [*раёшник*],' or storyteller, would twist a scroll depicting painted scenes, narrating them in an often humorous versified prose.

22 [Translator's note]: Dugin is referring here to the early 1980s in the Soviet Union.

cosmetically similar to Mamleev's work — flat and unfounded *chernukha*, unjustified and unrealistic American horror films, the synopses of idiotic crime serials — are most likely to simply ignore *Shatuny*. The crass modern Russian, having lost his late-Soviet virginity and watched his fill of thrillers and Stephen King film adaptations, has finally lost his last delicacy; this delicacy is the minimum prerequisite needed to experience revulsion, shock, horror…

Particularly egregious are the post-modernists, who have copied certain recognizable, intimately Mamleevan motifs, but diluted with kitsch, the desire to unnerve, insipid self-advertisement, uninhibited arrivisme, and a total insensitivity to the elemental character of the nation — both in its 'Sonnov-esque' and 'Padov-esque' aspects. It is clear that no one can stop the bastards. But one would like to.

One would also like for a young woman's gentle eye, as in the painting of the ingenious Pyatnitskii, to sparkle with a strange luminescence above the pages of a samizdat copy of *Shatuny*; in silence, in secret, in a sweet, deep, mad, Muscovian, weeping, crisis-stricken Russian underground where an eternal winter of flesh nurtures the paradisiac garden of a spirit exhausted by metaphysics.

A Girl Reading Mamleev. Thusly was Vladimir Pyatnitskii's painting named. At one time, whole delegations of metaphysicians were ushered in to look at it. It seemed to be an incredible paradox: it was Mamleev, and they were reading him! It was his book. The world had been inverted.

And now they have published it officially. Anyone who wishes to read it can do so. The world is not inverted. One feels a great, great sorrow because of this…

And not only because of this.

A Parallel Motherland

(Nikolai Kliuev)

I come of folk initiation,
Upon my flesh the mark is great,
The brow of nature takes oblation
I lay my blessings on its plate.[23]

— N. Kliuev
The prophet of transcendental Rus'

He considered himself not merely to be a poet, but a prophet. For Kliuev, this was not a metaphor. The fact is, within that Russian milieu of sects from which he emerged, there existed an official religious institute of 'prophets' and 'charismatics' which, in the eyes of the sect members, originated with the teachers of '*didaskalia*[24],' those 'charismatic teachers' who practiced glossolalia and other methods of direct contact with the world of the Divine; they expressed these states with the help of a special symbolic code. Speaking cautiously, it is possible that this institute was not a direct continuation of early Christian trends, but rather their latest artistic restitution. Though how can one know for sure whether these original Christian practices were not

---

23 [Translator's note]: "Я — посвящённый от народа, / На мне великая печать, / И на чело своё природа / Мою приняла благодать."

24 [Translator's note]: In early Christianity, the Greek term '*Didaskalia* [*Διδασκαλία*]' — derived from '*didasko* [*διδάσκω*],' to teach or instruct — was used in reference to the early sermonizers of both the Church and its apocryphal fellow-travelers.

preserved by the ancient Montanites[25], followed by the Messalians[26], the Bogomilists[27], and the Russian Strigol'niki[28], carried along on the secret road of initiatic organizations?

In principle, we encounter this exact relationship to poetry in all traditional societies. The poets in those times were a subset of the priestly caste, since the rhythm of language, the foundations of rhyme, and meter were considered to be the most sacred expressions of cosmic harmony. The very process of composing verses was seen as the poet's possession by a spirit or an angel, i.e., a sort of super-human entity which expressed its message in a ritualistic language. Even in the twentieth century, in the peasant milieu of the exiled Old Believers from which Kliuev emerged, we come across the very same ancient element. Kliuev himself was perfectly aware of the archaism of his worldview. After becoming familiar with 'secular,' profane culture, he did not reject this orientation toward the world but came even more to value and comprehend it. The poet would often compare the realities and states he described to those experienced by shamanic practitioners ("At a eucharist of shamans / I drank of blood and fire"[29]).

---

25 [Translator's note]: Montanism is a movement of early Christianity which derives its name from its founder, Montanus, a formerly pagan Phrygian priest. It was derided as heresy by the church for promoting novel prophetic revelations.

26 [Translator's note]: The Messalians were a dominant sect in Mesopotamia, known for their belief that the essence of the Holy Trinity is perceptible by the carnal senses; they did not recognize the need to submit to the regimentation of the Church and ecclesiastical rule, and exalted prayer as the ultimate divine act.

27 [Translator's note]: The Bogomilists were a gnostic, dualist sect of Christianity that was prevalent during the reign of the Bulgarian Tsar Peter I in the 10th century; they eschewed the church, did not use the cross as a symbol, and considered their bodies to be the temples of God.

28 [Translator's note]: The Strigol'niki were a heavily persecuted sect which appeared in Pskov around the middle of the 14th century; they completely disregarded the hierarchy of the Orthodox church, calling for a type of laymen's sermon that would bypass the religious ceremonies and rites then prevalent.

29 [Translator's note]: "За евхаристией шаманов / Я отпил крови и огня."

In addition, Kliuev constantly emphasizes the kinship of space between the mysterious Holy Rus' which he praises and the sacred civilizations of antiquity—Egypt, India, Israel, Ethiopia, etc. ("It is not without reason that Mecca is imagined as a grey hut in Olonetsk...").

As with all prophets, Kliuev immersed himself in a special state, a special world where the past, present, and future occur simultaneously, where the near and the far change places, where the dead and the living coexist in an Eternal Present and hold profound conversations—with myths, with a nature animated by the penetrative rays of Spirit, with familiar and unfamiliar objects. For the ancient Hebrews, this reality was called 'Merkabah' or 'the land of the wheel.' The prophets of the Old Testament (Ezekiel, Isaiah, Eli, Elijah, etc.) were immersed in this land and described it in their writings. In Islam, this world is called 'Hurqalya' or 'alam-al-mital,' the 'space of imagination'; it is a certain intermediate instantiation between the world of people and the world of the gods. One can find analogues of this prophetic cult in practically all traditions and religions.

In this light, the interpretation of Kliuev's poetry is more of a theological than literary problem. From metaphors, parables, hyperbole, images, rhymes, cultural allusions, and expressive devices, we move over to a completely different register, were we concern ourselves with esoteric doctrines and mystical terms adequate to the reality under discussion.

Russian Dualism

Kliuev's global worldview results from a principle dualism which defines the Russian soul and the paradox in which it has found itself over the past three centuries, since the schism. This dualism can be condensed as the conflict in Rus' between a pair of opposing points of departure—the actual and the potential, the extant and the possible, the manifest and the latent, the diurnal and the nocturnal. Starting from the fatal council of 1666 to 1667, Rus' was divided into two versions of itself.

One was the Rus' of officialdom which formally rejected its 'eschatological,' 'soteriological' function as Moscow, the Third Rome; this Rus' criticized the Stoglav assembly and the doctrine of Russia's national chosenness as the last Orthodox people; it parted ways with Holy Rus' and shunned antiquity as an epoch of ignorance, darkness, prejudice, and 'decay.' This was the Russia of the Romanovs, Saint-Petersburg, Peter the Great, the German settlement, French governors, the resort spa of Baden-Baden, and the European Enlightenment. This was the Russia that strove to be secular. It possessed an external, formally super-conformist kind of Orthodoxy, subject to the Synod (Hesychasm was viewed by this 'Orthodoxy' as an almost Athonite sect as early as in the clerical-historical works of the nineteenth century; and this is despite the canonization of St. Gregory Palamas). This was a desacralized monarchy which sought to emulate the Protestant north of Europe.

The second Russia is Ancient Rus'. But it is an underground Rus', one made of dreams and premonitions that lives in a parallel world, hidden and gleaming like the invisible city of Kitezh.[30] But this is not simply a legend, a sort of nostalgia, a cast of mind, or a cultural mirage. It has its own structure: Orthodox sectarianism, the bottom rungs of society, Cossack villages, political non-conformism. Even during the official persecution of the Old Believers under Nikolai I, when it was

30 [Translator's note]: The invisible city of Kitezh is a mythological place, said to have been built by Prince Georgii Vsevolodovich in the northern part of the Nizhegorodskii Oblast', near the village of Vladmirskii, on the banks of Lake Svetloyar. During the Mongol invasion of Rus', legend has it that the city of Kitezh spontaneously sank beneath the waters of the lake in order to preserve itself from destruction; it is said that only the pure of heart can find their way to Kitezh and that it will reemerge on the day of Final Judgment. Kitezh has, in some cases, been referred to as the 'Russian Atlantis.'

not safe for sectarians and Old Believers to publicly proclaim their faith, a third (just think of this proportion — a third!) of all Russian people professed their belonging to cults that, from the viewpoint of official Orthodoxy, were heretical; among these cults were those of the Old Believers, the Skoptsy, and the Khlysty. This Second Rus' was in spiritual and social opposition to secular Russia. This Rus' raved with its national alternative, analyzing the existent order in apocalyptic tones and longing passionately for the Second Coming.

Without a union with this Second Rus', without its active support, the October Revolution would never have happened. Kliuev's path, his semantics and the architecture of his prophecies, was the essence of this dramatic moment in the secret history of Russia. For Kliuev, the Revolution was an eschatological return to the pre-Petrine period: it is from here that we receive the striking formula: Soviet Rus'. This combination of words says all one need hear — it is precisely Rus' and not 'Russia.' Kliuev makes his sentiments explicit:

> In Lenin is the Kerzhenets spirit,
> His decrees bear the hegumen's shout.
> As if, in the Pomor Responses,
> He seeks the sources of destruction.[31]

In themselves, the *Pomor Responses* were a codex of norms for Orthodoxy in Holy Rus' after it had become a fugitive. This is a

---

31 [Translator's note]: "Есть в Ленине керженский дух, / Игуменский окрик в декретах. / Как будто истоки разрух / Он ищет в Поморских ответах." The Kerzhenets is a tributary to the Volga located in the Nizhegorodskii Oblast' which was associated with Old Believer settlements during their flight from persecution in the eighteenth century; The *Pomor Responses* [*Поморские ответы*] (known, in its extended title, as *Responses of the Wilderness Dwellers to the Hieromonk Neophyte* [*Ответы пустынножителей на вопросы иеромонаха Неофита*]) was a lengthy, polemical text written collectively by a group of Old Believer hermits in response to a text composed of a set of critical questions of faith written by hieromonk Neophyte.

testament for people of the underground. Revolution is an uprising. Lenin was the figure to continue the task of Father Avvakum and the Denisov brothers. He voiced not a doubtful tone, but rather a radical affirmation; more than this — he bore prophetic witness to something.

Naturally, the peasant poet's prophesying cannot be reduced to mere Bolshevism. Though one can never these incredibly important words of his: "The Red killer is more holy than the chalice."[32] This identification of the Bolsheviks with something sacred is not complete. But it was not pure folly, either (as anti-communist literary scholars believe). Everything relating to this matter is more subtle than that. The Second Rus' manifested itself in the Revolution. It brought itself to people's attention. But it was not entirely incarnated — somehow, it hung in the balance between obscurity and visibility. It was a sort of 'halfway Kitezh.' This is Platonov's 'Chevengur.'[33] *The victory is plain to see, but death has not vanished.* The enemy is annihilated, but the Second Coming is delayed.

The search for this gap — Kliuev's comprehension, his scrupulous investigation — constitutes the main problem in attaining the meaning of Russia's twentieth century. Kliuev — Russia's prophet — must help us in our attempt.

Personal Drama Has the Character of Witnessing

That which 'did not fit' into Bolshevism with regard to Kliuev's personal creative path is highly transparent. On the official level, the Bolsheviks saw their own approach as a sequential step forward and, consequently,

32 [Translator's note]: "Убийца красный святей потира".

33 [Translator's note]: Dugin, here, is referring to Andrei Platonov's 1928 novel *Chevengur* [*Чевенгур*] in which a proletariat composed of remote wanderers and outcasts comes to a village bearing the titular name in the midst of the Russian Civil War and creates a spontaneous, faltering utopia that is as apocalyptic and nightmarish as it is sacred and timeless; however, the fate of this utopia is quite grim at the novel's conclusion.

justified the previous 'bourgeois' stage as a necessary advancement from feudalism. Of course, in Engels's and Marx's evaluation, we see an unambiguous sympathy for capitalism over the feudal age. But on the level of rational Marxist discourse, this fact is not sufficiently clarified, and one even finds that the linear transitivity of the historical process is upheld; this idea goes against the grain of all traditional worldviews, based on the idea of cyclical time. Kliuev was in total solidarity with the Bolsheviks in every matter pertaining to the destruction of the 'Romanovs' Russia.' For the Old Believers, this was a 'casting down of the anti-Christ's throne.' The three-fingered cross [троеперстие] was seen as a desacralization and a profound perversion of Christianity. Therefore, the Bolsheviks' anti-church activities were often seen in a completely positive light. But when it came to modernization, the kolkhozes, and the naked aggression leveled against monuments to the distant past, the Old Believers arrived at their first point of divergence. At first, this may have seemed a misunderstanding, a distortion of the 'main line.' But, gradually, tragedy made itself all the more apparent. Once this had occurred, Kliuev wrote: "It is my opinion that the politics of industrialization is destroying the foundation and the beauty of folk life..."

Persecutions of Kliuev and peasant poets altogether (Esenin, Vasil'ev, Klychkov, Karpov, etc.) was not just a single episode. For they first time, they revealed the double meaning of Soviet socialism, the indeterminacy of its spiritual mission, the strangeness of its cyclical and metaphysical import.

It is possible that the secular bureaucratism prevalent under the Romanovs had silently entered Soviet life disguised in a new form. If this is the case, it did so through the specialists, the fellow-travelers, and, later, the NEPmen.[34] Later, the purely Soviet, Marxist bureaucracy

34 [Translator's note]: During the period of the New Economic Policy (NEP) in the Soviet Union (1921–1927), 'NEPman' was a pejorative term used to describe

made its appearance; for this latter group, the word 'revolution' had become a scarecrow or a nominal tribute to the past. The dark spirit of the 1666 council had found its way into Soviet Rus' and had made it into Soviet Russia.

The tragedy of Kliuev bears witness to that subtlest of processes which, in the remote 1920s, initiated the causes that would eventually lead to the collapse of Moscow in our 1990s.

The Ontology of Russian Nationalism

What are the fundamental lines of force in Kliuev's message? How does he describe the mysterious Rus'?

One immediately finds that Kliuev very simply identifies Rus' with 'prophetic reality.' 'Rus',' for him, is the same thing as 'Merkaba' for the Old Testament prophets, the 'Hurqalya' of the Islamic esoterics, the 'green land' of the Celtic vates, 'Hyperborea' for the ancient Greeks, or the 'Svetadvipa' of the Vedic Brahmins. This is why Kliuev refers to 'Rus'' as the 'White India,' i.e., the magical progenitor land, the sacred *Urheimat* of humanity. This is the source of his natural universalism; as long as there is 'Rus''—the 'folk [избяной] paradise,' the 'originary *Urheimat*,' and the 'archetype of the New Jerusalem'—then there is a kindred land for all peoples, for all races, and for all languages. Kliuev's nationalism (as with all the peasant poets, and maybe all representatives of the Second Rus' in general) is transcendent. It is for this reason that he describes blacks, Tatars, and Egyptians with such affection and ethnic familiarity... One recalls his famous "black Egorii on a white horse."

With the immediacy of a true prophet (who must, according to the norms of tradition, must be 'uneducated,' i.e., spontaneously and naturally selected by the spirit), Kliuev clearly speaks what the entire

merchants who took advantage of the limited entrepreneurial capitalism temporarily permitted by the state.

intelligentsia of the Silver Age were able to foresee, but were incapable of concisely formulating. Rus' is not a country, and the Russians are not a people in the usual sense of these concepts. Rus' is paradise and Russians are angels. But this luminescent reality is somewhat superimposed on its negative image, or rather shows through it. Everything is doubled. However, the real, immanent Russia is almost marked with a special sign. It is the bearer of *toska*, an all-consuming feeling of deprivation, loss. Even in the features of secular Russia, one can discern the image of the transcendent Rus' — not directly, but through its negation. Deprivation is obliquely indicative of fullness; the piercing feeling of loss reminds us of that which has been lost.

This is the ontological foundation of Russian nationalism. Heidegger (the theoretician of German ontological nationalism) almost perfectly incapsulates this idea in the following formula: "Unhappiness alludes to happiness, happiness calls up the sacred, the sacred hastens the Divine, the Divine reveals God."[35]

"The broom shrub moans about paradise."[36] Besides the striking poetic completeness of this line from Kliuev's poetry, one can practically discover a presentiment of the formula composed by the ingenious German philosopher. "The broom shrub moans about paradise" only in Russia. Only a Russian can perceive its message. And, so that there is no misinterpretation, it moans not about something remote which would need to be sough somewhere outside, but rather about something internal that is of the greatest intimacy and proximity.

This idea forms the basis for Kliuev's 'transcendentalization' of village life among the Old Believers and sectarians.

---

35 In German, we find even clearer etymological relationships between these words: *Unheil — Heil — Heilige — Göttliche — Gott.*

36 [Translator's note]: In Russian, there is a clear assonance at play in this phrase: "Ракитник рыдает о рае."

In the center of Kliuev's Holy Rus', there is not a cathedral, but a peasant hut. Externally, this is a typical anti-clerical motif. But it contains an even deeper aspect. The cathedral stood apart as a distinct cult device during relatively later stages of history. At one time, in the blessed times of the Golden Age, there were no differences between a cathedral and a standard domicile of any kind. Thus should it be in the 'age to come.' The Book of Revelation unmistakably speaks of how, in the 'New Jerusalem,' which will descend to earth at the moment of the Second Coming, "there will be no church." God will be with and in all. Only the Tree of Life will stand at the center of the Heavenly City.

Kliuev's Rus' is a combination of that which is most ancient (from the Golden Age) and that which is prophesied to come (the New Jerusalem). The peasant hut is sacred in itself. It, too, is a cathedral. ("The hut is shrine of the earth, / With its baked mystery and its paradise"[37]). In Kliuev's prophetic, supertemporal Rus', all objects are transformed (in the Orthodox liturgical, hesychastic meaning of this concept); they ascend to their luminous archetypes. In this way, the oven, windows, plants, flowers, and trees become sacred—especially the oven. This last plays the most important role in Kliuev's poetic universe.

Kliuev reinstates the fullness of the 'esotericism of the Oven.' In the traditional world, the hearth and the oven fulfilled the role of the domestic altar. This was the altar of the Feminine Divinity, the Greek Hestia, the Roman Vesta, etc. Public cults provided a zone of dominance for primarily masculine gods, protectors of social and religious systems relating to patriarchy. But in the private living space, where the woman had been driven from the beginning of the patriarchy, the most ancient matriarchal attributes—sacred cult objects used in veneration of the Great Mother—were preserved intact. These are the accoutrements of the Fiery Maiden, the White Lady. This is the Mother

37 [Translator's note]: "Изба—святилище земли, С запечной тайною и раем."

of the Sabbath, the Great Mother to whom Kliuev dedicated his great poem, the full text of which, alas, has been lost to us.

This is a crucial moment. The matriarchy, as Bachofen wondrously and convincingly demonstrated with the term *Mutterrecht*, preceded the patriarchy and corresponded to the Golden Age for the Indo-Europeans.

Later, the goddesses were replaced with masculine gods, but the traces of the most ancient ur-religion have been preserved in folklore, mythology, daily life, and so on. This is where we derive the plots of many Russian tales — Marya-Tsarevna, Tsarevna the Frog, etc. This is also where we get the demonized image of the Great Mother in the form of Baba-Yaga and, sometimes, in her daughters — the Amazon Yagishny. Corresponding precisely to this archaic cycle are the tales of Ivan the Fool's travels on his oven. In mythology and the collective unconscious, the Woman is identified symbolically with the Oven.

And in the world of Kliuev's "Russian Merkabah," his "paradisiacal peasant hut," the Mother reigns. His own mother (whom he loved madly) was fused with the Great Mother, and the latter, in turn, was fused with Rus', the sacred land. This is a surprisingly archaic motif which was especially developed in certain Old Believer interpretations, which prophesied 'salvation through the wife.' The 'Mothers of God [богородицы]' of the Khlysty are also associated with this theme.

It is remarkable that we also find the worship of divine femininity in early Christianity, at a time when women could become priests and the foundations of the dogma of the Mother of God [богородица] was being laid. In the framework of pre-Christian, Judaic religion, based as it was on strictly patriarchal principles, one can find no analogue; in relation to women, Christianity had made a return to long-forgotten original principles of Indo-European spirituality. As in the case of the 'charismatics,' Russian sectarianism returned, when it came to the question of sex, to early-Christian norms and esoteric doctrines which had faded or had even been outright excised by the official imperial church.

The Second Rus', with Kliuev as its prophet, is undoubtedly matriarchal. In Kliuev's verses, we almost never find mention of the Father. Rarely, we find grandfathers. But the grandfather is always described with emphatically white tones — he is completely grey, clothed in white, etc. The grandfather is not a man so much as a sexless or super-sexual saint; he is pure, sinless, and perhaps 'castrated [оскопленный].'

The Oven is the altar of the peasant hut, the symbol of Rus' herself, or of the Great Mother. The microcosm of the hut contains the macrocosm of the planet. Objects of sacred peasant life are equally as great as nations and civilizations.

From this Oven wind sacred paths, which go out and then return to their source. Its fire is the fire of the Old Believers' self-immolations, which received the blessing of Father Avvakum. This archpriest wrote of the flames just as Kliuev did, associating them with the End of the World and with the ontology of Russian nationalism: "the poor Russian sons, even if stupid, are glad: they awaited their tormentor; they braved the fires in their leagues for Christ the Son of God — of light." Or, as we read in a different place:

> Those dear Russian sons, it isn't so! — they crawl into the flames, but do not abandon the good faith…

This is no fire of utopia. It is terrible, but salvific. And therefore Kliuev, himself, is indifferent to the sufferings and blood instigated by the Revolution. There is no absolute death. In this question, the prophet (residing in a super-terrestrial world) has no doubt whatsoever. He possesses extreme confirmations of this fact. But the soul, nonetheless, can be cursed and lost. This fate is one hundred times more horrific than death, torment, tortures, suffering…

True horror begins when the peasant prophet clearly understands that the Bolsheviks threaten the Oven itself, the ancient spirit, the Russian peasant, the sacred land.

Kliuev interprets the modernization of the village as a monstrous spiritual catastrophe.

Kluiev's Great Mother is a crudely visible, authentically prophetic image of Woman-Russia-Sophia which, simultaneously, stood as the obsessive idea of the entire mystically oriented Russian intelligentsia of the time. From Soloviev to Blok, this holds true. But only with Kliuev does this theme take an operative, magical, esoteric character while, for the intelligentsia, everything stays on the level of dimly grasped intuitions or theoretical schemes. In both cases, the source is undoubtedly the same — the very fabric of Kitezh, of the Second Rus', striving to break forth from its narrow confinement of dreams and, in a moment of eschatological triumph, to explode into material reality. But none of the 'educated' people ever think to praise the crude peasant's Oven, doing so with sacred seriousness and prophetic ceremony. Irony and humor were always utterly alien concepts for Kliuev; he was ever grim in verse and in life.

Great Midnight

Kliuev lived in poverty, and his last years were spent in wild destitution. At the very end of his life, the Chekists shot him while he was in exile for having been the 'chief ideologue of the kulaks.' This was not simply a mistake, a misunderstanding, or unjustified pig-headedness. There was no way in which this poet-prophet's path could have been a sweet one. *La suplice est sur* (Rimbaud).[38] Poverty is an indispensable condition for the truth of one's revelations. The lightning of clairvoyance cannot strike the well-fed. Moreover, everyday delights such as

38 [Translator's note]: Fr.: "Torture is a certainty."

food, sex, and comfort are much more overwhelmingly felt when they are absent. Poverty is wealth. The poor man consumes all surrounding being, he is nourished by the elements, the luminescent energies of the parallel Motherland.

Kliuev had a clear vision of his poverty in old age and his eventual violent death ("And now that fate has gifted our heads to the executioner…"; "But the willow senses the running steps of the elk and the gunshot… Either into the stars or into the crown of the head"[39]). For the prophet, this is no surprise. It is the normality of things. In fact, he had nothing to do with the kulaks. He was much closer to the lower and middle strata in the villages. He had a wrathful hatred of capitalism, as did any Russian born from the Second Rus'. It was a different matter, though, when the Soviet reforms of the villages ignored their sacrality and archaism, introducing the utterly foreign ideas of rationality, pragmatism, and mechanization to the traditional provinces. Instead of a commune, organically woven with sacred knots — a brotherhood of the Great Mother — the Marxists artificially created a technical collective. This was better than Stolypin's[40] ideas of farming, but it was still not that which was prescribed in Kliuev's eschatological visions.

Kliuev was a peasant socialist, a National Bolshevik. In his fate, his path, his verse, and his prophesies, there are no contradictions. He stood unambiguously for Revolution as a true descendant of Stenka Razin, Father Avvakum, and Yemelyan Pugachev. But that which

39 [Translator's note]: "И теперь когда головы наши подарила судьба палачу…"; "Но тальник чует бег сохатый и выстрел… В звёзды или в темя."

40 [Translator's note]: Petr Arkad'evich Stolypin (b. 14 April 1862 — d. 5 (18) September 1911) was the chairman of the Council of Ministers under Nikolai II who, among many various fields of governmental reform, launched a program to reform the agrarian state of affairs which had spiraled out of control in the aftermath of the serfs' liberation under Alexander II. These reforms were widely considered to be a failure, but some historians have attributed this to the decade of tumult beginning in 1914 with the First World War and ending in 1922 with the conclusion of the Russian Civil War.

occurred later contained a major flaw. If suffering and incidental, individual injustices had been all that was at stake, the poet who had grown up on skeptical practitioners would not have been so aggrieved. But things were much more serious. A dark spirit, well-known to the Old Believers from the times of Nikon, had peeked out from behind the revolutionary mask of the Soviets. It was a gloomy visage: the First Russia, the usual moribund light in the eyes of the voivodes, gendarmes, and now the commissars.

> We are standing at the very brink of midnight. Or, maybe, we are not quite there yet. There is always that 'not quite.'[41]

Heidegger wrote these words. His relationship with National-Socialism is structurally reminiscent of that between Kliuev (and the Russian National Bolsheviks in general) with the Soviet authorities. What began as enthusiasm, engagement, and solidarity ended in doubts, suspicions, and alienation. Heidegger never publicly disavowed Nazism. People have famously referred to this as 'Heidegger's silence.' Kliuev never disavowed the Revolution, either. If the good manifested itself as the not-so-good, it would scarcely follow that the bad turned out to be not-so-bad. The Russia of St. Petersburg was an anomaly in the sacred history of our God-bearing people. There is no doubt of this. Whoever thinks otherwise can go to Baden-Baden and Gallipoli to become taxi drivers, princes, and gigolos. *Vite, mesdames et messieurs*![42]

The worldview of the prophet of Holy Rus' is profound and complex. But one must not attempt to grasp and decipher him in light of contemporary, one-dimensional cliches in politics and literature; rather, one should do so from that reality for whose name he stood and to which he gave expression.

---

41 [Translator's note]: Dugin's rendering: "Мы стоим вплотную к точке полуночи. А может быть, ещё нет. Всегда это 'ещё нет'."

42 [Translator's note]: Fr.: "Quickly, ladies and gentlemen!"

The Second Rus' is still with us here, even today. It is just as nourished with that gentle, terrifying, cruel, and holy *toska*. It calls on us with the very same colors of that Russian fall which steals one's breath; it triumphs with the very same grandeur of the white Russian winter; it frightens with the very same luxury of the Russian summer and the green wrath of the Russian spring. Holy Rus' is pounding in our hearts. This is not the official, urban, civilized Russia of the current minute. It is not 'Soviet,' but it is also not 'democratic' Russia. It is Kliuev's Rus'.

Soiled Russian faces… the Tatars… Space… An unfocused gaze… Blurred thoughts… And there is only this terrible, inexplicable pull… Through our bodies and through the sound of our native speech…

Our White India.

Our Paradise.

The Two-Headed Seagull

(Mark Zakharov)

A 'Strange' Play

Chekhov himself used to say that *The Seagull* was a 'strange play.' Even for him, to say nothing of the public, it came as something unexpected, new, unusual. Why? We shall attempt to understand.

Immediately, we notice that there are two generally accepted traditions when it comes to productions of the play. The first is classical. No matter how many successful or unsuccessful versions we've seen, one thing is obvious: there is no strangeness in these renditions. All of the characters and scenes are played in the usual Chekhovian style; the actresses give hysterical voice to their female delusions and the actors portray an eternal flitting between the impotence of the intelligentsia and the existential indifference of the local residents. We find this situation in every other Chekhov play. All that ever changes is the degree to which the acting convinces us and the purely technical habits of the director.

One may say practically the same thing when it comes to modernist productions of *The Seagull* (such the productions of the Theater on the Taganka). Here, we find the same even canvas of uniform dramaturgy; it is just that the hysteria takes a harsher form and comes with a Freudian cache — the members of the intelligentsia come off as unambiguous psychopaths. To put it more succinctly, if, in the first tradition, everything is dissolved in 'classicism,' then in the second tradition, everything is dissolved in 'modernism.' In both cases, there is a special, orthodox reading of Chekhov, but both camps are equally ignorant of the fact that this play was something extraordinary for the author and, therefore, problematic and distinct from the rest of his dramatic works. Therefore, the same difficulties appeared during the very first productions of *The Seagull.* At that time, the public still separated the performances they beheld into those which were comprehensible and those which were not. Back then, the theater had yet to acquire the quality of kitsch that one now derives from 'a night at the theater,' viewed as a pure spectacle without any attention paid to the conceptual side of events.

The rarest version of *The Seagull*, in which a certain strangeness is indeed to be found, is that produced by Mark Zakharov. In this version, one plainly encounters a rejection both of classicism and modernism; furthermore, we find here a rejection of the usual interpretation of Chekhov. And so, it is Zakharov's production which lays bare those aspects of the play which are often submerged in other treatments.

An Inexpressive Pair from a Different Play

There is one moment in Zakharov's production which leaps out at the viewer — this moment furnishes the 'strangeness' of the rendition.

This results from the dramatic difference in performance between two groups of actors: on one hand, we have the pair of Nina Zarechnaya (Aleksandra Zakharova) and Konstantin Treplev (Dmitrii Pevtsov); on the other hand, we have the remaining actors, with the pair of Arkadina (Inna Churikova) and Trigorina (Oleg Yankovskii) occupying the most important position in this latter group. At first glance, it may seem that the quality of acting is what gives the play its strange atmosphere, the experience and correspondences between characters. But, soon, one begins to understand that this is not so, that things are not that simple. A clear boundary passes not along lines of age or profession, but along the conceptual differences of the two separate worlds in Chekhov's own work.

It is entirely obvious that the thread of Arkadina and Trigorin (along with the rest of their party) remains within the confines of what is traditionally the 'Chekhovian': alienation, impotence in the intelligentsia, the existential dead-end of the human character, lost in a world bereft of meaning and direction. Their formula is impotence in the face of being, a complete collapse of hopes and wishes, the negative result of a deliberately failed path in life. It is the eternal lot of an intelligentsia suspended somewhere between the elites' exultation of pure being and the commoners' resignation. This theme can be adequately realized in both the classical and modernist modes, since the total disorientation and dead-end of our intelligentsia are extremely well-known. Of course, talented actors and a brilliant director can demonstrate this fact simply and protrusively, convincingly and comprehensively. In pseudo-classical Soviet renditions of *The Seagull*, this lack of escape was veiled under a disingenuous subtext: "this was the situation before the revolution, but now things are different." But, beginning in the 1960s, it was clear even to the uninitiated that there was 'nothing up the sleeves [фига в кармане]' of the intelligentsia. And as the intelligentsia was, so it remains. Churikova and Yankovskii are not only actors in The Seagull, they do not only demonstrate with their appearance, gestures, and mannerisms, under Zakharov's direction, that the theme of the intelligentsia's obliviousness is still relevant for Russia today. The 'New Man' is impossible. The old, decrepit characters, incapable both of igniting and being snuffed out, wander through the last few centuries of our history like insistent revenants who cannot be driven out by exorcisms of any kind.

It should be said that Zakharov casts this plot line in an extremely sympathetic manner—without any outmoded classicism, but also without the pseudo-contemporary banalities of the modernists. His play simultaneously captures both poles, both conservatism and freshness. But this is not the most important thing…

The point is that the Zarechnaya-Treplev thread is jarringly contrasted with that of the remaining characters. It falls, tumbles out, and hangs in the air. If Churikova and Yankovskii act out what is, convincingly, corporeally, then Zakharova and Pevtsov persist in some kind of vacuum. Who are they? Why are they? What are they doing? What has made them so distraught? We have absolutely nothing to go on.

Everyone—the viewer, the actors, and, apparently, the director as well—is left in the dark.

Could it really be that the unusual, super-passionate febrility of this play (of such antiquity for Chekhov) flows from nothing more than the banal amours between a young mediocrity and a hysterical two-bit actress, lacking brains, talent, and even the most elemental caution in life? If this were so, there would be nothing 'strange' about the play; to the contrary, this would be a straightforward spectacle of failure with a completely unfounded and unjustified pathos accompanied by an idiotic, vulgar symbolism.

The ambiguity of what Zarechnaya-Zakharova and Treplev-Pevtsov portray under the direction of Mark Zakharov bears witness to the fact that they are guessing at the special meaning of the 'Seagull,' at a certain meta-plot that departs from the framework of the strictly 'Chekhovian.' It is as though they remain suspended without gravity in some glass cupola that has been taken beyond the bounds of the play's basic course. They are pale, soiled, unreliable. They resemble the characters of that unwieldy play through which, in the beginning of *The Seagull*, the unlucky Treplev attempts to protest his mother and her notable beau.

Stop. This is a decadent play within a play... This is where the 'strangeness' comes in!

It is precisely thanks to this multiplicity that the characters' stability is shattered. The pair Zarechnaya-Treplev belongs to a different play; he is an author, and she is the main, sole actress. This is why they do not fit into the general 'scene [тусовка]' of Churikova, Yankovskii, Bronevoi and the rest of the hopeless company of intelligentsia. Their play belongs to a *different* order; set against the background of different sizeable, weighty images the play is rubbed away, becoming semi-transparent, subtle, and ceasing to belong to majoritarian reality. Zakharov recognizes this and draws a dramatic line in the sand; he sets up an apartheid between the young and the decorated and this is how he manages, most truly, to pose the metaphysical problem of *The Seagull*. This subtle director, eschewing the mainstream, is a sensitive person capable of separating the comprehensible from the incomprehensible. This is exceptional in our times. These days, everyone seems to think they understand everything. Instead of questions, they immediately find an answer (which, as a rule, is the dumbest one available).

Zakharov, bravely risking a desecration of the spectacle, prefers honesty.

The Scarecrow Achamoth[43]

Treplev's decadent little play is, naturally, not to be mistaken for a product of Chekhov's own dramatic principles. This is rather a depiction of Dmitrii Merezhkovsky's ideas.[44] The play's themes have practically nothing to do with the rest of Chekhov's characters. It concerns a cold, intellectual gnostic theory, perceptible only for transcendentally oriented minds. The Seagull of Zarechnaya is no primitive symbol of a romantic maiden in full bloom [в соку]. This is a character who represents profound esoteric doctrines — Sophia or Achamoth, Divine Wisdom, the gnostic Woman from above who has fallen into the material world of inescapable quantity, entropy, decay. Nina Zarechnaya, acting in Treplev's play, declares as much very directly. The Seagull is an image of the Soul, the Light from beyond, the first principle of ontology.

Treplev is a gnostic, a metaphysical adept of the Absolute who hastens his gaze toward what is beyond the visible; he is occupied with the soteriological mystery of the World Soul. He is called forth to free this soul from the shackles of disintegration, to restore its divine dignity, and, through this heroic act, to transform and renew the Universe. Between Treplev and this Soul are magical threads of initiatic, sacred Love. They have secretly, and before the appointed time, been endowed with the *Merciful Crown of the Tantra* (Jean Parvulesco).

---

43 [Translator's note]: 'Achamoth' (Greek: ''Αχαμώθ,' Hebrew: 'המכח [Chokhmah]') is a sacrificial being in many gnostic systems of thought, closely associated with the divine Sophia, who has fallen to the plane of the demiurge and, having created man, has also imbued him with a divine spark.

44 [Translator's note]: Dmitrii Merezhkovsky (b. 2 (14) August 1865 — d. 9 December 1941) was one of the key figures of the Russian 'Silver Age' and counted among the 'decadent' Symbolists; he was married to Zinaida Gippius (an equally important figure in this milieu) and was deeply embroiled in mystical, gnostic, and metaphysical ideas; he was a founder of the 'Religious-Philosophical' society, whose members held mystical councils relating to the future, religion, and society.

This pair has absolutely no place in Chekhov's oeuvre. One gets the impression that he has simply transposed them from the pages of other authors, along with their dialogues, glances, and gestures; but, in doing so, he has inserted his traditional anthropological context (which groans over gooseberries and sips on cordials). Zarechnaya and Treplev do not belong in this frame and look ridiculous in it, even to Chekhov himself.

What ought we say about the directors?

"I am the Seagull," says Nina Zarechnaya. This is not a tasteless metaphor for a lady emerging from puberty, but a strict gnostic thesis: "I am Achamoth, the transcendent Angel of extreme consciousness, a winged feminine archon of the luminous æons.[45] I am not a person. I am a fiery thought of the Absolute."

Treplev himself performs as a scribe having received a revelation, as the paladin of a non-intuitive, willful truth, as a Hermeticist, an alchemist, an adept of a secret Order, a Templar, or an Albigensian. For him, the phrase "I am a seagull" contains a clear metaphysical meaning, and it is precisely this meaning which determines his actions in the course of the plot. Treplev and Zarechnaya are unreliable and inscrutable only because their logic is so subtle that it gets lost behind the facets of the remaining characters' greasy existentialism, which presses out in every direction. It is for this reason that Zarechnaya appears to be the clueless one.

The Seagull is two plays, a dialogue between two authors and two visions of the world. On one hand we find the cold abstractions of Merezhkovskii's elitist soteriology while, on the other hand, we find the strikingly believable intelligentsia existentialism which falls strictly under Chekhov's purview.

---

45 [Translator's note]: In many gnostic systems, 'archons' are divine principles that have emanated from the Most High God (the invisible source of all things, the 'unmoved mover,' etc.); 'æons' are beings that have emanated from the 'archons.'

For the chosen, it is a gnostic myth and, for the profane, it is savory pessimistic realism. The subtle semi-fleshless marginal figures of Zarechnaya and Treplev are posited against the fleshly souls of Arkadina and Trigorin. It is curious that Zakharov is able to interpret Chekhov so perceptively. Nina Zarechnaya is a poor actress while Arkadina is an eminent one; Treplev is a mediocre romantic while Trigorin is a venerable writer. Zakharov forces his daughter Aleksandra to play the bad actress 'poorly,' and he transforms Pevtsov, the superman of post-Perestroika warriors, into a feeble mama's boy (as one looks upon these actors, it seems as though they are this way in real life). And, to opposite effect, Churikova and Yankovskii, having also fulfilled dozens of roles in which they have exhausted all of their strength in portraying existential hopelessness, seem this time in *The Seagull* to have surpassed themselves. The super-convincing, expansive, impressive villains which they play have come off as fantastically real.

Thanks to the dissonance present in the actors' play, Zakharov has unobtrusively and delicately commented on Chekhov himself, has deciphered his premise and accented the highway of his plot.

In the purely intellectual terminology of Merezhkovskii-esque authors, the entire problem is formulated in a dry and deliberately anti-egalitarian manner, provoking with its enigmas: "Achamoth fell into the clutches of dead matter." In The *Seagull*, Chekhov illustrates this thesis by his own artistic means. In the beginning is the static superposition of the first play (that of Zarechnaya and Treplev, performing as active figures) upon the main second play (whose primary figures are Arkadina and Trigorin—who begin as spectators). Nina Zarechnaya declares the gnostic myth. "The Seagull of the Soul at one time had descended into the spheres of a frigid hell." Later on, this script is manifested in practice. Treplev the Gnostic, along with his astral Fine Lady, cross from the sphere of pathetic esoteric declarations into immediate action. But this is also a realization of the following declaration: "Achamoth fell into the clutches of dead matter." The fact that these subtle young people are treated as a laughingstock by a gang of cynical bison in no way undermines their fundamental message. On the contrary, everything that occurs from this point in the play confirms the total rectitude of the beginning decadent. Zarechnaya falls into the clutches of the brute Trigorin, while Treplev hopelessly guards his gnostic symbol of faith, gradually identifying in the eyes of the profane with the second-order figure of the failed author (because he does not recant either his doctrine or his Love).

In the final scenes, we see that the divine woman, the early Nina, becomes an unlucky terrestrial woman who, in relief against the lucky terrestrial Arkadina, has utterly lost her game; however, the spirit of the latter is nothing more than a miscarriage. The battered Treplev also steels himself against the pendulum-lipped Trigorin; the supreme gnostic, set against the background of the inveterate writer, whose word-things are enchanted through their materiality (though, in light of this, their wielder is an extremely false and limited person), appears as an eternal dilettante. It is as if the characters of the first play have irreversibly transitioned into the second one, relinquishing themselves and giving up. In the weak mumblings of Zarechnaya — "I'm a seagull… no, that's not right. I'm an actress." — we see the final splashes of a memory of that which has never been.

We don't get a Churikova from a Zakharova, nor do we get a Yankovskii from a Pevtsov.

And nonetheless, it is not Chekhov with his constant unhappy ending and his convicted belief in the impossibility of renewal which is proven right, but precisely Merezhkovskii.

The Soul-Seagull has fallen. The intelligentsia is the spirit of hell. The frigidity of these social types, so habitually known to us, is the law of entropy (only Bronevoi makes allusive guesses at something else, and this may only be because he has played Müller). They are victorious and incredibly strong. But, as a result, they do not remain positive figures and do not dare to pretend to the construction of norms. A bastard will always be a bastard. This is being in the form of drama, of deprivation, of a descent into hell. But if there is suffering, that means there is a sufferer. And if there is a sufferer, that means there is a higher meaning which can reveal the gnostic arrangement of reality to us.

It is absolutely inescapable that the pale ghosts of Decadence experience a descent into the intelligentsia, into the disoriented, vampiric existentialism of the two-faced, godless provincials. Only then will the myth of Achamoth acquire its tragic meaning. The chaff will be separated from the wheat. The sufferer will display his ontological distinction from that which causes pain.

The scarecrow of the seagull coming out of the chest is not a stamp of anthropological pessimism, but the password to a secret order.

After the 'black work' comes the 'white work.' After *The Seagull I*, which has been so learnedly produced by Zakharov, there follows *The Seagull II*.

The Seagull II

Zakharov has stated the problem. The choice of actors, scenography, decoration, *gestuelles*, etc. — all of these have been tried and tested. Everything that can have been extracted from Chekhov has been. The 'strangeness' of both the play and the production are plain to see.

If everything ends with *The Seagull I*, then we might end the praise with it. But, with the prospect of *The Seagull II*, we should add a few additional comments. "Achamoth fell" is the first thesis of gnoticism. But, in that moment when it seems to everyone (including her) that all has been lost, she will rise again. "And the archons of the æons rejoiced and exclaimed: 'The Pistis Sophia is no more!'" The savior comes at the Midnight of the World, when everyone has forgotten to think of the sun and no longer even knows the meaning of darkness, since darkness seems synonymous with All. Chekhov's (and Zakharov's) first thesis is beautifully illustrated. Now the second thesis awaits its hour.

This is the hour of Revolution.

The 418 Masks of the Subject

(Sergei Kuriokhin)

> 72. There is no longer any room For us in this world where people's hearts have been coarsened like iron or the cement of a dead cathedral.
> 72. The crueler and wilder they become, the greater shall be their tortures and the more completely death shall grind them to dust.
>
> — Louis Cattiaux
> (*The Message Rediscovered*, Book XXII)

Two Postmodernisms

Postmodernism is not something strictly fixed, once and for all given and described. It should only be spoken of as a progressively greater awareness of the degree to which value systems and artistic methods, characteristic of the 'modern' epoch, have been exhausted. Postmodernism unilaterally negates modernism in an attempt to overcome it; but when it comes to the question of a new, alternative affirmation, this unilateral approach immediately collapses. Some postmodernists adhere entirely to the spirit of the 'new age,' seeing in the postmodern only a new (if unique) stage in an uninterrupted development of culture. But there are other carriers of the postmodern impulse who understand postmodernism to be the end of a whole period of civilization connected with the notion of a 'new age'; they see it as a suddenly discovered possibility of appealing (in a novel form) to those realities, upon whose negation civilization is based. The postmodern — in its sarcasm and ridicule of the avant-garde's serious reflexivity — establishes the possibility of a spiritual rehabilitation of the 'pre-modern,' i.e., the world of tradition with its culture, axiology, ethics, and so on. One can define this second variant of postmodernism as a version of Conservative Revolution.

It goes without saying that Sergei Kuriokhin belongs to this conservative-revolutionary tendency.

Pop-Mechanical 'Totalitarianism'

In his group 'Pop-Mechanics,' Kuriokhin combines practically every form of art — ballet, music, melodramatic declamations, the circus, theater, marionettes, erotic performances, painting, decorative art, and cinema. This fusion of diverse elements passes through his creative act with an obsessiveness that underlines the deliberation and profound groundedness of this method for the artist who employs it. It would seem that we are colliding with real chaos, with a totally syncretic mixture of all styles and genres, in a strange semi-comic, semi-mad presentation (in response to which it is unclear whether one should erupt in joyful applause and when one should grimace). Initially, such a mixture might appear as pure avant-gardism, or a step *forward* in relation to the delineation of genres, even in their modernist context, where the most radical attempts to transcend the boundaries of style are nonetheless subject to the internal logic inherent to a given sphere of the arts. For Kuriokhin — especially in his sweeping, totalizing, mass-oriented 'Pop-Mechanics — one is impressed by his striving to combine precisely *everything*, altogether as one. In accord with the degree to which 'Pop-Mechanics' has developed, not only has the quantity of elements that are used in the show mercilessly expanded, but also the number of genres and disciplines… The latest stages of Kuriokhin's creativity (having left many with the feeling of having come to a dead-end) are characterized by the gradual inclusion of (naturally, extremist) politics, ritual, and scientific experimentation into the mix. The units of performance are broadened from individuals to collectives, from objects to modes, from styles to genres, from personalities to disciplines.

It is in this will to totalize art that we find an explanation for Sergei's most recent fascinations. Those who have failed to comprehend the meaning of this orientation have clearly never paid any serious thought to the essence of what he was doing before. If they had, they would not perceive his appeal to politics, geopolitics, and esotericism as something strange and 'scandalous.' His expansion beyond the bounds of genre, his particular postmodernist 'imperialism' in art have logically trickled over into the sphere of the political, where they operate at especially large scales — in history, social discourses, and the masses. It is only natural that the Eurasian scope in politics would attract this 'imperialist' of art; his hastening to the limits of art has intuitively transformed into a fascination with political radicalism...

The Skomorokhs — Priests of the Pre-Modern

If, as regards the 'modern,' the mixture of all forms of art (and, more broadly, culture) into something unified is indeed new and unprecedented, then in larger historical context things appear rather different. The fact is that orthodox modes of modern art — music, ballet, painting, theater, literature, etc. — have only relatively recently (beginning with the Renaissance) been formed into inviolable, independent genres; and they have only just crystallized with the advent of the 'new age.' It turns out that 'modern' or contemporary art received its specification of genre (from which it longs to escape in postmodernism) beginning strictly from the moment of its transition from traditional society to the society of the profane.

But what came before?

It is with this question that we encounter a certain interesting detail. All modern art within Christian (and post-Christian) civilization has developed from a certain general complex in which the inheritance of the pre-Christian (or 'pagan) religious cult was concentrated. In Europe, this was the culture of the *Trouvères* or the *Minnesängers*[46]; in Russia (much more openly) it was the Skomorokhs [*скоморохи*] who fulfilled this function.

Christianity, and strict Orthodoxy especially, criticizes all extra-religious art (particularly music, dancing, secular songs, and theatrical performances), rightfully considering it as a continuation of pre-Christian sacrality. Having later on become little more than secular entertainments, musical instruments, dance, poetry, and theater were originally the instruments of magical and theurgic rituals. Special categories of priests and prophets were responsible for these activities (we recall the Celtic 'bards' and 'Vates,' who had previously belonged to the priestly hierarchy of the Druids). Up to now, certain primitive peoples, for whom shamanism was commonplace, have preserved a similar relationship to art. Singing, dancing, performances, and recitations of myths were exclusively a shamanic matter; in this respect, the shaman is the central and fundamental figure in the sphere of what, in profane civilization, has come to be known as 'art.' Even in the Old Testament, we see reference to such practices. For example, Elijah (the pupil of Eli) begins to prophesy when he hears a specially summoned musician play on the psaltery. But, in the very first society, the prophet and the musician were indistinct from each other — they were one and

46 [Translator's note]: The 'Trouvères' or 'Troubadours' (France) and the 'Minnesänger' (Germany and Austria) were traveling singers, instrumentalists, and poets — comparable to bards — who traveled the land and performed in through a multitude of media; the Trouvères oftentimes depicted hedonistic or Bacchic themes, while the Minnesängers took up a more pious, moralized poetics, frequently singing in worship of the 'Magnificent Lady.'

the same person. And so, in the circles of the Essenes, the concepts of a 'prophetic school' and a 'musical school' were synonymous.

Christianity removed the pre-Christian theurgic cults from social reality, but these did not disappear in their entirety; they became the domain of certain quite marginal groups who managed, despite everything, to safeguard the origins of a most ancient knowledge, the principles of occult practices. In Rus', the premier brotherhood of this sort, after the mages [волхвов] and their traditions had been uprooted, were the 'Skomorokhs'—the 'happy people.'

In their notions, the Skomorokhs synthetically incarnated everything that would later come to be called 'art' in its modern understanding. They played musical instruments, danced, put on theatrical productions, exposited their legends in verse form, trained wild beasts. But these elements of their activity were united through a common sacred knowledge of the cosmological order; their jokes (even the crudest ones) were a means of expounding a symbolic doctrine; their dances served as magical theurgic gestures; in their songs, they conveyed initiatic secrets which Christian doctrine had discarded. In doing so, they and their spectators would fall into a trance state, i.e., a special spiritual state (of pleasure) in which the presence of a world beyond was directly sensed. It is unsurprising that the use of alcohol and other psychotropic substances (possibly mushrooms) played such an important role in these proceedings.

It is none other than the Skomorokhs (and their tradition) which, for Russia, serves as an autochthonous synthesis of that which would later become art and its genres. Their dances became the ballet, their singing became opera, their instrumental music became the symphony, their telling of myth became literature, their taming of wild animals became the circus. It is important to note that the sacred side of the Skomorokh doctrine was also circumscribed within a specialized sphere—the occult sciences.

Because the secularization of Russian society occurred under the direct influence of the West, it was the products resulting from the disintegration of *Western* esoteric organizations (which, no less, were direct analogues to the Russian Skomorokhs) which bore the greatest influence on the emergence of secular culture. This led to a certain cultural dualism which remains to this day: the highest classes in Russian society treat the fractured aftermath of the unified complex of European 'Trouvères' or 'jugglers' as real 'culture,' while, in many respects, the folk masses follow the autochthonous 'Skomorokh' understanding of 'entertainment' or 'merrymaking' (this is particularly related to the cult significance of 'drunkenness,' but that is its own topic).

Malevolent Laughter

Sergei Kuriokhin's constant activity was not just an artistic search, but a determined and thorough recreation of that organic unity which preceded the classical, modern, and hypermodern periods (rock music, the avant-garde, etc.). It is shocking how consistently he was able to reproduce the foundational traits of the traditional, 'pre-cultural,' 'archaic' priesthood. By training a classical musician, pianist, and composer (in fact, one of the finest Russian Jazz composers), he was compelled from the very beginning to include wild animals in his concerts. This was no fleeting *épatage*, but an insistent confidence in the meaningfulness of displaying animals onstage as a self-signifying, deeply symbolic act. In tradition, beasts are calendric and cosmological symbols. Each beastly image is a letter in a sacred book, intelligible to priests. Kuriokhin's rabbits, lions, and cows (as with the bears, dogs, and she-goats of the Russian Skomorokhs) are essentially totemic and astronomical signs. Like the Roman augurs (those who told the future based on the flight patterns of birds), Kuriokhin is particularly interested in ornithological symbols — take, for example, his Sparrows'

Oratory (at one time, he was inspired to erect a grand monument to sparrows).

The theme of theater and performance has constantly emerged in the work of 'Pop-Mechanics.' These concerts have, on occasion, turned into full-on plays. The external absurdity of their plots (as with the Skomorokhs) obscures a deeper symbolic layer. This can also explain Kuriokhin's externally strange (and almost comic) television appearances (such as his famous declaration that Lenin was not a man, but rather a fly agaric mushroom); beneath the apparent nonsense, esoteric doctrines are hidden. Once certain texts by Terrance MacKenna (*The Food of the Gods*—about the influence of psychedelic mushrooms on the human psyche and their links to the sacred cults of ancient peoples) had been published in Russian, the idea that "Lenin was a mushroom" cannot have seemed all that delirious. The magical undercurrent of Bolshevism is becoming all the more apparent; Kuriokhin is merely outpacing the purely scientific studies of the matter, clothing the gravest doctrines in grotesque forms which provoke laughter.

Speaking of laughter: the phenomenon of laughter itself is not as obvious and simplistic as it seems. Tradition states that this act, common within human society, is in fact a form of contact with the beyond; in certain magical practices, spirits are summoned with the aid of laughter (compare this with the ban of laughter and smiling in many ascetic practices, and with the ritual character of laughter in medieval societies, an example of which would be alchemical, occult, operative-magical 'message' of Rabelais).

The laughter which Kuriokhin has evoked is strange and ambiguous. Whoever believes himself to understand the meaning of Kuriokhin's smile errs more greatly than he who admits to being mystified. There is something primal in this laughter, extremely grave. In principle, the Skomorokhs themselves often stood out in history as persons with a double significance. In embodying the archetype of the 'newcomer [пришельца],' the 'strange [иного],' and the 'alien [чужого],' the Skomorokhs provoked, simultaneously, interest and repulsion (and even horror). In a sense, they were messengers from 'the other side.'

There exists the opinion that, over the years, 'Pop-Mechanics' has become steadily darker, transitioning from its 'effulgent humor' to a 'malicious obscurantism.' In truth, Kuriokhin's original project has only clarified itself. Having become more comprehensible through the fulness of its realization, it has begun to frighten its onlookers.

The Dissolution of Personality

A plethora of celebrities have taken part in 'Pop-Mechanics'—musicians, singers, actors, artists, poets, and public figures. But they have all become, after a fashion, mannequins in Sergei Kuriokhin's strange production, taking on (in his consciousness) a special, functional occult meaning that is entirely removed from the status which they themselves hold. The light of some unique reality, of an undefined being, has begun to filter through them all… This is not the personality of the director, the organizer and manipulator of such a strange chaos, but something other—a 'magical presence,' the blurred but quite malign of 'someone else.' Kuriokhin himself once spoke, smiling, of the future birth in the cosmic midst of a 'new being' who must immediately take up a physiological covering. And, in this, we once again detect the notes of an archaic theurgy, the willful manifestation (in a quotidian context) of a terrible reality lying beyond our own…

The word 'Skomorokh' comes from the word for 'mask.' In the most recent iteration of 'Pop-Mechanics' (October 1995), all of the participants wore masks. For Kuriokhin, everything is becoming a mask, a strange carnival, a menacing whirlpool in which personality is dissolved, an unremarkable reality in which all expectations are deceived without exception. The Person is disappearing…

But let us recall the etymology of the word '*persona*'—in Greek tragedies, this word referred precisely to the 'masks' donned by the actors. Guénon emphasizes the initiatic meaning of the ancient theater—the alternation of masks on the face of one and the same actor illustrates the idea the individuum is not a thing in itself, a completed and absolute reality. Rather, it is merely a game played among the highest spiritual forces, a temporary image woven from crude elements which, at any moment, is prepared to dissolve. And behind all of this—coldly and immovably—stands the divine Presence, the eternal 'I.' Drawn into the maelstrom of absurd situations which lack any self-sufficient meaning, into a certain cosmic 'Pop-Mechanics,' the eternal 'I' forgets its nature and begins to identify with its mask. The sacred theater is called to remind it of the great folly inherent in such an act, to remind it that only the terrible Presence is of any importance and that people are nothing more than the shadows of objects in the beyond. Pop-Mechanics—like the *rayok* of the Skomorokhs—is a model of the world, a 'remake' of the archaic shrine.

418

Sergei Kuriokhin's vital project is ambitious to the highest degree. Pop-Mechanics must take its totalization to the uttermost conclusion. Beyond the modern, the features of a *new reality* are being traced all the more clearly. Art as it was in the time of 'modernity' has been exhausted. The culture, philosophy, and politics of modernity have been exhausted along with it... Modern man has come to fateful boundary (for him). The apocalyptic motifs of our current civilization have come almost to resemble advertisements for their obviousness.

And, from beyond the boundaries of this gloom, rays that are temporarily invisible have begun to break through. We are nearing the new æon, the new world, the new man.

The people with a 'soft' psychology see that which is to come in tones of infantile optimism — this is the logic of the new age, ecology, Zen Buddhism — leftovers from the hippies of yore. Kuriokhin is much more attuned to the apocalyptic shades of Aleister Crowley. The Age of the Crowned and Conquering Infant, of the discovery of runes, of the cosmic revolt of the Superman. "The Slaves Shall Serve."

The renewal of archaic sacrality, at once the most novel and most ancient synthetic super-art, is an important moment in the eschatological drama, of the 'storm of the equinox.'

In his *Book of the Law*, Crowley declared that only he who knows the meaning of the number 418 will pass on into the new æon, in which an era of authentic postmodernism — without any moaning compromise — shall arrive.

The latest 'Pop-Mechanics' was carried out under the sign of 418. This was effectively a Crowleyan performance, illustrating the end of the Æon of Osiris.

Something intimates that we shall soon find ourselves surrounded by strange signs.

The storm of the equinox.

Sergei Kuriokin's 'Pop-Mechanics' has played a particular role in the coming of the new æon.

My Name Is Axe

(Dostoevsky and the Metaphysics of Saint Petersburg)

The Writer Who Wrote Russia

Fyodor Mikhailovich Dostoevsky is Russia's principal writer. All of Russian culture and thought converges on him as if on a magical point. Everything preceding him foretold his arrival; everything after him flows from him. Without a doubt, he is Russia's greatest national genius.

The legacy of Dostoevsky is massive. But nearly all scholars agree that his novel *Crime and Punishment* is of central importance. If Dostoevsky is Russia's chief author, then *Crime and Punishment* is the chief book in Russian literature, the foundational text of Russian history.[47] As a result, there is not and cannot be anything accidental or arbitrary in it. This book must contain a certain secret hieroglyph in which Russia's entire faith is concentrated. To decipher this hieroglyph is to know the unknowable Russian Mystery.

The Third Capital — The Third Rus'

The action of the novel takes place in Saint Petersburg. It goes without saying that this fact is of symbolic importance. What is the sacred function of Saint Petersburg in Russian history? Once we have understood that, we can approach Dostoevsky's system of coordinates.

Saint Petersburg attains a sacred meaning only when compared to Moscow. Both capitals are associated with a special cyclical logic, a symbolic thread.

Russia has had three capitals in total. The first was Kiev—the capital of a national, ethnically homogeneous state belonging to the periphery of the Byzantine Empire. This northern limitrophic education did not play a terribly important civilizational or sacred role. It was a typical state of Aryan barbarians. Kiev is the capital of ethnic Rus'.

The second capital—Moscow—is of far greater importance. Moscow gained its special significance after the fall of Constantinople, when Rus' remained the last Orthodox Kingdom, the final Orthodox

47 We immediately note that many surmises of this article were influenced by a work of great interest: Vladislav Kushev's 730 Steps. In this text, the author formulates a paradigm of Crime and Punishment.

Empire. This is the origin of the phrase: "Moscow is the Third Rome." In Orthodox tradition, the concept of Kingdom takes on an eschatological role: it is that state which recognizes the fulness of truth in the Orthodox Church and which, in accordance with tradition, serves as a bastion against the arrival of the 'Son of Perdition'—the 'Anti-Christ.' The Orthodox state, constitutionally recognizing the truth of Orthodoxy and the dominion of the Patriarch, acts as 'katekhon,' the 'withholder' (from the apostle Paul's second epistle to the Thessalonians). The introduction of a Patriarch to Rus' became possible only once Byzantium had fallen as a kingdom; and, as a result, the Patriarch of Constantinople was stripped of his eschatological importance, which was concentrated not only in the hierarchy of the Orthodox Church, but in the Empire which recognized the authority of this hierarchy. It is this set of circumstances which endows Moscow with a theological and eschatological meaning—Muscovian Rus'. The fall of Byzantium, from the apocalyptic perspective of Orthodoxy, signified the rise of the age of 'apostasy,' widespread 'defection.' Moscow became the Third Rome for only a short time in order to delay the arrival of the anti-Christ, the moment in which his arrival becomes a universal phenomenon. Moscow is the capital of an essentially new state. Not a national one, but a soteriological, eschatological, apocalyptic one. Muscovian Rus', with its patriarch and Orthodox tsar' is a Rus' entirely distinct from that centered in Kiev. This is no longer the periphery of an Empire, but the last bastion of salvation, an Ark, a landing site that has been purified in preparation for the descent of the New Jerusalem. "There will not be a fourth."

Saint Petersburg is the capital of the Rus' which comes after the Third Rome, which is to say that this capital does not and cannot exist. "The Fourth Rome shall not be." Saint Petersburg affirms the Third Russia in quality, structure, and meaning. This is no longer a national state, a soteriological ark. It is a strange, gigantic chimera, a nation post mortem, a people living and developing within a system of coordinates beyond the bounds of history. Piter is the city of '*Nav*' [*нави*][48]' of the other side. This is why we find such assonance in the name for the city's main river, Neva, and in '*Nav*'.' It is the city of moonlight, water, strange buildings that are foreign to the rhythm of history, national and religious aesthetics. The Petersburg period of Russia contains the third meaning of Her fate. This is the time of particular Russians who lie beyond the ark. The last who made it onto the ark of the Third Rome were the Old Believers, who underwent a baptism of fire in their flaming huts.

Dostoevsky is a writer of Petersburg. Without Petersburg, he cannot be comprehended. But Petersburg, without Dostoevsky, would itself be nothing more than a virtual idea. Dostoevsky animated and actualized this mysterious city, baring its meaning (things, after all, only exist when their meaning shows forth through them).

Russian literature first appears only in Petersburg. The Kiev period was a time of epics and ancient tales. The Muscovian period was one of soteriology and national theology. It is Petersburg which brings literature to Russia — a desacralized remainder of unadulterated national thought, an exalted trace of that which had departed. Literature is a hull, a cosmetic sheen of sidereal waves, moaning over the inescapability of the vacuum. Dostoevsky was so profoundly able to heed this call of the void that the departed, erased, and forgotten is in some sense resurrected in his heroic spiritual creation.

---

48 [Translator's note]: '*Nav*' [*навь*]' is a cosmological category in Slavic paganism which refers to the chthonic realm — a veritable alternative universe to that of the visible, waking world (known as '*Yav*' [*явь*]') inhabited by humans. '*Nav*',' however, is opposed to the realm of '*Prav*' [*правь*]' which is the heavenly realm — the world where the gods of light dwell. In this distinction, '*Nav*" is also a dwelling of gods, but it is an underworld, and these gods are representatives of darkness. Altogether, the three realms — *Nav*', *Yav*', and *Prav*' — are considered to represent three fundamental states of being.

Dostoevsky is more than literature. He is also theology and epic. Therefore, his Petersburg recovers meaning. He makes a constant appeal to the Third Rome.

He gazes, torturously and unflaggingly, into the sources of the nation.

The last name of the main character in *Crime and Punishment* is Raskol'nikov. This is an unambiguous allusion to the idea of 'schism.'[49] Raskol'nikov is a man of the Third Rome who has been cast into the underworld [навий] of Saint Petersburg. He is a suffering soul which has awoken, according to a strange logic, after a self-immolation in the damp labyrinth of the Petersburg streets with their yellow walls, wet pavement, and gloomy, blue-grey heavens.

Capital

The plot of *Crime and Punishment* is a structural analogue of Karl Marx's *Capital.* It is a prophecy of the coming Russian revolution. At the same time, it is an outline for a new theology—the theology of abandonment by God, which would become the central philosophical problem of the twentieth century. This can be referred to as the 'theology of Petersburg,' underworld [навьими] thought. It is the intellectualism of ghosts.

The fabula of the novel is extremely simple. The student Raskol'nikov is deeply stricken by the revelation that social reality is evil. This is that unprecedented feeling so characteristic to certain gnostic, eschatological doctrines. The potassium cyanide of civilization. Degeneration and shame flourish in that place where organic ties, spiritual meaning, and anagogic spirals of hierarchy ascending unencumbered to the heavens are lost. This is a recognition of reality's desacralization. The loss of the

49 [Translator's note]: The Russian word for 'schism' is *raskol* [*раскол*].

Third Rome is unbearable. One feels horror in this encounter with the universal element of the anti-Christ, with Petersburg.

Raskol'nikov is entirely correct in his interpretation of the symbolic pole of evil—perverted femininity (Kali); usurious capital, condemned by religion, equates the living with the non-living and creates monsters; the result is the putrefaction and degradation of the world. This symbolism is ubiquitous in the novel—the old money-lending woman, this Baba-Yaga[50] of the modern world, Lady Winter, Death, the murderer. From her filthy corner, she weaves the web of Saint Petersburg, sending Luzhins, Svidrigailovs, Marmeladovs, yard keepers, the 'black brothers,' and the secret agents of capitalist sin out along its black streets. The threads of hell entangle taverns and brothels, dens of poverty and stammering, unlit flights of stairs and soiled gateways. Thanks to her old woman's charms, Sophia, the Lord's Wisdom, is transformed into the pitiful Sonechka with her yellow ticket. The center of the wheel that is the evil of Saint Petersburg has been found. Rodion Raskol'nikov carries out a form of ontological reconnaissance. Of course, Raskol'nikov is a communist. However, he is closer to the Social Revolutionaries than to the populists. He moves along the trajectory of his contemporary social discourse. He knows many languages and may easily have gotten acquainted with Marx's *Manifesto*, and even with *Capital*. The opening of the *Communist Manifesto* is of great importance: "A spectre is haunting Europe." This is not a metaphor, but a precise description of that special mode of existence which appears after the desacralization of society and the 'death of God.' From here on out, we are in a world of ghosts, apparitions, chimeras, hallucinations, and other phenomena of the infernal

50 [Translator's note]: Baba-Yaga is a common witch-like figure in Slavic mythology and folklore. Often, she is portrayed as a negative character, though she is sometimes helpful to the hero in certain tales.

[навьих] planes.[51] For Russia, this implies a 'journey from Moscow to Saint Petersburg,' an incarnation in the city on the Neva, the ghost city. This incarnation can never be complete.

The spectre of communism makes all of reality into something ghostly. Settling into the consciousness of a student in search of the lost Word, it casts him into a torrent of distorted apparitions: here, an old lecher drags a drunken youth behind him, there, Marmeladov is reduced to weeping after squandering his beloved's last shawl on drink, elsewhere, the demonic Svidrigailov, the messenger of cobwebbed eternity, watched over by the old money-lending woman, creeps up to Rodion's innocent sister. But is this a delusion? The ghost, having taken control of one's consciousness, actually cures it of its forgetfulness. The reality that is thereby revealed is horrific, intolerable, but true. Is the knowledge of evil itself evil? Is the observation of the world's illusoriness itself illusion? Is it madness to comprehend the fact that humanity does not live in accordance with logic? The spectre of

---

51 In his *German Ideology*, Max Stirner wrote: "*Mensch, es spukt in deinem Kopfe*!" This can approximately be translated as "Man, your head is obsessed with ghosts!" Father Seraphim gave us a relatively precise translation of the German verb *spuken*, derived from *der Spuk* (ghost) — an analogue of the French '*hanter*' and the English 'to haunt' — in the ancient Slavonic verb '*stuzhat*' [*стужать*],' which amounts to the German *spuken* — 'to be overwhelmed by an impure force, possessed, troubled by invisible beings.' As Jacques Derrida demonstrated in his *Hamlet and Hecuba* (1956), there is a similarity between Shakespeare's drama and Marx's *Manifesto*. In both cases, everything begins with a spectre, the expectation of its appearance. Derrida accurately notes that the "moment of the spectre does not belong to the usual version of time." In other words, time in the world of spectres has no commonality with the time which exists in the world of men. This bears a direct relation to the essence of Saint Petersburg, the ghost city which lives outside of the sacred time of Russian history, in a sort of subtle dream, an astral inebriation. This is Svidrigailov's ghostly eternity. This is the urban version of the 'Flying Dutchman,' its lamps, chandeliers, and candles; its Enlightenment is nothing other than St. Elmo's Fire, the fictive illuminations of a swamp's quasi-existence. It is the haunted city [*стужалый город*], *la ville hantée*... A place of madness, illness, mania, perversion, shame, and... illumination.

Marxism, narcotic of revelations, is a gnostic call to revolt against an evil demiurge... The bloody pain of the wounds it causes are fresher and more penetrative than a hall, brimming with sunlight, filled with decorous, twirling pairs.

In murdering the old woman, Raskol'nikov completes a paradigmatic gesture, realizes his Task, which is archetypically akin to Praxis as Marxism understands it. The Task of Rodion Raskol'nikov is an act of Russian Revolution, the résumé of all social-democratic, populist, and Bolshevik texts. This is the fundamental gesture of Russian history, which only unfolded after Dostoevsky's time while yet having been prepared long before him in the mysterious, primal knots of the national fate. Our entire history is divided into two parts — that which precedes Raskol'nikov's murder of the old money-lending woman and that which follows. But as a ghostly, super-temporal moment, this act throws its ripples back and forth in time. It reveals itself in the peasant uprisings, in heresies, in the revolts of Pugachev and Razin, in the schism of the Church, in the Time of Troubles, in the elemental depths, the complexities, the many planes, saturated with the metaphysics of the Russian Murder which has extended from the depths of the first Slavic tribes to the Red Terror and the GULAG. Every hand ever raised above the skull of its victim was moved by a passionate, dark, and profound rupture. It was taking part in the Common Task[52], and the philosophy thereof. The Murder of Death constitutes the hastening of the Resurrection of the Dead.

We Russians are a god-bearing people. Therefore, our every manifestation — high and low, noble and terrifying — is illumined by a meaning that comes from elsewhere, by the rays of a different City,

52 [Translator's note]: Dugin is referring to Nikolai Fyodorov's 'Common Task,' which is, generally speaking, the resurrection of all previous human generations from the matter of their disintegrated bodies, the abolition of death itself, and the cosmicization of humanity (which implies the transformation of planet Earth into a spaceship that can traverse the cosmos).

cleansed by a transcendent moisture. Good and Evil are combined into an excess of grace, flowing one into the other, and suddenly that which is dark illuminates, while that which is white becomes the pitch-black night of hell. We are as unknowable as the Absolute. We are an apophatic nation. Even our Crime is incommensurably greater than the good deeds of others.

Thou Shalt Not "Not Kill"

Between the middle of the nineteenth and the beginning of the twentieth century, the Russian consciousness was strangely obsessed with coming to a proper interpretation of the Old Testament commandment "thou shalt not kill." It was discussed as if it were the essence of Christianity. The ideas of our theologists, progressives, terrorists (particularly in the delirium of Boris Savinkov), the humanists, the revolutionaries, and the conservatives constantly returned to it. This theme, and the arguments surrounding it, was so central that it bore an influence on the whole of the modern Russian consciousness. Although, with the arrival of the Bolsheviks, the meaning of this formula noticeably faded; and, toward the end of the Soviet period, it once more ignited and began to 'haunt [стужать]' the brains of the intelligentsia.

As a commandment, "thou shalt not kill" does not strictly belong to Christianity and the New Testament, but is rather Judaic, originating in the Old Testament. This is an element of the Law, the Torah, which generally regulates the external, exoteric, ethico-social norms of being for the people of Israel. The commandment is not given any special status. We find something analogical in the majority of traditions, in their social codices. In Hinduism, this is called 'ahimsa' or 'non-violence.' This commandment of "thou shalt not kill," like all other points of the Law, regulates human freedom, guiding it into that stream which, in correspondence with Tradition, belongs to the good side, the 'right hand.' It is telling, in this light, that "thou shalt not kill" contains no absolute metaphysical meaning: like all exoteric decrees, this commandment serves a purpose only in tandem with others — to impose order on collective existence and preserve the socium from a fall into chaos (as the apostle Paul writes in Hebrews 7:19, "the law made nothing perfect"). In principle, if we compare the reality of the Old Testament with that of modernity, then the formula "thou shalt not kill" more closely resembles a no-smoking sign hanging in the foyer of a theater. It is recommended that one not smoke in the theater, it is a bad thing to do. Whenever a drunk lights up a smoke, it is a state of emergency for the ushers. Society judges these people and the guardians of order repress them.

It is revealing that the entirety of the Old Testament is teeming with instances of open defiance of this commandment. Murders abound there. It is not only sinners who commit them, but also the righteous, Kings, the anointed, even prophets — the disciple of Eli, Elijah, was a particularly bold case, not sparing even innocent children. People were killed in war; both kin and aliens were murdered; criminals and murderers were murdered; women were murdered, and no mercy was shown to the young, the old, the Goyim, prophets, idol worshippers, sorcerers, sectarians, or parents. Much was destroyed. In the book of Job, Yahweh himself, without any particular reason — besides a rather unimportant wager with the Morning Star — deals sadistically with his elected martyr. When Job, covered in leprous sores, bemoans his situation, Yahweh frightens him with two geopolitical[53] monsters — the land-bound Behemoth and the maritime Leviathan, i.e., he also kills him in a moral sense. New studies of the Bible convincingly prove that

53 In modern geopolitics, the Leviathan and the Behemoth refer, respectively, to sea and land powers. The Leviathan represents Atlanticism, the West, the USA, the Anglo-Saxon world, and market ideology. The Behemoth is a Eurasian, continental complex associated with Russia, hierarchy, and tradition. For more, see A. Dugin, *Conspirology* [*Конспорология*] (Moscow, 1992).

the original text of Job terminated at the peak of tragedy, while the naïve, moralizing conclusion was written much later by the Levites, who were terrified at the primordially harsh nature of this most archaic fragment of the 'Old Testament.'

In the context of Judaism, from which the commandment "thou shalt not kill" is directly drawn, this imperative is neither absolute, nor does it contain any special meaning. No one ever debated over it and, clearly, it never provoked anyone's contemplation. This is not to say, however, that it was not heeded. They heeded it, tried in vain to spill no blood. The council of Rabbi judges was still to be avoided. If someone was killed in vain, a reckoning swiftly followed. It was just like any other law, a commandment like any other commandment. There was nothing special about it. It was merely the rule of human cohabitation. Everything is different in Christianity. Christ is the fulfillment of the law. The law ends with Him. The mission of the law has been completed. In some sense, then, the law is removed. It is precisely removed, but not abolished. The problem of the spirit transitions into a radically different plane. Now comes the post-Law era, the era of Grace. "The shadow of the law has passed."[54] Strictly speaking, the emergence of such an era implies the irrelevance of the commandments. Even the first commandment about worshiping the Sole God is overcome by the New Testament, the Testament of Love for Him. Entirely new relations between Creator and creation take hold; the Divine Logos, by way of its incarnation, is introduced among the created themselves. From here on out, everything falls under the sign of Emmanuel and the gracious formula of 'God With Us." God is not in some remote, unreachable place and does not tower over us in the role of a Judge or Lawgiver, but instead takes on the role of the Beloved and the Loving.

---

54 [Translator's note]: [Old Church Slavonic]: "*Прейде сень законная.*" These words are found in the 'second voice' of the Theotokarion (hymns to Mary the Mother of Jesus).

The New Commandment does not repeal the former ten, but makes them superfluous.

The Humanity of the New Testament is cardinally different [иное] from that of the old, Judaic (or pagan) one. It is marked by the element of transcendent Love. Therefore, the dichotomy of the Law—'worship / non-worship,' 'the single / the many,' 'to steal / not to steal,' 'to deceive / not to deceive,' 'to kill / not to kill'—these no longer possess any meaning. In Christian sanctity, these are all cast in a positive light. The new man has no need of rules, for his lives only by one—sober, unsurpassed, undiluted Love, in prayer, meditation, and acts. This cannot be reduced simply to "thou shalt not kill"; a Christian saint would laugh at such a warning. Within him, duality has already been annihilated, the boundary between that which is and which is not him has already been broken. What's more, he would like to be killed. He strives to suffer. He thirsts for martyrdom. In any case, a full Christian existence has no relationship to the ten commandments of the Old Testament. They have been overcome, once and for all, in the holy baptism. Now, there shall only the a realization of grace.

But if we analyze the Christian not in sanctity, monkhood, ascesis, or selfless devotion, will the meaning of the Old Testament order stand for him? The answer is equally no. He has been baptized, which means that he is born again, which in turn means that God is also with him. God is within him, and not outside of him. And so, even though he is an unworthy sinner, he lives beyond the boundaries of the Old Testament man, in a new existence, in a current of undeserved, luminous grace. Regardless of whether he observes the laws of the Old Testament, this has no bearing on the intimate essence of his Christian being. Of course, for society, it is more pleasant to deal with obedient citizens who obey the rules. This holds true as well for Christian society. But this has nothing in common with the sacraments of the Church, with the mystical life of the faithful. This is where the most interesting aspect of Christianity begins. In transgressing any Old Testament commandment, the Christian in fact shows he has yet to realize within himself the mysterious nature of the New Man, the potential personality endowed by the Holy Spirit in the baptismal font. But who can boast that he has achieved total apotheosis? The holier a man becomes, the lower, more sinful, and more terrible he seems to himself in the face of the Shining Trinity. And so, as in the case of the holy fools, the debasement of the human, the fall, can serve as a paradoxical Christian path, a sacrament. Observation of the ten commandments holds no decisive importance for the Orthodox Christian. For him, only one thing matters: Love, the New, utterly New Testament, the Testament of Love. Without Love, the ten commandments are nothing more than a path leading to hell. And, if one has Love, then the commandments no longer have any meaning. This was all clearly comprehended by the radical Russian intellectuals. In Boris Savinkov's *Pale Horse*, the terrorist Vanya (a literary portrait of Ivan Kalyaev[55]) says the following before committing a murder:

> The path of Christs leading to Christ is a path apart… Listen, if you love immensely, if you truly love, then are you allowed to kill, or are you not?

And further:

> [O]ne must assume the torments of the cross, must resolve oneself to carry out any act out of love and for love. But necessarily, necessarily for love and out of love… That's how I live. For what? Maybe I live for the sake of the hour of my death. I pray: Lord, give me death in the name of love. But you don't pray for murder.

Savinkov did his living, thinking, writing, and killing after Dostoevsky's time. But he adds nothing to Raskol'nikov. Raskol'nikov does not

---

55 [Translator's note]: Ivan Kalyaev (b. 6 July 1877 — d. 23 May 1905) was a famous imperial poet and member of the Social Revolutionaries (SRs). He was executed after assassinating the Grand Duke Sergei Alexandrovich during the revolutionary period of 1905.

simply kill for the sake of humanity (even if he does so for humanity's sake in addition to his main reasons). He kills in the name of Love. He kills in order to suffer, to die, to kill death within himself and within others. Ivan Kalyaev, as well as Savinkov himself, are deeply Russian people, deeply Orthodox, deeply 'Dostoevskian'; they are clearly bearers of God like all the Russian people, infused with such a supreme, paradoxical, and Orthodox Thought, in comparison with which the finest and most profound Western philosophical schemes pale. This is a theology that passes through the pores, through the breath, through tears, dreams, and grimaces of anger. Through torment and torture. Through the blood-soaked, carnal, spiritualized elements of the New Life.

With love and for the sake of Love, everything is permitted. This is not to say that everything must be done, but that all commandments must be rejected and cast down. In no situation are they valid. All one must do is show, vitally show through a gesture that there is — and this is key — another dimension of being, a new light, the light of Love.

Saint Petersburg is the place where the old money-lending woman is murdered. Therefore, this is Russia's place of love, her *locus amoris*.

Rodion raises his two hands, two angular signs, two tapestries of tendons, two runes above the dry winter skull of Capital. And in his hands is a crude, indecently crude, uncouth object. With this object, the central ritual of Russian history and the Russian mystery is carried out. The ghost is objectivized; a moment removes itself from the fabric of earthly time (Goethe would slowly lose his mind, having seen what sort of moment this is…). Two theologies, two Testaments, two revelations converge into a magical point. This point is absolute.

Its name is Axe.

Labris

A brief genealogy of the axe:

As always is the case, it is Herman Wirth — the ingenious German scientist and specialist in the proto-history of humanity and ancient writing — who gives the most scintillating hypotheses regarding this object, its origins, and its symbolism. Wirth demonstrates that the double-headed axe was the original symbol of the Year, the circle in its two halves: one of them following the winter solstice and the other preceding it. The common (single-headed) axe, therefore, symbolizes one half of the Year; as a rule, this is the vernal, rising half. Wirth also claims that the utilitarian usage of the axe as a tool for felling trees relates to the symbolism of the Year; in Tradition, the Tree represents the Year: its roots are the winter months and its canopy represents the summer months. And so, the chopping down of a tree, in the symbolic context of sacred societies, corresponds to the arrival of the new year and the end of the old. The axe is simultaneously the New Year and the instrument with which the old one is destroyed. It is again a cutting implement which splits Time, severing the umbilicus of duration at the magical point of the Winter Solstice when the magnificent Mystery of death and the resurrection of the Sun is completed.

The rune depicting the axe in the ancient runic calendar was called '*thurs*,' was dedicated to the god Thor, and fell upon the first months following the new year. Thor was the God-Axe or its symbolic equivalent — the God-Hammer, *Mjölnir*. With this Axe-Hammer, Thor brained the head of the World Serpent, Jörmungandr, who swam in the lower waters of darkness. Once more, we find an obvious myth of solstice, associated with the point of the New Year. The Serpent is Winter, cold, the lower waters of the Sacred Year into which the polar sun is lowered. Thor — the Sun, the spirit thereof — defeats the clutches of the cold and liberates Light. During the later stages of the myth, the figure of the Light and the Sun is bifurcated into the saved and the savior; later it is trifurcated with the introduction of the implement of salvation: the axe. In their original forms, all of these figures were one and the same — god-sun-axe (the hammer).

Herman Wirth understood the first crude etchings of the sign of the axe in the most ancient paleolithic caves and on stones in light of a complete ritualistic, calendric complex; he traced the striking resilience of the proto-thought of the axe in the most temporally and geographically various cultures and names of the object. He showed the etymological and semantic connection between the plethora of words signifying the axe, with different symbolic concepts and mythological plots (even relating to the mystery of the New Year, the middle of winter, the Winter Solstice). Especially curious is his allusion to the fact that the symbolic semantics of the 'axe' are strictly identified with two other ancient hieroglyph-word-objects — the 'labyrinth' and the 'beard.'

The 'Labyrinth' is a development of the idea of the annual spiral, winding up toward the time of the New Year and, at the same point, beginning to unwind. The 'Beard' is the pure masculine light of the sun in the winter-spring half of the year's circle (hair, in general, represents the rays of the sun). It is for this reason that, in the runic circle, a different rune — *peorp* — is depicted as an axe, but refers to a beard. The minotaur lives in the center of the labyrinth, a monster, half-man and half-bull, equivalent to Jörmungandr the world serpent and... the old money-lending woman. In *Crime and Punishment*, Dostoevsky expressed a most ancient mythological plot, a mysterious paradigm of symbolic order; he described a primordial ritual which was practiced by our ancestors for several millennia. But this is no mere anachronism or the disparate fragments of a collective unconscious. In fact, we are speaking of a much more important eschatological picture, the meaning and gesture of the End of Time, the sacred apocalyptic moment when time collides with Eternity, when the tonguing flames of the Final Judgment erupt to consume.

Russians are a chosen people and Russian history is a résumé of world history. As if to a temporal, spatial ethnic magnet, the fateful meaning of the ages is drawn to us with growing force. The First and Second Rome only existed so that the Third might come. Byzantium was a proclamation of Holy Rus'. The apocalyptic Holy Rus' was extended into the ghostly city of Saint Petersburg, where the greatest prophet of Russia, Fyodor Dostoevsky, appeared. The principal heroes of his principal novel, *Crime and Punishment*, whose actions unfold in the labyrinth of the Petersburg streets, are the principal heroes of Russia. Most central among them are Raskol'nikov, the old money-lending woman, and the axe. And it is precisely the axe which acts as that ray which ties Raskol'nikov to the old woman. And therefore, the history of the world—through the history of Rome—through the history of Byzantium—through the history of Russia—through the history of Moscow—through the history of Saint Petersburg—through the history of Dostoevsky—through the history of *Crime and Punishment*—through the history of that novel's main characters—comes down to the Axe.

Raskol'nikov splits the skull of the capitalist hag. The name of 'Raskol'nikov,' in itself, already points to the axe and the event which it will bring forth. Raskol'nikov initiates the ritual of the New Year, the mystery of the Day of Judgment, the festivities of the resurrection of the Sun. Capitalism, crawling into Russia from the West, from the region of sunset, carnally represents the world serpent. Its agent—the old lady who is a spider weaving the web of usurious slavery—is a part of it.

Raskol'nikov carries the axe of the East.

The axe of the rising sun, the axe of Freedom and the New Dawn.

The novel should have ended triumphantly, with a full justification of Rodion; Raskol'nikov's crime is the old money-lending woman's punishment. The era of the Axe and Proletarian Revolution is declared. But...

Supplementary forces injected themselves into the matter. The investigator Porphyry revealed himself to be especially guileful. This representative of Kafka-esque jurisprudence—this Pharisee of pseudo-humanism—starts the complex intrigue of discrediting the hero and his gesture in his own eyes. Porphyry wretchedly trots out his facts and leads Raskol'nikov into the labyrinth of doubt, anguish, and torments of the soul. He not only tries to imprison Rodion, but seeks to crush him spiritually. One must deal with this sort of scum as Raskol'nikov deals with the old lady. "*Crush the head of the serpent.*" But the hero's strength has failed him...

From this point, the remaining fabric of the myth is obscured. In correspondence with the primordial scenario, Raskol'nikov should have rescued the Wise Sophia from the brothel as Simon the Gnostic did with Helen. And the scene in which the evangelical resurrection of Lazarus is recounted is a remnant of the original (virtual) variant: Sophia rescued by Love, freed from the shackles of debt slavery, preaches universal resurrection. But, here, she somehow enters into a conspiracy with the 'serpent-worshiping humanist' Porphyry and begins to insist to Raskol'nikov that he ought to pity the fate of the old woman—"*Not a trembling louse.*" This is the society which loves all animals, including the world serpent of infernal darkness. To belong to it is to sympathize with capitalist tears.

How are we to explain this?

Dostoevsky was a prophet and possessed the gift of foresight. He foresaw not only the Revolution (with his axe biting into a skull), but also its degeneration, its betrayal, its being sold out. The Sophia of socialism gradually degenerated into a slobbering, Pharisaic humanism.

The Porphyries infiltrated the Party and undermined the foundations of the eschatological kingdom which upheld the Soviet nation.

They refused Permanent Revolution, then the purges, and then Sonya, in the guise of the late-Soviet intelligentsia, once more raised a hue and cry with her idiotic "thou shalt not kill…" And blood gushed like a river—not the blood of old money-lending hags, but of truly innocent children.

There exists a virtual version of *Crime and Punishment* which ends in an utterly different manner. It has to do with the new, coming period of Russian history.

So far, we have been living along the lines of the first version. But that is now over. The new myth is incarnating. The crimson sword of Boris Savinkov burns the palms of a young Russia, the Russia of the End Times.

The name of this Russia is 'Axe.'

Mother Blood[56]

(Pimen Karpov)

A Total Loser

The name of Pimen Karpov is fully absent in our culture. This is as it should be. He was about as bad a writer as could be imagined; as a poet, he was below average. His life was a serious of unending failures. When the poet Karpov went to meet Aleksandr Blok, the latter took him for a chimneysweep; judging by his dark mug of the steppes, his wild gaze—he was a proper '*Chukhonets*[57].'

56 [Translator's note]: "Кровушка-Матушка"—diminutive, folksy versions of the words *krov'* [*кровь*] (blood) and *mat'* [*мать*] (mother).

57 [Translator's note]: The antiquated word *Chukhonets* [*чухонец*] was employed in the Middle Ages and in imperial times to refer to an inhabitant of the Finnish or

In 1909, he published his collection of essays entitled *Speech of the Dawns* [Говор зорь], which was both dim and of little meaning. Within this work, he naively defended the Russian peasants from the conceited arrogance of the intelligentsia. Only one person liked the collection — Leo Tolstoy, who was engaged at that time in the peak of his simplifications.

In 1913, he released the primary book of his life: *Flame* (*A Novel Concerning the Life and Faith of the Wheat-Growers*) [Пламень (роман из жизни и веры хлеборобов)].

I shall risk the assertion that nothing exists in Russian literature which can compare to this book in terms of its wildness, bareness, and unhidden insanity, paired with poor taste, unwieldy pseudo-folk language, and total artistic mediocrity. This infernal masterpiece stunned both the critics and the censors. The novel was decried by official organs as 'sectarian,' 'pornographic,' and 'sacrilegious.' A criminal case was opened against the author, and only his frail health and the impending revolution (until which he hardly managed to survive, pretending to be a defective) were able to save him from jail. Both those on the left and on the right were shocked by Karpov. They both saw in his novel a caricature — of the state, the people, the proletariat, the peasantry, the landowners, and the church — in short, a caricature of everything then conceivable.

But even less pleasant than this, Karpov failed even to become infamous, squandering this chance on account of an absolute incompetence in taking advantage of a critical situation pregnant in its popularity.

The novel was republished in 1924 after the revolution, but by then no one was paying attention to it (most likely due to its artistic worthlessness). Karpov continued to wander around Russia, begging for a room or some kind of honorarium (as he hated work and lacked any

Baltic region of Karelo-Finnic extraction.

and all know-how), but, always and everywhere, he came up against a complete indifference. It is unclear how he made it through to 1963, the year in which he died in total obscurity.

In 1991, the publishing house *Khudozhestvennaya Literatura* [Художественная литература] released *Flame* (for reasons unknown), as well as poems and excerpts from his biographical novella *Russian Ark* [Русский ковчег], in which Karpov described his acquaintance with the futurists, Khlebnikov, Sologub, Blok, Tolstoy, Severyanin, Grin, and other famous bohemian literary figures of pre-revolutionary Russia.

This 'Perestroika' publication was produced as a formal tribute to the awkward, third-rung author and, with this, his chapter was closed.

But, as always, the most interesting thing in his work has been overlooked.

The fact is that Pimen Karpov encrypted a unique esoteric message into his novel, a grandiose gnostic myth which prefigured the most brilliant visions of Platonov or Mamleev. Karpov had disseminated the mysteries of a profound Russian sacrality, had made a set of secret national doctrines a public possession, which unveiled the darkest and most beguiling aspects of our people's spiritual history with unprecedented clarity.

The Ringleader of the 'Zlydota'

Externally, the novel *Flame* is a heap of obscurantisms [мракобесия], blood-soaked crimes, unfettered sado-masochism, perversions, deaths, decompositions, black masses, sacrilege, blasphemies, and unqualified thanatophilia. Perversions, matricides, gang rapes, tortures — these all writhe one on top of another in unfathomable quantities until the novel's conclusion, with no consideration for plot, consequence, or logic. One gets the impression that the author has mechanically added another instance of rape or suffocation each moment his quill touched a fresh page.

Moreover, an unending horror is described without the slightest hint of humor; on the contrary, episodes of depravity alternate with metaphysical and theological surmises of the highest gravity. With careful scrutiny, on discovers that these bloody and pornographic pictures are summoned up only in order to illustrate certain complex gnostic conceptions which constitute the axis of the entire work. Karpov's intent gradually comes to clarify itself: he is not writing fiction, but an esoteric text camouflaged as literature and appointed for a special reader, a bearer of the Russian mystery.

The novel centers around certain sects that are dispersed among the usual peasant population in the outskirts of an estate owned by a malicious master — Gedeonov. Later, we learn that the main characters of the text are no people at all: one of them is a "messenger of the Supreme Light which has fallen in love with the earth"; another is the "son of a demon"; a third is a "prophet of the Sun."

One of the sects — that known as the 'Zlydotniks [злыдотники]' or 'Zlydota [злыдота]' — is headed by a certain Feofan, the "spirit of the lowlands." At a particular moment in the novel, it is revealed that he represents a paradoxical 'theophany,' as the name 'Feofan' is etymologically related to precisely this Greek concept.

At first, Feofan was a pious hermit, but then he was met with the howling injustice of 'God in the Heavens [Сущего].' His fate was changed in a single moment. For a long time, he had prayed that God in the Heavens would save two sick young children, living in great squalor and poverty, whom he allowed to live in his monastery out of pity; but, returning from an exhausting, solitary prayer lasting several days, he discovered their corpses, "black, rotting, and covered in slime." After this, everyone for whom Feofan prayed would thereafter die. It was then he realized that his was the black path of the earth, called upon to revolt against the "bright fire of heaven." Afterward, Feofan enters upon a path of unthinkably repugnant crimes — he murders his own mother with a kettle bell, pimps his sister out to border guards, and sells his daughter for a ruble to the perverted Gedeonov, so that the latter may subject her to erotic tortures. In doing these things, however, Feofan does not act out of some vulgar sentiment of 'Satanism.' He regards his accumulation of sins and his accepting a burden into his heart as a special path that leads to paradoxical holiness — to the City which lies beyond God in the Heavens. In the context of these optics, God in the Heavens himself appears as an ambiguous character. Karpov writes:

> But God in the Heavens is ferocious, jealous. And he subjects those more merciful and abundant in love than him to foul, unbearable punishments. In casting down the Angel of Life, who prayed for the forgiveness of Eve and Adam, he turned him into the Angel of Death.

The character of Feofan combines extreme evil with extreme sanctity. But his path is that of burden, torment, ever-increasing sin, suffering, torture, and evil, all for the sake of forcing God in the Heavens to step aside and unveil the secret sun of the Luminous City. Herein lies the meaning of the gnostic tradition, the 'left-hand path' (as it is called in Hinduism). It is no surprise that the 'burdensome path' is associated with sexual rituals; it represents an immersion into the 'lowlands,' the dark light of the earth. In the beginning, Feofan rises as the head of the sect of the Zlydotniks; then he disappears, reappearing later as an ascetic hermit, a prophet. It is then revealed that he is the 'herald of heaven,' who did not fulfill the order of God in the Heavens to punish the incarnate Christ and, "having taken him, resurrected, out of the earth, he united the heavenly with the earthly, the spirit with the flesh, love with hate."

When the peasant men and sectarians come together to revolt against the authorities, Feofan admonishes them with the following words:

> Who believes in me?… Who loves me?… Follow me!… Into the lowlands!… It will be wonderful there!… In the core of the earth!…

And further (in absolute accord with Nietzsche):

> 'Love the heart of the earth!' a harsh and prophetic cry sounded from the depths of the cave. 'He who does not come to know the earth will not see heaven… Do not fear evil! Do no fear hate! These are the igniters of love… Do you believe me?… Children!… Believe everything and everyone… How wonderful it will be!… This is true…'

(Think over this strange commandment, "believe everything and everyone." It is more terrible than the purely Satanic connotations of other openly heretical passages. Clearly, Pimen Karpov was anything but a simple author.)

The Brothers of Flame [Пламенники]

The second sect, in many ways opposed to the *Zlydota*, is the 'Flame' or the 'Brothers of Flame.' As in the first case, we find obvious, typical motifs relating to the Khlysty, though it is possible that the author is thinking of various branches of that sect. The Brothers of Flame, too, seek the Luminous City, and their relationship to God in the Heavens is also paradoxical. But their path leads elsewhere — it is not of the dualist, Manichean variety, but is rather pantheistic and pagan. They are sun worshippers. Their leader is Krutogorov, who later turns out to be Feofan's lost son.

Krutogorov is a prophet of the sun, of love, of unity. Just like Feofan, he rejects the moralistic dilemmas of sin and sanctity, proclaiming the unity of love and hate, life and death, etc. But his path is bright. He walks toward the non-dualistic Absolute through light, the spirituality of Russian nature, corporeal love, political revolt, and unending roundelays (Karpov writes that "the men in these places danced more than they worked").

Krutogorov is constantly occupied with promiscuous forms of eroticism, preaching the communal ownership of women and property. At the end of the novel, he comes to lead an uprising of villagers and peasants against the landowners and the city, the symbol of alienation. If Feofan passes through sin on his way to sinlessness, then Krutogorov's total solar sinlessness absolves him of all sins.

The chief principle of the Brothers of Flame is the omnipresent Fire, the herald of the Luminous City. At the novel's conclusion, the ecstatic sectarians perish precisely in flames.

> 'They're burning, the fortunate ones! They're burning!'
> 'The unknown one ascended above the mountain dale, beckoning with its flames like a boat in the sea, the Flaming City.'

This comparison with a ship is deliberate. This was the term which the Khlysty used to refer to their church. The fiery ship is the holy of holies for them — their 'inner church.'

The Maiden of the Luminous City

The feminine plays an important role in Karpov's doctrine. Described in the least convincing and schematic manner, the women in the novel *Flame* are nonetheless extremely important from a doctrinal perspective. They are the source of salvation, containing the highest spiritual paradox. The mixture of shame and sanctity within them reaches a maximal strain. They are bearers of the dark and deathly heat of unquiet flesh, but also give a tragic hint at the transcendent light of a lost, solar *Urheimat*. The original mother Eve, former instrument of the fall, must become the way toward salvation in accord with the universal scheme of heresies. This corresponds precisely to the Hindu doctrine of the Tantra.

Maria, the daughter of Feofan, whom he once sold to Gedeonov, plays a central role. She is a depraved hysteric and prophet who participates in all forms of incestuous sins and ecstatic orgies.

She, and no other, carries the mystery of the redemptive sacrifice. She is located between the Zlydotnik Feofan, the active creator of redemptive evil, and the sun-worshipping prophet of Flame Krutogorov (her brother).

Fulfilling her fate as a sacrifice of the divergent gnostic wills of her two kin, she burns along with other sectarians in the culminating moment of a sacred orgy. And she receives a crown of light.

This entire trifecta (Feofan, Krutogorov, and the hysterical Maria) alludes strangely to a comparison with the hierarchy of the Bogomils, at the peak of which stood figures representative of the three figures of the Trinity. Feofanov is the Father, Krutogorov is the Son, and Maria is the Spirit, since, in gnosticism, the spirit is the feminine principle. If this interpretation is accurate, then in the case of Karpov and his novel we find a holdover of the Bogomil tradition in Russia, which is officially considered to have been disrupted many centuries ago.

The Satanael Gedeonov

The landowner Gedeonov is the leader of yet another sect—the 'Satanaels' or worshippers of the 'Dark One [Тьмяного],' i.e., Lucifer. The name 'Satanael' once more points us toward the Bogomils, for whom it refers to Lucifer before his fall; the particle 'el,' present in all angelic names, translates from Hebrew as 'god'; the Morning Star [денница] was stripped of it after his fall from grace.

It would appear that, this time, we are dealing with an absolutely negative character. Gedeonov is a manifestation of total evil—evil for evil's sake. He tortures the peasant men, rapes and tortures the women and children, exterminates entire villages, and holds a public mass-execution by beheading in a broad field; he murders his mother, his daughter, and his wife among others. He has an illegitimate son: the 'friar [чернец]' Vyacheslav, abbot of the Zagorsk monastery, comes to replace him and organizes Satanic ceremonies of black magic in honor of the Dark One and of Gedeonov himself.

This is the antipode of Krutogorov. He possesses neither love nor life; instead, all he has is lust, envy, and venom.

But all is not so simple. Gedeonov is a Russian figure precisely comparable to the Marquis de Sade or Maldoror. Recall how profoundly Georges Bataille understood the meaning of sadism, describing the type of the 'sovereign man.' Gedeonov, the 'prince of darkness' who absolutized his 'I,' has exited the narrow boundaries of the human and discovered vistas of absolute madness, extending beyond the categories of good and evil.

> The unknown, the non-existent spoke to him from out of the darkness: 'You must either find… or create that which lies behind God in the Heavens.'

Once more, we go from trivial evil to non-trivial evil, the latter being gnostic, in parallel with the ideas and practices of Feofan. It's purpose is to facilitate the search for the transcendent which lies in the beyond…

Gedeonov, the 'sovereign man,' is a mystic of the far-right who is simultaneously reminiscent of the Baron von Ungern[58], Crowley, and Evola, seeking the Absolute in his own manner. As he says,

---

58 [Translator's note]: Robert Nikolaus Maximilian Freiherr von Ungern-Sternberg (29 December 1885 [10 January 1886] — 15 September 1921) was a general in the White Army during the Russian Civil War who fought primarily in the far east and, during a crucial point in the conflict, retreated to the areas of Mongolia, Manchuria, and China, where he formed the Asiatic Cavalry Division and embarked on a slew of unstoppable raids against the Reds and their sympathizers. During his time in Mongolia, he was initiated into an esoteric shamanic doctrine and thereafter sought to reestablish the empire of Genghis Khan. Eventually, in 1921, he was betrayed by a conspiracy among his own officers and soldiers which

> Man, generally speaking, is a mongrel: neither devil, nor god.

And further:

> Two camps are battling, the bastards… One in the name of god, but by devilish means (historical religions, sacred monarchies soaked in blood), the other in the name of the devil and also by devilish means, as well as godly ones on occasion… So, who's better?
> BOTH ARE BETTER!

Notice the genius of this—"both are better"—and meditate over its meaning. It is in concert with the idea which Merezhkovsky expounds in his trilogy *Kingdom of the Beast*, concerning the mysterious attraction between conservative monarchism and progressive revolution.

Gedeonov develops his thought:

> Throughout certain periods, these camps have switched roles, but their essence remains the same: the crowd desires to be delivered from its suffering and, in seeking a means of doing so, pile up a mountain of even worse sufferings, the bastards… And god and the devil are no more than the faces of a united truth of life, sides of one and the same coin—heads and tails. Who the hell wins?… The one who has an eagle [tails] on both sides—or the one with two pentagrams, two sides bearing the signs of winning, damnit… […].
> There they are, the backsides of the medal, damn your mother… In the cosmos: the beginning is the end, the end is the beginning (a closed circle); in religion, God is the devil and the devil is God; in society, the despot is chosen of the people, and the chosen of the people is the despot; in morals, a lie is the truth and the truth is a lie; so on and so forth. And so, at a certain period and in a certain measure, sin is sanctity and sanctity is sin. Do you understand what I'm leaning toward?…

The people to whom Gedeonov's question has been posed clearly have not understood him. For those of us who have experience with history

---

led to his arrest and execution at the hands of Red partisans. His figure and legend are of extreme importance to Dugin's esoteric Russian tradition.

and knowledge of religions, heterodoxy, and political doctrines, it is more comprehensible.

Gedeonov is alluding to the fact that the boundary between himself and Feofan is exceedingly fine.

Is there a boundary at all?

From Heresiology to Politology

At a particular moment in the narration, Karpov's purely mystical reality mingles with the social. The muzhiks, the Zlydota, the Krasnosmertniks, the Skoptsy, the Khlysty, the Plammeniki, and the Skrytniki, all in the end come to identify their mystical revolt against the 'evil demiurge' (God in the Heavens) with the social uprising of the proletariat and the peasants against the masters.

Gedeonov's far-right camp of Satanaels (Gedeonov constantly says the following about himself: "I am the iron vice of the state") are subjected to attacks from the socialist-oriented, sado-masochistic Wheat-Growers [хлеборобов], who have risen to search for the Luminous City and the sacred land in its political aspect.

An earth-shaking prophecy: the mystical 'fascist' (the 'sovereign man,' Maldoror) Gedeonov clashes with mystical communists of a Bogomil sect. It is a premonition of both the Russian Civil War and the Second World War. It is no surprise, then, that the Bolshevik Bonch-Bruevich was so outraged by *Flame*, having consciously striven to unite the Russian sects with the revolutionary movement; Pimen Karpov had exposed these forbidden plans too plainly to the public (luckily, no one had comprehended them). Gedeonov's great and terrible 'I', speaking with itself in the booming void beyond God in the Heavens, combines with the universal, collectivist, promiscuous, orgiastic ecstasy of revolutionary heresies in which the 'I' is dissolved in a unified rush toward the Luminous City. This combination is paradoxical, but its two terms are much less distant than are the gnostic (of any orientation) and the lukewarm semi-corpses living nearby (for whom there is neither a clearly expressed 'I' nor a clearly expressed 'we).

These are two types of mysticism which subtend the two most interesting political realities of the twentieth century.

But the dualism which Karpov himself seeks to accentuate constantly approaches a sort of vertiginous, threatening boundary where a paradox opens up in an even more horrifying, unforeseen light which troubles even the author.

The justification of evil on the part of the folk sectarians also justifies the opponents of their uprising. Evil is justified, the struggle with evil is justified, the methods of evil are justified, and the victory of either side is justified. The highest value is not immanent success, but rather the celebration of being, the triumph of a beautiful death, the victorious tidings of tortured flesh, blood, *krovushka-matushka*…

As Krutogorov says, "You have come to the world in order to burn in the sun of the City… The more vicious the evil, the brighter burns the flame of pure hearts!" In another place, he says, "If evil did not exist, people would not set about on their search for the City…"

It is clear that both tendencies are approaching each other all the more closely on the metaphysical level. Gedeonov's son Vyacheslav, the 'vile' informant, murderer (even though everyone in the novel is a murderer), plundering 'friar' 'repents' and ends his life in the purifying pyre among the Brothers of Flame.

But their kinship obviously goes much deeper; it is not exhausted with the external similarity in the methods of spiritual realization practiced by the Zlydota (the positive) and the Satanels (the negative). Beyond the fundamental front line of the spiritual-metaphysical and sociopolitical war, we catch the dull glimmer of a paradoxical possibility for a new political, ideological synthesis.

Pimen Karpov unambiguously approaches the theme of magical National Bolshevism, which pursued the consciousness of the most paradoxical and non-conformist minds of the twentieth century (let us recall Drieu La Rochelle: "Our problem is not the choice between a tsar' or a revolution; the problem we face is how to unite these concepts, how to realize the formula: 'Tsar' + Revolution,' 'extreme conservatism + extreme modernism'").

National Bolshevism: A Blood Pact

The idea of uniting the collectivist gnosis of the Russian sectarians seeking the Luminous City with the extreme right-wing ideas of Gedeonov's ("the iron vice of the state") 'Satanaels' is most clearly propounded in the dialogue between the 'friar Vyacheslav (loyal to conservative obscurantism [мракобесию]) and brother Andron, the Krasnosmertnik who has devoted himself to the social Revolution; it is significant that, in the course of the novel, we learn that both of them are Gedeonov's blood sons, which is to say that they are grandsons of the devil in a direct lineage, Gedeonov being the devil's spawn. Formally, Karpov portrays the proposition of the 'Satanael' Vyacheslav to the Khlyst-Bolshevik Andron as a temptation. But this reading is possibly the result of moral self-censorship, resulting from the interpreter's inability to recognize the dizzying metaphysico-political synthesis in its deepest implications, as Karpov calls for.

The entire dialogue is extremely important. Upon encountering his brother, the Bolshevik Andron says to him:

> 'Your world has come to an end!... The whole world belongs to us, the workers, the proletarians. And you—you're all simpletons, parasites, and aphids. Who do you speak for now?... Tell me. As for me, I'll tell you about how you, how all of you, will soon have a beautiful death. But if you join us, we'll have mercy on you...'
>
> 'I'm with you, brother Andron...' the friar cajoled him. 'We all serve only the Dark One... We will rule the whole world together... Only by way of the Russian god—the Dark One... There is no god equal to him! Soon, the whole world will believe in him! The planet will be ours! We share

> a union… […] Ho-ho! The terrestrial globe will be the domain of one unbroken state! And at the head will be the Russians… Have you really not heard about the union of the terrestrial globe? It is our Russian union!… The spirit lives where it wishes…'

In this instance, Vyacheslav is hinting at the existence of a secret far-right organization with gnostic underpinnings and emphasizing its connection with Russia (recall the specialist of Albigensian heresy and colonel of the SS Otto Rahn; his books about the Cathars were listed among required texts for the SS cadres; In his book *Hitler and the Cathar Tradition*, the French historian Jean-Michel Angebert generally confirms that the influence of Albigensian gnostic thought on National-Socialism was decisive).

This becomes even more explicit when Vyacheslav says the following:

> We have already captured Europe. Now it's time to go after America. Why? Because Europe has bowed down before the Dark One… the Russian god of hidden powers and delights, the god of life, and not death… And the East has long belonged to us… In that region, the Dragon and Muhammed are hypostases of the Dark one…

The phrase, "Europe has bowed down before the Dark One" jumps ahead to twenty years in the future, as Otto Rahn's book *The Court of Lucifer* (which was also recommended by Himmler and Wiligut/Weisthor to the SS for study) only made its appearance in 1935.

Later, we find a key passage which serves as the axis of National Bolshevism:

> And you, proletarians without realizing it, have bowed down to the Dark One—to material. So wherein lies our quarrel?

The Dark One, god of blood and life, unites the extreme right and the extreme left in a single front against the petrified liberal civilization.

Both the German Conservative Revolutionaries and the Russian Eurasianists came to this conclusion in the 1920s and 1930s. But Andron perceives this all as a provocation. Despite the depth of his attraction to gnostic paradox, his worldview remains conditioned by a moralistic dualism. Therefore, he cannot understand the dizzying depths, the alliance proposed to him by his 'black brother.' And rattles off his own position:

> 'It's the rich who betray beautiful death, the Russians, and everything else!' Andron hooted, his red beard trembling. 'And you bugs, you're the minions of the rich—your own brother...'
> 'By no means! We wish to award poverty! Only, first, we must do so for Russian poverty, for god is Russian and nothing else... American poverty can look after itself... the same goes for the Europeans. Understand me! We are speaking not just about bread, but of the most profound profundities... A freedom which man has not known from the beginning of the world... What does bread matter?... You've stuffed your belly and croaked out of boredom...'

Vyacheslav expresses the essence of National Bolshevism in concise terms ("first we'll worry about Russian poverty" and "you've stuffed your belly and croaked out of boredom").

And yet, Andron continues to insist:

> 'You dog, with your Russian Kostoglots[59]—you will never know a beautiful death...'
> 'Do we have a blood pact?'
> 'What blood pact?'
> 'This one: we shall give up all power to the proletarians, all of our factories and plants... We will give the land up to the muzhiks. Not to betray the

59 [Translator's note]: In the Russian literary tradition, the last name Kostoglot [Костоглот] serves the parodic and sometimes absurd function of showing a certain character to be ridiculous or worthy of derision; the name derives from the verb *glotat'* [*глотать*] ('to swallow') and the noun *kost'* [*кость*] ('bone') and refers to a glutton who eats so uncontrollably that he even swallows the bones.

> beautiful death of Russians, but of others... Pass that along to your committee members... If they agree, we'll have a peaceful blood pact... If they don't agree, then it'll be blood for blood to the furthest degree... vengeance unto extermination! But if you smooth everything over, we'll make you a minister... Adding a simple water carrier to the ministries — that will be the first point of our peaceful pact... And further, step by step, we'll promote the poor and demote the rich. It's as easy as taking a drink of water. This will encapsulate the east and the west, the heavens and the earth, the underworld of America — the whole terrestrial globe will be under Russian power... that is, the power of the Russian god, the Dark One. The world will be delivered! It will be a marriage without measure, without limits!'

And yet the dullard Andron continues his insistences:

> Just wait until we deliver it from the dogs.

At this symbolic phrase, the sacred meaning of which is lost on the speaker ('dogs' represent the 'guides of the soul,' magical beings in the boundaries who allow the elect to move through the critical point of being — the winter solstice of the spirit), Vyacheslav gives an ingenious answer in its succinctness and fateful character whose contemporary understanding and interpretation might have cardinally changed the course of Russian history:

> JUST WAIT.

Indeed, we could absolutely have waited for what he foretold; moreover, on this could have brought on a 'deliverance of the world' and have given us a 'wedding without measure.'

But the prophetic conclusion of the scene of a sorrowful one:

> And the friar walked away with nothing.

The 'Underworld of America,' bastion of all things non-Russian and anti-Russian, of anti-gnostic gloom, was conquered after all. The National Bolshevik synthesis has not been completed; the nation remains fractured along a fine, paradoxical, and profound, but all the same moralistically dualist line — 'white terror / red terror,' 'the black hundred / the red commissars,' 'Bolsheviks / monarchists.'

The marriage of the 'Reds' and the 'Browns,' which provides the key to the global rule of the immanent spirit, has yet to occur.

Venge Yourself, Rus'!

Pimen Karpov reveals a plethora of mysteries. He describes secret rituals — the 'great stamp' carried out by the razor of the Skoptsy, the burning out of eyes by the gnostics of the 'inner path,' the female crucifixions and collective orgies of the Russian tantrists, the redemptive sacrifices of youths on the dark altar of the Satanaels, the 'whispering over bread and wine' of magical conspiracies, smoking of 'heretical grass,' incest, matricide, and patricide on the part of the Zlydotniks. But it is Blood which plays the prime role in all of these acts.

In Tradition, blood is considered the chief principle of life; it is associated with fire, the flame — especially in its properties of heat. This explains the name of the novel — *Flame* — which is synonymous with the concept of 'Blood.' In a completely traditional context, relations to blood (whether it be animal or human) are highly nuanced, surrounded by several sacred interdictions and taboos. In the Bible, it is generally forbidden to include animal blood in one's food. It is the ritual slaughterer's bloodletting of the animal which distinguishes the 'pure (kosher) food' of the Jews from the impure (terefah). But we are concerned here not with the curse of blood, but with its misuse, which is equated with sacrilege.

In the modern world, where almost no trace of sacred tradition remains, the picture is entirely different. This world is fatally incapable of grasping inner life. Civilization, as it grows ever more technological, efficient, and automated, is on a course of accelerated petrifaction. The juicy fabric of reality is being replaced with a flat image of itself, a system of representations which expels the flesh of things. Humanity is falling into apathy. Pragmatism is wiping out passion. Reality is becoming 'kosher,' empty, and lifeless after having passed through the surgical hands of a gigantic, invisible, omnipotent slaughterer. This is what leads to such monstrous compensation — eruptions of world war, a sea of crimes, the illusory cruelty of youth culture, and the abundance of blood on the television screen (war films, horror films, coverage of conflict zones and catastrophes). But this is not *that blood*. This latter blood is diluted, cold, and lacking redness; it can neither horrify, nor renew, nor resurrect. It is the blood of a fictive light, the morose secretions of an exhausted planet. It is an artificial, deaf, counterfeit blood...

The 'Union of the Terrestrial Globe' of which Vyacheslav speaks in Pimen Karpov's novel is a global conspiracy against petrifaction. It is the concord of the Plamenniks, a 'blood pact.' Its participants are those who are tormented inside by the voice of being which has not disappeared, who rise up against the ice, unfazed by its totality.

Undoubtedly, this is a paroxysm of heresy, heterodoxy — the path of an unauthorized, forbidden, inadmissible revolt (and this is the source of its Luciferian features). But the Hindus aver that, at the end of the dark age (the Kali-Yuga), the usual roads of spiritual realization are no longer effective; the problematic of recent times discounts any metaphysical guarantees; the dangerous, precarious, and paradoxical path of the 'left hand,' the 'path of blood,' is the only hope that remains for a cherished union with the Absolute. Orthodox traditions are degenerating in conformity with the petrified world, becoming a hollow moralism, a 'warm disintegration' that perverts that original fiery truth on which they are based. Standing against these bloodless vampires of orthodoxy are the blood-drenched vampires of heresy. Against the fictive electric light of a flat verbal demagoguery — a living, passionate, fanatic, and frantic Flame of perilous spiritual insurrection.

There can be no doubt that the path of blood—the secret doctrine described by Pimen Karpov—poses an immensely great danger. But its risk comes not from the monstrous irreversibility of crime; the risk comes from the fact that, at a certain point, the mind may reject this trajectory, and then the being of the one who revolts will be forever lost in inescapable labyrinths of outer darkness. Stupidity is the most terrible impediment on the dangerous path toward the Luminous City. But a truly 'flaming mind,' a 'violet mind,' is born of the union between consciousness and madness. Plain rational thought is as useful here as the stunted brains of the local villagers.

Thus, Pimen Karpov's conclusion is as follows: there is no spirit without politics; the political is the field in which profound spiritual forces unfold and in which bloody, heavenly-abysmal energies combine.

Russia is a bewildering country, and the beings who populate Her (the 'Wheat Growers,' the 'Krasnosmertniki,' the 'Prostetsy,' the 'murderers,' the 'proletarians,' the 'conservatives,' the 'iron vice of the state,' and all the rest) are overshadowed by a metaphysical meaning which hearkens from elsewhere, by an intuition of the 'depths of the depths.' It is this which obliges, terrifies, and gives hope…

Pimen Karpov's commandments are addressed to us, are more relevant than ever today:

> Each of you, made brothers through the Dark One, possesses his own light—dark, invisible, learned—ultraviolet… We shall hoist above the planet we share… But the Russians must be at the head…

Blood against petrifaction. A Russia of roundelays and angelic madness against 'infernal America.' The deafening howl of *toska* for Tradition against conciliation with the silent degeneration of the cooling dead. World Revolution cannot be avoided; neither can we avoid the Day of Judgment and the fiery eucharist.

> But the Russians must be at the head…

And, once again, a mysterious voice can be heard—the voice of the 'depths of depths,' of Pimen Karpov:

> Remember, Rus'! The Fatherland! Remember it! Secure its revenge!

Mountains of the tormented, poisoned by the lead of your sons who have saturated your fields with a burning, mortal blood, knock at the roofs of their coffins with their bones: "Revenge!"

The storm clouds of your sons, mangled, blinded, driven insane, with torn arms and legs, crawl across the squares and streets; they dispatch their mute, wailing cry to you, mixed as it is with frothing blood: "Revenge!"

For the offense of death! For the poisonous lead! For the slaughter of the wounded and the unarmed! Millions of fathers, mothers, orphans, and widows, in *toska* and irreducible woe pledge themselves to you, Rus'. Why, why have you forgiven this abuse, accursed Motherland?!

O Rus', venge yourself! Venge yourself with blood, with the sun of the City, with torments! Like the Luminous City, venge yourself with untold torments upon your abusers…

"It Seems to Me That the Governor Yet Lives..."

There are beloved frontiers.
My frontier is a crimson sword.

— Boris Savinkov

Few these days take interest in the Social Revolutionaries (SRs), radical, revolutionary terrorists who were the primary actors of Russian history between the end of the nineteenth and the beginning of the twentieth century. Those on the right count them as agents of a Russophobic, Judeo-Masonic conspiracy; the liberals accuse them of radicalism and potential totalitarianism (seeing in them the seed of the Stalinist system); even the communists and the far-left disavow them as extremists who discredit their ideas. The result is that there are no successors of Russian terror, just as its defeat has no fathers.

But there is someone new who has yet to reveal his face — he leafs through the pages of Savinkov's books and greedily soaks up those likes written in the blood of the author and others.

Pale Horse is an ingenious text in which existential, mystical, philosophical, and social motifs are woven into a single organic whole. This is a testimony. This is literature. These are instructions for action. What did this paradoxical riddle of a man wish to say, having sent more than one dozen Whites, Reds, Greens, and others lacking a color?

We clearly see in Savinkov's work a dominant motif of apocalypse. "I will give you the morning star." This line is hypnotically repeated by the terrorist author in his diary. In Latin, the 'Morning Star' is 'Lucifer.' The fallen but unbroken angel — the first creation of God — is the timeless archetype of a true revolutionary.

The 'Morning Star' is a covenant of double significance, a symbol both of election and cursedness. It pursues the dry imagination of the man who has made death his profession, his object of study, his fate.

The 'Morning Star' is the reward of the merciless punisher, he who bears the mystery of absolute vengeance which must afflict both the just and the unjust.

Savinkov justifies terror with appeals to the 'social good' and 'justice.' The terrorist's inflamed soul poses a more global, more radical question — what is death? If it is inescapable for living beings, then can we justify delaying our encounter with it? Savinkov brilliantly describes a spiritual portrait of his friend, the terrorist Kalyaev. This latter took the terrorist act to be a sacrifice by which one lays one's own life (and only after the fact the lives of others) on the altar of the great metaphysical question. Kalyaev — Vanechka — wants to 'suffer' and to die. That is why he kills:

> And so the business of peasants, of Christians, of Christ is carried out. In the name of God. In the name of love… I believe in our people, the people of God. Love is in them. Christ is in them… I go forth to do murder, but I myself believe in the Word; I swear to Christ. It's painful for me… Painful…

We find here the ingenious intuition of Death's unity beyond the fictive dualism of the executioner and the victim. Killing and dying are the same act. But to voluntarily kill-die is not simply to subordinate oneself to the all-consuming element of death as an object, but to enter into an active dialogue with it, to initiate a process of courting, matchmaking and, at the far extreme, to bring about a Marriage.

In the case of Russian terror, to 'kill' is to allow for the profound, excruciating philosophical question of Being.

Revolutionary terror also existed in the West. But the French (or, more broadly, European) anarchists were something entirely different. They had a separate culture, a different spiritual milieu. Knowing the fatal limitations of the French, as well as that of Westerners in general — their one-dimensionality, shallowness, and vulgar rationality — one can imagine that the terror in Europe is equally as cosmetic and narrowly rational as everything else. To kill in order to decide social questions; to kill in order to proclaim one's political views. And nothing more.

A Russian kills in a different manner. Behind him is a deep layer of national Orthodox metaphysics, the whole tragic drama of the apocalypse, the schism, suffering, the hysterically and piercingly comprehended Christian paradox.

The Russian terrorist is a sacrifice. He carries out a magical act, called forth to save not only society, the people, the class, but all of reality.

In *Pale Horse*, Savinkov meticulously describes an assassination attempt made on a governor's life. The attempt is difficult, dreary, and fraught with hitches. It is accompanied by hysterics, love plots, psychological breaks, and class friction. Flashes of cowardice and indecisiveness ruin the entire undertaking several times. During one unsuccessful attempt, the best cadres are lost — to include the worker Fyodor who fires his weapon from behind a wood pile until the last moment, but who is ultimately defeated by the gendarmes. But the plan is realized in the end. The Orthodox student-mystic manages to fling a homemade bomb into the governor's carriage. The Servant of the System is shredded by an explosion. Joyously and obediently, beautifully and submissively, the murderer victoriously gives himself up to his executors. It would seem that the target has been hit. The sword of the dark angel has fallen. The tyrant has been overthrown.

And in this moment, after having prepared the whole operation, a terrible thought enters Savinkov's head. It seems to him that the "governor yet lives."

Of course, he is alive. The idiotic personality of the monarchical servant, bastard, and oppressor is but a mask. The essence of the System is not in it, nor in the tsar' himself.

The Evil Demiurge is ungraspable. He is beyond the realm of social marionettes.

It is not so easy to catch ahold of him.

A horrifying vision leads Savinkov toward yet newer and newer political groups. He — the jealous partisan of Labor's freedom, the heroic avenger of the disenfranchised and oppressed peasants and workers — joins the Whites, the 'masters [барам],' at a certain moment, even though he has bombed and slashed them in their dozens. Later, he is drawn toward Fascism and Mussolini. Then, in Bolshevik Russia, he notes his proximity to the communists.

This alternation of political convictions makes him an organic National Bolshevik. He is beyond all narrow party doctrines. He is a hero devoted to a metaphysical idea, the Paladin of Death. He is a cold-blooded murderer with the soul of a lamb.

His enemy surpasses the usual political barricades. It is the System and its hidden essence. The Evil Demiurge, the secret agent of Alienation. In order to understand it, one must pass through the entire political spectrum in a circle. In doing so, one only derives value in the instance that every step is paid for with blood.

'Whites,' 'Reds,' 'Blacks,' 'Browns,' 'Greens'... What is the difference when you get right down to it?! The only thing that matters is transgressing the boundary.

> If a louse in your shirt
> Shouts that you are a flea,
> Go outside
> And kill!

Kill, so as to suffer afterwards.

Kill, so as to perish.

Kill, so as to be cursed.

Kill, so as to kill. So as to die. So as to live.

Boris Savinkov is a practitioner of that profound form of thought developed by the great Dostoevsky. That principally undecided problem. That great dream. Rodion Raskol'nikov, in murdering the old moneylending woman, struck a blow at the skull of Capital and the cosmopolitan banking system, breaking the chains of 'usurious slavery'... Boris Savinkov sank his bullets into the very same 'old woman.'

The Bolsheviks at one time believed that they had once and for all 'murdered the governor.' That Alienation had been bested. That the Demiurge had been toppled. But the spirit of decay resettled itself in them. They had forgotten the pain and the risk in their naïve optimism. Revolution and blood had been betrayed, sold out, given up. With what misunderstanding, loathing, suspicion, and indifference did they write about terror, about Savinkov, about the S.R.s, and about the populists during the last years of their rule. The names of streets—'Kalyaevskaya,' 'Bakuninskaya,' etc.—no longer spoke to anyone. The bureaucrats had effaced the memory of the zigzag belonging to those shoulders which once lobbed bombs.

They paid for this treachery.

And, once more, the bastards celebrate their triumph on the ruins of socialism. Once more, the merchant's ugly mug shines; the lazy pimp stretches out, dealing in minors and girls; the scum wipes off its hands after felling the last cherry orchard...

We are discovering the books of Boris Savinkov. *Pale Horse.* We breathe in the story of his life, his eroticism, his struggle.

We so passionately desire the Morning Star.

And, again and again, it seems to us that *the governor yet lives.*

CJ

OTHER BOOKS PUBLISHED BY ARKTOS

Sri Dharma Pravartaka Acharya	*The Dharma Manifesto*
Joakim Andersen	*Rising from the Ruins*
Winston C. Banks	*Excessive Immigration*
Alain de Benoist	*Beyond Human Rights* *Carl Schmitt Today* *The Ideology of Sameness* *The Indo-Europeans* *Manifesto for a European Renaissance* *On the Brink of the Abyss* *The Problem of Democracy* *Runes and the Origins of Writing* *View from the Right* (vol. 1–3)
Armand Berger	*Tolkien, Europe, and Tradition*
Arthur Moeller van den Bruck	*Germany's Third Empire*
Matt Battaglioli	*The Consequences of Equality*
Kerry Bolton	*The Perversion of Normality* *Revolution from Above* *Yockey: A Fascist Odyssey*
Isac Boman	*Money Power*
Charles William Dailey	*The Serpent Symbol in Tradition*
Ricardo Duchesne	*Faustian Man in a Multicultural Age*
Alexander Dugin	*Ethnos and Society* *Ethnosociology* *Eurasian Mission* *The Fourth Political Theory* *The Great Awakening vs the Great Reset* *Last War of the World-Island* *Political Platonism* *Putin vs Putin* *The Rise of the Fourth Political Theory* *The Theory of a Multipolar World*
Edward Dutton	*Race Differences in Ethnocentrism*
Mark Dyal	*Hated and Proud*
Clare Ellis	*The Blackening of Europe*
Koenraad Elst	*Return of the Swastika*
Julius Evola	*The Bow and the Club* *Fascism Viewed from the Right* *A Handbook for Right-Wing Youth* *Metaphysics of Power* *Metaphysics of War* *The Myth of the Blood* *Notes on the Third Reich* *Pagan Imperialism* *Recognitions* *A Traditionalist Confronts Fascism*

OTHER BOOKS PUBLISHED BY ARKTOS

Guillaume Faye	*Archeofuturism* *Archeofuturism 2.0* *The Colonisation of Europe* *Convergence of Catastrophes* *Ethnic Apocalypse* *A Global Coup* *Prelude to War* *Sex and Deviance* *Understanding Islam* *Why We Fight*
Daniel S. Forrest	*Suprahumanism*
Andrew Fraser	*Dissident Dispatches* *Reinventing Aristocracy in the Age of Woke Capital* *The WASP Question*
Génération Identitaire	*We are Generation Identity*
Peter Goodchild	*The Taxi Driver from Baghdad* *The Western Path*
Paul Gottfried	*War and Democracy*
Petr Hampl	*Breached Enclosure*
Porus Homi Havewala	*The Saga of the Aryan Race*
Lars Holger Holm	*Hiding in Broad Daylight* *Homo Maximus* *Incidents of Travel in Latin America* *The Owls of Afrasiab*
Richard Houck	*Liberalism Unmasked*
A. J. Illingworth	*Political Justice*
Alexander Jacob	*De Naturae Natura*
Jason Reza Jorjani	*Artemis Unveiled* *Closer Encounters* *Faustian Futurist* *Iranian Leviathan* *Lovers of Sophia* *Novel Folklore* *Prometheism* *Promethean Pirate* *Prometheus and Atlas* *Uber Man* *World State of Emergency*
Henrik Jonasson	*Sigmund*
Edgar Julius Jung	*The Significance of the German Revolution*
Ruuben Kaalep & August Meister	*Rebirth of Europe*
Roderick Kaine	*Smart and SeXy*
Peter King	*Here and Now* *Keeping Things Close* *On Modern Manners*

OTHER BOOKS PUBLISHED BY ARKTOS

James Kirkpatrick	*Conservatism Inc.*
Ludwig Klages	*The Biocentric Worldview* *Cosmogonic Reflections* *The Science of Character*
Andrew Korybko	*Hybrid Wars*
Pierre Krebs	*Guillaume Faye: Truths & Tributes* *Fighting for the Essence*
Julien Langella	*Catholic and Identitarian*
John Bruce Leonard	*The New Prometheans*
Stephen Pax Leonard	*The Ideology of Failure* *Travels in Cultural Nihilism*
William S. Lind	*Reforging Excalibur* *Retroculture*
Pentti Linkola	*Can Life Prevail?*
H. P. Lovecraft	*The Conservative*
Norman Lowell	*Imperium Europa*
Richard Lynn	*Sex Differences in Intelligence*
John MacLugash	*The Return of the Solar King*
Charles Maurras	*The Future of the Intelligentsia & For a French Awakening*
John Harmon McElroy	*Agitprop in America*
Michael O'Meara	*Guillaume Faye and the Battle of Europe* *New Culture, New Right*
Michael Millerman	*Beginning with Heidegger*
Maurice Muret	*The Greatness of Elites*
Brian Anse Patrick	*The NRA and the Media* *Rise of the Anti-Media* *The Ten Commandments of Propaganda* *Zombology*
Tito Perdue	*The Bent Pyramid* *Journey to a Location* *Lee* *Morning Crafts* *Philip* *The Sweet-Scented Manuscript* *William's House* (vol. 1–4)
John K. Press	*The True West vs the Zombie Apocalypse*
Raido	*A Handbook of Traditional Living* (vol. 1–2)
Claire Rae Randall	*The War on Gender*
Steven J. Rosen	*The Agni and the Ecstasy* *The Jedi in the Lotus*
Nicholas Rooney	*Talking to the Wolf*
Richard Rudgley	*Barbarians* *Essential Substances* *Wildest Dreams*

OTHER BOOKS PUBLISHED BY ARKTOS

Ernst von Salomon	*It Cannot Be Stormed* *The Outlaws*
Werner Sombart	*Traders and Heroes*
Piero San Giorgio	*CBRN* *Giuseppe* *Survive the Economic Collapse*
Sri Sri Ravi Shankar	*Celebrating Silence* *Know Your Child* *Management Mantras* *Patanjali Yoga Sutras* *Secrets of Relationships*
George T. Shaw (ed.)	*A Fair Hearing*
Fenek Solère	*Kraal* *Reconquista*
Oswald Spengler	*The Decline of the West* *Man and Technics*
Richard Storey	*The Uniqueness of Western Law*
Tomislav Sunic	*Against Democracy and Equality* *Homo Americanus* *Postmortem Report* *Titans are in Town*
Askr Svarte	*Gods in the Abyss*
Hans-Jürgen Syberberg	*On the Fortunes and Misfortunes of Art in Post-War Germany*
Abir Taha	*Defining Terrorism* *The Epic of Arya* (2nd ed.) *Nietzsche's Coming God, or the Redemption of the Divine* *Verses of Light*
Jean Thiriart	*Europe: An Empire of 400 Million*
Bal Gangadhar Tilak	*The Arctic Home in the Vedas*
Dominique Venner	*For a Positive Critique* *The Shock of History*
Hans Vogel	*How Europe Became American*
Markus Willinger	*A Europe of Nations* *Generation Identity*
Alexander Wolfheze	*Alba Rosa* *Rupes Nigra*

www.ingramcontent.com/pod-product-compliance
Lightning Source LLC
Chambersburg PA
CBHW020820270326
41928CB00006B/385

* 9 7 8 1 9 1 5 7 5 5 2 4 7 *